MICHELANGELO
ANTONIONI

THE ARCHITECTURE
OF VISION

WRITINGS AND INTERVIEWS
ON CINEMA

Edited by Carlo di Carlo
and Giorgio Tinazzi

American edition
by Marga Cottino-Jones

MARSILIO PUBLISHERS
NEW YORK

Original Italian title: *Fare un film per me è vivere*
(Marsilio: Venice, 1995)

Copyright © 1991 & 1992 by Cinecittà International, Rome
Copyright © 1994 by Marsilio Editori, Venice

Translation copyright © 1996 by Marsilio Publishers, with the exception of the
following articles, reprinted here by permission:

"Making a Film Is My Way of Life" © 1962 *Film Culture*; "Reflections on the Film Actor"
© 1966-67 *Film Culture*; "The Event and the Image" © 1963-64 *Sight & Sound*;
"Reality and Cinema Verité" © 1965 *Atlas*; "What This Land Says to Me," © 1969 *Atlas*;
"Antonioni on the Seven-Minute Shot" © 1975 *Film Comment*;
"A Conversation with Michelangelo Antonioni" © 1960 *NY Film Bulletin*;
"An Interview with Michelangelo Antonioni © 1969 Grossman Publishers.

Preface to the American Edition copyright © 1996 by Marga Cottino-Jones

Of the present edition copyright © 1996
by Marsilio Publishers, 853 Broadway
New York, NY 10003

ISBN CLOTH 1-56886-012-9
ISBN PAPER 1-56886-016-1

Library of Congress Cataloging-in-Publication Data

Antonioni, Michelangelo.
    The architecture of vision : writings and interviews on cinema /
Michelangelo Antonioni : American edition by Marga Cottino-Jones.
        p.   cm.
    Simultaneously published in Italian under the title: Fare un film è
per me vivere.
    ISBN 1-56886-012-9 (hc). -- ISBN 1-56886-016-1 (pb)
    1. Antonioni, Michelangelo--Interviews. 2. Motion picture
producers and directors--Italy--Interviews. 3. Motion pictures.
I. Cottino-Jones, Marga.   II. Title.
PN1998.3.A58A5   1996
791.43' 0233' 092--dc20   95-49019
                                                           CIP

Distributed in the United States by
Consortium Book Sales and Distribution
1045 Westgate Drive, Saint Paul, MN 55114

CONTENTS

PREFACE TO THE AMERICAN EDITION

by Marga Cottino-Jones

In the Spring of 1995, Michelangelo Antonioni was presented with one of the most coveted prizes a motion picture director can ever receive: the honorary Oscar for a lifetime commitment to cinema. This recognition has highlighted Antonioni's unique contribution to the world of cinema and has confirmed his reputation as an artist whom, in the words Roland Barthes, "toute une collectivité s'accorde pour reconnaître, admirer, aimer."

Antonioni's professional career has been characterized by a firm conviction that filmmaking had to be constantly renewed, in both subject matter and techniques, in order for cinema to keep up with the changes and innovations taking place in the real world. A director's role is comparable to a writer's, who communicates his views of the world to his readers through words. Antonioni has admitted several times that his is a world of images, not of words, and that it is through images that he communicates his ideas and feelings to his audience. At the same time, he has often used his pen and his voice to speak of his films, his interests, his choices, his views on cinema.

This collection was first published in Italian in 1994 as the first volume of a larger series to be issued under the aegis of Cinecittà International as the offspring of the French editorial project in six volumes already in publication.* The writings presented here, most of which have been translated into English for the first time, bring to the English-speaking readership a very precious testimony of

---

1 See Carlo di Carlo's Preface to the present volume for more detailed information. The second volume of the Italian series has been published at the end of 1995 by Marsilio Editori, with the title *I film nel cassetto* [Films in the drawer] and containing Antonioni's scripts and subjects that, for various reasons,were never made into films.

Antonioni's complex and multiform view of his works and of the world that is behind them. The essays have been grouped in four parts: the first two, "My Cinema" and "My Films," consist of Antonioni's own writings. The other two, "Interviews on Cinema" and "Interviews on Films," contain the texts of several of his interviews with important Italian and French journalists and critics.

Carlo di Carlo's preface to the Italian edition explains how the idea of the collection came about, and how it is connected with other initiatives taken by the film community to celebrate Antonioni's work and make it better known to his viewers and the reading public. Giorgio Tinazzi's introduction, "The Gaze and the Story," prepares readers for what they will find in this volume by introducing the main topics Antonioni discusses in his writings and interviews.

This material gives readers the opportunity to see past several of the misconceptions about Antonioni and his work that have been maintained by the press. It also offers a better understanding of his extraordinary personality as a director and a human being, and a better appreciation of his critical sharpness and his insatiable curiosity for new personal and professional experiences. Many readers of Antonioni's writing have been amazed to find such an important director so unpretentious toward himself and his achievements, and at the same time so generous in evaluating the works of other directors or so restrained in commenting upon the often unfair views of his critics.

Antonioni has often been accused of "coldness" or of "technicalism." Several of his essays challenge the validity of such accusations. In these writings Antonioni discusses his ethical and professional motivations for not sympathizing with his characters, or for choosing certain techniques that purposefully draw attention to themselves. For example, in *The Vanquished*, an early film in which he investigated the issue of crime among youth, the director took a strong professional stand against sympathizing with characters involved with crime, thus showing his ethical opposition to violence. "I absolutely did not want my heroes to be likable," he explains. "It is so easy to make an individual with a gun in his hand likable. . . . The detachment that I am being accused of was aimed at avoiding the possibility that the story could influence the public even in an involuntarily negative way."

Similarly, Antonioni's personal explanations for his use of technical innovations show the reasoning behind his repeated use of the special technique of the "long take" in *Story of a Love Affair*—a reasoning that reveals his determination to innovate on traditional cinema: "I was able to free myself from it [traditional cinema's old method], by way of a very long crane movement that followed the characters until I felt the need to stop." His complex use of color is made clear by what he says in his interview with Jean-Luc Godard about *Red Desert*, where he used color for the first time. As he explains in the interview, Antonioni saw color as a very important technique that opened up completely new possibilities in filmmaking, especially in relation to character and dialogue: "Let's say that they [the passages of dialogue] have been reduced to the bare minimum, and in that sense they are linked to the use of color. For example, in the scene in the hut where they are talking about drugs and stimulants, I couldn't *not* use red. In black and white it would never have worked. The red puts the viewer into a state of mind that allows him to accept such dialogue. It's the right color for the characters—who, in turn, are entailed by the color—and also for the viewer."

Antonioni also reveals his preferences concerning the subject matter of his films, and his own yearnings for what is different and new in the world. He often stresses the important connection between narrative and film. For Antonioni, it is always a question of finding a story in the real world and telling it well, whether in writing or on film. He himself is a very good fiction writer; he has not only written most of his scripts, but has also authored several short stories, published in a collection called *That Bowling Alley on the Tiber*. Antonioni is also greatly fascinated by all new forms of technology, and even by the world of science fiction. "The range of possibilities which technology gives to a filmmaker is infinite," he says. "We can do absolutely what we want with . . . these new technologies. . . . It's not a limiting device; just the opposite." However, he also feels his own limitations when faced with the changing world of technology: "I really wish I were already part of that new world. Unfortunately, we are not there yet, and for older generations, such as mine or that of people born just after the war, that is a real tragedy."

Throughout all of these essays and interviews, Antonioni's personality, his thoughts and his beliefs, come alive in an endearing and engaging way. Through them readers will be able to reach a new level of appreciation and respect for this unique "man of images."

August 1995
Los Angeles

PREFACE TO THE ITALIAN EDITION

by Carlo di Carlo

The "Antonioni Project" was first presented in May 1988 at the XLI Cannes Film Festival as a multimedia project. It was promoted initially by the Ente Autonomo Gestione Cinema and later by Cinecittà International. Under my curatorship, the project received partial funding from the Ministry of Tourism and the Performing Arts.

It was decided that the project would embark upon a journey throughout the world, making twenty stops over the span of five years. This journey would take the project from Cannes to Montreal, from Montpellier to Istanbul, from Paris to New York, from Rome to Los Angeles, and from Geneva to Ferrara. New prints were issued of all of the films by Michelangelo Antonioni (both his short films and his feature length films), in addition to some unreleased films and the documentaries that the director has produced in recent years, since his illness.[2] Two hundred and twenty images, among the most significant from his films, were presented in a photographic exhibit that offered a visual reading of his work. Thirteen seminars were promoted under the auspices of the project; among the most significant ones, worth mentioning are the one that took place at the Louvre Auditorium, chaired by Alain Robbe-Grillet, and the one that took place at the Italian Cultural Institute of New York, chaired by Furio Colombo.

Alongside the rerelease of Antonioni's cinematographic work (in versions with French and English subtitles, since the entire project has benefited from public

[2] After suffering from an ictus that caused serious impediment to his legs and speech, Antonioni has decreased his filmmaking activity. However, he just completed, with German director Wim Wenders, a film entitled *Al di là delle nuvole* [Beyond the Clouds].

funding "for the dissemination of Italian cinema abroad"), a publishing project is about to be completed. The centerpiece of this project is a six-volume series called *L'Œuvre de Michelangelo Antonioni* (five of these volumes have already been published; the sixth is to be completed in 1995), which also includes other publications, not of this series, which were previously available only in French.

The Centro Sperimentale di Cinematografia in Rome should be credited for the timely publication of the third volume of the series—*Album Antonioni: Une biographie impossibile*, edited by Renzo Renzi—during the Roman leg of the project in December of 1992. It is clear that the project of reissuing Antonioni's work as a whole, in a series unique in bothe size and composition, constitutes a fundamental contribution to the analysis and dissemination all of its aspects.

Today, the Italian edition finally releases its first volume. In agreement with the publisher and the directors of the series, we have modified its overall plan, which will will have a different sequence from the French one. We believe, in fact, that this first volume, dedicated to Antonioni's cinema and his films, should precede the others, in order to fill a gap in our cinematographic culture.

Unlike many other great authors, Michelangelo Antonioni, has avoided telling his story throughout his life, and has thereby avoided debating about himself, and about the significance of his cinema and work. "What I had to say," he has always maintained, "I said through my films, and I have nothing to add to these."

Besides the articles that he wrote as a critic—from 1936 to 1950, when he made his first feature film, *Story of a Love Affair*—and that will be published in the next volumes in this series, Antonioni's writings on cinema number no more than thirty, written over the span of thirty-five years.

At the same time, we have realized that his interviews—either of a general nature, and/or concerning a single film—are almost all of great importance. They are unsuspected sources of information, observations, and even of rare revelations about his own life and work, which complete and enrich his biography as man and as artist. In collecting them for publication we have come to the conclusion-that they should be considered "oral writings."

The research that Giorgio Tinazzi and I have carried out has allowed us—before everything else—to reconsider the composition of this volume, and of the next one, in light of these facts.

This volume has, therefore, been subdivided in the following manner: the first part, "My Cinema," contains essays, articles, and reflections on cinema, along with two seemingly anomalous texts—"My Experience" and "A Talk with Michelangelo Antonioni on His Work"—which originated in two meetings with students of the Centro Sperimentale di Cinematografia. Because they are at the same time narrative and testimony, they have become two absolutely fundamental references for anyone who wishes to understand Antonioni and his cinema. The director's writings on his films are gathered in the second part, "My Films." General interviews appear in the third part, "Interviews on the Cinema," whereas "Interviews on Films" appear in the fourth.

All of Antonioni's writings have been published in [and translated from] Italian or French, with the exception of those texts which Antonioni reserved for initial publication either in England or in the United States. The criterion for classification within each part is chronological.

THE GAZE AND THE STORY

by Giorgio Tinazzi

"I don't believe that what an author says about himself and about his own work would help make sense of his work." This is a statement that Antonioni has often repeated and that, by the way, is likely to be true for all authors. Therefore, in looking at Antonioni's own statements, we are not seeking any authoritative interpretation or analytical assistance. We will find there, however, indications of his tendencies, of his interests, and of his poetics. At times we will find these things indirectly, most often when Antonioni is not discussing his films, but rather in his travel journals or in passages from his stories.

Potentially, at least, a critical attitude on the part of the author presupposes a creative work with little residue of past experiences, with no ambiguity, and with no open meanings—in short, a creative work very different from Antonioni's cinema. ("But, after all," Antonioni himself once said, "this difficulty of reading, this lack of clarity, aren't they—how shall I put it—a quality?") Likewise, a more controlled, less "instinctive" creativity might be considered essential to a filmmaker. But for Antonioni, "a shot is never the product of a process of reasoning, it is an instinctive choice." And the same is true of other technical and expressive elements: "They are often unconscious factors, natural creative events, and as such they often refuse a rational explanation." He has also stated: "I have never liked questions when they are directed at me, because they imply a specific meaning and force me to the level of reason, while instead, when I work, I am always at a deeper level."

For this "man of images," working on the set does not involve the working out of a ready-made thought, "but of an idea in the making, that creates itself on the spur of the moment," leaving ample room for improvisation prompted by direct interaction with the environment. That is where the film is written, directly on the camera. For this reason, Antonioni's scripts are mere traces, sometimes notes. They belong to the language of words, which has serious limitations: "This is the limit of the script: to give words to events that reject words."

For Antonioni, to provide interpretive keys to critics and spectators would mean to "coldly" examine this meeting place of forces—and in the end it would mean a change of vocation. "Words do not come easily to me," he says, "images do!"

On the other hand, Antonioni's modest refusal to judge his own films reflects, in some way, the same attitude taken by his films toward the subject matter they visualize. They do not interfere with the events presented, but rather observe them closely, taking in subtle connections and picking up continuities and disturbances. Why ask him for an historical evaluation of these events, in addition to a value judgment on the films, when his prevailing interest is toward the individual? Antonioni said many times that he is not a sociologist, a moralist, or a politician, thereby laying claim to his rights as narrator: "I am not offering messages, I am telling stories that I *see* around me" (emphasis added). He has also noted that *Zabriskie Point* is a "fable"; it is "just the story of an emotion, mine, as I came in contact with America." The dimension of the fable would have become even more apparent, and thus different (because it was "a world which had never been mine"), with the production of *L'aquilone* [The Kite], written with Tonino Guerra.

To tell stories then, is what Antonioni does in his films. These stories are the outcome of an attitude in which involvement and detachment alternate, both toward the subject matter and toward the biographical material that nourishes it. It would be enough to reread his review of Visconti's *La terra trema* to understand how, for Antonioni, the need for "detachment" is part of an artist's assets: "Perhaps in this primary detachment between author and environment, between author and character, we can find the reason for such a lyrically pure effect." For Antonioni there is also a personal matrix which he has to take into account—the social environment where he grew up, the city. Hence, the attempt to objectify these subjective factors in the stories (which, as soon as they are created, become "object") and to make his own feelings or moods or residual images flow in them. Ferrara[3] exists as an indistinct backdrop, an

---

[3] Ferrara is the town where Antonioni was born and raised. See Antonioni's own description of the city in the interview "Conversation" (p. 215 below).

atmosphere; its outlines continuously fade out and thus remain unexpressed and almost undercover. It may happen that he is reminded of it on a trip ("I was breathing a little of the air of Ferrara in Prague"), or else that he speaks of an attitude of sorts, almost a state of mind, without giving too much weight to it ("only a person from Ferrara can understand a relationship which has lasted eleven years, yet had never existed"). The middle-class environment—the environment Antonioni knows best—above all helps him investigate some of the processes involving the individual and his quest for identity.

What about the director's subjectivity? Some traces of this subjectivity can still be found in his films. And, although they remain somewhat unexpressed, on the margins, traces can also be found of other impulses—such as violence, which Antonioni has many times insisted is a component of his character that he has evidently diverted, or sublimated, through his bent toward formal expression. In this way, the impulse has turned into impatience, into an urge to understand and question: "When a film is finished, an unexpressed violence always remains, a sort of brute matter and wickedness which drives us to pick up the quest again, from one place to another—to see, question, and fantasize about things which are more and more elusive, in anticipation of the next film."

Hence, mediation takes over, and with it a sense of indeterminacy. It would be an act of coercion to insist that Antonioni be a critic of his own work. Yet certainly, in his writings and in his statements, we find much that is illuminating. There can be curious correspondences between written images. Antonioni writes in the "Preface to Six Films": "A girl lives down there. . . . She isn't even in love with me. Where did I read this sentence?" This seems to suggest the ending of the Portrait, written in 1938, of a girl "that I was not familiar with, but everybody was talking about": "Truly, she was so transparent that I no longer knew why everybody was talking about her. Only one thing was important to me back then: that she loved me, that she loved me."

There are even recurring situations in his writings, like the sketch of the boy sent to look for his sister on the walls of the city, which is identical to the situation in the Six Films preface, and also in Une Journée. Then there are cases in which the writing foreshadows the films. When Antonioni writes, in 1964, "One day I will invent a film while looking at the sun," how can one not think of the ending of Identification of a Woman, made twenty years later? But this game of allusions or inlays is scarcely productive. Nor does it help much to ask for explanations of formulas (alienation, crisis, incommunicability) from someone who is so very distant from definitions and classifications.

Antonioni also tends to play down, if not avoid, critical questions of an historical nature. This is the case with his complex relationship with neorealism. According to his point of view, he is right in emphasizing certain coincidences. For instance, he was filming *People of the Po Valley* at the same time and in the same area where Visconti was setting his film *Ossessione*. "I had to invent neorealism little by little on my own, nobody had taught it to me." Later on, he will point out, accepting a formula coined by French criticism, that his effort was toward *interiorizing*—toward looking at what is inside the individual, at his feelings, after the story and the external elements have been examined. Behind these assertions of a deliberately general nature there is, however, the perception that the cultural and political "climate" has nevertheless represented a fundamental experience. The question is, for whom? For Antonioni's cinema, or for the Italian cinema after the war?

If, from the context, we go on to focus on the single texts, the first characteristics of Antonioni's cinema that emerge are recognizability and consistency. In fact, there are clear stylistic traits that recur in his work, often accompanied by thematical predilections.

It is an *œuvre* which develops coherently—also through recurrences, distortions, and variations, under the sign of continuity and innovation. The director realizes this; and although he also realizes that the continuity is not a sign of monody, but rather of inquiry, he seems, nonetheless, almost afraid of recurrences. He frequently insists upon the elements of diversity, if not of disjunction, in his works: "*The Vanquished* does not represent a close examination and development of the themes from which I started, and which are dear to me. Rather, it is a deviation which has allowed me to clear up for myself a series of technical and aesthetic problems." Thus, the intention to bring back themes and techniques for further clarification and distillation is settled from the beginning at the formal level. If Antonioni, while filming *Blow-Up*, stated that the film was "entirely different from its predecessors," later on he considered *Tecnicamente dolce* [Technically Sweet] (a project that was never completed because of producer Ponti's sudden change of mind) impossible to make after *The Passenger*: "There is a certain resemblance between the characters of the two films, and this is the reason why today, after having completed *The Passenger*, I no longer feel like filming *Tecnicamente dolce*." But the connection, even if the films differ, persists, and it almost seems as though Antonioni still feels the need to deviate. "This will be my last *Antonionian* film," he said during the shooting of *Identification of a Woman*, "in the sense that I would like to free myself from the burden of feelings in order to keep more to the facts. I feel the need to start moving in different directions."

Movement and new directions. As these words imply, it is not by chance that a constant in much of Antonioni's cinema is a narrative structure based upon the age-old idea of the journey, in the sense of adventure, revisitation, escape, and the search for identity. But these words also describe his need to explore different environments, places, and spaces in which to situate his characters, while carrying with him long-established beliefs and deep obsessions, never renouncing his original intention to follow up on what comes after the events and on how they filter through the emotions. So there is the "variation" of *The Vanquished*; there is, above all, the London of *Blow-Up* ("they are the avant-garde, not just of a way of life, but also of a way of thinking, of feeling"); and there is the America of *Zabriskie Point*. In this last case, two are the themes that interest Antonioni: on the one hand, the continuous change to which reality is subjected ("something I like about America is the continuous movement and renewal that one perceives there"), the inner repercussions caused by that change, and a propensity toward *adventure*; on the other hand, the contrast, or the presence of two incompatible aspects: innocence and violence, openness and closure.

Along with these themes, there are elements that belong to form, "strong" factors that stand out: the vastness of spaces, with the consequences this can have (as we shall see) for the "American soul," and the constant presence of images, of a world of communication that takes you in and lashes out at you. It is "a country where images jump out at you with every step."

In this sense, *Chung Kuo: China* represents the confrontation with something radically *different*, historically new, which one has to observe, without aiming at narrative construction, before being able to interpret. In many ways, this film is a return to Antonioni's documentary phase. Today, after so many unnecessary controversies, we can look at the film for what it was meant to be—a series "of traveling notes, more on the Chinese than on China." But it would be misleading to search for continuity—however partial—with the other two "new" films. Not only, obviously, for the absolute impossibility of seeing a connection between the historical contexts being dealt with, but also because the director's attitude has not remained the same. Facing a reality, such as that of the Chinese, that is totally other, he abandons the "individualist" key, and all stimulations to which he had always been so receptive. In a certain sense, he frees himself from them, and frees his ability of observation, which privileges the dimension of the everyday routine, of work, and of the rhythms of life: "Here, every morning, between five-thirty and seven-thirty, the streets take on a blue hue." Before everything else, those rhythms, gestures, and behaviors are generators of images: "The first image that I have of China is of a dozen red caps on the heads of men dressed in blue, unloading goods off of a wagon, at the border of Lo Wu." What the author wants to offer us is the "proximity" of things and people seen in such a way, "a great repertory of faces, gestures, habits."

If Antonioni does not want to, and probably cannot be, his own critic, he is nevertheless fully willing to show some of his propensities, some of his uppermost interests: "I think that the inspiration of filmmakers must always be anchored in their time, not so much to express it or interpret it in its more crude and tragic events . . . but rather to grasp its reflection within ourselves." Both the events themselves and their internal ramifications are important; and even more important is the relationship between historical and subjective time. From their dissonance, from their division, from a separation of their *logic*, a crisis is born: the difficulty of relationships between subjects, between characters, environment, and events. Internal time sees its project flawed, and the recovery of memory impossible, so that lived time becomes "suspended" time. In such a sense, *The Cry* seems to be symptomatic of this crisis, whence Antonioni's distillations, amplifications, and repetitions originate, together with the recognition of the similar in the different. The main contrast is in the dissonance of time, and Antonioni reveals his ability to assimilate naturally, without rational explanation, the individual impact of changing events ("one eye opened to the outside and one turned toward the inside"). However—and herein lies the complexity—what he depicts is a loss that leaves behind its residues, because events and environments have a sense of legacy that remains present.

Change and contrast prevail. In the background there is the general type of change or contrast, between the old and the new, that one finds in things and environments. "To take for granted the end of the forest," Antonioni wrote apropos of *Red Desert*, "to turn empty what was full, to subject this ancient reality, by discoloring it, to a new one, that is equally suggestive—hasn't this been going on here for years in a neverending flux?" But the inner self does not hold up to change. The interchangeability of feelings reveals their fragility. Some of these feelings (I'm thinking of eroticism) both mask and reveal. What emerges is the inner-self's refusal to adapt to the evolution of the cognitive instruments of experience. It is this profound difference between the inner-self and the external world which provokes separation and defeat: "Today," Antonioni said in 1961, "the world is jeopardized by a very serious unbalance between a science completely and consciously projected into the future, ready to repudiate itself daily in order to acquire a fraction of this future, and a stiffened, stylized, moral world, that everybody recognizes as such and yet everybody contributes to keeping alive, either out of cowardice or out of laziness." Change and inadequacy remain the leitmotif.

But it is important to reiterate that we are not asking for a key to interpret this crisis (a formula which Antonioni has almost never used), or precise diagnosis. The director operates at a different level, and [Renzo] Renzi is right to talk of "states of the mind in representational form," of *blues* around a crisis situation.

Even if they maintain their individual origins, these secret moods (perhaps, one might say, this biography) and their complex ambiguities often need to externalize themselves, because the characters are always "set," and because the change, as I noted, is above all in the physical world. The maladjustment originates from this. It would be enough to think of Giuliana in *Red Desert*, or of the protagonists of *Zabriskie Point*. In *Red Desert*, there is the Ravenna that industrialization has transformed by ravaging the landscape; in *Zabriskie Point* there is the America of many contradictions ("the waste, the innocence, the immensity, the poverty"), of radical transformations, of full and empty places, of outbursts and losses—"an arm-wrestling contest with the most beautiful and the most disgusting reality in the world.".

Although with the radical difference discussed earlier (difference in subject matter and in attitude), China has an impact, too, and becomes hostile because of its changes. "Perhaps there is a deeper reason that my notes remained notes, and that is the difficulty for me to have a definite idea of that reality in constant change that is popular China."

What we are touching upon, here, are the inclinations and predispositions of the filmmaker, which are primarily revealed by his films; his words can, at most, bear them out. These words mainly serve to clarify an attitude toward formal elements, or rather, toward the elements of his language. On this level, it is acceptable to ask more of the director, even if, as he insists, "what I say on theoretical grounds doesn't have any pretensions of being one hundred per cent right."

First of all, a general consideration in terms of the technical apparatus should be emphasized. On the one hand, there is the tendency to propound its lack of difficulty ("Technology? It has no importance, because you can avail yourself of a medium that is like the word"), and at the same time the need to discredit it

("I adopted technology to eliminate technology"). On the other hand, there is constantly—from the beginning of his career—a dissatisfaction with rules, and with the practices that they have encouraged. Therefore, the need for change grows, the need to find a more flexible form of expression, more fluid and "freer." In any case, Antonioni tends to connect technology (which is, after all, the form) to a meaning, to the urgency of something that excludes any fetishization of the technical medium.

The preoccupation with "technicalism unto itself" was present, in Antonioni the critic, just as—vice versa—"inventive technology" attested to functionality and modernity. The comparison was brought out, for example, in relation to *La terra trema* and *Hamlet*. In Visconti's film, as Antonioni notes, there are "shots that really express something, even a simple mood, and a photography that always and powerfully creates an atmosphere. We would be following in Olivier's footsteps if here it were not a question of a technicalism in and of itself. In Visconti technology is really at the service of poetry."

With these premises in mind, it was natural that Antonioni the author would reject the accusation of being a formalist, which for a long time was imposed on him on the basis of a completely schematic critical formula. Indeed, at that time, critics were speaking of form without differentiating between technical exhibitionism and the ability or necessity of an author to question his own language, thus revealing his own "project." Antonioni perceived this particular need as his own, and consequently was displaying justified "defenses": "They were accusing my first films of being overly refined. I, on the contrary, was spasmodically searching for the right image for what I wanted to express. Technical exhibitionism seems to me to be the opposite of what I wanted to do."

It is really the search for a "right" form that feeds Antonioni's impatience for a well-established, and therefore regulated, expressive apparatus, and spurs him to search for technical novelties. *The Mystery of Oberwald* is in this sense the terminal point of a preceding tension. Symptomatically, the director chooses a thematic basis quite "distant" from himself, and a story structure not in tune with his predilections—almost as if he wants to experiment (technically) on material which is, if not alien to him, then at least "independent" of him. (He speaks of "detached respect.") The technique of electronic reproduction, fascinates him because it is tendentially less bound to presupposed naturalistic image representation, because it makes (or can make) the sign more arbitrary, and particularly the color more "inventive": "What a sense of lightness I have experienced in front of those events which lack the complexity of the real which we are accustomed to. . . . It was like recovering a forgotten childhood." The future possibility that "poetry and technology" may walk hand in hand will naturally influence the method of storytelling. Showing and narrating, as I will emphasize, have always proceeded on parallel levels for Antonioni: "Who knows what one will be able to do in the future? In any case, all of this will change not only the technical means, the configuration of the image, but the subject matter of the story as well. The very method of storytelling will be different. "

So Antonioni shows a strong interest in form. It is important to pay attention, then, to the constitutive elements of his films, beginning with the "original" relationship between character and environment. "I like to thoroughly know where a story is placed," he has said many times. He has also stated that, "It is part of my craft to observe people in the context of the situations they are in," and that, "The subject of my films is always born of a landscape, of a site, of a place I want to explore." A story, therefore, always has its setting; a character always has his space.

The traditional relationship can also be inverted: "A story can also be born by observing the environment, which will then be the outline." The fruitful temptation of abstraction appears more than once: "The subject of *The Cry* came to my mind while I was looking at a wall." Meaningful setting, dramatic agent, narrative occasion; the space becomes complex and charged with meaning.

The entire visual dimension of Antonioni's films has its precise functionality: "A certain line spoken in front of a wall or against the setting of a street, can change in meaning." Framing a shot and choosing its depth always express a need: "I have made much use of the telephoto lens," the director declared to [Jean-Luc] Godard apropos of *Red Desert*, "so as not to have depth of field, which is an indispensable element of realism. What interests me now is setting characters in contact with things, because today things, objects, matter have weight."

On the level of meanings, talking about characters and environment signifies investigating the relationship between the individual and reality. *Blow-Up* emerges as a crucial film also under this rubric, as apoint of arrival as well as a junction: "It will seem strange to say it, but *Blow-Up* was, to some extent, my neorealist film about the relationship between the individual and reality, even if it had a metaphysical component in the abstract rendering of appearances."

The "right" image becomes more and more influent; especially on space, which has to be also "right"—that is, precise. ("In Prague," he wrote in a travel note, "nothing is curved.") It is important "to attribute to a person his own

xxii \ THE ARCHITECTURE OF VISION

story—that is, the story that coincides with his appearance, with his position, his weight, his weight in a space." The suspended fragments and the empty spaces of the final scene of *The Eclipse* correspond to the "disappearing" of the story and of its actions. Antonioni's interest in architecture does not need to be emphasized.

What he tells us about architectural space is also valid for landscape. In *The Cry*, the landscape is like a character; its permanence is the evocative memory which becomes fixed, *crystalized*. The locations denote a story, but, even before that, a reality. "The vastness," Antonioni wrote regarding America, "is the other experience. And I believe that it has much to do with the American spirit. A country of this vastness, with these distances and this horizon, cannot but be conditioned by its dimensions for that which concerns dreams, illusions, tensions, solitude, faith, innocence, optimism, and desperation, patriotism and revolt."

The attention to the modality of *showing* proceeds hand in hand with *narration*. There is evidence from the very beginning of Antonioni's preoccupation with the traditional system of storytelling, including dissatisfaction with the rules generally accepted by the authors, and with the habits of the audience. The traditional ways of cinema had provoked an "instinctive tiredness" in him. He showed intolerance for the order of the sequences, for the forced connections that seemingly had to be made among them, "jumps from sequence to sequence, with one acting as a trampoline for the next."

Therefore, the conventional development seemed to him, if not an obstacle, then certainly a hindrance. He felt he needed to look for a new freedom in telling a story, for connections that reflected other (more "internal") forms of articulating thought. It was necessary to find new ways of visualization, of manipulating time, without fear of "making literary, even figurative, cinema."

Because of these impulses, which the director defines as "instinctive," Antonioni's cinema comes to settle itself into a sort of intermediate zone, which finds its originality, its "lesson," in its narrative articulation. Each time, two forces set it in motion differently. On the one hand, there is a force that connects events, articulates them—in short, tends to build a story. On the other hand, there is force that sections off the events and stretches them out in time, that disassembles and penetrates the meshes of the story to amplify them as much as possible, to gather the echo, the refractions, and the eccentric waves of the events.

Antonioni seems to allude clearly to this duplicity, even if—in theory but above all in practice—it was the expansion which has prevailed and which, therefore, has primarily characterized his work. In fact, he states that he is "always telling a story," although he then takes issues with some details—he has an aversion to key scenes (and one understands why *Oberwald* was "foreign" to him), and he has increasingly felt the need to break up the action (inserting, for example, as in *L'avventura*, "shots even of a documentary type"). As far as characters are concerned, he tends to reject those defined as "main"—and it is revealing that he actually said this regarding a film based on a literary source, *The Girlfriends*. In any case there is the tendency to "lower" the high points of a story, to thin out the narrative fabric. This occurs all the more as the second force intervenes, which favors the moments when the narrative development doesn't move forward (the so-called "dead times," upon which Antonioni's critics have long lingered). The action then goes on beyond conventional time, because there is an afterward which is of interest. One understands, therefore, the preference Antonioni once accorded to Bresson: "I liked *Les Dames du Bois du Boulogne*; I liked the way of "dodging" the main scenes; Bresson only showed the consequences of the main scenes."

Between the story's "passages" there is no necessary connection: the narration slackens, it becomes more "fluid," more connected to "particular circumstances." They are the "apparently secondary moments"; the incidental, the contingent, the motiveless enter into the story. Other portions of reality become involved. With regards to di Carlo's stylistic search,[4] Antonioni has spoken of "an attempt to give meaning to the meaningless," and it seems almost as if he were speaking of himself. Manipulation of narrative time, along with a stripping-down process are described as characteristic elements of his type of cinema.

In Antonioni's work, the entire narrative span is being questioned. How can one forget the ambiguous, "suspended" endings of so many of his films? Can it be any accident that, in recounting a discussion held on *Red Desert*, he will recall Chekhov's claim that whoever invents new endings for dramas will have initiated a new era?

This method of storytelling will also give expression to zones of thought and of consciousness which had little space in the conventional narrative. They are moments of experience which are recovered. Indeed, the referent of a story is to be found, for Antonioni, in experience, in "life." This new way of relating narrative materials isn't programmatically "abstract." He once said: "The rhythm

[4] A close collaborator of Antonioni's, and the coeditor of the present volume, Carlo di Carlo is a also a filmmaker inh his own rights.

of films in which sequences must connect themselves to each other is a false rhythm—a rhythm that is not true to life. Why did *L'avventura* make such an impression when it came out? Because the film had a rhythm closer to life." He also said: "Stories can be made of passages, of fragments, they can be unbalanced, like the life we live." Abstraction and experience, then, are one of the polarities of Antonioni's cinema.

With these progressively established requirements, it was logical that Antonioni would find himself—or did find himself—reckoning with the problem of the "strong" codifications of the cinematic narrative apparatus, and then with the possible "derivations" from other languages. Under the first heading, the relationship with traditional "genres" is of interest. From Antonioni's standpoint, it wasn't just a question of a denial, but also—and in a more complex way—of a particular usage, characterized by expansion and deviation. It has been noted several times that Antonioni has not been alien to formulas connected with the structure of the "thriller": one has only to think of *Story of a Love Affair*, *L'avventura*, *Blow-Up*, and *The Passenger*. But those mechanisms, with the implications they entailed both on the level of narrative and on that of the "expectations" of the viewer, have been employed with modifications, alterations, and deviations so that the outcome is different. "What was certain," says the director with apropos of *The Passenger*, "was only my need to reduce the suspense to the minimum—a suspense, however, that had to remain and that did remain, I believe, an indirect, mediated element." The resulting narrative balance is still a difficult one, between something that stays and supports the story, and a series of centrifugal forces that pull away.

And what about the ancient problem of literary "adaptation"? The autonomy of the director is not up for discussion, the problem of "loyalty" does not exist. "I have never even had the preoccupation of loyalty to Pavese," Antonioni wrote regarding *The Girlfriends*. "When one separates a story from the words that express it and that make it an artistic whole, what remains? A story remains that is equivalent to a news item read in a newspaper, to a story told by a friend, to an event we have been a part of, to a figment of our imagination." The text can even be obstructive—even if it is loved, as it was in Pavese's case—just by virtue of its stylistic aspect. The problem is how to transfer from one form of writing to another; "hybridizations" do not suit the director's conception of cinema: "We all agree, it seems to me, that there is nothing worse than literary painting, literary music, or cinematographic literature." The exchanges with other languages, so noticeable in many of Antonioni's films, are really another thing altogether..

In this continuous pendular motion between telling and showing it is almost natural to arrive at the nucleus of Antonioni's cinema: *vision*, with all of its problematic issues and its implications. One has to deal with the complex connections, the subtle plottings; the sometimes deep-set clashes of image, vision, and representation—the articulation of a unique authorial *project*. The journey begins immediately, with *People of the Po Valley* ("Everything that I did after, good or bad as it might have been, started from there"), and arrives at the critical point of *Blow-Up*, where the image-representation becomes the film's own object of investigation, and, according to the critic Lorenzo Cuccu, "the gaze that made the film came to directly question itself." The journey continues with further questioning (*Zabriskie Point*, *The Passenger*) until the conclusive *Identification of a Woman* ("and after?"). The self-reflexive dimension of Antonioni's cinema has already been sufficiently brought to light by his critics, so there is no need for me to expound upon it.

The major premise of this cinema, and consequently of the poetic statements of the author, is an antinaturalistic or antimimetic premise; the concept of reproduction is that of construction, "not cinema at the service of reality, but reality at the service of cinema." At this point one notices that there are several connections with certain statements that Antonioni made in old reviews. Imitation, Antonioni recently confirmed, is death for an artist. At another time he stated that at the origins of art there is "violence."

For the director, reproducing on film actually means transfiguring. Just think of Antonioni's use of color—one of the key factors in the reproduction process—which must be "invented," which must be "dynamic" ("I like Pollock so much for this reason"), and with which new relationships are to be searched out ("I believe that there is a relationship between camera movements and color"). His openness to technology is rooted in this antimimetic potential of the camera. Technology could grant the old wish of "painting a film as one paints a picture," which was talked about at the beginning of the 1960s.

This premise, therefore, precedes any relationship with the image. At the beginning, in the phenomenological sense, there is the ability of the eye—its faculty of seizing the mutable—and its ambivalence between *fixing* and *losing*. It is not by chance, obviously, that in the "Preface to *Six Films*" Antonioni speaks of the connections between eye and brain, instinct, and consciousness: "Here is an occupation that never makes me tired: watching." And to anyone who questioned him on his readings, he declared, almost with irritation, that it would be necessary to first ask a director what he observes, and then ask what he reads.

Faced with the written page, Antonioni is not afraid to state that "writing for me is a deepening of the gaze." His is an "instinctive and sincere need to reduce everything to image." In a travel journal he noted about Leningrad: "Never before have I felt as satisfied with watching as I do here. One has the sense of being in a place built according to one's own desires."

The gaze is the generator of images; which in turn generate tension, faith ("I still believe, after so many years of cinema, that images have a sense"), because the connections between images and imagination are subtle. There may be disagreements, too, between images and the world—and in fact, perhaps it is here that the so-called Antonioni contrast is found, and therefore Renzi is right when he writes that duplicity resides in the refusal of the content of a world whose form we love.

The connections between images produce the story: the organization of the vision (the "putting together . . . of observation's miscarriages") is the organization of the story. The "natural" course of things can also be modified: "When I don't know what to do I begin to look around. There is also a technique for this—or, more precisely, there are many of them. I have mine, which consists in moving from a series of images up to a state of things."

Things, events, tend to assume an imaginative consistency, to go *beyond* seeing, to make it *exceed*, and it is not by chance that Antonioni cites Wittgenstein: "An image has the form of a reality that does not exist." Thus, *trust* is not separated from the consciousness of this *exceeding*, which can express itself in falsification: "The greatest danger for anyone who makes films lies in the extraordinary possibility that the cinema offers of lying." It is a danger, but it conveys also the ability to ascertain the unavoidable ambiguity of our relationship with the world.

Every idea of vision as mere receptivity is banished from Antonioni's world, because vision is necessarily selection, intervention, inclination (for him, the author) to "move from the detail to the whole." It is a process—that is, duration; and time can be described as a fundamental category of his cinema. Duration—approximating the flowing of time in an investigation—qualifies the new perception of the director: "While for the painter it is a question of discovering a static reality, or even a rhythm, but a rhythm that has stopped in the sign. For a director the problem is taking a reality that grows and wears itself out, and to propose this movement, this arriving and proceeding, as a new perception, . . . a whole that is indivisible and spread out in duration. And this duration informs it and determines its very essence." This complex vision is the particular way of staying in contact with the director's reality, of "adjusting the facts of our personal experience in time with those of a more general experience."

It is still a question of "going beyond," of arriving at the irreducible depths of the image, which is a mysterious depth: "We know that under the revealed image there is another one that is truer to reality, and under this yet another, and yet another under this last one—until the true image emerges of that reality, absolute, mysterious, which nobody will ever see. Or, perhaps, until every image, every reality are shattered." Reality and appearance intersect: we are at *Blow-Up*. And the form of image taken into consideration (the photograph), apparently the most objective of all, helps to bring forth the value of that interaction.

The circle widens to the point of knowledge. More questions also revolve around the process of representation. The question of "what film to make" on which *Identification of a Woman* (and, for now, Antonioni's work) ends refers us to broader questions. What is disturbing is that *aftertime*, on which the end of the film questions itself. Those dispersed images might confirm that the cinema can no longer place itself in direct relation to experience, and will definitely be "other." In the end, an ancient doubt remains, or a point of arrival—that is, the image stands for *what it is*. It seems useful to reread the first lines of *The Dangerous Thread of Things*,[5] and to ask whether Antonioni's statement about how a film is born isn't also a final question: "When they ask me how a film is born, what I don't know is precisely how the birth itself comes about—the delivery, the big bang, the first three minutes—and whether the images of those first three minutes have a spirituality. In other words, whether the film is born first as an answer to a need of its author, or rather, whether the question that those images posit is destined to be nothing more than that—to stand, ontologically, for what it is."

---

[5] A short story from Antonioni's collection *That Bowling Alley on the Tiber*.

THE ARCHITECTURE OF VISION

MY CINEMA

MY EXPERIENCE[1]

The most important factor that, I think, has contributed to making me the director that I am—good or bad, it is difficult for me to say—is perhaps the middle-class environment where I grew up. My family was from the middle-class and we lived in a middle-class world. It was this world that predisposed me toward certain themes, certain characters, certain problems, and certain emotional and psychological conflicts. Evidently, as happens to everybody and in every field, everything I have experienced influenced me in thinking of certain stories, rather than others. This much I can say, but if I had to show precisely which experiences, be they cinematographic or not, have contributed to my formation, I wouldn't be able to do so.

It is also difficult to say how a story is born, how the subject of *Story of a Love Affair* or *The Cry* came into my mind. For me, films are born in the same way that poetry is born for poets; I don't want to pose as a poet, but I would like to make an analogy. Some words, some images, some concepts come into the mind, and they all mix together and become poetry. I believe that the same thing happens with the cinema. Everything that we read, hear, think, and see at a certain moment sets itself in concrete images, and stories are born from these images. Many times

[1]"La mia esperienza," from a meeting held on March 31, 1958, with the students of the Centro Sperimentale di Cinematografia, Rome; originally published in *Bianco e Nero* 6, June 1958. Translated by Allison Cooper.

these stories are prompted by specific facts or events, but this seldom happens to me—or rather, it happened just once, with *The Vanquished*.

Another question deals with Ferrara. I haven't used it much in my films, and even *The Cry* was filmed more in the Veneto region than in Ferrara. The reason? I think that we are more at ease in certain environments than in others. And I believe that to look at things, characters, and landscapes with an interest that is deeper because it comes from those experiences that we had during our adolescence, during our youth, and that continue to live unconsciously inside ourselves—I believe that all of this is very useful, since it allows us to more easily find the motives and the solutions of the stories that come to our minds. Also, there are certain characters that we understand better than others. I would find myself at a disadvantage, for example, if I had to film in the south [of Italy], because I feel very different from the people who live there; I don't understand them.

There is a question concerning Pavese and his diary.[2] I am asked whether or not I find similarities in my films to Pavese's book. I wouldn't know—not intentional ones, anyway. I have read the Pavese's diary, and it could be that something of it stayed inside of me, or that some of his experiences coincide with mine. It is evident that, in one's own films, one always puts in something autobiographical. The very fact of being sincere equals being a little autobiographical. A director who works with sincerity is, before being a director, a man. As such, if he is sincere, he puts all of himself into that film, and therefore includes his own morality, his own opinions. And I believe that one must not start from preconceived ideas, from premises, because this mechanizes everything, it cools everything down. Rather, it is necessary to follow the story itself, the characters themselves—who are what they are—and, in this way, express a certain morality.

2 Cesare Pavese's diary, entitled *Il mestiere di vivere*, was published in Italian in 1952; it was translated into English with the title *The Burning Brand: Diaries 1935–1950* in 1961.

What about my literary preferences? It is a question people often ask me. It seems easy to reply: Flaubert, Hemingway, Scott Fitzgerald, one can say them all. But I think it is a poorly put question, because there are some moments in life when one is interested in a certain cycle. You like bourgeois novels, so you read Fitzgerald; you like popular novels, so you read Steinbeck. I had a great passion for Gide. I read him avidly, I recall—with a ferocious eagerness. I knew him by heart. Today he no longer interests me; it is all over. I can no longer take anything from his work. The same thing with Eliot, whom I have read and reread, and who has been very useful to me. But today I prefer Pasternak. What I mean is that you mature, you evolve, you defer to reality, you keep in step with the times. You assimilate certain literary experiences and that's it. Then you turn to other experiences.

What film do I prefer? And which one of mine? When you answer the first question, you always forget the most important films: it seems to me, however, that one must cite Eisenstein—I liked *Que viva Mexico!* very much; and [Renoir's] *Grand Illusion*, too. I also have great admiration for Dreyer, *Joan of Arc* and other films. And I also like the films of [F.W.] Murnau. There are many other directors and films that I like; for example, [D.W.] Griffith's *Broken Blossoms*.

Which one of my own films? None of them—at least, I don't have a particular predilection for any of them. This is because I have never succeeded in making a film under normal conditions and, therefore, I have never succeeded in saying everything that I wanted to say. When that happens, I will feel satisfied, at least I hope so. All of my films leave me unsatisfied. When I see them again there is always something that irritates me, because I remember the difficulties that I faced, and not having known how to deal with them better makes me angry.

Am I a neorealist director? I really couldn't say. And is neorealism over? Not exactly. It is more correct to say that neorealism is evolving, because whenever a movement or a current ends, it gives life to what comes after it. This goes on all the time. The neorealism of the postwar period, when reality was what it was, so intensely present, focused on the relationship between characters and reality. What was important was that very relationship, which created a cinema based on "situations." Today, instead, since reality has—more or less, for better or worse—been normalized, it seems important to me to look for what is left inside the characters of all their past experiences. That's why, nowadays, it's no longer important to make a film about a man whose bicycle has been stolen—that is, a film about a character who is important because his bicycle has been stolen, and just for this, above all for this; and not to find out if he is shy, if he loves his wife, or if he is jealous, and so on. (These things are not interesting, because the important thing is that particular experience, the mishap with the bicycle that prevents him from working; therefore we must follow him in his search for the bicycle). Here is why, I was saying, such a film no longer seems to me important. Today, once the problem with the bicycle has been eliminated—I am speaking metaphorically, try to see beyond my words—it is important to see what is inside this man whose bicycle was stolen, what are his thoughts, what are his feelings, how much is left inside of him of his past experiences, of the war, of the period after the war, of everything that has happened to our country, a country which, like so many others, has just come out of such an important and serious experience.

This, then, is how the technique that I use (which, by the way, is instinctive to me—I don't make a special project to film in a certain way) seems to me very closely related to the interest I have in following the characters until their innermost thoughts are revealed. I delude myself, possibly, in thinking that staying on top of them with the camera means making them talk. But I believe it is much more cinematic to try and capture the thoughts of a person through an ordinary visual reaction, rather than enclose them in a sentence, that is, in a verbal, didactic form. One of my concerns in filming is to follow the characters until I feel it is time to stop. To follow them not for the sake of it, but because I think it is important to establish, to capture the moments in the life of a character that appear to be less important. When all has been said, when the main scene is over, there are less important moments; and to me, it seems worthwhile to show the character right in these moments, from the back or the front, focusing on a gesture, on an attitude, because they serve to clarify everything that has happened, as well as what is left of it inside the character.

I am trying to film my scenes along this line. I don't read what I have to film in the morning; I know the script by heart, and therefore I don't need to study it each morning sitting at my desk. When I arrive at the studio I ask everybody to leave and I stay alone for fifteen, twenty minutes—as long as I need to try out the camera movements, to master them in order to solve the sequences at the technical level. I do not film several versions of the same scene. I don't have doubts about the position of the cameras. Of course, these are problems I am concerned with; but I solve them at the outset and then I don't think about them any more. For me, camera movements cannot be solved at the desk; they have to be taken care of with the camera itself. I always use the dolly, even if I have to film a fixed frame (and anyway, I prefer to make vertical movements rather than lateral ones). I follow the characters with the camera the way I have planned, making adjustments whenever they are needed. I frame the shot from behind the camera. Some do it differently, even famous directors like Clair.[3] It is a legitimate system, I am not saying it isn't, but how they succeed in filming from little drawings and little sketches they did on paper is a mystery to me. I think that frame composition is a plastic fact, a figurative fact that must be seen in its correct dimension. The acting has value in its relation to the frame composition: A line spoken by an actor at three-quarters is different from the same line spoken at full face or in profile; it takes on a different value, a different meaning.

At this point, we have arrived at the discussion of the actors, and some of the problems of acting. And here, understandably, your questions are

[3] French director René Clair (1898–1981) made films in the 1930s and 1940s that later proved strongly influential on Italian neorealism. Some of his best known titles are: *The Italian Straw Hat, A nous la liberté,* and *Children of Paradise.*

many. I will try to answer as methodically as possible. Here too, evidently, as with the frame composition which we have just discussed, absolute truths do not exist. [Fred] Zinnemann, for example—to mention a director who's working here in Rome—recently said: "I want the actor to pull through by himself. Once it is clear what the character is, who he is, what he wants, what he must represent in the film, the actor must then invent everything by himself. If an actor asks me what he should do, I am in trouble." I find myself in a position opposite to that of Zinnemann. That is, I don't believe that it is necessary to make everything perfectly clear for the actor. I'm not saying that we shouldn't be in agreement over the character, because this is obvious. However, it isn't necessary to define it in detail. It is necessary that the director make the actor understand what he must do, what he has to represent in the film. But I don't believe it is necessary to do what is often done in Italy, both in the theater and in the cinema (I am referring, for example, to Visconti and De Sica), which is to define everything that is behind a certain line, clarify the psychological movements of the various passages, illuminate all of the implications and, in short, thoroughly investigate all the psychological details of that line, set the actor's brain in motion, trying to make him a part of all that seems to be behind every line, every scene, every story, and every single episode of the story. Because if this were true, it would also be true that the best actor is also the most intelligent one, because the actor who is more intelligent is the one who has the greater capacity to understand. On the contrary, this is not the case. To begin with Duse, who was not a woman with exceptional gifts of intelligence, up to the best actresses of our times who, as women, are absolutely of no account, while on the stage (who knows how) succeed in expressing certain sentiments so well, with exquisite psychological sharpness. I believe that, more than intelligence, it is necessary to stimulate the actor's instinct, in whatever way, even with tricks. By trying to make the actor understand what he must do by defining the most remote reasons to him, you risk making the actor's action mechanical, or making him direct himself, which is always wrong because the actor cannot see himself, he cannot judge himself, and therefore he risks not being natural.

Harmonizing the different backgrounds of the actors—this is the problem that a director most frequently has to face. The solution is to have what you want quite clear in your mind. You choose a foreign actor because he has the face of the character you need. If the character is Italian, that actor must become Italian. There is little to be done—either he becomes Italian or he doesn't. It is a question of taking whatever he has of his own country away from him, of making him become Italian in his gestures, in his behavior, in his way of walking. It is a question of instinct; it is a question of progressively polishing him. I could cite numerous experiences in which I found myself having to solve serious problems in my relationship with actors. Going back to the question of intelligence, I should at least mention my relationship with Betsy Blair. She is a very intelligent actress who needs very thorough explanations. I must confess that I spent one of the most terrible and upsetting moments of my cinematographic career with her, when she wanted to read the script of *The Cry* together with me. She claimed that I uncovered the message behind every sentence in the script, which is not possible. The sentences that an actor speaks are things that come out of instinct. They are suggested by the imagination, not by reason, and therefore many times they have no explanations, other than the director's need to have them spoken by a character. It is, very often, an unconscious factor, a natural event, creative and as such it refuses explanation. And therefore, with Betsy Blair, I had to completely invent things in order to give her what she wanted to know, and explain things that in no way corresponded to what I wanted to say. In this way, I was only trying to put her in the condition to play the character better than if I had not explained it to her. With Steve Cochran I had to do something quite different. He—who knows why—had come to Italy expecting to find a directing job—which was just absurd! Therefore, every once in a while he would refuse to do something, saying that he didn't feel that it was necessary. So I was forced to direct him with some tricks—not letting him know what I wanted from him, but trying to get it through means that he absolutely didn't suspect.

Photography is also very important for me because it allows me to establish—something I have always worried about—a more precise relationship between characters and landscape. Gray tones and overcast skies are often characteristics of my films. Is this a figurative preference? Not really, and not exactly. The fact is that when there is no sun, I can film with greater freedom; and that is a choice dictated also by practical considerations. In the sun, the camera's angles are fixed. If the sun is behind, the camera's shadow is there; if the sun is in front, it enters the camera and therefore there are fixed angles, fixed planes. Since one of my concerns is following the character at length, it is clear that without sun I can do so more easily, and in more depth.

I am asked what I think of the relationship between the filmmaker and the public, and whether or not the general public understands my films. To the second question I would answer no, while the reply to the first is a little more complex. There are several ways of making films. There are directors, even at a high level, who pay attention to this relationship; and there are directors who, on the other hand, try to make a film responding to an internal urge. A colleague of mine, very highly thought of, was telling me that he always had in his films a shot showing a large crowd. This statement presented in this way, has very little impact, but in practice I can see how it works. Evidently, this is a way of taking the public into consideration. It is clear that such a shot breaks the monotony of the film; it gives it another rhythm; it allows a greater tension. I believe, in short, that it is a very clever move. If I then tell you that this director is Fellini, you immediately understand that he truly succeeds in transforming a practical need into an aesthetic one. Lucky is he who succeeds in doing it.

The first day that I arrived in France to be Carné's assistant (in the film *Les Visiteurs du Soir*),[4] I was stopped in Nice. I had to stay there for a

---

[4] French director Marcel Carné (1909–) is the author of such films as *Le Jour se lève, Les Visiteurs du soir*, and *The Law Brokers*.

month waiting for the visa to cross the border [with Occupied France]. When I arrived in Paris, it was a Sunday, and it was raining. A sad day, a city which made a tremendous impression on me—it was the first time I saw it. I arrived in this empty studio. There was only a little crew that was filming in an enormous theater. In a corner, there was a little construction, and Carné was filming there. As soon as he saw me he wanted to send me away: "Who is that person?" he shouted. "Get out!" And I said, "But—please—Scalera sent me, the production company that is coproducing the film. Scalera sent me." I had a contract for the film's codirection in my pocket, which I certainly avoided showing Carné. I couldn't tell him, "Look, I count as much as you do." I was embarrassed about it, and it would have been ridiculous to say this to him. I just told him that I was supposed to be his assistant—that Barattolo had sent me to be his assistant. Carné still protested a bit, then said, "OK, I understand. OK, you have eyes: Watch." And then he left. This was my welcome, and there I stayed for a week as an intruder—because you mustn't forget that it was 1942, and France had been occupied by the Italians, and therefore we weren't very popular. Carné, who belonged to the left, disliked me, but he would not even give me the chance to explain to him that, more or less, my political views were no different from his. Therefore, it was very difficult to get along with him. And I must say that I didn't even like his way of filming or of directing the actors. I don't believe I learned much from him. I must say that he worked on instincts and that he was a great technician, and this is what was most useful to me. I think I learned from him how to use the camera at a certain angle.

Making a Film Is My Way of Life[5]

The first time I put an eye behind a camera (a 16mm Bell & Howell), it was in a lunatic asylum. The head of the institution was a great big hulk of a man with a face so ravaged by time that it resembled those of his patients. I was still living then in the quiet old town of Ferrara where I was born, a wonderful little town in the Po Valley. A number of my friends and myself had decided to make a documentary on the insane. The director of the asylum was most anxious to be of service, he even went so far as to roll himself over the floor to show us how his patients reacted under certain provocations. But I was determined to make a documentary that would include the inmates themselves; I was so insistent on this point that he finally said: "Okay, let's try it."

So we set up the camera, got the lights ready and placed the inmates around the room in preparation for the first shot. I must say that they were very cooperative in following our instructions and extremely careful not to make any mistakes. They helped us move things around and I was really quite surprised by their efficiency and good will.

Finally, I gave the order to turn on the lights. I was a bit nervous and anxious. Suddenly, the room was flooded with light, and for an instant the inmates remained absolutely stationary as though they were petrified. I have never seen such expressions of total fear on the faces of any actors.

---

[5] "Fare un film è per me vivere," from *Cinema nuovo* 138, March-April 1959. Originally translated in *Film Culture* 24, Spring 1962.

The scene that followed is indescribable. The inmates started screaming, twisting, and rolling themselves over the floor-just as the head of the asylum had demonstrated earlier. In no time at all the room became an inferno. The inmates tried desperately to get away from the light as if they were being attacked by some kind of prehistoric monster. The same faces that had kept madness within human bounds in the preceding calm, were now crumpled and devastated. And this time we were the ones who stood petrified at the sight. The cameraman didn't even have the strength to turn on the motor, nor I to give an order. It was the head of the asylum who yelled, "Stop, off the lights!" And as the room became silent and subdued, we saw a slow and feeble movement of bodies which seemed to be in their final stages of agony.

I have never forgotten that scene. And it was around this scene that we unconsciously started talking about neorealism.

This all happened before the war. Then came the war and we were witness to many scenes of violence, not to say madness; so the habit became fixed. But that documentary, which was never completed, always remained in my mind, during our postwar discussions on filmmaking in Italy, as a classic representation of neorealism. It seemed that Italian cinema would remain chained to one standard reality, the Real, always more real. The camera was camouflaged in the streets or placed against a keyhole to capture the most hidden aspects of reality. All the esthetic concepts learned in school were swept away in the rush, in the need to overcome theory with facts and with films. Needless to say, many of those films achieved success, for the truth is that the reality around us was exceptional and controversial. How could it be ignored?

Making a film is not like writing a novel. Flaubert once said that living was not his profession; his profession was writing. Making a film, on the contrary, is living—at least it is for me. While I am shooting a film, my personal life is not interrupted; in fact, it is intensified. This total commitment, this pouring of all our energies into the making of a film-what is it if not a way of life, a way of contributing to our personal heritage something of value whose worth can be judged by others? Obviously, when a film is shown to the public, one's own personal concerns which are reflected in the film, also become public. And in the immediate post-war years, which were so full of dire events, so full of anxieties and fears for the world's future, it was impossible to talk of anything else. There are such times when to ignore certain events would be dishonest for a man of intelligence, because an intelligence that absents itself at a crucial moment is a contradiction in terms.

I think filmmakers should always try to reflect the times in which they live; not so much to express and interpret events in their most direct and tragic form (we can also laugh at them, and why not? I love comedies, even though I haven't made any myself yet, and among the comic actors I like most are Danny Kaye and Alec Guinness), but rather to capture their effect upon us, and to be sincere and conscientious with ourselves, to be honest and courageous with others. In my opinion, it is a singular way of living. However, I do feel that the standard of the real, which is the basis of Italian neorealism, must now be met in a wider and deeper sense. In today's return to normal conditions (for better or worse), the relationship between an individual and his environment is less important than the individual himself in his complex and disquieting reality and in his equally complex relations with others.

What is it that torments and motivates modern man? Of all that has happened and is now happening in the world, what are the repercussions inside a man, what are the consequences in his most intimate relationships and dealings with others? Today, more than ever, these are the questions we should keep in mind when we prepare ourselves to make a film.

In discussing my film, *The Cry,* the French critics referred to it as a new form of filmmaking which they called "internal neorealism." Ever since those early days of that documentary about the insane, I have never thought of labeling what for me was always considered a necessity, *i.e.,* to observe and describe the thoughts and feelings that motivate a man in his march to happiness or death. Nor do I ever concern myself with introducing "themes" into my films; I detest films that have a "message." I simply try to tell, or more precisely, show certain vicissitudes that take place, then hope they will hold the viewer's interest no matter how much bitterness they may reveal. Life is not always happy and one must have the courage to look at it from all sides. However, the finished film in itself should contain the meaning. If we are sincere in our narration, the ideas we have will sooner or later always get across. The important thing is that the story should be told with a firm and impassioned conscience. The films I like best are those in which the images convey a sense of reality without losing their force of persuasion. Films that are made without affectation, without indulging in romantic extravagance or intellectual excess, films that look at things exactly as they are: not backwards or forwards, of from the side, but face to face.

ACTORS AND PARADOXES[6]

The critics often note the continuous and intense search for a style in your films. What do you think of this assessment? And what weight do you give to a stylistic search in the laying out of a film?

It is quite accurate that I am seeking out a style. I am of the opinion that it is always necessary to find, for every film, a language that has its own originality. And not only with regard to how to frame certain shots or how to build sequences, but to all the "material" that we use for a film, such as photography, sound, noises, music, and actors.

In what sense do you think of actors as "material"?

In the fullest sense. It may seem, in the phase of preparation for a film or even during the shooting, that I never talk to the actors, that I don't "explain their part to them," as people say, that I don't clarify the obscure points of the characters they have to play. If I do act this way, it is because I intend to consider the acting as one of the means that helps the director express an idea, be it figuratively or strictly conceptually. I force myself, in short, to press the actor for instinct, rather than intelligence. Then I will be th one to select what I need. In short, if I am wrong, it is in saying: "This works and this doesn't." It is a matter of an error of judgment, not of approach.

[6] In *Mondo Nuovo* 27 (December 1959), reprinted in *L'avventura*, edited by Thomas Chiaretti (Bologna: Cappelli, 1960). Translated by Allison Cooper.

One might think that you consider all the actors as indistinguishable, anonymous, brute matter.

Really, no. I know very well that there are intelligent actors, as well as unintelligent ones. But I would like to propose a paradox. On the set, I am more mistrustful of the intelligent ones, because they themselves become directors.

In short, actors should trust their instincts, and the director his brain?

Not exactly. Often I also trust my instinct. If it weren't so, I would not have worked in the absurd conditions that I have worked in. The important thing, however, is not to do exactly what is written in the script, nor to go to the extreme of constantly changing, responding to the demands of the day, of the landscape, of the mood. The important thing is to start off the first shot with the entire film fully developed in mind. It has been said that I am very pedantic and drawn-out in shooting. In reality, I am even more pedantic and drawn-out in the preparation of the film, which is the most difficult time in the making of a film. The day that what you want to do, and what you want to say, becomes clear, then you can relax, and confidently trust your instinct. All of this, you understand, is part of the marvelous world of good intentions.

We began by talking about a constant search for technique. In what way do you conduct this search?

First of all, I would say that one starts from a negative fact, from a weariness of current techniques and methods. I have changed many things in my way of storytelling. I would still like to change more. My idea, for this film [*L'avventura*], would be to build every sequence in a peculiar, particular way. I would like the film to be born under the stimulus of a continuous invention, even if this invention will change the substance in certain areas.

For example?

For example, look at the problem of landscape. In this film the landscape is not only an indispensable component, but almost paramount. I have felt the need to break up the action a lot, inserting in many sequences frames that might seem formalistic or inessential—that is, documentary-type shots (a tornado, the sea, the passage of dolphins, things like that)—but that for me are in reality indispensable, because they "help" the idea of the film.

And what is this idea?

The idea is the observation of a fact. Today we live in a period of extreme instability—political instability, moral instability, social instability, and even physical instability. The world around and inside us is unstable. I am making a film on the instability of feelings, on the mystery of feelings. These characters find themselves on an island, in a rather dramatic situation; a girl in the party is lost. They start to look for her. The man who loves her should be worried, upset, anxious. And, really, at the beginning, he is. But then, slowly, his feelings grow weaker, because they have no strength. And he doesn't want to look for her; by then he isn't worried about it. He is attracted by other feelings, by other "adventures," by other experiences just as unsteady and unstable.

Is it the observation of a moral situation, without judgment?

It's obvious that I, personally, am a man who has his own ideas about the world. If somebody finds that the film has another meaning, more explicit, beside this, it means that things have gone in that direction.

A Talk with Michelangelo Antonioni on his Work[7]

ANTONIONI: Someone once said that words, more than anything else, serve to hide our thoughts. Nevertheless, in answering your questions, I will try to be as direct and honest as possible, as I try to be when I'm working on a film. I didn't come prepared to make a speech, so I've been asking myself what should I say to you and what is it that you want to know about me. I am a filmmaker who began making feature films about ten years ago, and who forced himself to follow a certain direction, to maintain a certain coherence. Now I'm not saying this to pat myself on the back, but I'm saying it because it was the only way I would have been interested in making films. Had I done them in any other way, I probably would have made worse films than the ones I did make.

Now, if you ask me what were the motives and the reasons that led me to make films in this particular manner, I think I can say today that I am motivated by two considerations. (And bear this clearly in mind, these statements are being made *ex post facto* and not *a priori*, that is, I had conception of them until I actually became involved in making feature length

[7] This article is based on the transcript of an open discussion that took place at the Centro Sperimentale di Cinematografia of Rome on March 16, 1961 after a retrospective screening of Antonioni's films for students and faculty members, arranged by the Centro's director, Leonardo Fioravanti. It originally appeared in the school's monthly periodical, *Bianco e nero* with the title: "La malattia dei sentimenti." Originally translated in *Film Culture* 24, Spring 1962.

dramatic films.) The first had to do with those crucial events that were taking place around us immediately after the war, and even later, in 1950, when I first started working in films; the second was simply a technical matter more closely related to cinematography per se. With reference to the first consideration, I will most certainly say that as far as their particular period was concerned, all those so-called Italian neorealistic films, among which are some genuine masterpieces, were representative of the most authentic and the most valid cinematic expression possible, and they were also the most appropriate. After all, it was a period in which everything happening around us was quite abnormal; reality was a burning issue. The events and situations of the day were extraordinarily unusual, and perhaps the most interesting thing to examine at that time was the relationship between the individual and his environment, between the individual and society. Therefore, a film such as *The Bicycle Thief*, for example, where the main character was a laborer who lost his job because someone had stolen his bicycle, and whose every motivation stemmed from that specific fact, and that fact alone, which in itself was the most important aspect of the film and around which its entire story was centered—this, I say, was the type of film necessary and appropriate for its time. (I know I've said this all before, but I don't mind repeating it because it's something of which I'm profoundly convinced.) It really wasn't necessary to know the protagonist's inner thoughts, his personality, or the intimate relationship between him and his wife; all this could very well be ignored. The important thing was to establish his relationship with society. That was the primary concern of the neorealist films made at that time. However, when I started making films, things were somewhat different, and my approach therefore was also different. I had arrived a little late on the scene, at a time when that first flowering of films, though still valid, was already beginning to show signs of exhaustion. Consequently, I was forced to stop and consider what subject matter was worth examining at that particular moment, what was really happening, what was the true state of things, what ideas were really being thought. And it seemed to me that perhaps it was no longer so important, as I said before, to examine the relationship between the individual and his environment, as it was to examine the individual himself, to look inside the individual and see, after all he had been through (the war, the immediate postwar situation, all the events that were currently taking place and which were of sufficient gravity to leave their mark upon society and the individual)—out of all this, to see what remained inside the individual, to see, I won't say the *transformation* of our psychological and emotional attitudes, but at least the symptoms of such restlessness and such behavior which began to outline the changes and transitions that later came about in our psychology, our feelings, and perhaps even our morality.

And so I began with *Story of a Love Affair*, in which I analyzed the condition of spiritual aridity and a certain type of moral coldness in the lives of several individuals belonging to the upper middle class strata of Milanese society. I chose this particular subject because it seemed to me there would be plenty of raw material worth examining in a situation that involved the morally empty existence of certain individuals who were only concerned with themselves, who had no interest whatsoever in anything or anyone outside of themselves, and who had no human quality strong enough to counterbalance this self-centeredness, no spark of conscience left which might still be ignited to revitalize themselves with a sense of the enduring validity of certain basic values. It was this, unfortunately, which led the French critics quite innocently to define my style of filmmaking as being a kind of internal neorealism. At any rate, this seemed to be the right road for me to follow at that time. Later, I will also tell you how and why I had adapted a certain technical approach that was directly in line with this choice.

The second consideration that led me along this particular road was an everincreasing feeling of boredom with the current standardized methods of filmmaking and the conventional ways of telling a story. I was already instinctively aware of this feeling when I first started working on my early documentaries, especially *N.U.*, which I had filmed in a somewhat different manner than what was then considered the orthodox way of making a film. (You will recall, however, that in 1943 I had already started shooting my very first documentary, which wasn't completed until 1947. Ever since then, in addition to making films about landscapes and places of interest, which were the usual kind of films being done in Italy at that time, I began making films about people, and in a way that was much more intense, much more sympathetic, much more involved.) As far as the documentary form was concerned, and especially with *N.U.*, I felt a need to avoid certain established and proven techniques. Even [Giovanni] Paolucci, who was then one of the most noted documentarists, was making his documentaries in accordance with the set standards of the day, that is, in blocks of sequences. Each one of these blocks had its own beginning, its own end, and its own order; when joined together, these blocks constituted a certain parabola that gave the documentary a unity of its own. And they were impeccable documentaries, even from a formal point of view; but I felt somewhat annoyed with all this sense of order, this systematic arrangement of the material. I felt a need to break it up a little. So, having a certain amount of material in my hands, I set out to do a montage that would be absolutely free, poetically free. And I began searching for expressive ways and means, not so much through an orderly arrangement of shots that would give the scene a clear-cut beginning and end, but more through a juxtaposition of separate isolated shots and sequences that had no immediate connection with one another, but which definitely gave more meaning to the idea I had wanted to express and which were the very substance of the documentary itself; in the case of *N.U.*, the life of street-cleaners in a particular city.

When I was ready to start work on *Story of a Love Affair,* I found myself with these observations already acquired and with this basic experience already assimilated. So, as I was saying before, when I used that particular technical approach which consisted of extremely long shots, of tracks and pans that followed the actors uninterruptedly (the longest shot in *Story of a Love Affair,* 132 meters and it was the one taken on the bridge), I did it perhaps instinctively, but reflecting upon it now I can understand what led me to move in that particular direction. In effect, I had the feeling that it wasn't quite right for me to abandon the actor at a time when, having just enacted an intensely dramatic scene, he was left alone by himself to face the after-effects of that particular scene and its traumatic moments. Undoubtedly, those moments of emotional violence had had a meaningful effect upon the actor and had probably served to advance him one step further psychologically. So I felt it was essential for me to follow the actors with the camera a few moments after they had completed their performance of the written scene. And though this may have seemed pointless, it actually turned out that these moments were exactly those which offered me the best opportunity to select and utilize on the moviola screen certain spontaneous movements in their gestures and facial expressions that perhaps could not have been gotten in any other way. (Many times, of course, I had the camera follow the actors even without their being aware of it, that is, at a time when they had thought the shot was finished.)

All this experimentation provided the basis for the results achieved in *La notte*. And I want to say this, that ever since then I believe I have managed to strip myself bare, to liberate myself from the many unnecessary formal techniques that were so common at the time. I am not using the word "formal" in the sense that I had wanted to achieve results that would be strictly figurative. That wasn't the case at all. In fact, this has never been of any interest to me. Instead I have always tried to fill the image with a greater suggestiveness—by composing the shot in a way that would assist me to say precisely what I intend, and at the same time to assist the actors to express exactly what they are required to express, and also to assist in establishing a working rapport between the actors and the background, that is, the activity going on behind them as they perform their particular scene.

So, film by film, I gradually began to divest myself of certain precious and professionalized techniques. However, I must say that I don't regret having had them, for without them perhaps I would not have been able to finally arrive at what I feel is a greater simplicity. Now I can actually permit myself to make some minor technical errors. And I do make them. In fact, sometimes I even do it on purpose, in order to obtain a greater degree of effectiveness. For example, certain unorthodox uses of "field" and "counterfield," certain errors regarding position or movement. Thus, I have rid myself of much unnecessary technical baggage, eliminating all the logical narrative transitions, all those connective links between sequences where one sequence served as a springboard for the one that followed. The reason I did this was because it seemed to me—and of this I am firmly convinced—that cinema today should be tied to the truth rather than to logic. And the truth of our daily lives is neither mechanical, conventional nor artificial, as stories generally are, and if films are made that way, they will show it. The rhythm of life is not made up of one steady beat; it is, instead, a rhythm that is sometimes fast, sometimes slow; it remains motionless for a while, then at the next moment it starts spinning around. There are times when it appears almost static, there are other times when it moves with tremendous speed, and I believe all this should go into the making of a film. I'm not saying one should slavishly follow the day-to-day routine of life, but I think that through these pauses, through this attempt to adhere to a definite reality—spiritual, internal, and even moral—there springs forth what today is more and more coming to be known as modern cinema, that is, a cinema which is not so much concerned with externals as it is with those forces that move us to act in a certain way and not in another. Because the important thing is this: that our acts, our gestures, our words are nothing more than the consequences of our own personal situation in relation to the world around us.

And for this reason it seems most important nowadays for us to make these so-called "literary" or "figurative" films. (Obviously, these terms are paradoxical, because I am absolutely sure that no such thing as a literary film or a figurative film exists. There exists only cinema, which incorporates the experience of all the other arts.) I think it is important at this time for cinema to turn toward this internal form of filmmaking, toward ways of expression that are absolutely free, as free as those of literature, as free as those of painting which has reached abstraction. Perhaps one day cinema will also achieve the heights of abstraction; perhaps cinema will even construct poetry, a cinematic poem in rhyme. Today this may seem absolutely unthinkable, and yet little by little, perhaps even the public will come to accept this kind of cinema. I say this because something of the sort is already taking shape, something which even the public is becoming aware of, and which I think is the reason why certain so-called difficult films today are even achieving commercial success; they no longer remain in the film libraries, they no longer remain in the can. Instead, these films are reaching the great masses of people; in fact, I would say the more widespread they become, the more they are being understood.

ENZO BATTAGLIA [*student of the Centro's directing class*]: With reference to that shot in *La notte* where Jeanne Moreau, at a certain point, moves along that white wall against which she appears almost crushed—was this a planned shot, one that was in the original script, or was it improvised there on the spot? In other words, what I'd like to know is to what extent you plan your shots in advance and to what extent you let yourself be influenced by the locale during the actual shooting.

ANTONIONI: I believe that in every form of artistic endeavor, there is first of all a process of selection. This selection, as Camus once said, represents the artist's revolt against the forces of reality. So whenever I'm ready to start shooting a scene, I arrive on location in a fixed state of "virginity." I do this because I believe the best results are obtained by the "collision" that takes place between the environment in which the scene is to be shot and my own particular state of mind at that specific moment. I don't like to study or even think about a scene the night before, or even a few days before I actually start shooting it. And when I arrive there, I like to be completely alone, by myself, so that I can get to feel the environment without having anybody around me. The most direct way to recreate a scene is to enter into a rapport with the environment itself; it's the simplest way to let the environment suggest something to us. Naturally, we are well acquainted with that area in advance, from the moment we have selected it, and therefore know that it offers the proper setting for the particular scene that's being shot. So it's only a matter of organizing and arranging the sequence, adapting it to the characteristic details of the surrounding environment. For this reason, I always remain alone in the area for about half an hour before I start shooting a scene, whether it's an indoor scene or an outdoor scene. Then I call in the actors and begin testing out the scene, because this too is a way of judging whether the scene works well or not. In fact, it's possible that a well-planned scene that was written while sitting behind the desk, just won't work anymore once it's laid out in a particular locale, so it has to be changed or modified right there and then. Certain lines in the script might take on a different meaning once they're spoken against a wall or against a street background. And a line spoken by an actor in profile doesn't have the same meaning as one given full-face. Likewise, a phrase addressed to the camera placed above the actor doesn't have the same meaning it would if the camera were placed below him. But the director (and, I repeat, this is my own personal way of working) becomes aware of all these things only when he's on the scene and starts moving his actors around according to the first impressions that come to him from being there. So, it is extremely rare that I have the shots already fixed in my mind. Obviously, in the various stages of preparing a film, a director creates images in his mind, but it is always dangerous to fall in love with these formulated images, because you eventually end up by running after images abstracted from the reality of the environment in which the scene is being shot and which are no longer the same as they first appeared while sitting behind the desk. It is really much better to adapt yourself to a new situation, and this is especially so since the nature of film scripts today, as you know, are becoming less and less detailed and less and less technical. They are the director's notes, and serve as a model on which one works during the course of the shooting. So, as I was saying a short while ago, improvisation comes directly from the rapport that is established between the environment and ourselves, from the rapport between the director and the people around him, both the usual professional collaborators and the people who just happen to be gathered in that particular area when the scene is being shot. In other words, it is possible that the rapport itself could suggest the outcome of a scene; it could suggest the modification of a line; it could suggest so many things inasmuch as it too is a method of improvisation. So, I repeat, for this reason I very seldom give much advance thought to the shot but prefer to think about it when I'm there on the scene and when I put my eye behind the camera.

GIULIO CESARE CASTELLO [*film critic and member of the Centro faculty*]: This pertains to a natural setting, but what about the studio where the set is constructed according to a preconceived design?

ANTONIONI: What I said also applies to a studio set.

CASTELLO: Certain reciprocal stimuli inherent in a scene that is shot in a natural environment do not exist in one that is shot in a studio, which, to some extent, always creates a kind of limitation, if for no other reason than there exists a scenography; the set, therefore, is constructed in a specific way and there are certain movements which you simply cannot make, unless you plan and construct the scenography in a different way.

ANTONIONI: Aside from the fact that I've been working less and less in a studio (I've now made two films without once setting foot in a studio), I can say that even there the situation I described holds true. Of course, when preparing a set within a studio, I sketch out an idea for the designer or architect as to what I think the scene should be like, establishing thereby a certain rapport with the surroundings. But not until I actually find myself on the finished set, at that moment and that moment only, do I have the exact feeling of what the scene should really look like. And to some extent even those surroundings, which I myself to a certain extent have set up, can offer me surprises and suggest some changes, some new ideas. And I never reject those suggestions. Even here, before I start shooting, I remain alone by myself for a period of twenty minutes, a half hour, and sometimes even longer.

ANTONIO PETRUCCI [*member of the Centro faculty*]: If I'm not mistaken, you once wrote somewhere that just before you start shooting a scene, you put yourself in a state somewhat similar that of a writer in front of a blank page. And yet, undoubtedly, you must have some clue in mind as to what you want to do, just as a writer does; he doesn't sit down in front of a blank page unless he first has a definite idea what he wants to write about.

ANTONIONI: No, but to continue your metaphor, you might say it's more like a writer who has an idea in mind as to what the house in which his character lives should be like, but has not yet begun to describe it. The creation doesn't take place until he describes it. Just as a scene in a film isn't depicted until the actual shooting of that scene takes place. Now there are more than a thousand ways an actor can enter a room and slap someone across the face. But there is only one right way; the other fifty thousand are all wrong. It's a matter of finding the right way. So, when I enter upon a new environment, I feel as though I were in front of a blank page—I have no idea where to begin. And I'm pursued by doubts right up until that moment when I see the material on the moviola screen. Therefore, I would think that even the studio can offer some surprises. Because the moment you place the actors on the scene, then, from the rapport established between the actors and their surroundings—a rapport that is absolutely new and spontaneous—you get an idea as to what should follow, depending on how the situation effects you. If every detail in the sequence were foreseen, well, then there wouldn't be any need at all for the dolly. Today a film is made while in progress; it is written right there on the spot, with the camera.

CASTELLO: This method makes it necessary for you to shoot much more than the usual amount of footage. For example, how many feet of film did you shoot for *L'avventura* and *La notte?*

ANTONIONI: Not so much. At least, not an extreme amount. For *L'avventura*, I shot about 170,000 feet; for *La notte* about 140,000. So that's not much.

CASTELLO: I would like to ask another question of a more general nature. There being no doubt that everything you did to date was done the way you wanted to do it, inasmuch as you never have had to compromise yourself with the producers, is there anything in your films that you your-self reject, anything with which you are dissatisfied, not in the sense that every artist is always more or less dissatisfied with almost everything he has done in the past, but rather something you feel you shouldn't have done or which you should have done differently?

ANTONIONI: Although I'm not completely satisfied with everything I've done—which is something natural and logical—I believe there's no particular film that leaves me more dissatisfied than any other. However, there are certain parts in some films that displease me more than other parts. For example, in *The Vanquished*, and also some sections in *The Lady without Camellias*, which is a film I consider to be a mistake, mainly because I started off on the wrong foot from the very beginning of the film by concentrating on a character who then turned out to be the wrong one. Others may find that this is not so, but for me, knowing what I had in mind, I felt very bitter over the fact that I had to make so many changes from the original idea. However, there are some sequences in the film which I would do exactly the same way today. In *I vinti*, I was particularly dissatisfied with the Italian episode. And even in the French episode, I would now change many things, since I have come to know France a little better since then. Perhaps I'd leave the English episode as it is. But it's very difficult to judge this way, because even in *L'avventura* it seems to me there are certain things that I don't like anymore; even in *La notte*. And then, with *La notte*, I'm still so close to it that I haven't come to like it yet, and I'm not sufficiently detached from the film to really judge it.

FIORAVANTI: In *L'avventura*, what are the parts that least satisfy you?

ANTONIONI: Well, for example, today I would do the entire party scene at the end in a different way. I don't mean it's not good as it is now: I mean I would just do it differently, perhaps worse, but in any case, differently. Then, certain scenes on the islands, for example, certain things with the father, certain things with the helicopter.

KRYSTYNA STYPULKOWSKA [*student in the Centro's acting classes*]: First of all, I would like to speak about *L'avventura*, or more precisely, about the significance of its ending, its conception.

I understand one should never put such questions to a director, and for this I apologize, but some of us have spent many hours, actually entire nights, in discussing this very problem because every one of us saw it in a different way. Some said it dealt with an almost Pascalian conception of life, which lays bare the solitude of man, his perpetual failure, his humiliation, his attempt to escape from a world in which there is no way out. Others found in this ending, however disconcerting, a conception of life that is perhaps more optimistic than any of your other films. What are your thoughts on the subject?

My second question, though banal, interests me enormously inasmuch as I'm a student of acting. I would like to know how you work with actors. To be more precise, do you change your methods according to the personality of the actors? For example, let's take three actresses who have worked with you and who are quite different from each other: Lucia Bosé, Jeanne Moreau, and Monica Vitti.

ANTONIONI: I think it would be appropriate at this time to read you a statement I made at a press conference given for the opening of *L'avventura* at Cannes. It pretty well reflects my thoughts regarding the motives and the considerations that moved me to make *L'avventura* and, in a general way, sort of answers the young lady's question, which I will reply to more directly later on.

"Today the world is endangered by an extremely serious split between a science that is totally and consciously projected into the future, and a rigid and stereotyped morality which all of us recognize as such and yet sustain out of cowardice or sheer laziness. Where is this split most evident? What are its most obvious, its most sensitive, let us even say its most painful, areas? Consider the Renaissance man, his sense of joy, his fullness, his multifarious activities. They were men of great magnitude, technically able and at the same time artistically creative, capable of feeling their own sense of dignity, their own sense of importance as human beings, the Ptolemaic fullness of man. Then man discovered that his world was Copernican, an extremely limited world in an unknown universe. And today a new man is being born, fraught with all the fears and terrors and stammerings that are associated with a period of gestation. And what is even more serious, this new man immediately finds himself burdened with a heavy baggage of emotional traits which cannot exactly be called old and outmoded but rather unsuited and inadequate. They condition us without offering us any help, they create problems without suggesting any possible solutions. And yet it seems that man will not rid himself of this baggage. He reacts, he loves, he hates, he suffers under the sway of moral forces and myths which today, when we are at the threshold of reaching the moon, should not be the same as those that prevailed at the time of Homer, but nevertheless are.

Man is quick to rid himself of his technological and scientific mistakes and misconceptions. Indeed, science has never been more humble and less dogmatic than it is today. Whereas our moral attitudes are governed by an absolute sense of stultification. In recent years, we have examined these moral attitudes very carefully, we have dissected them and analyzed them to the point of exhaustion. We have been capable of all this but we have not been capable of finding new ones, we have not been capable of making any headway whatsoever toward a solution of this problem, of this ever-increasing split between moral man and scientific man, a split which is becoming more and more serious and more and more accentuated. Naturally, I don't care to nor can I resolve it myself; I am not a moralist and my film is neither a denunciation nor a sermon. It is a story told in images whereby, I hope, it may be possible to perceive not the birth of a mistaken attitude but the manner in which attitudes and feelings are misunderstood today. Because, I repeat, the present moral standards we live by, these myths, these conventions are old and obsolete. And we all know they are, yet we honor them. Why? The conclusion reached by the protagonists in my film is not one of sentimentality. If anything, what they finally arrive at is a sense of pity for each other. You might say that this too is nothing new. But what else is left if we do not at least succeed in achieving this? Why do you think eroticism is so prevalent today in our literature, our theatrical shows, and elsewhere? It is a symptom of the emotional sickness of our time. But this preoccupation with the erotic would not become obsessive if Eros were healthy, that is, if it were kept within human proportions. But Eros is sick; man is uneasy, something is bothering him. And whenever something bothers him, man reacts, but he reacts badly, only on erotic impulse, and he is unhappy. The tragedy in *L'avventura* stems directly from an erotic impulse of this type—unhappy, miserable, futile. To be critically aware of the vulgarity and the futility of such an overwhelming erotic impulse, as is the case with the protagonist in *L'avventura*, is not enough or serves no purpose. And here we witness the crumbling of a myth, which proclaims it is enough for us to know, to be critically conscious of ourselves, to analyze ourselves in all our complexities and in every facet of our personality. The fact of the matter is that such an examination is not enough. It is only a preliminary step. Every day, every emotional encounter gives rise to a new adventure. For even though we know that the ancient codes of morality are decrepit and no longer tenable, we persist, with a sense of perversity that I would only ironically define as pathetic, in remaining loyal to them. Thus moral man who has no fear of the scientific unknown is today afraid of the moral unknown. Starting out from this point of fear and frustration, his adventure can only end in a stalemate."

That was the statement I read in France. I believe one can deduce from its premise the significance of the film's ending, which, depending on how you look at it, might be considered either optimistic or pessimistic. Georges Sadoul has made a little discovery which I later found to be in agreement with what I had intended when I shot the final scene. I don't know if you still remember it. On one side of the frame is Mount Etna in all its snowy whiteness, and on the other is a concrete wall. The wall corresponds to the man and Mount Etna corresponds somewhat to the situation of the woman. Thus the frame is divided exactly in half; one half containing the concrete wall which represents the pessimistic side, while the other half showing Mount Etna represents the optimistic. But I really don't know if the relationship between these two halves will endure or not, though it is quite evident the two protagonists will remain together and not separate. The girl will definitely not leave the man; she will stay with him and forgive him. For she realizes that she too, in a certain sense, is somewhat like him. Because—if for no other reason—from the moment she suspects Anna may have returned, she becomes so apprehensive, so afraid she may be back and still alive, that she begins to lose the feeling of friendship that she once had for Anna, just as he had lost his affection for Anna and perhaps is also beginning to lose it for her. But what else can she do but stay with him? As I was saying before, what would be left if there weren't this mutual sense of pity, which is also a source of strength. In *La notte* the protagonists go somewhat further. In *L'avventura* they communicate only through this mutual sense of pity; they do not speak to one another. In *La notte*, however, they do converse with each other, they communicate freely, they are fully aware of what is happening to their relationship. But the result is the same, it doesn't differ. The man becomes hypocritical, he refuses to go on with the conversation because he knows quite well that if he openly expresses his feelings at that moment, everything would be finished. But even this attitude indicates a desire on his part to maintain the relationship, so then the more optimistic side of the situation is brought out.

CASTELLO: I find it a bit ridiculous, this wanting to establish whether an ending is optimistic or pessimistic. However, I have noticed there is a certain divergence of opinion. I find the ending of *L'avventura* far more optimistic than that of *La notte*. And yet there are some who find *La notte* more optimistic.

ANTONIONI: Once, in a situation similar to this, Pirandello was asked some questions about his characters, his scenes, his comedies. And he replied: "How should I know? I'm the author." Now for the young lady's second question about acting. With actors, I use certain ideas and methods which are strictly personal, and I don't know if they are right or wrong. Looking back at what has been my experience with actors, I can say that I directed them in a certain way only because I didn't care to work in any other way since my way seemed to give me the best results. And then, I am not like those directors, such as De Sica and Visconti, who can "show" the actor exactly how the scene is to be enacted. This is something I wouldn't know how to do inasmuch as I myself do not know how to act. I believe, however, that I know what I want from my actors. As I see it, an actor need not necessarily understand everything he is doing. In this respect, I always have a great deal of trouble when I first begin working with my actors, especially with some foreign actors. There is a general belief that actors must understand everything they do when enacting a scene. If this were so, then the best actor would be the one who is the most intellectual, which is simply not the case; the facts show us that often the reverse is true. The more an actor forces himself to comprehend the meaning of a scene, the more he tries to achieve a deeper understanding of a given line, a sequence, or the film itself, the more obstacles he sets up between the really natural spontaneity of that scene and its ultimate realization. Aside from the fact that by doing such, he tends to become, in a certain sense, his own director; and this is more harmful than beneficial. Now, I find it's not necessary for a director to have his actors rack their brains; it's better, in every respect, for them to use their instinct. As a director, I shouldn't have to consult with them regarding my conception of the way I feel a scene should bell done. Otherwise, by revealing to them what is after all my own personal plan of action, they automatically become a kind of Trojan horse in what is supposed to be my citadel, which is mine by virtue of the fact that I am the one who knows what I want from them and I am the one who knows whether their response to what I ask for is good or bad. Inasmuch as I consider an actor as being only one element in a given scene, I regard him as I regard a tree, a wall, or a cloud, that is, as just one element in the overall scene; the attitude or pose of the actor, as determined under my direction, cannot but help to effect the framing of that scene, and I, not the actor, am the one who can know whether that effect is appropriate or not. Furthermore, as I said previously, a line spoken by an actor where the camera is facing him from above has one meaning, while it has another meaning if the camera is facing him from below, etc., etc. Only the director can judge these things, not the actor. And the same applies to intonation, which is primarily a sound and only secondarily a line in a piece of dialogue. It is a sound that should be made to integrate with the other sounds accompanying a given image, and at that moment, when the actor speaks his line, all the sounds, including his delivery of that line, that combine to make up the total sound pattern appropriate to that image or sequence, are not there yet. The actor pays no attention to all these details, but the director does. And that's not all. Even improvisation is a factor in connection with this particular subject. For instance, when an actor makes a mistake in delivering a line, I let him make that mistake. That is, I let him go ahead with his mistake because I want to see how it sounds, how it works, before he goes ahead and corrects that mistake. I want to see whether I can somehow utilize that mistake. Because at that moment his mistakes are the most spontaneous things he can give me, and it is that spontaneity of his which I have need of, even though he gives it to me against his will. When going through a scene before shooting it, I often try out certain pieces of dialogue or certain actions which may not have anything to do with the actual scene itself, and I am forcefully embarrassed when the actors ask me for explanations. Because beyond a certain point, I don't want to tell them anything. When I was doing *The Cry*, that excellent actress Betsy Blair wanted to go over the script with me, and she would ask me for an explanation of every line. Those two hours I spent with her going over that script were the most hellish hours of my life, since I was forced to invent meanings that weren't there at all. However, they were the meanings she had wanted me to give her, so she was satisfied. And this should also be taken under consideration.

There is another reason why I feel it really isn't necessary to explain every scene to your actors, for if you did so that would mean you'd have to give the same explanation to each actor. And this would not do, at least not for me. In order to get the best results, I know that I have to say one thing to one actor and something else to another actor. Because I am supposed to understand his temperament, I am supposed to know how he reacts, that when affected a certain way, he reacts a certain way, and when affected another way, he reacts differently. So it's not possible to use the same approach with every actor. To the director, the scene itself remains always the same, but when I approach the actors, in order for me to obtain the desired results, my explanations to them have to vary in accordance with the nature and temperament of each actor.

STEFANO SATTA [*student of the Centro's acting classes*]: Although *L'avventura* and *La notte* both end with a new awareness on the part of the protagonists (you mentioned a mutual feeling of pity) while *The Cry* ends with a suicide, it seems to me that *L'avventura* and *La notte* are more imbued with agony and despair than *The Cry*. Is this merely coincidental or is it actually because of the different social climate involved?

ANTONIONI: This is a question the critics can answer more efficiently than I can. You are not really asking me a question, you are making an observation. In other words, what you're telling me is that *L'avventura* and *La notte* succeeded in achieving their aims while *The Cry* did not. When the critics said—with regards to *The Cry*—that I was cold, cynical, and completely inhuman, they evidently weren't aware of what I was trying to say. Perhaps I was not precisely aware of it myself at the time, and it only became clear to me after having done the other two films. Perhaps *L'avventura* and *La notte* help somewhat to explain *Il grido*, which, if shown in Italy today might receive a greater success than when if first came out. I would say that *The Cry* is a more pessimistic film, more full of despair, which may be due to the fact that I myself, at that particular moment in my life, was in a certain state of depression. So if the film didn't reflect this, I'd really be surprised.

SATTA: I would like to express myself more precisely. In *The Cry* I found a greater feeling of human warmth than I did in *L'avventura* and *La notte*.

FIORAVANTI: I think he means that *The Cry* ends in a more dramatic and tragic manner, that is, with a suicide; but, in certain aspects, he finds this film is actually more optimistic than either *L'avventura* or *La notte*, which seem colder to him in spite of the fact that they contain certain glimmers of hope.

ANTONIONI: But insofar as this human warmth is no longer of any value to the protagonist, insofar as it doesn't help to prevent him from destroying himself, the ending of this film is more pessimistic than the others. I don't know. In spite of everything, this quality of human warmth as expressed by the main character in *The Cry* doesn't serve him at all as any link to the rest of humanity. He is a person who is no longer attached to life.

SATTA: I would like to ask you another question. Regarding the final scene in *La notte*, I feel that you have departed from your usual style; in the sense that whereas you have been accused at times of making your characters say so very little to each other, in the final scene of *La notte* almost the opposite is true. With that final conversation between the husband and wife it almost seems that you want to give an explanation for the benefit and comfort of the spectators.

ANTONIONI: I don't know if it gives that impression or not. Actually, that conversation, which is really a soliloquy, a monologue by the wife, is a kind of summing-up of the film to clarify the real meaning of what took place. The woman is still willing to discuss, to analyze, to examine the reasons for the failure of their marriage. But she is prevented from doing so by her husband's refusal to admit its failure, his denial, his inability to remember or unwillingness to remember, his refusal to reason things out, his incapacity to find any basis for a new start through a lucid analysis of the situation as it is. Instead, he tries to take refuge in an irrational and desperate attempt to make physical contact. It is because of this stalemate that we do not know what possible solution they could come to.

CHRISTA WINDISCH-GRATZ [*student of the Centro's acting classes*]: Between *L'avventura*, *La notte*, and *The Cry*, I particularly liked *The Cry*. I liked the ending of *Il grido* because it clarifies something, it arrives at a definite conclusion, one that is perhaps too cruel, that needn't be so, but nevertheless that's the way it is. Whereas *L'avventura* and *La notte* leave me cold because they don't come to any definite conclusion.

ANTONIONI: Lucretius, who was certainly one of the greatest poets who ever lived, once said, "Nothing appears as it should in a world where nothing is certain. The only thing certain is the existence of a secret violence that makes everything uncertain." Think about this for a moment. What Lucretius said of his time is still a disturbing reality, for it seems to me this uncertainty is very much part of our own time. But this is unquestionably a philosophical matter. Now you really don't expect me to resolve such problems or to propose any solutions? Inasmuch as I am the product of a middle-class society, and am preoccupied with making middle-class dramas, I am not equipped to do so. The middle class doesn't give me the means with which to resolve any middle-class problems. That's why I confine myself to pointing out existing problems without proposing any solutions. I think it is equally important to point them out as it is to propose solutions.

BANG-HANSEN [*student of the Centro's directing class*]: I would like to know to what extent you believe lucidity could be a form of salvation or a way out.

ANTONIONI: Now, look, lucidity is not a solution. In fact, I would say it puts you at a greater disadvantage, because where you have lucidity there is no longer any reason for the existence of a scale of values, and therefore one finds one's self even more at a loss. Certainly, I am for lucidity in all things, because this is my position as a secular man. But in a certain sense I still envy those who can draw upon their faith and somehow manage to resolve all their problems. But this is not so with everyone. You ask me questions of such magnitude that I feel I'm much too small to answer them.

PAOLO TODISCO [*student of the Centro's acting class*]: To go back to your experiences with actors, you said that you try to create a characterization, giving the actor a minimum amount of directions, and then wait to see how he himself develops a certain theme.

ANTONIONI: No, that's not quite right. If never let the actor do anything on his own. I give him precise instructions as to what he is supposed to do.

TODISCO: Okay, then here is my question: In your films, you have worked with the following three actors: Lucia Bosé, Steve Cochran, and Monica Vitti. Three kinds of experiences, three different types of actors: Lucia Bosé, who has done very little before she started working with you; Steve Cochran, whose experience is that of a school much different than ours; and Monica Vitti, who comes to films from the stage. Which of the three gave you the most difficulty?

ANTONIONI: Steve Cochran. Because he is the least intelligent of the three.

CASTELLO: Just a moment. Only a short while ago you said you didn't want intelligent actors; you wanted it this way yourself, so why do you regret it now?

ANTONIONI: Let me explain. He was less intelligent in the sense that when I specifically asked him to do something, he simply refused to do it. If I gave him certain directions and told him to follow those directions to the letter, would abruptly tell me, "No." "Why not?" I would ask him. And he would reply, "Because I'm not a puppet." Now that was too much to tolerate—after all, there's a limit to everything. As a result, I had to direct him by using tricks without ever telling him what it was I wanted.

GUIDO CINCOTTI: But it was resolved one way or the other. Either Cochran finally resigned himself to following your directions or else this underhand method you used went well. Because the end results were excellent.

ANTONIONI: No, because he just went ahead and did everything he wanted—only he never became aware of the tricks I had to use in order to get what I wanted from him. With regards to Lucia Bosé, I had to direct her almost with a sense of violence. Before every scene, I had to put her in a state of mind appropriate to that particular scene. If it was a sad scene, I had to make her cry; if it was a happy scene, I had to make her laugh. As for Monica Vitti, I can say she's an extremely serious actress. She comes from the Academy, and therefore possesses an extraordinary sense of craft. Even so, there were many times when we were not in agreement on certain solutions, and I was forced to beg her not to interfere in my domain.

TODISCO: It is said that a stage actor generally creates some difficulties for the director of a film. Now have you had such difficulties with, for example, Monica Vitti who was originally a stage actress?

ANTONIONI: No, I wouldn't say so. Because Monica Vitti is a very modern actress, so even in her theatrical career she never had those attitudes which can be defined as "theatrical." Therefore, I didn't have any great difficulty with her. And then Monica Vitti is extraordinarily expressive. This is a great quality for a film actor. Perhaps on stage this expressiveness was of less value to her; that is, if an actor does have such a quality, it is all the better, but if he does not, it doesn't really matter much; what is more important for the stage is the actor's attitude. At a distance of one hundred feet, the actor's facial expression is lost, but in a film what counts the most is the actor's expressions. And Monica Vitti has an extremely expressive face.

MARIO VERDONE [*film critic and member of Centro's faculty*]: Currently, what is your opinion about the contribution music can make to a film? I say currently because it has seemed to me this contribution has diminished in your last two films.

ANTONIONI: I think music has had and can continue to have a great function in films, because there is no art form which the film medium cannot draw upon. In the case of music, it draws directly, and therefore the relationship is even closer. It seems to me, however, that this relationship is beginning to change. In fact, the way music is being used today is quite different than it was used ten years ago. At that time music was used to create a certain atmosphere in order to help get the image across to the spectator. Earlier, of course, in the period of the silent film, there was the old pianola which was originally used to hide the noise of the projecting machine and then, later, as a means to emphasize the images that passed over the screen in absolute silence. Since then, the use of music in films has changed a great deal, but in certain films today it is still being used that way, that is, as a kind of external commentary. Its function is to establish a rapport between the music and the spectator, not between the music and the film which is its proper function. Even to this day, especially in certain films from Hollywood, a battle scene is accompanied with violent symphonic crescendos from a full orchestra; a sad scene is always accompanied with violin music because it is felt that violins create an atmosphere of sadness. But this seems to me to be a completely wrong way to use music, and has nothing whatever to do with cinematography.

There are, of course, certain films where music is used in a more meaningful way, as a means to complement the images, to heighten and intensify the meaning of the image. And this has been done with certain scenes in *L'avventura* and in [Alain] Resnais's *Hiroshima, mon amour*. And I must say that the music really worked well in these cases, that is, it expressed what the images themselves intended to express, it was used as an integral part of the image. Having said this, however, I must also say that I am personally very reluctant to use music in my films, for the simple reason that I prefer to work in a dry manner, to say things with the least means possible. And music is an additional means. I have too much faith in the efficacy, the value, the force, the suggestiveness of the image to believe that the image cannot do without music. It is true, however, that I have a need to draw upon sound, which serves an essential "musical" function. I would therefore say that true film "music" has not yet been invented. Perhaps it might be in the future. Until that time comes, however, I feel that music should be spliced out of the film and spliced into a disc, where it has an autonomy of its own.

PETRUCCI: In connection with this, I want to bring up the entire sequence in *La notte* that takes place in the streets of Milan. It is clear that when those street sounds, those automobile horns, etc., are isolated from their corresponding images, they have no meaning in themselves.

At the same time, however, when heard in relation to those images, their function is exclusively a musical one.

ANTONIONI: Of course. But there must be a mutual rapport. That is, the images cannot stand alone, without those sounds—just as those sounds would have no meaning at all if they were detached from the images.

VERDONE: I seem to find a certain predilection in your films for contemporary art. Not so much with regards to the paintings of [Giorgio] Morandi which are seen in *La notte* or of the abstract paintings seen in *The Girlfriends,* but more so in your framing of the image itself, in your manner of seeing things, for example, a white wall or a gravel path or some wooden boards nailed to a window. That is, you seem to have a predilection for a kind of painting which might be called non-painting, like that of [Alberto] Burri, or a sculpture by [Pietro] Consagra, or similar artists—I could cite [Emilio] Vedova, [Lucio] Fontana, etc., etc. I would like to know if this is accidental (and I'm sure it's not since it seems to me nothing is accidental in your films) or is there a definite rapport between contemporary art and your latest films?

ANTONIONI: I have a great love for painting. For me, it is the one art, along with architecture, that comes immediately after filmmaking. I'm very fond of reading books on art and architecture, of leafing through pages and pages of art volumes, and I like to go to art shows and keep in touch with the latest work being done in art—not just to be *au courant* but because painting is something that moves me passionately. Therefore I believe all these perceptions and this interest have been somewhat assimilated. And, naturally, having followed modern art, my taste and my predilection for a certain style would be reflected in my work. But in framing a shot, I certainly don't have any particular painter or painting in mind; that's something I avoid.

PETRUCCI: I'd like to ask you a question about something you mentioned before, concerning your earlier work and its particular tendency, from a technical point of view, toward using long shots, long tracks, long pans, etc. We have not seen any widespread indication of this in your latest films. Can we therefore assume that a change has taken place in your method of expression, that you are now using your technical means of expression in a different way?

ANTONIONI: When I began *Story of a Love Affair*, as I said a short while ago, I did not consciously intend to make a film in that particular way, that is, it was not a preconceived style that was evolved while sitting behind the desk. But when I started climbing on the dolly to follow the actors around in the first scene, I saw that it wasn't essential to cut right at the specified end of that scene, so I continued shooting on for a while longer. As I already said before, I felt an urge to keep the camera on the actors even after the prescribed action was completed. Evidently, I did this because I felt the best way to capture their thoughts, their states of mind was to follow them around physically with the camera. Thus the long shots, the continuous panning, etc. Later, however, as I went along (and here I should say that even in making this film I worked quite instinctively) I became aware that perhaps this was not the best method after all, that perhaps I was concentrating too much on the external aspects of the actors' states of mind and not enough on the states of mind themselves. Perhaps it would be better, I thought, to construct the scene and try different camera movements and montage so that by setting up the camera at one level, then using a certain pan in a preceding or following shot, I could obtain the results I wanted. In short, I realized that just one specific technical approach was not enough to obtain the particular type of shots I would need to go beyond the literal aspects of the story, but that it was necessary to work more closely with the material itself, selecting those particular objects in the scene by various methods.

FRANCO BRONZI [*student of scenography*]: When speaking with some of the student directors here at the Centro, there are certain times when we students of scenography meet up with some rather strange notions. We find that student directors or young directors have the feeling that scenography is not very important. It seems that as far as they are concerned, to shoot a scene against a natural wall of a building is more or less the same thing as shooting a scene against a wall constructed in a studio. According to your way of thinking, is scenography an important contributing factor in the successful realization of a film?

ANTONIONI: I wouldn't say it isn't. It could be. It depends on the type of film you make. For example, in the next few months I'll be doing a film where I don't think I'll have any need of a studio, but immediately after that, at least if I don't change my mind and start something else, I'll be doing another film entirely inside a studio. For it will be done in color and I want to inject my own color scheme, that is, I want to paint the film as one paints a canvas; I want to invent the color relationships, I don't want to limit myself by one photographing natural colors. In this case, scenography becomes an extremely important element. There is also something to be said for scenography when one shoots a film outdoors and wants to obtain a specific kind of background—then scenography is as important as it is in a studio. Today there are several filmmakers who are working in somewhat the same way I have and will be working. Resnais, for example, is one of these, as well as several young filmmakers like [Jean-Luc] Godard and others. They actually intervene and change the natural setting of the environment, and even go so far as to paint walls and add trees. It's not a matter of merely selecting a place and accepting it exactly as it is. A natural setting provides you with enough of an idea of the background required for the realization of a scene, but even outdoors one should intervene and make what changes are necessary. So therefore scenography important.

GIAN LUIGI CRESCENZI [*student of the Centro's acting school*]: In the film, *The Girlfriends,* we have the portrayal of a painter who is going through a certain crisis. In *L'avventura,* we have the portrayal of an architect who neither plans nor designs but merely calculates figures and draws up estimates for construction materials. In *La notte,* Mastroianni is a writer in crisis. I would like to know if these three characterizations, which are analogous to one another, not only in terms of their professional crises but also with regard to their personal affairs, were conceived by you for the purpose of examining a certain type of individual in order to draw some conclusions about his particular situation, or was this similarity in your choice of character type simply coincidental?

ANTONIONI: It seems rather odd that you would think it could be a coincidence. Obviously, when I select the profession of a character for one of my films, I know very well what I'm doing. I choose intellectual types mainly because they have a greater awareness of what is happening to them, and also because they have a more refined sensibility, a more subtle sense of intuition through which I can filter the kind of reality I am interested in expressing, whether it be an internal reality or an external one. Furthermore, the intellectual, more than others, is the type of person in which I can find the symptoms of that particular kind of crisis which I am interested in describing. If I take an insensitive type, a rough and rugged type, he wouldn't have any of the particular problems I'm concerned with and the story would end right there. So I don't quite know what you mean. Do you want to know if I'm searching for a single character type that would be representative of everyman? I don't understand.

CASTELLO: Perhaps he means to ask if there exists a certain development from one character to another; whether your ultimate objective is to create a general character who would be representative of the intellectual in crisis, or if each character is independent of the other.

ANTONIONI: No, I don't believe the individual characters in the various films are meant to be representative of a certain type of man. Naturally, I shall make a film that will bring an end to this cycle of films which are dedicated, so to speak, to the emotions. As a matter of fact, at a certain point in the film I'm now working on—although it too is mainly concerned with the relationships of human sentiments—due to the very nature of the story itself, this particular theme is given less prominence than it had in the other films and paves the way for the introduction of other themes.

Reflections on the Film Actor[8]

The film actor need not understand, but simply be. One might reason that in order to be, it is necessary to understand. That's not so. If it were, then the most intelligent actor would also be the best actor. Reality often indicates the opposite.

When an actor is intelligent, his efforts to be a good actor are three times as great, for he wishes to deepen his understanding, to take everything into account, to include subtleties, and in doing so he trespasses on ground which is not his—in fact, he creates obstacles for himself.

His reflections on the character he is playing, which according to popular theory should bring him closer to an exact characterization, end up by thwarting his efforts and depriving him of naturalness. The film actor should arrive for shooting in a state of virginity. The more intuitive his work, the more spontaneous it will be.

The film actor should work not on the psychological level but on the imaginative one. And the imagination reveals itself spontaneously—it has no intermediaries upon which one can lean for support.

It is not possible to have a real collaboration between actor and director. They work on two entirely different levels. The director owes no explanations to the actor except those of a very general nature about the people in the film. It is dangerous to discuss details. Sometimes the actor

[8] "Riflessioni sull'attore," from *L'Europa cinematografica,* supplement to *L'Europa letteraria* 9-10, July-August 1961. Originally translated in *Film Culture* 22-23, Summer 1961.

and director necessarily become enemies. The director must not compromise himself by revealing his intentions. The actor is a kind of Trojan horse in the citadel of the director.

I prefer to get results by a hidden method; that is, to stimulate in the actor certain of his innate qualities of whose existence he is himself unaware—to excite not his intelligence but his instinct—to give not justifications but illuminations. One can almost trick an actor by demanding one thing and obtaining another. The director must know how to demand, and how to distinguish what is good and bad, useful and superfluous, in everything the actor offers.

The first quality of a director is to see. This quality is also valuable in dealing with actors. The actor is one of the elements of the image. A modification of his pose or gestures modify the image itself. A line spoken by an actor in profile does not have the same meaning as one given full-face. A phrase addressed to the camera placed above the actor does not have the same meaning it would if the camera were placed below him.

These few simple observations prove that it is the director—that is to say, whoever composes the shot—who should decide the pose, gestures, and movements of the actor.

The same principle holds for the intonation of the dialogue. The voice is a "noise" which emerges with other noises in a rapport which only the director knows. It is therefore up to him to find the balance or imbalance of these sounds.

It is necessary to listen at length to an actor even when he is mistaken. One must let him be mistaken and at the same time try to understand how one can use his mistakes in the film, for these errors are at the moment the most spontaneous thing the actor has to offer.

To explain a scene or piece of dialogue is to treat all the actors alike, for a scene or piece of dialogue does not change. On the contrary, each actor demands special treatment. From this fact stems the necessity to find different methods: to guide the actor little by little to the right path by apparently innocent corrections which will not arouse his suspicions.

This method of working may appear paradoxical, but it is the only one which allows the director to obtain good results with nonprofessional actors found, as they say, "in the street." Neorealism has taught us that, but the method is also useful with professional actors—even the great ones.

I ask myself if there really is a great film actor. The actor who thinks too much is driven by the ambition to be great. It is a terrible obstacle which runs the risk of eliminating much truth from his performance.

I do not need to think I have two legs. I have them. If the actor seeks to understand, he thinks. If he thinks, he will find it hard to be humble, and humility constitutes the best point of departure in achieving truth.

Occasionally an actor is intelligent enough to overcome his natural limitations and to find the proper road by himself—that is, he uses his innate intelligence to apply the method I have just described.

When this happens, the actor has the qualities of a director.

The Event and the Image[9]

A filmmaker is a man like any other; and yet his life is not the same. *Seeing* is for us a necessity. For a painter too the problem is one of seeing: but while for the painter it is a matter of uncovering a static reality, or at most a rhythm that can be held in a single image, for a director the problem is to catch a reality which is never static, is always moving toward or away from a moment of crystallization, and to present this movement, this arriving and moving on, as a new perception. It is not sound—words, noises, music. Nor is it a picture—landscape, attitudes, gestures. Rather it is an indivisible whole that extends over a duration of its own which determines its very being. At this point the dimension of time comes into play, in its most modern conception. It is in this order of intuition that the cinema can acquire a new character, no longer merely figurative. The people around us, the places we visit, the events we witness—it is the spatial and temporal relations these have with each other that have a meaning for us today, and the tension that is formed between them.

This is, I think, a special way of being in contact with reality. And it is also a special reality. To lose this contact, in the sense of losing this *way* of being in contact, can mean sterility. That is why it is important, for a director even more than for other artists, precisely because of the complexity of the material he has between his hands, to be committed

9 "Il fatto e l'immagine," from *Cinema nuovo* 164, July 1963. Originally translated in *Sight & Sound* 33 (1), Winter 1963–64.

morally in some way. It is almost superfluous to point out that our effort as directors must be just that of bringing the data of our personal experience into accord with that of a more general experience, in the same way as individual time accords mysteriously with that of the cosmos. But even this effort will be sterile if we do not succeed in giving, by this means, a sincere justification of the choices which life has obliged us to make.

The sky is white; the sea-front deserted; the sea cold and empty; the hotels white and half-shuttered. On one of the white seats of the Promenade des Anglais the bathing attendant is seated, a [black man] in a white singlet. It is early. The sun labors to emerge through a fine layer of mist, the same as every day. There is nobody on the beach except a single bather floating inert a few yards from the shore. There is nothing to be heard except the sound of the sea, nothing to observe except the rocking of that body. The attendant goes down to the beach and into the bathing station. A girl comes out and walks toward the sea. She is wearing a flesh-coloured costume.

The cry is short, sharp, and piercing. A glance is enough to tell that the bather is dead. The pallor of his face, the mouth full of saliva, the jaws stiff as in the act of biting, the few hairs glued to the forehead, the eyes staring, not with the fixity of death but with a troubled memory of life. The body is stretched out on the sand with the stomach in the air, the feet apart and pointing outwards. In a few moments, while the attendant attempts artificial respiration, the beach fills up with people.

A boy of ten, pushing forward a little girl of about eight, shoves his way through to watch. "Look," he says to the girl, "can you see?" "Yes," she says, very quietly. "Can you see the spit on his mouth?" "Yes." "And the swollen stomach? Do you see? It's full of water." The little girl watches as though fascinated, in silence. The boy goes on, with a kind of sadistic joy. "Now he's still white, but in a few moments he'll go blue. Look under his eyes; look, it's starting." The girl nods in assent, but remains silent: her face shows clearly that she is beginning to feel sick. The boy notices this and looks gloating. "You scared?" "No," the little girl replies in a thin voice. "Yes you are," he insists, and goes on almost chanting, "You're scared—you're scared—" After ten minutes or so the police arrive, and the beach is cleared. The attendant is the only one who remains with the policeman. Then he too goes off, summoned by a lady with violet hair for her usual lesson of gymnastics.

It was wartime. I was at Nice, waiting for a visa to go to Paris to join Marcel Carné, with whom I was going to work as an assistant. They were days full of impatience and boredom, and of news about a war which stood still on an absurd thing called the Maginot Line. Suppose one had to construct a bit of film, based on this event and on this state of mind. I would try first to remove the actual event from the scene, and leave only the image described in the first four lines. In that white sea-front, that lonely figure, that silence, there seems to me to be an extraordinary strength of impact. The event here adds nothing: it is superfluous. I remember very well that I was interested, when it happened. The dead man acted as a distraction to a state of tension. But the true emptiness, the malaise, the anxiety, the nausea, the atrophy of all normal feelings and desires, the fear, the anger—all these I felt when, coming out of the Negresco [Hotel], I found myself in that whiteness, in that nothingness, which took shape around a black point.

REALITY AND CINÉMA VÉRITÉ[10]

The camera is a gossipy eye, hidden behind a keyhole, that records all it can. But how about what happens beyond the keyhole's range? If one keyhole is not enough, then make ten, a hundred, two hundred; put the same number of cameras behind them and shoot miles of film. What will you end up with? A mountain of material which captures not only the essential aspects of an event but the marginal, absurd, or ridiculous ones; your task then is to cut and select. The actual event included these aspects, all the nonsense, the extraneous matter. But selection falsifies it—or, as they say, interprets it. It's an old problem. Life is not always simple, or intelligible; even history, taken as a science, cannot comprehend it completely: a conclusion which both Strachey and Valéry reached their separate ways, the one a historian who wrote history as an art, the other a poet who deprecated history.

Furthermore, the Pudovkin experiments, which at the editing stage changed the meaning of certain close-ups by reversing their order, are now almost commonplaces. A smiling man looking at a bowl of soup is a glutton; if he looks at a dead woman with the same smile, he is a cynic. But why have a keyhole, two hundred cameras and a mountain of material? This kind of film, a derivative of Italian neorealism, is now called *cinéma vérité*, "truth film" or "living film." Its proponents claim that it is

---

[10] "La realtà e il cinema diretto," from *Cinema nuovo* 167, January-February 1964. Originally translated in *Atlas* 9 (2), February 1965.

absolutely objective. From which we might conclude that their ideal tool would be a machine that would merely observe and describe.

But there is one fact that cannot be ignored: such a machine must first be programmed. Indeed it could take innumerable stands: the descriptive, the ethically or aesthetically evaluative, the explanatory-predicative, the sympathetic or antagonistic; and certainly there will be even more possibilities in the future. In time, this sort of machine will replace the reporters and columnists of daily newspapers. It may even drive cars. But we will always have to give it the address to which we want it to go. In short it must have a reservoir of ideas and commands.

Nothing is changed when directors of *cinéma vérité*, their cameras tucked under their arms, mingle with the crowds as they film their investigations. They must always be guided by an idea, a controlling point of view, without which their cameras would remain as inert as the mightiest computer were it deprived of a program—and this despite its superhuman memory and unlimited data. I recently watched the shooting of a scene that purported to record a woman's extemporaneous replies to questions being put to her in the street. The answers were typed out and the woman had to memorize the script. Only then did they shoot the scene. The falsity of the result was disregarded.

Not long ago in a town near Valdagno [in the Veneto region], I stopped at a bar on a big, windy square. Wind is very photogenic. Surrounding the square were a few widely separated houses, and the wind swooped between them raising clouds of dust, which first assailed me and then flew on over the roofs, turning white against the light. Indoors, the scene was even more expressive. Through a huge front window one could see practically the whole square, closed on the far side by a wall cutting horizontally across the landscape. Above the wall was blue sky which appeared discolored by the dust. As the clouds of dust dissolved, the blue regained its intensity, like a fade-in. It was eerie. I moved around the room, looking for the best angle, and couldn't find it. I would have been in a quandary if I'd had to frame what I saw. The problem may be that unless the visual imagination has a tale to tell, it operates in a void.

I turned to the bar, where a girl had been making my drink. She was dark, with light, melancholy eyes. About twenty-eight, badly built. Slow, precise gestures. She looked outside at the pieces of paper and the trees blowing in the wind. I asked her if it was always like that here. She answered: "You kidding!?" Nothing more. Then she sat down on a stool, leaning her arms on the espresso machine, her head on her hands. She seemed tired, sleepy, indifferent, preoccupied with serious problems. In any case she was motionless, and so began to be a character.

I think this is a way of doing *cinéma vérité*. Attributing a story to a person—a story that coincides with his appearance, his posture, his weight, with the volume of space he fills. I moved slowly to the end of the bar until I reached a position behind her shoulders, thus moving her into the foreground. Behind her was an oblique window and the dust which poised against the glass, then slipped down it like liquid. From this angle, with the girl's shoulders in front of me, there was a harmonious relation between the outside and the inside; it was a meaningful image. The white outside, an almost nonexistent reality, and the dark spots inside, including the girl, had some meaning. She too was an object. A character without a face, and without a story. The frame was so beautiful that you needed hardly anything else to know her.

Nevertheless, I approached her while she was making me another drink and asked her name. "Delitta." "What?" "De–lit–ta." "Like *delitto*?" "Yes, but with an *a*." I looked at her, astonished.

"It was my father's doing," she explained. "He said it was a *delitto*, a crime, to have children when life was so hard. My mother insisted, though, and finally he said all right, but I'm going to name him 'Delitto.' I turned out to be a girl, so—"

I could have pestered her with questions, followed her all day long through the streets of her windy town and into her home, which would probably have been clean and ordinary, and I am convinced that there would have been no surprises and that the single absurdity in her life would still have been her name: Delitta, like *delitto*, but with an *a*.

PREFACE TO *SIX FILMS*[11]

What did you want to say? That is the question that people ask me most often. The temptation is to respond: "I wanted to make a film and that's it." But if you try to understand why I made it, what I thought about while I was making it, what I wanted to say: if you expect that I summarize my reasons and explain that which is almost impossible to explain—that is, certain impulses or intuitions, or moral and figurative choices—you risk arriving at just one result: To spoil the film itself.

I do not believe that what a director says about himself and his work helps in understanding the work itself. When Manzoni talks about the historical novel, it doesn't add anything to what he already said in *The Betrothed*.[12] The route that a director follows in completing a film is full of errors, doubts, and sins. For this reason, the least natural thing that one can ask of that director is to talk about it. In my case, as selfconscious as I am, my words will serve at the most to specify a particular state of mind, a vague awareness. In short, the answer I prefer to the above question is this: "In that period, certain events happened in the world, I saw certain people, I was reading certain books, I was looking at certain paintings, I loved X, I hated Y, I didn't have any money, I wasn't sleeping much."

[11] "Prefazione," from *Sei film. Le amiche, Il grido, L'avventura, La notte, L'eclisse, Deserto rosso*, Turin: Einaudi, 1964. Translated by Allison Cooper.
[12] Alessandro Manzoni (1785–1873) was one of the most influential writers in nine-teenth-century Italy. His masterpiece, the novel *The Betrothed* (1840), as well as some of his theoretical writings were inspired to the then fashionable ideas on the historical novel.

But the publisher asks me for a preface and I can't say no, even though writing is not my business, even though talking about myself requires much effort. It will be a fragmentary and insufficient preface, but I don't know how to do any better.

I believe that something all filmmakers have in common is this habit of keeping one eye open to the inside and one open to the outside. At a certain moment the two visions approach each other, and like two images that come into focus, they are superimposed upon one another. The motivation to speak, to show that something comes from this agreement between eye and mind, between eye and instinct, between eye and consciousness.

As far as I am concerned, at the beginning there is always an external, concrete element. Not a concept. Not a thesis. And there is also a bit of confusion at the beginning. Probably, the film is actually born out of this confusion. The difficulty consists in putting some order into it. I am convinced that it depends not just on a way of thinking, but also on being accustomed to letting your imagination work.

I remember very well how the idea of *L'avventura* came to me. I was on a yacht with some friends, and I would awaken before them and sit up on the deck in a state of complete relaxation. One morning I found myself thinking of a girl who, years before, had disappeared, and nothing more was ever heard of her. We had looked for her everywhere for days and days, but to no avail. The yacht was sailing toward [the island of] Ponza, by then nearby. And I thought, "What if she were there? That's it!"

However fascinating it might appear to me, I am unable to immediately accept an idea. I leave it. I don't think about it; I wait. Months, even years go by. It has to remain afloat in the sea of things that accumulate through living. If it does, then it is a good idea.

A director does nothing but look for himself in his films. They are documentaries, not of an already-made thought, but of a thought in the making.

London 1952. A dead-end alley. Houses of blackened bricks. A pair of shutters painted white. A street light. A gutter pipe painted red, very glossy. A motorcycle covered with a tarpaulin, because it is raining.

I want to see someone pass by on this street who will remind me of Chaplin. The first passerby will suffice for me. I want an English character for this English street.

I wait three and a half hours. Darkness begins to draw the traditional cone of light around the street light when I go away without having seen anybody.

I believe that these little failures, these empty moments, these abortions of observation, are, all things considered, fruitful. When we have put quite a few of them together—not knowing how, not knowing why—a story emerges. The subject of the *The Cry* came to my mind while looking at a wall.

Rome, the fourth day of a garbage collectors' strike. Rome flooded by rubbish, heaps of colored filth on the street corners, an orgy of abstract images, a never-seen, figurative violence. And, on the other hand, the trash collectors' meeting among the ruins of the Circus Maximus, about a thousand men dressed in bluish coats, silent, ordered, in expectation of I don't know what.

A story can also come forth in this way—observing the environment, which will then provide the background. In cinema it is often an effective method, because it allows to attain a figurative coherence in an easier way.

1962. I am in Florence, to see and film a solar eclipse. Unexpected and intense cold. Silence different from all other silences. Wan light, different from all other lights. And then darkness. Total stillness. All I'm capable of thinking is that during an eclipse even feelings probably come to a halt.

It is an idea that has vaguely to do with the film I am preparing—more a sensation than an idea, but a sensation which defines the film even when the film is far from being defined. All the work and the shots that came after have always been related back to that idea, or sensation, or premonition. I have never been able to leave it aside.

I should have put these verses of Dylan Thomas in the opening credits of *The Eclipse*:

> ... some certainty must as well exist,
> if not to love well, at least not to love.

The ideas that are good for films might not be good enough to help one in life. If it were so, a director's way of life would coincide with his way of *forming* a film, and his practical experiences could coincide with his intellectual ones. Instead, however autobiographical one might be, there is always an intervention by our imagination that translates and alters the material—and in saying this, I am not saying anything new.

We are our characters to the extent that we believe in the film we are making. But between us and them there is always the film; there is this concrete fact—precise, lucid. There is this act of will and force that identifies us unequivocally, that sets us free from abstraction and places us with our feet firmly on the ground. In this fashion, we are transformed from proletarians into bourgeois again; from pessimists into optimist; from solitary and alienated people into people who want to open a dialogue and communicate.

I have never claimed to define what I do in the cinema in a philosophical way. The word "alienation" was not invented by me; for years it has been part of European critical and philosophical terminology, from Marx to Adorno. Therefore, it expresses a real phenomenon, a concrete problem of mankind, that has probably grown acute over the last few years.

Now, I am not dismissing these themes: My films are there and they speak—in the literal sense of the term—for themselves. Perhaps I didn't immediately realize the road I was taking, but one thing is certain: I immediately tried not to remember it, or to forget about it. What I dismiss is the accusation of "alienation" made *ad personam*—as though, in creating a film, in living in this period of time at the service of a story, I was not stating all of my problems and resolving them by objectifying them. But, while I make a film I am conscious, present to myself, to my environment, to my story, and I am alienated to the extent that this event induces me to suffer alienation, to fight it and overcome it by making the film.

The greatest danger for whoever makes films lies in the extraordinary possibility that the cinema offers of lying.

Books are part of life, and so is cinema. Nothing changes, whether a story comes from novel, from a newspaper, or from a real or invented episode. A reading is a fact. A fact, when you think about it, is a reading.

Authenticity, or invention, or lie. Invention precedes the chronicle. The chronicle provokes invention. Both of them are joined together in an identical authenticity. Lie may be seen as a reflection of an authenticity yet to be discovered.

In the immediate postwar period, I asked the most important Italian producers if they would send me traveling throughout the world to film a documentary. I was thinking also of filming a revolution, one of those revolutions that take place in South America every so often. The film that I most regretted not making was *The Happy Girls of '24*, set during the revolutionary years of fascism.

I also proposed a few novels. But, above all, original subjects. Dozens of proposals. (It is long and painful, this discussion of time wasted in waiting rooms, or telling stories, or writing page after useless page. However useful our experience may have been, we must remember that for my generation it always had to be added to another experience, that of the war—a fearful addition!)

One day I invented a film while looking at the sun: the meanness of the sun, the irony of the sun.

For years I have had these verses of MacNiece in my head:

Think of a number, double it, treble it, square it, and sponge it out.

I am sure that they could become the nucleus, or at least the symbol, of a curious comic film. They already indicate a style.

I also thought—in a moment of exasperation—of writing a film version of the first chapters of [Bertrand] Russell's *Introduction to Mathematical Philosophy*. A very serious book, but, in my opinion, rich in comic cues. For example: "The number three is not identifiable with the trio composed of Mr. Brown, Mr. Jones, and Mr. Robinson. The number three is something that all trios have in common." For the trio of Mr. Brown, Mr. Jones, and Mr. Robinson is reserved a part already colored with the ridiculous. And then: "The relationship *wife-husband* is the reverse of that of *husband-wife*." You see them already, these two inverse and friendly couples and the circumstances in which they would be involved. And again: "The number two is a metaphysical entity, we can never be sure if it really exists in itself, or if we have discovered it." This is a hallucinatory affirmation from the point of view of the number two. Of a number two protagonist.

These are games, naturally—*divertissements* that indicate, nevertheless, how the most singular things might suggest a film. A professional bias that is, nonetheless, also an instinctive and sincere need to reduce everything to images.

Some time ago, the pop-art sculptor [Claes] Oldenburg was at my place. He made an observation that struck me: In Europe, one writes more than one visualizes. The opposite of the United States. I have to say that, in this sense, the influence of cinema has been beneficial. The war and the postwar period, for example, have found in the cinema illustrations of a sometimes disconcerting strength and truthfulness. This depends on the nature of the means itself, but also on the fact that nobody, more than us filmmakers, is inclined to look.

Here is an occupation that I never get tired of: looking. I like almost all of what I see: landscapes, characters, situations. On the one hand, it is dangerous, but on the other, it is an advantage, because it allows for a complete fusion between life and work, between reality (or unreality) and cinema.

You cannot penetrate events with *reportage*.

During the postwar period there was a great need for truth, and it seemed possible to photograph it from street corners. Today, neorealism is obsolete, in the sense that we aspire more and more to create our own reality. This criterion is even applied to films of a documentary character and to newsreels, most of which are produced according to a preconceived idea. Not cinema at the service of reality, but reality at the service of cinema.

There is the same tendency in feature films. I have the impression that the essential thing is to give a film an almost allegorical tone. This means that every person moves in an ideal direction, which is irrationally in agreement with everyone else's directions, until a meaning is formed that *also* includes the story being told, but that goes beyond it in intensity and freedom of solutions.

By submitting the exposed film to a determined procedure known as "latensification,"[13] it is possible to bring out elements of the image which the normal development process is incapable of revealing. For example, a street corner illuminated by the weak light of a lamp becomes perfectly visible, right down to the details, only if the film is "latensified;" otherwise it is not.

This has always dumbfounded me. It means—I was thinking—that the impression of the things weakly illuminated by the light of the street lamp is there, on the film. It is there concretely. Pushing this reasoning, we can argue that the film is more sensible than the photoelectric cell, whose needle doesn't even move at that light. Pushing even further (at a theoretical level, however, as at a practical one, we could not ignore other considerations), perhaps the film records everything, in any light, even in the dark—like cats' eyes, like an American military apparatus recently invented—and only our technical backwardness prevents us from revealing all that there is on the photograph.

We know that under the revealed image there is another one which is more faithful to reality, and under this one there is yet another, and again another under this last one, down to the true image of that absolute, mysterious reality that nobody will ever see. Or perhaps, not until the decomposition of every image, of every reality.

Therefore, abstract cinema would have its reason for existing.

---

[13] Latensification is an intensification of a latent photographic image by chemical treatment or prolonged uniform exposure to low-intensity light.

A girl lives down there—she is not even in love with me.

Where did I read this sentence? I could make it a symbol of our—mine and my contemporaries'—youth in Ferrara. We had no other worries. The smell of the hemp (today, in the countryside near Ferrara, hemp has been replaced by other crops), the smell of the remains of beets on the wagons as they went to and fro the sugar factories, the smell of the river, of grass and mud. In the summer, all of these smells mixed together with that of a woman—in the winter, with low-quality perfumes at the popular dances. The long and wide streets, the streets of a flat city, beautiful and still, like invitations to elegance, to dissipated idleness. The interminable chats on the corners of these streets at night with friends, and the topic would always be a woman. Certain nights we would go to taverns to drink wine. But I didn't like getting drunk, losing consciousness as a result of those brief escapades.

Some other nights I would go, by myself, to a popular block of flats, and I would stay there all night, with a girl. I don't regret having wasted away so many hours of my life in that way, and so I can talk about it. We would sit down on the staircase and stay there in the dark. I could see, by the light of the moon, a stupendous arch and, behind it, a sixteenth-century courtyard. I would hear footsteps, voices in the dark. I remember a child pushed out of a door like this:

"Go look for that slut of your sister!"

"Where is she?"

"Along the city walls. She's the first one you'll find with her legs open."

The girl that was with me was sweet and faithful. She wouldn't let me go before sunrise for fear that the youths of the apartment complex would beat me up. At dawn I would return home listening to the rolling of the wagons on the pebbles. Sprawled out on the wagons, the carters would sing. They had slept soundly, plunged their heads into a bucket of water, drunk a shot of grappa in a bar, and now they were singing, without happiness, and soon their song would give way to curses. At times I, too, would get on one of those wagons and have them take me along with them. I don't remember what we talked about anymore, but at the time those dialogues seemed extraordinary to me.

I would also go to other houses, solid houses with their brickwork eaves—spacious, safe—and almost all of the "respectable" girls of the city would be there. And here, also, it would almost always be the same thing as in the tenement house, perhaps with more circumspection, but with a complex and ancient broadmindedness, well within the artistic and historic tradition of the city.

Why am I relating these things and not others, certainly more interesting? Maybe because it is these things that I feel belong to me. The rest fell on top of me like an avalanche, and I could only endure it. And also because, in some way, I feel that these things are behind *Story of a Love Affair*, *L'avventura*, and *Red Desert*.

In other words, I happened to discover the disease of feelings before the feelings themselves.

I don't know why, in cinema, I started becoming interested in feelings rather than in other, more burning issues—such as the war, fascism, our social problems, our lives at that time. It is not that these other issues left me indifferent. I was inside of them; I was living them, even if in a rather solitary way. It must have been because of a sentimental experience of mine that ended in an inexplicable manner. I could not ask anyone but myself for the "why" behind this ending. And this "why" joined up with all the others, and together they became a single immeasurable "why," a massive show that had mankind as its protagonist. Mankind facing his environment and mankind facing mankind.

This is my only presumption: of having entered the path of neorealism by myself. It was 1943. [Luchino] Visconti was filming *Ossessione* on the banks of the Po river, and, also on the Po river, a few kilometers away, I was filming my first documentary.

Po di Volano[14] belongs to the landscape of my early childhood. To the Po of my youth. The men who would pass on the levees, dragging along the barges with a rope at a slow, rhythmic pace; and later the same barges

---

[14] Located on the delta of the Po river, Po di Volano is the village where Antonioni filmed his first documentary, *People of the Po Valley*.

dragged along in a convoy by a tugboat, with the women intent on cook-
ing, the men at the helm, the hens, the clothes hanging out—true wandering houses, touching. They were images of a world of which, little by
little, I was becoming conscious. That landscape, which until then had
been a landscape of things, motionless and solitary—the muddy water, full
of whirlpools, the rows of poplars that would get lost in the fog, the Isola
Bianca which, in the middle of the river at Pontelagoscuro, divided the
current in two—that landscape was moving, it was filling up with people
and regaining strength. The things themselves were claiming a different
attention, acquiring a different significance. Looking at them in a new
way, I was taking control of them. Beginning to understand the world
through the image, I was understanding the image, its force, its mystery.

As soon as it was possible for me to do so I returned to those places
with a camera. This is how *People of the Po Valley* was born. Everything
that I did after that, good or bad as it was, started from there.

The film was finished, the first copy was ready. Doubts, misgivings,
regrets. Enclosed within our own limits, we wish to go back and start all
over again. Nothing is as finished as a film when it is finished. Maybe a
building. One is undefended, exposed to the looks and irony of everyone,
without being able to tell anybody about one's own personal adventure,
which is recorded neither on the film, nor in the script—a memory, but
a curious memory, like a premonition, of which the film gives only a partial, insufficient evidence.

Returning to *Red Desert*, I remember what I told Monica Vitti: "Maybe
I wasn't mean enough." And I meant this; I didn't put the film to the test
before starting it, I didn't check to see if it was mean enough. It is always
necessary to do such a test. What will happen to the story is what happens to a substance placed in contact with its natural reagent, which
reveals it; its composition, its truth.

When the film is finished, an unexpressed violence always remains, a
remainder of matter and meanness that pushes us to take up the pil-
grimage again, from place to place to see, to interrogate, to dream about
things that are increasingly elusive, with the next film in mind.

Under the rotunda of the Grand Hotel in Rimini, still enclosed by the barbed wire that encircles it during the winter, two ten-year-old girls are playing. One goes around the rotunda on a bicycle. The other nimbly puts her hands forward, and, placing them on the sand, stiffens herself up into a handstand, skirt on her face, skinny legs straight up in the air. She then falls down on the other side and starts over again. They are two fairly poor girls. The one going around the rotunda on her bicycle calls to her friend, "Edna—Edna—," with every passage. And then she continues, in a sing-song voice, "What love—what pain!"

She disappears. She reappears. "What love—what pain!"

It is early morning. There is nobody on this beach except for these two girls and myself. There is no other sound but that of the sea and this thin voice that sings of love and pain.

For that entire day, this was a film for me.

Told in this way, the episode cannot be too meaningful, and it isn't easy to understand how it could have suggested a story. One would have to hear the intonation of that voice to understand. It was a special intonation, fresh and agonizing at the same time. It gave a certainly unconscious but deep dimension to those words—all of the world's love and all of its pain. In the mouth of that character, the words were absurd, but not the intonation.

These are the limits of scripts: to give words to events that refuse words.

To write a script is a truly tiresome job, just because one must deal with describing images with provisional words, words which will no longer do, and this is already unnatural. The description cannot be anything but generic and patently false, because very often it concern images lacking concrete references.

When I reread these scripts, what I feel most is the memory of the moments that brought me to write them. Certain location scoutings, interviews with people, time spent in the places where the story would then come to life, the gradual discovery of the film in its fundamental images, in its colors, in its rhythm. This is perhaps the most important moment. The script is an intermediary phase, necessary, but transitory. For me, the film, while I am filming, must connect back to those moments in order to turn out well. I need to find that emotional charge again, that conviction.

The discussions with my collaborators in the scriptwriting phase, the often dispassioned and competent search for a structure, for a solution suggested by experience certainly contribute to articulating the story in the best way. But they risk dampening the initial emotional charge. This is why during the scripting phase there is always a moment of crisis, in which you lose the sense of what you are doing. Then there is nothing to be done but to break off and to set about thinking of the film as you imagined it while scouting for a location.

Another sensation I have had reading these scripts is rather curious: a type of astonishment, mixed with irritation. Because by now, having the films imprinted in my head, too many things no longer coincide. And even those that do coincide are exposed in a pseudoliterary form that truly irritates me. Whoever asserts that the script has a literary value is wrong. One could argue that some don't have it, and that others do. That could be so. But then they are true and proper novels, with an autonomy of their own.

A movie not imprinted on film doesn't exist. The scripts presuppose the film. They don't have autonomy; they are dead pages.

MY FILMS

"Attempted Suicide"
Episode of *Love in the City* (1953)

SUICIDES IN THE CITY[1]

Dearest Guido,[2]

I am happy that you liked the interview. It is so hard for me to talk about myself. And now you are asking me to begin again by responding to your review of *Love in the City*. I believe, all things considered, that it would be wrong to do so. I have just commented on the criticism of *The Vanquished* in that very interview. It would make sense if we were dealing with a sketch that had been successful, or at least had given rise to discussions, to clashing opinions. But not on your life. Everyone is in agreement in classifying my episode as the least meritorious on a hypothetical merit list. And it could very well be that they are right; it is not up to me to judge. The only person from whom I have heard a completely favorable opinion is Ennio Flaiano; and actually [Cesare] Zavattini seemed to be well-disposed, if you overlook the moral reservations.[3]

---

[1] "Suicidi in città," from *Cinema nuovo* 31, February 1954. Translated by Allison Cooper.
[2] The letter is addressed to Guido Aristarco, one of the foremost Italian film critics of the past four decades, particularly as the editor of the magazine *Cinema nuovo*.
[3] A writer and a journalist, Ennio Flaiano (1910–1972) was also active as a scriptwriter, including work for Rossellini's *Open City* and a long partnership with Fellini, from *Variety Lights* (1951) to *Juliet of the Spirits* (1965). Cesare Zavattini (1902–1989) was one of the most important figures of Italian neorealis. As a scriptwriter, he worked on many of De Sica's films, including *The Bicycle Thief* and *Umberto D*.

Now, how can I bring up certain topics without running the risk of being accused of self-conceit, of having merely pious intentions that never change? In short, I would prefer to let bygones be bygones, and not talk about it anymore. In addition, what I would say would be very unpopular. Those types of suicides, as soon as I understood their exhibitionist complex, no longer distressed me. Except, perhaps, two of them. The rest were happy to have tried to take their lives, and to be there to talk about it in front of a camera; they were happy to earn some money in such a simple way. They even began to flirt among themselves. "Sir," one said to me one day, "do not tell Z. that I'm married, I'm trying to go out with her." Z. was also one of the group.

And they were keen—again, except, perhaps, for two truly touching cases—on making me believe that they had really wanted to die, and that they had tried it over and over again, and that, all things considered, they had been unlucky not to succeed. And not only that, but also that they were ready to try it again, if they found themselves in that very same position.

I am sure this is not true. I am sure that they were not telling the truth, that they were exaggerating on account of who-knows-what form of vanity, or of masochism. Those were cases that had to do with psychology, not morality. I cannot bring myself to sharing the opinion that if someone kills himself it is to some extent everyone's fault. Suicide is such an enigmatic gesture; it exists in every place and time since man and animals have existed. You can examine it from so many points of view—anatomical and physio-pathological, statistical and sociological, psychological. It is true that suicide has a moral significance and that psychology cannot ignore morals, but it is also true that morality cannot ignore the teachings of psychology. Someone wrote that suicide is a total act of psychology. Which also means that every act of suicide has its story. The commander who goes down with his ship comes to be considered a hero. We may like or dislike heroes, and yet society honors them and worships their memory. The Church itself grants its sacraments to a suicide affected by madness. This demonstrates that it is not possible to leave special causes aside, and the special is the proper domain of psychology.

You can clearly see that it was not such an easy theme. As soon as you begin to scratch the surface of the topic, difficulties leap out. Faced with these difficulties, within the very restricted limits of the film length granted to me, what could I do? I tried to provoke an aversion to suicide in the public through the spiritual squalor of the characters. In other words, I aimed directly at the content, at the substance of the theme. This is why I do not agree with your accusation of "elzevirism."[4]

Dear Guido, after the experiences of *The Vanquished* and *The Lady without Camellias*, what should I think? That the cinema is angry with me? I do not believe it. I feel that I have an excellent relationship with the cinema, and I forgive it for this and more.

Kindest regards.

[4] "Elzevirsism" comes from "elzeviro," the journalistic term given to the main article of the cultural page (usually page 3) on major Italian newspapers. The "accusation" Antonioni tries to reject, here, was one of cultural elitism, which had come to be associated with the writing of such articles.

The Girlfriends (1955)

LOYALTY TO PAVESE[5]

Dear Calvino,

Just a few days ago your letter was brought to my attention, published in the Einaudi news bulletin. I am very late in responding to you, but maybe it is better this way; at least every polemic intention shall have disappeared. Not toward you (your letter was very flattering to me), but toward criticism in general.

Such conflicting and often inaccurate, even if positive, things are being written about my films, that in reading them a form of irritation lingers in me—not so much toward those who wrote them as toward myself, in that I have not been quite clear, precise, persuasive, or suggestive enough.

I have even followed the controversy around "my" version of Turin, which did not satisfy the Turinese. According to some of them, who wrote outraged letters to a local newspaper, I have chosen "the ugliest streets" rather than represent the "unmistakable face" of the city, its "coquetry and grace," etc. Evidently, each Turinese sees and loves the city in his own way, which is always a legitimate way. But, with all due respect for these manifold ways, I have to say that in coming to film in Turin, the last thing I thought of doing was concern myself with the city from a tourist point of view, to concern myself with the city *tout court*.

---

5 "Fedeltà a Pavese," from *Cinema nuovo* 76, February 1956. Translated by Allison Cooper. Antonioni's letter is addressed to Italo Calvino.

The background had a relative importance in a film so specifically psychological. I will say more: I never even worried about being loyal to Pavese. The only words that I recall having uttered on the subject were to reassure [Carlo] Muscetta, and with him Einaudi, that I would do my best not to betray the spirit of the story.[6]

Apparently it was not a question of doing one's best. This was not the problem. When you detach a story from the words that express it, that make it a story artistically complete in itself, what is left? You have something equivalent to a newspaper story related by a friend, an event that we have had the chance to attend, a product of our imagination. This is the new point of departure. Then it is a question of developing, forming, and articulating in another language this artless matter, with all of the consequences that the event brings with it. As a matter of fact, at this point the original text can actually get in the way. I believe I am a fairly good reader, if for no other reason than that in reading I succeed in forgetting my profession. So it happens that certain pages exert a strong influence over me, but it is an influence of a necessarily literary nature, which means nothing in terms of its adaptability to the screen. When that happens, the decision of whether or not to turn away from those pages becomes very difficult. However, it is very easy to be seduced by those pages, and make mistakes.

In Pavese, the danger was always latent—above all in a story like *Among Women Alone*, written in such an enchanted, allusive prose; motionless in a world of feelings; miraculously still in a whirlwind. To bring the story as it is to the screen would have been not only impossible, but even damaging to Pavese himself. A change in medium inevitably brings about substantial modifications. I don't want to affirm the existence of a "specific" cinematic quality; but if nothing else, the term does have a practical significance. It might have been possible to follow another path, that of the complete submission of cinema to literature—for example, by adopting a "speaker" who

---

[6] Carlo Muscetta is a well-established Italian literary critic and editor of literary series. At the time, working for the Turin-based publisher Einaudi, he was responsible for the series that included Pavese's novels.

would read Pavese's words, and illustrating these words with images. Anything is possible. But I don't believe in such hybridisms, and since I don't believe in them I would have never succeeded in sincerely adopting them. The illustrations of a literary work have an artistic value to the extent that they are not merely illustrative. It is the same with the cinema. Loyalty to Pavese could not have been an *a priori* and literal fact. If I chose this story rather than another, there was evidently a reason. "Reason" is perhaps the least appropriate word. It was rather a question of something that escaped reason, and therefore it was impossible to think about it rationally. One critic wrote that *The Girlfriends* is an intelligent film. I can say that it was done under the thrust of a something other than intelligence—naturally, within the limits that such a thing is possible. If a film, to use this same critic's words, gives "a fundamentally correct interpretation" of Pavese, it means that the choice itself is a guarantee of loyalty, the only one that I could give in good faith. And that it was right not to make an issue out of this, the real issue being something else: that of the autonomy of the film, of its validity. That is why the critics who persist in comparing film and story risk going astray. It even happened, in my opinion, to Filippo Sacchi, one of the best of such critics. According to him, giving a concrete sense to Rosetta's suicide, has diminished its impact. As if one suicide could be more beautiful than another, outside of the way it is presented. Sacchi can argue that he refers to the suicide in the film, to the way it was presented. In that case I have nothing more to say, beyond expressing my disappointment, the irritation I was talking about at the beginning. I believed that I had given the character of Rosetta a sincerity of its own, and, I would say, a figurative restraint that would spare it from banality. And by the way, we should remember that love as a motive for suicide, in the film, is nothing more than the last straw in a boredom with living, an inability to connect with life, which are also Pavese's motivations. But the suicide in the story, if conveyed as such to the screen, would have remained literary, in any case. And we all agree, it seems to me, that there is nothing worse than literary painting, literary music, or literary cinematographic literature. That is why his criticism seemed to me to be one of the most perceptive among those I read.

As far as the moral content of the film is concerned, a similar point can be made. Certain critics reproved me for not having made Carlo a dialectical character. I have no hesitation in declaring that I detest key characters. My craft is being a director, but also, as Pavese says, living. Living in a society, in an environment, having relations with fellow men, having experiences. I certainly cannot forget all of this in directing a film. My experiences, my opinions, my own errors—these are what is most personal. They will all filter through my film in spite of me, if I am sincere. If the film succeeds, anybody will be able to extract them. If they cannot be perceived, it means that the film has failed. But it has failed on an aesthetic level, which is what I want to emphasize. So, when you criticize the character of Celia as confused, this is a criticism that I can share or not (and I do share it), but it is legitimate.

If I could, I would redirect at least a third of *The Girlfriends*. It was produced under the worst conditions. It started with one film company, it was then taken over by another after two and a half months of interruption. Two and a half months of interruption is a considerable amount of time. But the worst thing is that all of this time was spent in financial negotiations, talks, and discussions—face to face, that is, with the prosaic side of cinema, which a director, at least while filming, should ignore. It is sad to verify with your own eyes that a story about characters, an emotional and psychological conflict, a development of moods and of atmospheres, can become a business deal—that feelings, moods, and atmospheres weigh in on the scale of financial speculation.

It is discouraging to have to explain the story dozens and dozens of times to unknown faces (I don't know why, but I just can't tell certain stories to certain faces); to find oneself confronting reactions, confronting the most unthinkable of expressions; to hear the strangest remarks, such as the following: "Why don't we make Momina have a dog that later dies in the Po river? It's more touching."

The behind-the-scenes doesn't count, I agree. But I can't forget it. What I wish for is to be able to someday make a film in full agreement with the producer, without scandals, without interruptions—in other words, under normal conditions. Normal: nothing more. I have never had this luck.

L'avventura (1960)

THE ADVENTURES OF *L'AVVENTURA*[7]

There are many ways to talk about a film, and there are many people that can do it. Critics, writers, philosophers, psychiatrists, spectators, even painters and architects. But there is only one way for the author to do it: to talk about himself. It can be easy or difficult. For me it is impossible. Furthermore, I am convinced that whatever a director says about himself or his work is of no help in understanding the work itself—especially if it is about an old film. And so an episodic story of what was happening around the film, during the shooting, is better. Perhaps it is more illuminating, however fragmentary and incomplete. Is this how films are made?

No, not like this. But this is what it was like at the time of *L'avventura*.

I could begin with the tornado, and how—when I saw it arrive, flaring up over the sea, vanishing up above like a very tall mushroom with its hat lost among the clouds—I shouted to the cameraman to take the camera immediately and film. But Monica Vitti was afraid; so, one of the fishermen who was working for us told her that he knew how to cut down the tornado. His father had given him the magic words, in church, on a Christmas night years ago. And in fact, when he uttered them, the tornado disappeared. And I was angry because that tornado was exactly

<hr>

[7] "Le avventure dell'*Avventura*," from *Corriere della Sera*, 31 May 1976. Translated by Allison Cooper.

what I needed—an impressive plastic material, to convert the mystery of the island. And the next day I wanted to fire the fisherman, but I could not do it. He had put a bandage around his head to protect from the wind a cheek that was swollen like a balloon—a sudden toothache that was a divine punishment because the fisherman had taken God's place in dispelling the tornado.

But perhaps I should specify that all of this was happening on Panarea, in the Aeolian islands,[8] and that every morning we would go by boat to film on a rock called Lisca Bianca, twenty minutes from Panarea. When the sea was calm you could see puffs of mist coming out of the water and dissolving in many little sulfurous bubbles. But it was never calm. It was always stormy. In that brief trip to go to Lisca Bianca we were literally risking our lives. I believe I came to hate it, that sea.

The liners had suspended their service, and we were eating carob beans and moldy cookies. There were wild rabbits on the island, but they were sick. No cigarettes, not even pay. At a certain point the workers went on strike and decided to return to Rome, but they couldn't go until the liners resumed service. We were forced to hire others, who were supposed to come in on the same boat. This took place, if I am not mistaken, about a month later. But the two groups met on the boat, and when the second group learned from the first how things were, they didn't even disembark. There were six or seven of us left behind: the actors, the cameraman, the production director, and my assistants.

We had learned to load cameras and lights on our shoulders and to build platforms sheer above the sea. One night the sea prevented us from returning to Panarea and we were forced to camp on the rock. While we were trying to embark, a wave tore one of the rafts away from its moorings and pushed it offshore with two men in it. I spent the night watching that hell that was the sea, with the nightmare of those two at its mercy. I could hear the waves beating against the rocks and I could see their spray, illuminated

[8] The Aeolian islands (also called Lipari) are a group of volcanic islands in the Tyrrhenian Sea, northeast of Sicily.

by the moon, coming almost up to me, in a leap of almost eighty meters. The raft was recovered at dawn, with the two exhausted men. The sky was clear, the sun shining, the sea slightly calmer.

I also remember the crossing to go to Lipari to preview the rushes, after two months of shooting. We watched the waves come toward us as if we were at the bottom of a valley, and it seemed impossible that a little boat like ours could climb over them. Nevertheless, we succeeded in doing it—wave after wave, like a car going around curves.

We saw the rushes. To me it seemed dreadful.

From Panarea you could at least phone out [to the continent]. There were two radios, receiver and transmitter, American leftovers from the war. The motor that provided them with energy was one of those hand-crank types, like on old cars. The postal worker [who operated it] often had his arm in a sling; he would break it starting the motor. But when he was all right you could use the radio and communicate. It happened that whoever had a portable radio on the island could tune in to the transmitter's wavelength and listen to the conversations. In this way, everyone's mood circulated through the air. The little streets of Panarea would fill up with loving phrases at full volume. Or with insults. Such as mine to Rome for taking such a long time in finding a new producer. The first one had disappeared with the first problems, and there was no longer anyone backing us. But I didn't care. I had twenty thousand meters of film with me, I could continue filming. I was concerned with another problem: How could I tell the truths of the film and keep the other truths—which were swarming at the margins, which were pushing with such force—silent? By weighing the one set of truths against the others?

Naturally I would have preferred to hide my worries and my bitterness from my coworkers—the discouragement I was feeling for being forced to impose that absurd way of living and working on them. If this was cinema, what was cinema?

Some films are pleasant and some films are bitter; some are light and some are painful. *L'avventura* is a bitter, often painful film. It is the pain of feelings that come to an end, or in which you catch a glimpse of the end at the same moment when they are born. All of this is recounted in a language that I have tried to keep stripped of effects. They say that a film is "articulated in a distended rhythm, in relations of space and time that adhere to reality." These are not my words. I have very few words at my disposal with which to say these things. I will give an example.

After seeing the film, everyone wonders: What ever happened to Anna? There was a scene in the script—which was later cut, I don't remember why—in which Claudia, Anna's friend, is with other friends on the island. They are making all possible speculations about the disappearance of the girl. But there are no answers. After a moment of silence, one says: "Maybe she simply drowned." Claudia suddenly turns to him: "Simply?" They all look at each other, dismayed.

This is it. This dismay is the meaning of the film.

Red Desert (1964)

My Desert[9]

Up until now I have made nine films, plus one episode: *Attempted Suicide*, which is in *Love in the City*. Let's just say ten films in fifteen years. Is that many? Is that few?

I am doing some calculations in order to understand how in the world, right now, I feel the need to abandon black and white. That is a medium which, up until a short while ago, I thought was the most suitable for my mentality and for my way of explaining the events of life. With *Red Desert* I have never had doubts about the necessity of using color. After all, it doesn't seem to me to be a big deal if other cinema authors who, until now, had been faithful to black and white—like Bergman, Dreyer, Fellini, and Resnais—have experienced this same need of color, and almost all of them at the same time. For me, the reason is this: Color has, in modern life, a meaning and a function that it never had in the past. I am convinced that before long, black and white will truly become the stuff of museums.

This is also the least autobiographical of my films. The one in which I have kept my eye turned most to external things. I told a story as if I were seeing it happen before my eyes. If there is still some autobiography, it is precisely in the color that it can be found. Colors have always thrilled me.

9 "Il mio deserto," from *L'Europeo* 16 August 1964. Translated by Allison Cooper.

I always see in color. I mean, I am aware that they are there, always. I dream, the rare times that I dream, in color.

In my films, naturally, I have tried to use colors that would satisfy my own taste. It could not be any other way. Unfortunately, I have not always succeeded in doing it. The difficulties, with color, are three times greater than with black and white.

Adopting color, nevertheless, is a thrilling experience. You just have to forget about it, and never lose sight of the story. I am also convinced that the best results can be achieved if the public no longer notices the color as a fact in and of itself, but accepts it as a figurative component of the story itself.

Finally, there is another reason why I consider *Red Desert* to be very different from my previous films: It does not discuss feelings. I will go as far as saying that feelings have nothing to do with it. In this sense, the conclusions of my previous films here are taken for granted. Here I was interested in talking about something else. The story I had in my hands presented different issues: take neurosis, for example. And perhaps, the fact that I detached myself from vague themes, like the theme of feelings, allowed me, this time, to better develop the characters. Monica Vitti certainly felt closer to this type of woman than to the type she played in *The Eclipse*. In fact, it seems to me that her contemporary and nervous acting style portrayed this character with an extraordinary sincerity, and also gave her a particularly realistic physiognomy.

Why the title *Red Desert*? In these last few months, I have often been aked this question. From the beginning I had thought of *Blue and Green*, but then it seemed a little too attached to the issue of colors. Therefore, I preferred *Red Desert*. The explanation is simpler than it seems, and it goes also for the titles of my other films, which nobody discusses any longer today. Because it is about intuitive definitions, which assume their meaning and value only later. I hope that these images are also seen as a summary introduction to a film that one perhaps should feel more than understand. Nothing difficult or mysterious. In any case, nothing more difficult or mysterious than the lives that we all live.

THE WHITE FOREST[10]

It is very cold. I know it. I see it in the others. The ice would enter my bones if I let it pass through—that is, if I'd get distracted. But I have too much to do. Not that I have specific things to do. As a matter of fact, I am doing absolutely nothing—that is, whoever looks at me certainly thinks this. But it is not true. I am observing the forest, which, little by little, is becoming white. I also have other minor practical tasks, such as to ascertain that every job is done properly, to indicate the points of the underbrush and the still-green tops of the pines to the painters—they know that I do not want dark spots, but one always escapes notice. Painting a bush is simple; but the top of a forty-meter-tall pinion pine which looks, from the gound, like a small patch of green, becomes, for the painter who sees it from the ladder pushed far up in the tree, a tangle of branches that you cannot finish whitewashing. The man leans out as much as he can on the ladder, which twists frighteningly, and I hold my breath because that man is in danger for me, and even though it may appear so, I am not insensitive to these things.

But beyond these simple tasks there is another one that occupies me completely, and it is watching the forest change color. In the dark, or better, in the artificial light, I am trying to understand what these white—or rather dirty, gray—trees will be like tomorrow, against the gray sky (a layer of clouds has covered it for a week), near the cement of the factory, near its towers. Since for now, as it stands, this question cannot have anything but an intuitive answer, I keep asking myself, more and more insistently. To be honest, I began to formulate it just a little

10 "Il bosco bianco," from *Il deserto rosso*, Carlo di Carlo ed., Bologna: Cappelli, 1954. Translated by Allison Cooper.

while ago. The question was not there when I said that I wanted a white forest, the sentence came out of me spontaneously, suggested by an image that flashed in my mind. I had not even the shadow of a doubt. Not even when, as soon as I said that the forest had to be white, I noticed that they looked at me as though they had just heard this color named for the first time (if white is a color). And immediately they wanted to know why. As if changing the color would have been enough to make them agree with me. As if with red, or blue, or yellow—which are, perhaps for the time being, the three fundamental colors of the chromatic scale—that question would not have had any reason to exist. I have never liked questions when they are directed at me, because they imply a well-thought-out meaning, and they force one to put oneself at the level of reason, while, instead, when I am working I am at a deeper level. And in this sense, it occurs to me that questions are pure sound, without meaning. Those are the moments in which I most feel myself an animal—that is, they look at me as though I were one, and perhaps I truly am one. This state also has its advantages, I have to admit it, because you are left in peace. But this is not the case tonight. This time, whoever passes by here—attracted by the light, the noise, the white cloud, and I don't know by what else, because the things that make people curious are never the same for everyone—gets in line with the others, out of curiosity, and asks: Why white? He also looks at all those workers who are handling an enormous pump mounted on a truck that is producing, as I was saying, a huge white cloud; and there are others who are getting up on very tall ladders that get lost in the dark, or are moving lights and generators or are filling up drums of paint; or they are burning the grass on the lawn (which should not be white, but dark) with hand pumps that throw burning gas, like flame-throwers. It's a real spectacle, above all because it is seen across the veil of mist produced by the cloud of paint. We are all white, like millers. The passers-by stop, observe, enjoy themselves, and after a while come closer and—with the air of saying OK, I understand, it's wonderful, marvelous, but I would just like to have one thing explained—they ask: Why white?

It may seem strange that the first time that I happened to stop there while surveying the location where I was going to shoot the film, I immediately formulated many hypotheses on what might have been, shall we say, the poetic meaning of this forest, which at first glance unquestionably excluded every idea of forest. I was trying to understand this, and at the same time to find the angle from which I might frame it. Most important was the silence, which was completely missing. When I entered it, which I did immediately, the forest did not reveal any of its typical sounds or smells. The forest was forced to accept the sounds and smells of the city, of its outskirts, onli slightly muffling them. The forest was surrounded, besieged, by streets: the sound of cars, trucks, and motorcycles, constantly, and even a train, against the background of the drone of machinery mixed with the hiss of vapors; and as for smells, the yellow smoke full of acids that pestered the whole area. Hissing and smoke came from the huge factory (with three thousand workers), built in the middle of an enormous pine forest, of which this actual forest is all that remains, for the moment. The factory works day and night. Once I asked its manager if he could interrupt that smoke, which was disturbing some of my takes, for a few minutes. He answered: "Do you know how much a minute would cost me? One hundred and fifty million lira."

It is known that Ravenna was surrounded until about twenty years ago by immense pine forests, and that today these pine forests are dying. You can see it with the naked eye: dry, benumbed trees, which are really growing without hope. What I am talking about is the green area closest to the city, which I would cross every day in my wanderings. Little by little, interested as I was in looking at everything that was around the forest, and that, as a matter of fact, the forest was often hiding from me—I didn't notice it any longer. I let it go by the window of the car, hoping to find the by-now familiar scenery that would come after. In this fashion the forest lost, each day a bit more, its natural characteristics. No, it is not exactly right to say natural; rather, its long-time-gone characteristics— the characteristics of a forest, of a perfect and unique nature that had, by then, become expendable. What was natural, now, was for the forest to disappear to make room for a new space to be filled with other shapes, other volumes, other colors. In other words, this forest was disintegrating as an idea; only to become, subsequently, the scenery that one saw from the office of X in the scene numbered as such, the backdrop of the first outdoor scene, and so on. Until it finally took on—and I say finally, because it was the result of a work of clarification—a new aspect, that of a problem, the number one problem of the sequence that I was imagining. In fact, one thing was certain: That green had to be eliminated if I wanted the scenery to acquire something of an original beauty, made up of arid grays, imposing blacks, and even pale pink and yellow spots—distant pipes or signs. There was also some green, but it was a question of a very thin chimney that cut across the factory horizontally, then rose to a prodigious height, elegant and powerful in its slenderness, higher than almost any tree. And so when the production manager announced to me, some time after, that the following Sunday we would be able to film the scene in front of the forest and asked me what I would need, I was suddenly certain, to the extent one can be certain in this order of things, that the forest should be painted white, a dirty white that, at best, would turn out gray in Technicolor, like the sky of those days, or like the fog, or like the cement.

These similarities in the gray sky, the fog, and the cement (which by the way is made here, close by, in enormous quantities) are similarities of which I am thinking only now, tonight, in an attempt to find at all costs a justification for the mass of work I have unleashed, and to silence the doubts or worries that are assailing me from every side. First doubt: Will the white forest make the type of suggestion I am expecting? Second doubt: Won't it look like snow? First worry: If we have frost, the paint will go. Second worry: If tomorrow the sun—with one of those jokes that this very mysterious object is used to pulling on us—comes out, all of this work will have been in vain, because from the point where I will put the camera for the long shot of the whole forest, I will be against the light, and the trees, instead of being white, will be dark. Nor can I change my angle, because we only painted one side of the forest. If I had said—I try to think, not without a certain reluctance, almost wishing to cease thinking—if I had said brown, the rotten brown of the winter earth, that is, of the lifeless earth, what effect would I have obtained? I close my eyes for a moment. Without any emotion whatsoever, I imagine the brown forest. I reopen my eyes. I look at the workers, still half unfinished; it is three in the morning, they have been working since six o'clock yesterday. I work with them, after all, but mine is a work that makes no impression, as far as effort is concerned. The cold has intensified. The huge pump mounted on the truck has broken, the painters' work has become exhausting. Manual laborers are becoming necessary. We send a townsman to look for some of them, to pull them out of bed. A hand pump, with its forty meters of hose, falls from the top of a ladder. No, it didn't fall, it was thrown on purpose by the workman who was controlling it. He is a hardy type, but he can't take it anymore. He comes down to the ground and says: "I want a half-million." The production inspector turns to the onlookers: "Who has a half-million here to give to this man?" Nobody laughs. The painter leaves, dragging his helper along with him. And what if others follow him? What if parts of the forest remain unpainted? The anguish of this prospect is enough to erase all of my doubts. Why white or dirty white or gray? Because that is how it is and that is all. If I wanted to I could talk to you about it at length and tell you that nobody cares about the trees of this area, and that the waste of the factories turn up in the marshes and the canals, where the waters are black or yellow, and they aren't really waters anymore. Ask the fish who have stomachs full of oil. Among the trees, there is today a canal for the ships to sail. Ravenna is the second port of Italy, did you know that? The myth of the factory conditions everyone's lives, it strips it of unforeseen events, it strips it of all flesh. Synthetic materials dominate, sooner or later they will end up reducing the trees to nothing more than antiquated objects, like horses. To take for granted the end of the forest; to make something full into something empty; to submit this old reality, by discoloring it, to a new one, a new reality that is just as suggestive—sn't this what has been happening here for years, in a flux that never stops?

But I don't want to talk about it. I don't want to explain why. All that I can say—that I must say to my production director, with mourning in my heart, now that it is morning and that a beautiful sun has come out and it is impossible to film—is that I give up on this scene. No white forest in the film. And that is the reason why I write about it.

IT WAS BORN IN LONDON,
BUT IT IS NOT AN ENGLISH FILM[11]

My problem with *Blow-Up* was to recreate reality in an abstract form. I wanted to question "the reality of our experience." This is an essential point in the visual aspect of the film, considering that one of its main themes is to see or not to see the correct value of things.

Blow-Up is a performance without an epilogue, comparable to those stories from the twenties where F. Scott Fitzgerald showed his disgust with life. While I was filming, I was hoping that no one in seeing the finished film would say: "*Blow-Up* is a typically British film." At the same time, I was hoping that no one would define it exclusively as an Italian film. Originally, *Blow-Up*'s story was to be set in Italy, but I realized from the very beginning that it would be impossible to do so. A character like Thomas doesn't really exist in our country. At the time of the film's narrative, the place where the famous photographers worked was London. Thomas, furthermore, finds himself at the center of a series of events which are more easily associated with life in London, rather than life in Rome or Milan. He has chosen the new mentality that took over in Great Britain with the 1960s' revolution in lifestyle, behavior, and morality, above all among the young artists, publicists,

---

[11] "È nato a Londra ma non è un film inglese," from *Corriere della Sera,* 12 February 1982. Translated by Allison Cooper.

stylists, or musicians that were part of the pop movement. Thomas leads a life as regulated as a ceremonial, and it is not by accident that he claims not to know any law other than that of anarchy.

Before the production of the film, I had lived in London for some weeks during the shooting of *Modesty Blaise*, a film by Joseph Losey starring Monica Vitti. In that period I realized that London would be the ideal setting for a story like the one I already planned to do. But I never had the idea of making a film *about* London.

The same story could certainly have been set in New York or in Paris. I knew, nevertheless, that I wanted a gray sky for my script, rather than a pastel-blue horizon. I was looking for realistic colors and I had already given up, for this film, on certain effects I had captured in *Red Desert*. At that time, I had worked hard to ensure flattened perspectives with the telephoto lens, to compress characters and things and to place them in juxtaposition with one another. In *Blow-Up*, I instead opened up the perspective, I tried to put air and space between people and things. The only time I made use of the telephoto lens in the film was when I had to—for example in the sequence when Thomas is caught in the middle of the crowd.

The greatest difficulty I encountered was in reproducing the violence of reality. Enhanced and ultra-soft colors often seem to be the hardest and most aggressive. In *Blow-Up*, eroticism occupies a very important place, although the focus is often placed on a cold, calculated sensuality. Exhibitionistic and voyeuristic trends are particularly underlined. The young woman in the park undresses and offers her body to the photographer in exchange for the negatives she wants so much to retrieve. Thomas witnesses a sexual encounter between Patrizia and her husband, and his presence as spectator seems to increase the young woman's excitement.

The risqué aspect of the film would have made filming in Italy almost impossible. Italian censorship would never have tolerated some of those images. Let's not forget that, even though censorship has become more tolerant in many countries in the world, Italy remains the country of the Holy See.

In the film, for example, there is a scene in the photographer's studio where two twenty-year-old women behave in a very provocative way.

Both are completely naked, although this scene is neither erotic nor vulgar. It is fresh, light, and, I dare hope, funny. Certainly I cannot prevent viewers from finding it risqué. I needed those images in the context of the film, and I did not want to give them up only because they might not meet with the taste and morality of the audience.

As I have written other times in reference to my films, my narratives are documents built not on a suite of coherent ideas, but rather on flashes, ideas that come forth every other moment. I refuse, therefore, to speak about the intentions I place in the film that, at one moment, occupies all my time and attention. It is impossible for me to analyze any of my works before the work is completed. I am a creator of films, a man who has certain ideas and who hopes to express them with sincerity and clarity. I am always telling a story. As far as knowing whether it is a story with any correlation to the world we live in, I am always unable to decide before telling it.

When I began to think about this film, I often stayed awake at night, thinking and taking notes. Soon this story, with its thousands of possibilities, fascinated me, and I attempted to understand where its thousands of implications would take me. But at a certain point, I told myself: let's start making the film—that is to say, let's try, for better or for worse, to tell the story and, then.... Today I still find myself at this stage, even if I am nearly finished filming *Blow-Up*. To be frank, I am still not completely sure of what I am doing, because I am still in the "secret" of the film.

I believe my work depends on both thought and intuition. For example, just a few minutes ago, I was all by myself, thinking about the next scene, and I tried to put myself in the shoes of the main character at the time when he finds the body. I stopped in the shade of the English lawn; I paused in the park, in the mysterious clarity of the London neon billboards. I approached this imaginary corpse and I totally identified with the photographer. I strongly felt his excitement, his emotion, the thousands of sensations that were released in my "hero" by the corpse's discovery. And then I experienced his way of coming back to his senses, of thinking, and reacting. All of which lasted only a few minutes, one or two. Then the rest of the cast joined me and my inspiration, my sensations, vanished.

Zabriskie Point (1969)

What This Land Says to Me[12]

My way of working is the diametric opposite of that enormous bureaucratic machine, Hollywood. Of course I'm not talking just about opposite methods, but an opposite approach to life itself, a refusal to accept embalmed ideas and clichés, or affectation and imitation. Besides, how could I have worked with my hands tied by a rigid scenario when America, the location of my film, was continually changing and transforming, even physically, and therefore required continual change?

Adaptation and acceptance embrace everything, from the misery of the ghetto to Vietnam. And liberty ends up meaning the liberty to buy a new car. In this sense I can say that my relationship with America consists in having sampled its best and its worst. In fact I think that what our civilization and our generation represents and produces can be seen here on its highest and purest level as well as on its lowest and most brutal. If I had to sum up my impressions of America, I would list these: waste, innocence, vastness, poverty.

Waste in this country, as a mental attitude, habit, and article of faith, is on a fantastically inconceivable scale that is impossible to get used to, whether it involves making a movie or the way of life among the rich.

More than anywhere else in the world, there is innocence in the eyes of so many people here: honest boys who dream of another kind of life,

---

[12] "Che mi dice l'America," from *L'Espresso*, 6 April 1969. Originally translated in *Atlas* 18 (2), August 1969.

soldiers who don't want to fight a war, disciplined middle-class citizens barbecuing steaks and waving to each other. An unsuspicious innocence that can also carry them unaware to a great tragedy that they will accept with good will, like one of those many obligations they accept silently every day. Perhaps this is the difference between the white people and the [Blacks], that the [Blacks] are the only people, aside from the most committed groups among the youth, who know what could happen, the only ones with the ability to refuse to accept, the only ones who are not afraid.

Like waste, there is poverty of incredible proportions, and on an extent one would never have guessed. Why so much poverty in a land that can and does produce the highest standard of living in the world? For poverty here is real, tangible, a hard, everyday fact accessible to everyone except for those who are by now too far gone in dream and stupor.

Vastness is the other impression and I think it has a great deal to do with the American character. A country of such vastness, with such distances and such horizons, could not help but be molded in its dreams, illusions, tensions, its solitude, faith, innocence, optimism and desperation, its patriotism and revolt, its dimensions. Personally, from the point of view of my work, this experience of vastness counted and is counting a lot. How can I go back, I sometimes ask myself, how can I return to Italy?

In the midst of this chaos of products and goods, of waste and poverty, acceptance and revolt, flows a current of continuous, tumultuous change. Europe felt to me like a far-off museum. I don't mean Europe with its intellectual presumptions, its cynical illusions of knowing everything beforehand.

My film is, in one way or another, about all this. It was filmed (and I'm still editing it) with difficulty, with anger, and also with love and great passion. It was a wrestling match with the most beautiful and the most disagreeable reality in the world.

My next film must be an Italian film, because I must find my own roots again. But I'm not going to pretend it won't be difficult, very difficult, to find the right track and the right tone.

LET'S TALK ABOUT *ZABRISKIE POINT*[13]

Writing is not my business. I know that I'm not a good judge of myself or of my films. Each time I must put something down on paper about myself, the same embarrassment returns. The questions put to me are always the same: why did you make that film? What were you trying to say? I'm tempted to reply: I wanted to make a film and that's that. But if you want to know why and how I did what I did, what prompted me to do it, what I was thinking while doing it, what I wanted to say—in other words, if you want me to summarize my reasons and explain what is almost impossible to explain (impulses, intuitions, figurative choices), you will only come to this: you will come to spoil the film itself.

I think that what a director says about himself and his work does not help to understand the latter. In my case, what little knowledge I have of myself, words can, at best, clarify a particular moment, or a state of mind, a vague awareness. The answer I prefer to the above question is that, at a certain period when a film was being prepared and shot, I saw certain people, read certain books, loved X, hated Y, had no money, did not sleep well. . . . But even in saying that much, perhaps I am supplying involuntary explanations.

Let's talk instead about *Zabriskie Point*. Talk about it now, long before these words will see print. There are marches on Washington. American universities are in revolt, four youths have been killed on an Ohio campus and two more in Jackson. It is difficult, unfortunately, to reject the temptation of feeling like a prophet. I would prefer, however, to reflect on some of the psychological aspects of violence.

[13] From *Esquire* 74:2, August 1970.

I'm convinced that a policeman does not have death on his mind when he enters a university or faces a mob. He has too many things to do, too many orders to follow. The policeman is not thinking of death anymore than a hunter is thinking of the death of a bird. Astronauts, in the same way, are not afraid, not because they do not know the dangers, but because they do not have the time. If the policeman gave some thought to death he probably would not shoot.

Making a picture in America brings with it one single risk: the risk of becoming the object of a discussion so wide in range that the quality of the film itself is forgotten. I went to America because it is one of the most interesting, if not the most interesting country in the world. It is a place where some of the essential truths and contradictions of our time can be isolated to their pure state. I had many images of America in mind, but I wanted to see it with my own eyes, not as a voyager but as an author.

My film certainly does not pretend to say all there is to say about America. Even if the film's content is complex, the story is simple. It is simple because it sets out to achieve the aura of a fable. Now, even if critics may object, I do believe one thing: fables are true. Even when the hero destroys an army of dragons with his magic sword.

If I had wanted to do a picture about student dissent, I would have continued the direction I took at the opening with the student-meeting sequence. If ever the day comes when young American radicals realize their hopes to change the structure of society, they will come from that kind of background and have faces like those. But I left them there, and I followed my protagonist on a completely different itinerary. The itinerary does run through a bit of America, but almost without touching it, not only because the young man flies over it, but because from the moment he steals that airplane, America for him coincides with "the earth," from which, precisely, "he needed to get off."

That's why you can't say that *Zabriskie Point* is a revolutionary picture, although it may seem so from the point of view of abstract dialectics.

Some say that to do a picture in a foreign country you have to know that country in depth. This doesn't strike me as a valid aesthetic criterion. If it were so, how could American or Japanese critics judge and praise, as they did pictures like *L'avventura*, *Fellini Satyricon*, *The Damned*, themselves knowing very little, I suppose, about Sicily, ancient Rome, or the Germany of the Krupps? I should like to ask Americans: How many of you, crossing one of your astonishing deserts, have stopped at a ghost town longer than for a normal tourist visit?

And anyway, why should I be coercively confined to speak of "what I know," which ultimately would mean (following Aristotle) what the average audience believes it knows, within the patterns of verisimilitude, current majority opinion, tradition, and so on.

Certainly, judged by such ancient critical standards, my picture, especially the finale, may even look delirious. Well, as an author I claim my right to delirium, if for no other reason than today's deliriums might be tomorrow's truths.

I am not an American and I shall never tire of repeating that I do not claim to have done an American film. But why deny legitimacy to a foreign, detached observation? A famous French philosopher and aesthetician wrote: "If I look at an orange hit by a side light, I do not see it as it actually appears to me, i.e., with all gradations of color from light to shadow; I see it as I know it to be, uniformly colored. To me it is not a sphere with graded nuances of color; it is an orange."

Well, let's put it this way: I have looked at America as it has appeared to me, without knowing what it was. Eventually, as I kept looking at the orange, I may have felt like eating it; but this urge is a fact which strictly involves my own personal relationship with the orange.

In other words, this is the problem: whether I have managed to express *my* feelings, impressions, intuitions; whether I have been able to raise them—if you permit the expression—to a poetic level; and not whether they correspond to those of Americans.

Why Americans saw in *Zabriskie Point* a film against their country remains a mystery to me. "Antonioni has given us his contempt, we give it back to him," they even said, echoing Ivan Karamazov. What, contempt? I must be dreaming. Are the two protagonists seen with contempt? Or maybe they are not American themselves? Perhaps the Paris *Herald Tribune* critic is right when, astonished by the reactions of his fellow

American critics, he wonders: "Did they perhaps watch a different picture?"

That an author should analyze his own political and social choices, and manifest them in his work—in my case, a motion picture which relates back to them through the channel of imagination—does not justify taking those choices as the only basis for judgment. The course of the author's imagination is the real issue. The questions are: whether the word *poetry* acquires special weight today (can the word by saved by poets?) and whether this word applies to *Zabriskie Point*. It isn't up to me to pass judgment, but I believe that poetry is the criterion for others to do so.

I insist on this argument, because I want to be understood. I've always detested the role of the non-understood. If there is something enigmatic in what I do or say or write, I am in the wrong. (The trouble is that my errors are perhaps the most personal element I have put in my films.)

If one is instinctively brought to make common cause with America's rebellious youth, perhaps it is because one is attracted by their natural animal vitality. When in Chicago kids with blankets over their shoulders and flowers in their hair are seen being bashed by grown men wearing helmets, you come very near to forming, without reservations, a total alliance with them. I wasn't able to avoid wishing these youths great success. For they know what the adults ignore. They know that reality is an impenetrable mystery, and it is in the nature of today's children not to succumb passively before this mystery nor calmly to accept the adult vision of reality which seems to have produced monstrous results. These are the experiences and impressions which have caused some personal symbols to emerge in my films. But after each new film, I'm always asked what the symbol means, rather than how it was shaped and inspired.

My films are always works of research. I do not consider myself a director who has already mastered his profession, but one who is continuing his search and studying his contemporaries. I'm looking (perhaps in every film) for the traces of sentiment in men and of course in women, too, in a world where these traces have been buried to make way for sentiments of convenience and of appearance: a world where sentiments have been "public-relationized." My work is like digging, it is archaeological research among the arid material of our times. That is how I started my first film and that is what I am still doing.

It has never been my intention, in any film, to show the conflict between the human mind and technical progress. My interest is not in man facing machine but in man facing man, with his acts, his story, his attempts at love, according to the style, the pace, the place, and the occasions which today's civilization allows. It is not the command of the machine which is slipping away from man, but the control of his sentiments, his beliefs. In answering a question put to me about *Red Desert*, I said once, more or less, the following: "In this film, machines, with their intrigue of power, beauty, and squalor, have an enormous effect and they have taken the place of the natural landscape. But machines are not the cause of the crisis of the anguish that people have been talking about for years. I mean that we must not long for the more primitive times, thinking that they were a more natural landscape for man. I prefer to believe that man must struggle to try and mold and restrict the machines to man's measure, not try to negate technological progress."

Color has a psychological and dramatic function for me. This point is not an Absolute, nor is it valid for everyone. It is a rapport between the object and the light, the object and its observer, the position of the latter in regard to the object, and even its physical state. At times we have a desire for color and we find it or even see it where it is not. These are not my discoveries, they are findings of scientists expert in that field.

Nor should the psychological effect of color be overlooked. There is a psychology of color which has been proved by hundreds of texts. There are scenes and dialogue in my films which would not have been possible without the presence of walls or backgrounds of particular colors.

But theoretic discourses are useless. One simply must use in a film only those colors which are right for the story one has to tell. Exclude all others. A painter doesn't ask what color that tree before him should be, but lets his fantasy tell him. He has his good reasons for dong what he does, but do not ask him what they are. Most of the time, he cannot give the answer. But there is one thing I must tell you: you cannot argue that a film is bad but that the color is good, or vice versa. The image is a fact, the colors *are* the story. If a cinematic moment has colors which appear right and good, it means that it has expressed itself, that it achieved its purpose. The blue spread over Picasso's painting, evident during his blue period, *was* the painting.

A director does nothing but search for himself in his films. They are documents not of a finished thought but of a thought in the making. Often one is asked: How is a film born? The probable answer is that it is born in the disorder which is in us all; the difficulty is in finding the order, in knowing how to pull the right thread from the skein. I'm convinced that it depends not only on an attitude, but also on an attitude of one's fantasy.

A story idea can be born in a moment like this: Rome, the fourth day of a strike of garbage collectors. Rome flooded with garbage, heaps of colored refuse at the street corners, an orgy of abstract images, a symbolic violence never before seen. And, contrasting this, the meeting of the garbage collectors in the ruins of the Circus Maximus; two thousand men dressed in bright blue blouses, silent, orderly, waiting for I don't know what. Observing this scene, it came to mind that in that moment, it wasn't anymore the garbage collectors in the midst of the garbage, but all the citizens of Rome.

When one is in certain moods one should not be alone. People help you by taking your mind off yourself. They even make you less "sensitive." They force you to be a hypocrite, they stir up the air around you, polluting it. In a mob everyone can be exalted, at a party everyone is a little bit of a fool. Among people who know nothing of me, I even forget myself a little. "Ignorance," said Joubert, "is a bond between men." There I go with a quotation. I detest myself when I assume the airs of an intellectual. Naturally, I've read a quantity of books but I've always tried to hide this fact. Modesty? Diffidence for culture? I don't know. Read a book carefully and do not think of it again. A book works inside you, like food.

Talking about it is like writing a new book. But, then, I get little pleasure out of talking. Today I've decided not to do anything which does not also give me great pleasure. Shooting gives me pleasure. I should not let too much time lapse between films.

Traditional images are no longer capable of representing the world. One can say that the ideal image of the world is that which coincides exactly with a world which must be canceled as an image. For an image no longer exists which gives form to the world because the world itself can no longer be represented other than by approximation. There's the need, I think, to recommence from zero to experiment with new ways of representation. It is a process already underway.

Saying this, one realizes that the tasks of the spectator also are modified. It cannot go on, as it has till now, that the image enters through the eye to reach the brain, the spectator must operate on his own, almost creatively. One says *seeing* a film, *reading* a film. These words now are no longer suited. Today, it is the rapport between image and image which counts. So it is more right to say that today we must *feel* a film. Let's put ourselves down in front of the screen no longer as men of culture (our culture is almost at the zero point anyway) but simply as men.

A screenplay is never definitive for me. It is a director's notebook, nothing more. In a screenplay there is no technical plan, where to place the camera, which lens to be used; these are things to be seen to during the shooting. That's the system for all directors now, I think. Even the dialogue must be heard spoken by the actors, or rather by the characters, within the scene being shot, before I can be sure of the validity of the lines.

And there's another factor. I believe in improvisation. It is not my habit to prepare myself for a business encounter, a love encounter, or a friendly encounter. I take them as they come, adapting myself in the course of things, making use of the unexpected. The same system works in shooting a film. A propos of improvising: when I think of the past I can say that I have always lived from minute to minute. It is my way, even now.

Each moment of the day is important to me because it constitutes a new experience. And this does not change while making a film: the stimulants of reality during the filming, the chance encounters, the rapport between working companions, all these things influence the film and lead to sudden choices and even to radical changes. That's what I mean by improvising.

My relations with my actors are rather curious. Rather friendly I would say, even if the opposite is often presented as the case. The *métier* of an actor is something I would never attempt to learn, since any form of exhibitionism is against my nature. Nor could I support being in the position of being chosen, rather than being the chooser. The actor must always compromise with the personalities of the roles to be interpreted.

Maybe that's the reason why I can tolerate without much trouble an actor's sudden shift of humor. I understand their problems: the good profile for close-ups, the right stills for publicity, things of that sort. I realize too that actors and actresses often feel uneasy with me, they feel as if I've shut them out of my personal creation. In a certain sense, they are right. But that is the kind of collaboration, and no other kind, which I ask of them.

Only one person holds in his head a clear idea of the boundaries of the film and that is the director. Only one person mentally fuses the various elements which compose a film and is in a position to foresee the results of this fusion, and that is the director. The actor is one of these elements and sometimes not even the most important. For example, one thing the actor can never do is see himself in the scene. Consider how many ideas for his acting he could get, if that were possible. This limitation will partly be eliminated the day we film on magnetic tape, but i don't believe that it will change the actor film-relationship. It will always be the director who must manipulate the "actor-element," following precise criteria which only he knows.

Methods for directing actors are many, each director tends to have his own. For my part, I think that it isn't necessary, in order to achieve a certain comportment, or certain expressions and intonations, that the actor must be in a corresponding state of mind. In fact, this could even lead to putting us at cross-purposes, because it would be the result of his sensibility being different from mine and thus committed differently in the film.

I never think of the public. I think of the film. Obviously, there is always an interlocutor, but it is the ideal interlocutor (who may really be another me). If it weren't that way, I do not know how I would manage, inasmuch as there are as many publics as there are continents and human races, not to mention nations, cities, villages, social classes, sexes and generations.

The number of new directors in America, Germany, Italy, Hungary, Czechoslovakia, everywhere, could be much larger than it is. Young directors do not yet have the power they merit in the cinema because the resistance to the novelty which they offer is very strong. The commercial and industrial network of the cinema is like an enormous dike which is holding back a sea of talent. Things are moving even in America, but much too slowly. How much longer will it take the producers to realize that the majority of the public is made up of young people and they want to see films made by their own generation?

Why talk about costs? Money spent on a picture is never seen by the director. And a great part of the expenditure is not even wanted by the director. Filming in America, I had contrasting opinions: on one side it seemed that money did not matter, or mattered less. But then, it wasn't true. It is true, instead, that more is consumed in America, more than one can imagine. I think they must teach it at school—how to consume. And when you grow up, it gets worse, you consume that much more. And since the cinema is run by grown-ups, the result is that there is a squandering of material and money such as I've never seen in Europe.

Zabriskie Point is certainly the most costly film I've made. And not only because of the reason I've just given, but also for the absurd laws which the American unions have. For example, in Arizona once, I saw that there was a doctor and a nurse hovering around the set. I didn't know what they were doing. No one was ill; if anything I was somewhat concerned about the doctor's health. He might have had sleeping sickness because he was out cold and snoring all day. The nurse, however, was busy taking snapshots. On another day, shooting in Los Angeles, I asked for an extra. They brought me thirty. When I asked why, I was told, "Just in case."

The movie camera hidden behind the keyhole is a gossipy eye which records what it can. But what of the rest? What is happening beyond the visual range of the keyhole? So one hole is not enough. You make ten, one hundred, two hundred holes, place that many cameras behind them, and let several miles of film roll through. What will you have? A mountain of material in which not only will there be the essential aspects of an event, but also the marginal, absurd, and ridiculous aspects. Or the less interesting aspects, I mean to say. Then your job is to reduce and select. But the actual event really did include all these aspects. In selection, you will be falsifying. So you say, I am interpreting. That's an old question. Life is neither so simple nor always so intelligible and even history-as-science does not come near to completely expressing it: Strachey and Valéry came to the conclusion via different routes; the historian who made history an art, and the poet who despised history.

Pudovkin's experiments also are well-known. He changed the meaning of certain shots by rearranging the sequences in the editing. A smiling man who looks at a bowl of soup is a glutton; if he is shown with the same smile eyeing a dead woman he is a cynic. Why then the keyhole and the two hundred cameras and the mountain of material?

Some lines of MacNeice have been running through my mind for years: "Think of a number, double it, treble it, square it, and sponge it out."

I'm convinced that this could become the nucleus, or at least the symbol, for a curious film. The lines already indicate a style.

Probably the best film is one which is born from many diverse ideas, not from one alone. But the problem is in recognizing these ideas in the chaos of sensations, reflections, observations and impulses with which the world surrounds us, or our own imagination provokes in us. Why, among so many possibilities, do we isolate some ideas and not others? There are several answers but none of them satisfactory.

The good ideas for a film may not be the same ideas which serve us in life. Otherwise, the way a director lives would coincide with his way of *forming a film*. Instead, however autobiographical these ideas may be, there is always the intervention of our fantasy which translates and alters what we see and what we want to see. We are our own personages to the extent in which we believe in the film which we are making. But between us and them there remains the film. There is that concrete, precise, lucid fact, that act of will and of strength which qualifies us unequivocally, which releases us from the abstraction to let our feet rest firmly on the ground. Thus from being proletarians, let's say, we re-become bourgeois, from pessimists we re-become optimists, from solitary and alienated persons we re-become desirous of opening a dialogue and of communicating.

I read something written by an American philosopher some years ago which left an impression on my memory. This philosopher had gone to spend a city in what we'll call a model city. First-rate schools, splendid music halls, stadiums for all the sports, fountains, parks, theaters, no germs, no poverty, no drunks or addicts, no criminals and no policemen.

Moral: He returned to New York and what a relief! "Give me," the philosopher said, "something primeval and savage, even if it must be something perfidious like a massacre of Armenians, just to restore the balance. I want to run all the risks of the world, with all the inherent suffering and crime. Here there is many times more hope and help than in that quintessence of all mediocrity."

One can share, fully or not, the position of our philosopher and it is true that some films are like that model city: insupportable, dull. You can't go wrong in asking yourself, when you are preparing a film, if there is enough nastiness in it. If there isn't, put some in. What will happen is what happens when a substance is put in contact with its natural chemical reagent, which makes it reveal itself, its composition, its truth.

The first time I stood behind a movie camera was in an insane asylum. The supervisor was a tall, imposing man and he had a face which, with the passing of time, was beginning to look more and more like that of one of the inmates. I was living then in my hometown of Ferrara, a fine little city in the Po Valley, silent and ancient. Together with some friends, we had decided to make a documentary film on the insane.

The supervisor went out of his way to be helpful, even rolling on the floor to illustrate how some of his patients reacted to outside stimuli. I wanted to make the documentary with the truly insane, and after some insistence on my part, the supervisor said: "Try it."

We set up the camera and the lights and we placed the inmates in the room as we wanted them for the first shot. I must say that they took our orders with humility and took care not to make mistakes. They were very touching in their sense of cooperation and I was delighted with the way things were going. Then I called for the lights to be turned on. I was excited myself. All at once the room was flooded with light. For an instant, the patients remained immobile, like stone statues. I've never seen on any actor's face an expression of such thorough, total fright as I saw then. This lasted only a second, and was followed by an almost indescribable scene. The schizophrenics began to roll on the floor, just as their supervisor had done. In a moment, the entire ward became a pit in Hell. The insane tried desperately to hide from the light, as if it were some prehistoric monster which was assaulting them. Their faces, which a minute before had seemed composed, now were distorted and devastated. Now it was our turn, behind the camera, to freeze like stone statues. The cameraman didn't have the strength to start the camera rolling and I could give no orders. It was the supervisor who finally shouted to us to put out the lights. In the semidarkness of the ward we could see bodies huddled together which were still twitching as if they were in the last throes of agony. I'll never forget this scene. It was that day (just before the war) and that scene which started us talking about neorealism in the cinema.

Every time I enter a strange office, public place, or private home, I get the urge to rearrange the scene. I go out to meet someone and the conversation puts me ill at ease. Because I feel that neither of us is properly placed in the room. He is on a divan, whereas he should be in an armchair, which would be less free, more enclosed. I'm seated next to him, when I should be opposite. And instead of his having his back to the wall, I feel it would be more fitting if there were a window or a door behind him, leaving some possibility for escape.

Is this professional distortion, or the instinctive urge to feel myself in physical harmony with my surroundings? I believe more in the second hypothesis. In fact, I cannot shoot a scene without first being alone in the room, or the set, in order to understand it and sense the various possible camera angles.

A book is read in a few days, you keep it next to the bed, you carry it with you, you reread it. A painting or a piece of music you enjoy all your life. A motion picture you lose at once, or almost. It is placed in the memory and then after only a few weeks the demolition work begins: you erase, add, change, retain the best, or retain the worst. The film then belongs to you. And that is why, when after a few years you see the film again and you find that it is different, you might not like it anymore.

There are moments when I seem to perceive, however confusedly, the *why* of certain things. When this happens, I become a combative optimist. How many times, however, do I hear myself being accused of pessimism. Some years back, when I made a movie based on a book by Cesare Pavese, I was bracketed with him.

Now, I've read Pavese with interest and with love, but I cannot say that he is my favorite italian writer. And one reason for this is the tragic conclusion of his life, his suicide, a conclusion which made his intellectual experiences coincide with his practical experiences.

But am I not still here, making films (good ones, bad ones, whatever) which are always against something and someone? Isn't this obstinacy? And isn't this obstinacy itself a kind of optimism?

Chung Kuo. China (1972)

Is it Still Possible to Film a Documentary?[14]

Once again, I had promised myself I would write a diary about my trip, and once again, I did not do it. It might be because of my disorganization, of my frenetic work pace (fifty takes a day), or of the new images that overwhelmed me. But perhaps there is a deeper reason; perhaps it is because I find it difficult to have a definitive idea of that reality in constant change that is contemporary China. To understand China, it is perhaps necessary to live there for a long time. And yet a famous Sinologist, during a debate, observed that every person who spends a month in China feels capable of writing a book, but after spending a few months he may write just a few pages, and eventually, after a few years, he prefers to write nothing at all. It is a witticism, but it confirms how difficult it is to perceive in depth the truth of that land.

The famous revolutionary writer Lu Hsün used to say to young people: "Truth, naturally, is not easy. It is difficult, for instance, to behave in a truthful way. When I am giving a speech, my attitude is never completely true because I speak differently to friends than to children. It is possible, however, to say things that are quite true in a voice that is quite sincere." After my return, I have answered infinite questions. I believe I have

14 "È ancora possibile girare un documentario?" from *Chung Kuo. Cina,* ed. Lorenzo Cuccu, Turin: Einaudi, 1974. Translated by Allison Cooper.

never said so many words on one subject, and this is because I was hoping, in some way, to clarify China for myself. At times, the people who were asking me questions, especially if they had never been in China, would already have an answer of their own. I say this without irony, because it is natural that it should be this way. For the men of our time, that immense country typifies contradiction. In most of us there is a "Chinese temptation," just as in Ling W.Y., that character of Malraux, there was a "Wetern temptation." Political movements that were inspired by that great revolution are called "Chinese," and because of the habit of referring to the Maoist militants with this adjective, I often found myself having to specify whether I was talking about the Chinese from Canton or the "Chinese" from Rome or Paris. There is an idea of China based on books, on ideology, on political faith, that does not need to be verified through a journey like the one I was so fortunate to take. And there are questions that I do not know how to answer directly. But among the comments made about my documentary, there is one which has repaid me for all I went through: "I felt as if I actually had been to China." It was exactly what I had hoped to obtain, and I do not venture to say that I have succeeded, because in my five-week stay with the Chinese I should have learned a little bit of modesty. "Reflect often upon your weak points, faults, and errors," wrote Mao to his wife, and it is a useful piece of advice for everyone.

I, too, before going there, had in my mind a predetermined idea of China, resulting not so much from recent books, from the impact of the cultural revolution, or from discussions about Maoism, but rather from images, and particularly, for me, fabulous images: the Yellow River; the Blue Desert, the place where there is so much salt that they make houses and streets out of salt, and therefore they are all white; the deserts; the mountains with animal shapes; the farmers dressed in fanciful clothes. I did not find this China in my trip, except perhaps for a moment when I arrived by plane in Peking on a cold and windy evening, and I saw an enormous square full of boys and girls who were singing and dancing in the lights of the airport. They were welcoming a Somalian chief. Also the Honan farmers, from the center of China, looked right out of a fairy tale in their white or black clothes. But these are exceptions. The China I saw is no fairy tale. It is a human landscape, very different from ours, yet also concrete and modern. These are the faces that have invaded the screen of my film.

I do not know what sense there is in remembering the somewhat infantile fantasies that I brought with me from Italy. But I would like to escape from the temptation, so common after having finished a job, to make results coincide with first intentions. And to me it seems positive that I did not want to go on searching for an imaginary China, and that I entrusted myself to visual reality. After all, I decided from the very beginning to take the Chinese—more than their accomplishments or their landscapes—as the protagonists of the film. I remember having asked, on the first day of conversation with my hosts, what, in their opinion, symbolized most clearly the change which came after the liberation. "Man," they answered. I know that they meant something more than, and different from, the images of man that a camera can capture. They were talking about the conscience of man, his ability to think and to live in justice. At the same time, this man also has a look, a face, a way of speaking and of dressing, of walking in the city or in the countryside. He also has a way of hiding himself and of pretending sometimes to appear better—or different, anyway—than what he is. Is it an act of arrogance to approach this multitude of men and film thirty thousand meters of film in twenty-two days? I believe it would be if the director said: "Here it is, this is China, this is the new man (or the opposite), this is his role in world revolution (or the opposite)." But I knew this (or I guess) before I went to China. If, on the other hand, I say: "These are the Chinese that I was able to film in a few weeks of work, on a trip that has given me unforgettable emotions. Do you want to follow me on this trip, which has enriched my life and which could also enrich yours?" If I say this, I think I am making a legitimate proposition.

I have been asked, upon my return, whether the Chinese authorities limited my possibilities of movement, whether they obliged me to see a reality that coincided with their propaganda. One journalist remarked that in the film, "while in the preestablished scenes the Chinese are always smiling, in the impromptu scenes they are more serious, sometimes even frowning." It is true, although not always. But I do not believe that the documentary would be closer to reality if "preestablished" scenes were absent. The children who sing in the nursery school, and all the rest of the "mise en scène," are evidently the images that the Chinese want to give of themselves, and it is not an image uprooted from the reality of the country. When they show us the bust and the works of Mao in plain sight atop a chest of drawers, they don't care to know if, in the West, they will be subscribing to the "cult of personality." It is propaganda, but it is not a lie. Mao's name is rarely uttered and, when it is, it is said with an enormous respect. Sometimes, when I happened to utter it, they would look at me as though I were talking nonsense, perhaps not solemnly enough. At any rate, they would watch me with suspicion.

[Alberto] Moravia is right in saying that we are dealing with a modern form of cult. For the Chinese, the history of China begins with Mao. "To find men of style and genius / turn to our time." These are verses from one of his poems.

Perhaps it is a good thing to talk about my dealings with the Chinese bureaucracy, because they are among the few things that did not become images in the film. They had told us at the embassy in Rome that we would have to propose an itinerary. And so, in our first meeting in Peking with the functionaries of Chinese television, we showed a map of China, upon which we had marked what were to be the stops in our imaginary journey—which was to remain as such. It was, in fact, an ideal, and therefore absurd, itinerary. To cover all of it, it would have taken six months. And this was the reason that the Chinese put forward in refusing it. But it was not the real reason. Our itinerary had already been established by them, and it was completely different. We discussed it for three days. Three entire days, closed up in a room of the hotel, seated in armchairs arranged along the walls, in front of coffee tables and cups of tea, which a girl was continuously passing out and filling up. The center of the room, empty, was an immense space that made one uneasy, as though the ten thousand kilometers that separated China from Italy were all concentrated there. Peking and China were outside, and I had a frenetic curiosity to begin seeing them, to go out and wander around, but instead I had to stay there and turn down their proposals, make new ones, accept some of them, and so on, in an exhausting seesaw of argumentation.

I realized afterwards that those conversations and the faces of my interlocutors, their unforseeable laughs and their strange way of reacting and getting excited, were also part of "China," and that the verbal and sometimes sanctimonious labyrinths in which I felt I was losing my way were much more "Chinese" than the streets that awaited me outside, which, in fact, are not very different from our own.

Only after gaining a certain familiarity with the Chinese can one begin interpreting and having a feeling for their behavior, if such a thing is ever possible. At times their customary gentleness suddenly vanishes and leaves in its place a harshness that strikes you as totally unyielding. When negotiations reach a breaking point, they themselves ask for a recess, only to present themselves again a few hours later, or the next day, as though nothing has happened. It may remind you of a type of Jesuitism, but it is not. And it is not true that never saying no, changing instead the topic or laughing to conceal a refusal, is only a tactic. Ignoring the "no" is a law of qualitative, or analogical, thought, which is at the base of Chinese reasoning. The collision with a quantitative way of thinking like ours is inevitable, and all of the misunderstandings that take place at the rational level stem from this point. I am not saying that they are less rational than we are. They are rational in a different way.

It was a harsh and courteous battle that had neither winners nor losers. A compromise came out of it, and the film that I filmed in China is the fruit if this compromise. I must add that I am not all that sure that a compromise is always reductive in view of the results—first of all because those results could also have been the fruit of an erroneous intuition, and also because I believe that the limits imposed by the compromise, corresponded, in my case at least, to a greater tenacity in watching and choosing. Anyway, it was a compromise that had to do with time and also with their "bureaucracy." I use this word unwillingly because it makes me thing of a bureaucratic pyramid, of waiting, in a Kafkaesque way, for orders that had to come from higher up and far away. But, in my experience, the

Chinese bureaucracy is reminiscent of the "Emperor's Message." One day in Shanghai I wanted to see the Huang Pu (the river that cuts through the city and flows into its harbor), from the side opposite to the one I was accustomed to. I persuaded one of my escorts to take me to the other bank. Once I was there I understood why my escort had hesitated. The other bank was occupied by an uninterrupted series of factories, and it was impossible to reach the river without crossing through one of them. In order to do so, it was necessary to ask permission of the revolutionary committee of the factory. At that moment only the vice-president of the committee was present, a stout young man in his late twenties, with a volitive face, and cold and penetrating eyes. "Cinema? . . . Photographs?" he commented, smiling. He turned his glance to the dark building that towered above us and then looked at us. "No, no. . . ," he said. My escort explained to him that we were from Italian television and we came from Peking, and it seemed to me that Peking's authorization, meaning the government's, should be enough. I could not understand why in the world my escort was not using this argument to force the other one to give in. But this was not an argument for them. In a society like the Chinese one, the only person whose business it was to decide in that moment was that young man, and my escort, by not insisting, was only respecting his authority, his responsibility. But I do not believe that his authority was consecrated in a written document, or that it ensued from a legal one.

For millennia the Chinese state has succeeded in developing one of the greatest cultures in the world with a minimum number of legal principles, formal laws, or functionaries. In place of laws you had the morality and the wisdom of life, and it seems to me that this still constitutes an aspect of Chinese reality today. Certainly, Mao Tse-tung is not Confucius. "Mao's Marxist-Leninist-thought" wanted to represent a break with Confucianism, and for this reason it sped up to the highest degree the process that brought millions of men to be protagonists on the world scene. But Mao, too, is a teacher of morality. I am truly convinced that the Chinese, in their everyday life, more than just obeying formal laws, are conditioned by a common idea of what is right and wrong, from which they gain a greater simplicity of life—that is, a greater serenity in human relations.

For example, one sees a few policemen who direct traffic in white jackets, but one does not notice the presence of the police, at least not in the form of military police. Every district has its representatives charged with maintaining order, and they are almost always women. If something happens they immediately turn up and maintain order. They are respected and listened to; they represent power, but in an unassuming way. Certainly, in a very different way than our own, in which even a traffic officer is a man who receives from the uniform a perhaps excessive authority.

I was told that this unassuming image of power could hide a different reality. I find it, however, very significant to the understanding of China, just as the image of the Italian police force, with all its weapons and its apparel, could be significant to an understanding of Italy. I still believe, after so many years of cinema, that images have meaning.

For this reason I do not know what I should think when I read in a review that "socialism is not something one sees," and that once it is understood that revolution is a mental, material, and moral thing, but not necessarily visible, one cannot make a documentary like Antonioni's or Ivens's, nor a feature film like Godard's.[15] The author of the review, usually a serious and committed writer, watched the film well. He remembers a great number of its details, recognizes that it is an "honest monologue," and then concludes with: "Enough with cinematographic documentaries, and long live the Chinese republic." As if there were a cause-and-effect relationship between the death of the documentary and the long life of the Chinese republic. But if we want to better understand his intentions, we should draw a conclusion from this statement that I refuse to believe; that almost any form of cinema is devoid of meaning,

15 Dutch filmmaker Joris Ivens (1898–1989) shot a series of documentaries on China, *How Yukong moved the Mountains* (1974-76), which is often compared to Antonioni's *Chung Kuo*. Jean-Luc Godard's film is probably *La Chinoise* (1967).

and that for the "most bourgeois and positivistic of all arts," it is impossible to do any better. If Antonioni's film is wrong, it is Antonioni's fault, not the fault of that faceless ghost, that abstract concept, that is the cinema.

I remember that once, in Suchow [Suzhou], I wanted to film a wedding scene. The interpreter answered that, in those days, at Suchow, nobody was getting married. "All I need is a boy and a girl," I said, "to reconstruct a wedding scene." So the interpreter replied that in those days at Suchow, nobody was getting married. I insisted that all I needed was for them to pretend to get married. But he concluded that it was not right that they pretend to get married given that they were not getting married.

This is why, in the film, you do not see a Chinese marriage scene. None of the documentary scenes was created with closed-studio criteria.

Maybe the interpreter was simply naive, but I wanted to remember this small incident because it seems typical of the importance that one can give to the image and how it can be captured. The Chinese have a very earthly, concrete, visible idea of reality.

CHINA AND THE CHINESE[16]

I do not like to travel as a tourist. One arrives in a place, begins to wander around, following the advice of a guidebook that is rarely up-to-date. One tries to phone people whose address one got from friends who were in that same place years ago; sometimes those people are not there any longer, sometimes they are. And so you meet them and they tell you,

[16] "La Cina e i cinesi," from *Il Giorno*, 22, 25, 26 July 1972. Translated by Allison Cooper.

often with the air of wanting to get rid of you, that you must see this and that. And you go there and you see everything with their eyes, or better, you let yourself be taken by the hand in looking at the place; you endure the bombardment of impressions that come from the outside, at least until you begin to choose and evaluate what you see by yourself. Indeed, it happens that while you look around, you discover other things on your own account, and this is a step forward, and then you meet other people who give you other suggestions, and that is another step forward. Little by little, you learn how to look completely with your own eyes.

This is a way of traveling, but I do not like it. Furthermore, it makes me very sad, because of these worlds that you are not permitted to enter, since your very presence is enough to modify their workings, and because of these shells that close up in front of you and offer your only a kind welcome, and the story—always biased—of how one lives inside that shell.

The first image I have of China is of a dozen red caps on the heads of men dressed in blue who are unloading some goods off a wagon, on the border of Lo Wu [province]. The blue is not the color worn by porters (porters do not exist in China, each person traveling carries his own baggage); it is the dominant color of the clothing of the Chinese: blue, green, gray, and, less common, beige. Certain blues and certain discolored greens would stir envy in those of us who love to dress with shabby elegance.

The jackets are military style, but generally they are worn open at the collar. A Western tailor would say that they are too large, that they "do not fit well." In fact, they are all commercially manufactured. Only in the countryside are they made at home to save two bucks.

In the country they use different colors. Raw or dyed black cotton is used for the elderly. The style also changes: It is more old-fashioned, the jackets have braided loops instead of buttons, the pants are tighter at the bottom and are shorter. The women wear high-collared shirts, buttoned on the side. According to Western taste, I would say that the farmer's clothes are more beautiful.

Here, every morning, between five-thirty and seven-thirty, the streets take on a blue hue. Thousands, tens of thousands of blue jackets on bicycle are going to work, uninterrupted lines that take up the whole street, the whole city. You have the impression that 800 million blue Chinese pass before your eyes. [...]

The film is entitled *Chung Kuo*, which means "China". In reality I did not make a film about China, but about the Chinese. I remember having asked, on the first day of our discussions [with our hosts], what, according to them, most clearly symbolized the change which happened in the country after the liberation. "Man," they had replied. Therefore, at least in this, our interests coincided. And I tried to look at man more than at his accomplishments or at the landscape. Let me be clear on this: I think of China's contemporary socio-political structure as a model, perhaps inimitable, worthy of the most attentive study. But the people are what struck me the most. What precisely struck me about the Chinese? Their candor, their honesty, their reciprocal respect. [...]

One day in Nanking, I am on my way to the post office to send a telegram. They give me the usual form—which in China is a much larger piece of paper than [the one we use in Italy] because the character-based handwriting requires more space—and I begin to write the text, in Italian. At a certain point I feel a weight on my right arm, which prevents me from writing. I raise my eyes and I realize that a small crowd has gathered around me. There are many children. (Chinese children are extraordinary, and would require a whole separate discussion.) They climb up on each other and up onto the table. My form is surrounded by heads whose noses are right on my pen, to see it up close, writing Western letters, one after the other. I do not know how to describe the wonder of those eyes. The eyes of the children in China—and often, also, of the adults—are always full of wonder, like those of infants who are just beginning to see.

The clerk asks me in hesitant English where the telegram is going. "Italy," I say. She does not understand. She does not know what it is. I write it for her. She reads it and runs into another room laughing. Through the glass door I see her turn to the other workers with my little piece of paper in her hand. And all of them go toward a wall where there is a map, and they begin to look, and finally they find Italy. One of them points it out and all the others burst into laughter: This country is so small that you can hardly see it.

The concept that there is a component of pleasure in work is not generally a part of our ideology. If there is any place where you can verify the truthfulness of this assertion, it is China. It is common to see male and female workers come out of the factories and, rather than rush right home, linger in the courtyard of the factory, sitting in a circle, to discuss work problems. After all, they are the owners of the factory, and it seemed to me that everyone is conscious of this.

It turned out that I was able to see and film a scene of this type. It was not an organized scene. Nothing of what I filmed in China is organized. In seeing the film, the viewers will be able to see on the faces of those girls who are discussing or reading a newspaper together (only one man among them) not the expression of someone who is carrying out a duty, but a real and sincere interest, mixed with pleasure.

I had the impression, observing people work, that each of them accepts the duties he has, even the most onerous, in peace, and with the consciousness of doing something useful for the community—a deep-seated feeling in the Chinese of today. In my brief stay in that country (little more than a month), I did not notice that this feeling entered into conflict with individuality.

Suchow is a little city reminiscent of Venice. Narrow lanes, small squares, bridges, canals, low houses, stillness. Contrary to Venice, Suchow's inhabitants smile voluntarily, they are kind and curious, with discretion. I remember the spasmodic but calm, composed curiosity of a crowd of five or six thousand people assembled in front of a restaurant where I was doing some takes. When I turned the camera to the outside and asked that the street be cleared for a few minutes, the crowd dispersed obediently. And then it was a problem to convince someone to walk by so that the street would not be completely empty.

In Suchow I wanted to record a soundtrack of women's voices: greetings, calls, chattering—and I said so to one of my escorts. He was a very courteous and efficient person, and he spoke English perfectly. His name was Sing. We went with him one night in search of a silent place where we could carry out the recording. We chose a courtyard surrounded by blocks of flats two or three floors high, a few lit-up windows, and the sound of radios. But this did not turn out to be a problem. Everyone was asked to turn off their radios, and in just a few minutes we obtained silence.

The four women obviously were not actresses. We would call them housewives. They were lively and eager to be of help. They already knew what I wanted. I arranged certain movements in advance to create different sound levels and we began. The first try did not convince me. I made some comments and we tried again. Three, four times. The fifth still left me unsatisfied, but I did not have the courage to say so. For a couple of minutes I spoke of something else. Then I raised my eyes and saw the silhouettes of the people who were watching us at the windows standing out against the light from the interior. And all at once the situation seemed so absurd that I felt an acute sense of shame. In my career I have directed films in French and in English, and even [given instructions to] a Turkish seaman, and I never felt uncomfortable. But to direct in a language that never has, in any word, a sound or a tonality that resembles ours, is humiliating as well as absurd. I looked at my sound technician, who was bustling about with his Nagra [tape recorder]. I looked at my interpreter, who was smiling as always. I looked at the women and I said that it went well. They seemed very happy.

However, now I can say it: I was not happy. It seemed like the four women overdid it in trying to comply with my wishes, losing the naturalness in their movements. Like accomplished actors, they spoke with a certain drawl. Chinese, but a drawl.

Hunan is a province situated almost in the center of China. It is famous for an artificial irrigation system, built at an enormous cost in manual labor, which has allowed the entire area to become one of the most fertile of the country. When you get there by train, you can see a beautiful and soft countryside, interrupted every once in a while by the twinkling of the rice paddies. Not a square yard uncultivated.

The city where we stayed is called Linshien, a small, lively, industrious city, where, unlike in the northern cities where the houses are enclosed in courtyards, life unfolds in the open. A little like in the South [of Italy]. Personally, I find it very agreeable to eat seated on a rock, talking with the neighbors and with passers-by, surrounded by playful children, rather than locked up in a room. That is what happens in these cities that are far from the large centers, and also in the outskirts of the large cities—for example, in Shanghai, where these outskirts take up two-thirds of the city.

Linshien has a provincial and oldish air about it that puts one at ease. Few Westerners have reached these parts, and in the villages scattered in the surrounding countryside, Westerners have never been seen.

We went into one of these villages with the camera on our shoulders (the cameraman's shoulder, obviously), and we walked along a few streets, the main streets. It was not possible to go down the other small, narrow, suggestive streets, so professionally inviting. I do not know whether what we filmed will reveal the commotion that our presence caused. Dismayed people who hid in the entryways of houses, or ran away and came back with a group to watch us. Semi-hidden faces and eyes in the darkness of interiors. Generally, in China, the crowd applauds the Westerners who pass by. Here they were paralyzed; they did not even dare to approach us.

One curious detail: The president of the revolutionary committee of the city had given us permission to carry out the shooting, and was walking ahead of us. And as soon as he saw an old man, he approached him and told him to go away, to hide.

The "Passenger" that You Didn't See[17]

I have always thought that scripts are dead pages. I have also written it. They are pages that presuppose a film, and without the film they have no reason to exist. They don't even have literary value. The following sequence was not included in *The Passanger* for reasons of length. Therefore, there should be no reason to publish it. But I filmed it, and therefore it is a sequence that exists somewhere, inside a box at the bottom of some warehouse, and it exists in my memory and in the memory of whoever saw it screened—for example, of whoever edited it with me.

I confess that I liked this sequence, not just because it was splendidly acted by Jack Nicholson and the German actor, but also because, in supporting the theme of the film, it also gave quite an unreal dimension to the reporter's character. Carried out on the ambiguous thread of memory—you know that memory offers no guarantees—this sequence opened for Locke, the journalist, with daydream moments he enjoyed exploring. The name of an unknown woman, Helga, brings unexpectedly to his mind the memory of a red bicycle. Helga and the bicycle never encountered one another, but the fascination of the game issues exactly from that. For a man like Locke, who has already given up his own identity to

[17] "Il 'Reporter' che non avete visto," from *Corriere della Sera*, 26 October 1975. Translated by Allison Cooper.

assume another's, it cannot but be exciting to run after a third one. He doesn't even need to wonder how it will end.

I filmed the scene with sinuous and barely perceptible camera movements. To think of it now, it seems clear to me that I was unconsciously trying to carry out a movement similar to that of our imagination, when it attempts to give life to images that don't belong to us, but that, little by little, we make our own. We color them, we give them sounds—glimmers of color and sound—but lively, just like our memories. Or like dreams, which are inadequate and laconic as far as content is concerned, but very rich in sensations and thoughts.

Munich, in Bavaria. A square dominated by the apse of a church, and by the imposing side of another. A square that would resemble an interior if it weren't for an airy sound of bells that fades away as Locke moves away from the churches. One begins to notice a chorus of young voices coming from another building, hardly disturbed by the sound of a street sweeper's broom dragging on the pavement. Locke stops to listen for a moment, and then goes on walking again. With his hands in the pockets of his pants, and his shirt unbuttoned, he lets his heels lightly tap over the stone pavement without a precise rhythm. Perhaps he is even looking for a new way to walk.

He starts down a street. He stops in front of a storefront that was once a window. Just a few objects; old and exotic stuff, sophisticated. They stand out against the darkness of the store as though they are actually illuminated by an inner light. Inside there is a tall, fat man, about forty-five years old, with a big, childish, red face. The man stops in the middle of a gesture when he realizes that Locke is on the other side of the window. He seems to recognize him. He says, as if to himself, "Charlie." And then louder, to Locke: "Charlie!" Naturally, there is no reaction on Locke's part. The man calls again, and this time Locke bends down and looks to see where the voice is coming from, inside the store. And he sees the man set off towards the door next to the shop window, then go out into the street and come meet him with the happy expression of someone who is having a pleasant, albeit unexpected, encounter. Extending his hand, the man repeats, "Charlie!" Locke turns, thinking that the other man is speaking to someone behind him, but he doesn't see anyone. So, a bit hesitantly, he in turn holds out his hand, which the German shakes vigorously. "What a pleasure—what a pleasure! What are you doing here? It has been centuries since we have seen each other." He has a hardy voice, appropriate to his physique. Locke observes him, forcing himself to recognize him, but it is evident that the slightly coarse features of that face are totally unknown to him. And he limits himself to saying, "I am just passing through." "But what a pleasure," repeats the German, "you can't believe—after such a long time."

He gives Locke a slap on his left shoulder and continues to stare at him, visibly submersed in a wave of memories. "We should celebrate this meeting. Let's go drink something." "Let's go," Locke responds with good-natured resignation. "Just like old times," the other concludes. They set off. Their footsteps are brisk, youthful. Locke responds to the German's second slap by taking him under his arm. They cross a crowded street. On the sides are yellow and pink houses. The air is clean, calm. Locke is more agile, and reaches the opposite sidewalk at a run. The German, on the other hand, hesitates; he is afraid of the traffic. Locke waits for him and together they enter a pub.

It's a typically Bavarian place, heavily decorated with empty barrels, trophies, copper objects. Faces weighed down by beer. The glasses are filled up in some sort of cellar and then handed over to girls, who bring them upstairs. One of these girls comes over to greet them. The German turns to Locke and says in a vaguely complicitous tone, "Campari and soda?" Locke agrees, "Campari and soda." The girl leaves and the two sit down. The German continues to stare at Locke with a slightly obtuse and open grin. He seems truly happy to be there with an old friend. "So, how has everything gone for you?" he asks. Locke shrugs his shoulders. The German continues: "With all of those projects that you had going—to keep up with you was mind-boggling, you know?" He laughs.

He talks and laughs loudly. Locke, on the other hand, maintains a quiet countenance, almost creating a barrier between himself and the unknown friend. He no longer feels uneasy. Rather, his recent embarrassment begins to melt away. Nevertheless, he feels that this is an experience that he should have by himself, not in the company of that man—who, in the meantime, has begun to imitate his old friend Charlie by emphatically citing the witty remarks that have evidently remained in his mind. "'We will build a new world'—'The human spirit is ready to be freed'—I will always remember it." Locke avoids looking at him.

A few yards away from them, on the staircase that leads to the upper floor, the legs of those who are walking upstairs can be seen. The sound of the footsteps on the wooden stairs has a strangely military rhythm. Locke looks away and glances outside, beyond the windows, at the bustle on the street. It is a carefree street. It is morning. The German breaks the silence: "No children?" "No. I adopted one but it didn't work out." "You were always saying that you would never have children." Locke turns to look at him. "I don't remember having ever said anything like that," he observes quietly. "I do," insists the German. Meanwhile, he pulls a photograph out of his wallet. "Mine have grown up, you know?" He lays the photograph on the table in front of Locke. "This is Maria—and this is Heinrich. Heinrich is a big fan of pop music." Locke gives a cursory glance to the picture. The girl arrives with the Campari and sodas. Each takes a sip of his.

Putting down the glass, the German literally changes his expression. He becomes sly, allusive. He lets a couple of seconds go by before saying, "Do you remember Helga?" Locke smiles. Now he is beginning to have fun. "Helga? What a name." "She's married. Remember the policeman? Surely he would have arrested me if it hadn't been for you—and everything would have been out in the open, my trafficking, my little adventures. All of it. Now she is married. She is a housewife."

Locke lights a cigarette, to react to a light sadness that seizes him. After a minute he begins to speak, always in a low voice: "Yes. It's strange how you remember certain things and forget others. If, all of the sudden, we remembered everything that we have forgotten and forgot everything that we remember, we would be completely different people."

The German, without having understood well, has an approving air. He changes the subject. "Do you remember the song that we used to sing?" "No, I don't think so." The fact that Locke doesn't remember, while he himself does, seems to give the German a certain satisfaction, so much that he starts to sing, moving his hand to the song. "Living doll—a walking talking living doll—Remember?" "I remember a bicycle that I had," Locke replies. "Red." The German's face darkens. "A bicycle? No, I mean—when we were together." Locke becomes more and more ironic. "When we were together? What was it like?"

Now the German seems dismayed. He looks Locke right in the eyes, for a long time, with a consternation that makes it clear that the atrocious suspicion of a misunderstanding has flashed into his mind, although it was then thrown out. Locke, on the other hand, is impassive, and the German can find nothing better to do than explode into a roaring laugh, which slowly dies down in unison with the swaying of his head. Locke also laughs. "Helga," he murmurs, "how fun she must have been!" "Ah yes," echoes the German.

Again silence. The German finishes drinking and then drums the table with his fingertips. Now it is he who is embarrassed. After a while he gets up, saying: "I have to go. Work, you know." He looks for money in his pocket to pay for the drink, but Locke stops him. "No, no—I've got it." The German sighs, almost as if he wanted to show his regret at having to leave. "So—come back and visit me," he says. Locke nods yes. The German leaves. He crosses the room which, in the meantime, has almost emptied out. He reaches the door. He turns. Locke replies to his goodbye, waving his hand. "Goodbye," he says softly. But the German can't hear, he is already on the street, intent upon finding the right moment to cross the street.

Locke lowers his head and looks at what is left of the Campari and soda in the glasses.

ANTONIONI ON THE SEVEN-MINUTE SHOT[18]

The second-to-last take of the film, which lasts approximately seven minutes, called for the use of a special camera, a Canadian invention.

I also tried other ways of getting the same idea, but all were shown to be less practical and more artificial.

The problem was not so much getting out of the window, but panning the full semicircle of the piazza to end up before the window again.

This was made possible by the use of a camera mounted on a series of gyroscopes. Inside the room, the camera moved hanging from a track attached to the ceiling. The cameraman pushed it with his hands on the large curving handles seen in the photo.

Once the camera arrived at the wrought-iron grating, the worst problem arose. The grating was hinged, and swung open a second after the bars went off-camera at the sides of the shot. Obviously, I controlled everything—including commands for the zooms and pans—on a monitor that was in a van. From here I gave orders to my assistant with a microphone, and the assistant transmitted them to the actors, extras, cars, and everything else which made the "movement" in the piazza.

Behind the hotel there was a huge crane, more than a hundred feet high, from which hung a steel cable.

Once the camera was outside the window, it left the track and was simultaneously hooked onto the cable. Naturally, the shift from a fixed support, like the track, to a mobile one, such as the cable, caused the camera to bump and sway while a second cameraman, experienced in this

[18] "La penultima inquadratura di *Professione: Reporter*," from *Professione: Reporter*, edited by Carlo di Carlo, Bologna: Cappelli, 1975. Originally translated in *Film Comment* 11 (4), July-August 1975.

work, took over. This is where the gyroscopes came in: they completely neutralized the bumping and swaying.

The shooting of this take required eleven days. There were other difficulties, primarily the wind. The weather was windy and stormy, and a wind storm soon arrived, doing much damage. In order to be independent of the weather, this special camera normally operates in a closed sphere. But the sphere was too big, and would not pass through the window. Doing without the sphere meant exposing ourselves to the vagaries of the weather. But I had no choice. Furthermore, I had shoot between 3:30 and 5:00 p.m. because of the light, which at other hours would have been too strong. You must remember we came from inside to the outside, and the ratio of internal to external light governed the diaphragm opening for the whole shot. Another problem: the camera was a 16mm one. After much discussion, the cameraman was persuaded to try 35mm. They asked me to mount a 400-foot reel, but, as I thought, it was not long enough for the sequence. To use a thousand-foot reel required a new adjustment of the whole gyroscopic equilibrium of the camera.

The photos show the work we did to get the final result.

A big crowd followed our efforts each day. When, finally, on the eleventh day, we succeeded in obtaining two good takes, there was a long and moving outburst of applause, such as, on the field, greets a player who has made a goal.

The Mystery of Oberwald (1980)

ALMOST A CONFESSION[19]

After years of thinking about it, I finally shot a film on video. It is called *The Mystery of Oberwald*, and is the adaptation of a play by Jean Cocteau, *The Two-Headed Eagle*, which is vaguely based on the story of Ludwig the Second of Bavaria and that of the Empress Elizabeth of Austria. Cocteau combined the two together, inventing a third story which, without retaining the morbid fascination of the other two, has at least the ambition, as Cocteau himself stated, of combining the "human drama" with the "grand roles." In fact, the drama was written expressly for two actors: Edwige Feuillère and Jean Marais.

Why this choice? It isn't a choice, it is fate. You can also make some irony out of this by saying that the "mystery" is actually in the "why" I made this film. It is, in fact, the first time that I have taken on a tragic drama, and the impact has been anything but smooth. Let's say that I have done some of my best work to soften the blow.

First of all, I set the story free from all historical ties by moving it to another time period. The costumes are evidence of this. We are in the year 1903, in an unidentified kingdom. In the second place, I brought some modifications to the dialogue. With Tonino Guerra's help, I shortened it and rid it of the emphasis with which Cocteau had padded it.

[19] "Quasi una confessione," from *Il mistero di Oberwald*, edited by Gianni Massironi., Turin: E.R.I., 1980. Translated by Allison Cooper.

In short, I faced the subject from a position of respectful distance, at the same time trying to avoid disappearing as director. I hope that, here and there, I made my presence known. I don't want to defend Cocteau— I consider him a talented writer, gifted, yet limited and far removed from modern literary taste. And yet, a certain air of up-to-dateness runs through his play. It's understandable that I tried to define it more precisely, above all by adopting a terminology that vaguely evoked the sad stories of our time. Words like "anarchist," "opposition," "power," "chief of police," "comrade," and "group" belong to our everyday vocabulary. It is true that the conclusion of the story is much more romantic than what one might have imagined, but this has to do with the stylization and formulation of the melodramatic genre to which Cocteau wanted to remain loyal.

Therefore, my distance was completely justified. But this justification carries along with it—now, while I am writing—a confession. What a sense of lightness I felt in facing those events, so devoid of the complexity of the real, to which we are accustomed! What a relief to escape from the difficulty of a moral and aesthetic obligation, from the haunting desire to express yourself. It was like rediscovering a forgotten childhood.

But there's more. That position actually allowed me to dedicate greater attention to the problems pertaining to the technical medium. The electronic system is very stimulating. At first, it seems like a game. They put you in front of a console full of knobs, and, by moving them, you can add or take away color, meddle with its quality and with the relationships between various tonalities. It is also possible to obtain effects forbidden to normal cinema. In short, you realize quickly that it isn't a game, but rather a new world for cinema. Not for television, for cinema. A new way of finally using color as a narrative, poetic means.

The problem of color in cinema doesn't exist in and of itself. Cinema exists, as always, and color is part of it. Too often it happens that, not being accustomed to looking at color as an integral part of film, we think of it as of something additional, or even marginal. Producers are used to reading scripts in black and white. The screenwriters themselves, most of the time, write them without even taking colors into consideration. A script can therefore be made into film, according to a common opinion, in black and white or in color, indifferently.

With video this is no longer even an issue. Television is in color. In front of a small black-and-white screen, the television viewer knows, or unconsciously feels that he is defective. With video cameras, you start with the premise that they reproduce colors with absolute faithfulness, or, if so desired, with absolute falseness. And you must think about this in order to put together images in connection with the story you want to tell.

As far as I am concerned, I think I have just begun to scratch the surface of the very rich range of possibilities that electronics offers. Others will be able to do even more. One thing that I can say is that the magnetic tape is perfectly equipped to take the place of traditional film. In a decade, the game will be over, with great economic and artistic advantages for everyone. In no other field do poetry and technology walk hand in hand the way that they do in the field of electronics.

INTERVIEWS ON CINEMA

A CONVERSATION WITH
MICHELANGELO ANTONIONI[1]

You are the author of all the stories of your films. Is that because you haven't found any other way of illustrating what you have in mind; or is it that, for you, to create a film story and to direct it become one and the same thing?
   For the principle of the cinema, as for that of all the arts, there is one choice. As Camus says, it is the revolt of the artist against actuality. If you stick to that principle, how important are the means by which reality is disclosed? Whether the author of a cinema finds it in a novel, in a news item or in his own fantasy, what counts is his way of isolating it, of stylizing it, of making it his own. If he achieves that, the source has no importance. The plot of *Crime and Punishment* without the form which Dostoevskij gave it is a mediocre plot. It could become either a very beautiful—or very ugly—film. That is why I have almost always written my own films. Once I was struck by one of Pavese's novels. As I worked on it, I knew that I loved it for reasons entirely different from those which had originally made me think of it as a film. And the pages which had interested me the most were those which lent themselves least to a

[1] From *Cahiers du Cinéma* 112 (October 1960). This interview took place under particular conditions. An initial conversation had been taped during the 1960 Cannes Film Festival, the day before the *L'avventura* "affair." Thus, the circumstances were far from normal, and it was impossible to publish the remarks of that evening. It was necessary to revise them, or at least, take a closer look at them. But Antonioni left Cannes the next day. The interview published here was done through correspondence.
   Originally translated in *New York Film Bulletin* 2nd series, 8 (34), 1960.

cinematic translation. On the other hand, it is very difficult to find one-self an original story line, since the original material is already selected in terms of a very definite narrative style. Finally, I find it much simpler to invent the story completely. A director is a man, therefore he has ideas; he is also an artist, therefore he has imagination. Whether they are good or bad, there are so many stories to tell, it seems to me. And that which I see, that which happens to me is constantly changing these stories.

The subjects of your films resemble one another curiously; they always revolve about the same problem: the couple, the woman, solitude. Why?

The characteristic choices of a director answer to the same logic which determines his limits: if you accept the latter, it is much easier to evaluate the first. It is possible that the public (at least the part of the public which is interested in my work) is tired of seeing me constantly returning to the same subject. But, if it is true that, up to now, I have only produced vari-ations on the same theme, it is also true that I have tried to develop this theme, to enrich it, to renew it in the light of my own experience. I have been making films for ten years. I began with *Story of a Love Affair*, here in Milan, where I am now making *La notte*. The places, the atmosphere, are the same. The characters belong, more or less, to the same social class. However, this film seems so different to me—if I didn't know that it is much more autobiographical than *Story of a Love Affair*, I would say that *La notte* is the film of another director. Probably, just like the surround-ings, I have also changed countenance.

Take *The Cry*, for example. In that film, while you will find my favorite theme, I pose the problem of the emotions in a different aspect. If, before this, my characters usually accepted their failures and emotional crises, this time we meet a man who reacts, who tries to overcome his unhappi-ness. I have treated this character with much more mercy.

The landscape also has a different function. If in my other films I used it to add better definition to a situation or a spiritual state, in *The Cry* I wanted it to be the landscape of memory: the countryside of my child-hood, seen through the eyes of someone returning home after an intense cultural and emotional experience. In *The Cry*, this return takes place in the most appropriate season: winter—when the wide, open horizon becomes a counterpoint to the psychology of the film's central character. *L'avventura*: this is the story of a cruise on a yacht. The disappearance of a girl during the period of several days is meant to symbolize the fragility of emotions in a real situation. In a certain sense, it is the answer to *Il grido* provided by the characters who peopled my preceding films. To make a play on words, you might say that *L'avventura* is *The Cry* of *The Girlfriends*. At any rate, it is not a question of truth seen from different perspectives, but of two different ways of seeing the same truth. The result is the same: solitude. With *La notte* I will arrive at one result of compromise; the compromise that is found today in morality and even in politics. The characters this time find themselves, but they have trouble in communicating because they have discovered that the truth is difficult, that it demands great courage and decision—impossible to achieve in their way of life.

What does your work bring you? What would you do if you could no longer make films?

If you have an enemy, don't try to beat him up, or curse him, or humiliate him, or hope he will have a traffic accident. Simply hope that he will be left without work. It is the most horrible fate that can strike a man. Every vacation, even the most marvelous, makes no sense except as a way to counteract fatigue. I consider myself privileged in this: I do work that pleases me. I don't know many Italians who can say as much. This work is the most important thing in my life. It is superfluous to ask me what it gives me. It gives me everything. It gives me the chance to express myself, to communicate with others. Being inept at speaking, I would have the sensation of not existing at all—without the cinema.

The other things I would have been able to do are, in order: architecture and painting. As a kid I didn't design puppets as most children of my age did; I designed doorways, capitals, plans of absurd battlements; I constructed city districts in cardboard and painted them in violent colors. I have always loved colors. The few times that I dream, it is in color. The thing that strikes me first about a face is its coloring. I don't say this to make myself singular: it's simply a characteristic like any other. I am naturally very impatient to make a film in color.

What does the word "directing" mean to you?

Authoritative critics have written essays and books on that subject. I am not a theoretician of the cinema. If you ask me what directing is, the first answer which comes to mind is: I don't know. The second is this: My opinions on that are all in my films. And then, among other things, I am against the separation of various phases of the work. This separation has only a practical value. It is valuable for all who participate in the work: all but the director, especially if he is also the author of the film story and directing the picture. To speak of direction as one phase of the work is to carry on a theoretical discussion which seems to me antithetical to the concept of unity of creation to which each artist dedicates himself during his work. Doesn't one edit and do the montage during the shooting these days? And during the shooting, isn't everything automatically in question: from the story to the lines of dialogue which reveal their true meaning only when heard in the voices of the actors?

To be sure, there is always a moment when—from ideas, images, intuitions about movements, whether psychological or physical—you must arrive at a concrete realization. For the cinema, as in all the other arts, it is the most delicate moment; when the poet or the writer puts his first words on paper, the artist his brush to canvas, or the director arranges his characters in their setting, makes them speak and move, establishes by composition and framing a reciprocal harmony between people and things, between the rhythm of the dialogue and that of the entire sequence, makes the movement of the camera follow the psychological situation, etc. But the decisive moment above all is when he receives from all these and all that surrounds him all possible suggestions in such a way that his work acquires a more improvised direction, becomes more personal and even, in the broadest sense, more autobiographical.

What importance do you give to Italian neorealism? Do you consider yourself attached to it, for example, by the sketch in Love in the City, *and in what way?*

To answer a question of this kind, I would have to write an entire essay on Italian neo-realism. At present I am engaged in making a film. I find myself in a creative period and not a critical one. All I can say is that Italian neorealism has produced some very beautiful films; in that way it has been important. For me the sketch in *Love in the City* belonged completely to the neorealistic current. But how can one judge from the fragment of a film which the exigencies of length forced me to mutilate so much. I should have and I wanted to—related so many stories, I even shot certain others. There was one in particular that I had to cut out because of the unbearable ugliness of the principal character: a servant. Nevertheless it was a strong, dramatic story. And it is precisely then during the shooting of *Love in the City* that I learned how much can be discovered while making a film. These people who tried to commit suicide were great characters. They were that during the making of the film itself by virtue of the understanding they established among themselves and because of what they told me. They were terribly proud of their deed, but at the same time so happy (almost against their will) that they were still alive, that they were truly touching. I should have put all that on film there, right away: Perhaps that would have been the true neo-realistic film that Zavattini talks of so much.

What is the most important moment for you in the creation of a film?
I've already answered that in discussing directing. All the moments in the creation of a film are of equal importance. It's not true that any sharp distinction between them can exist. They are all in synthesis. Thus, during the elaboration of the story, it can happen that you decide on a tracking shot, or while planning scenes you may change a character or situation, and even during recording change one or more cues. From the moment when the first idea of the film came to mind—still formless—up to the projection of the rushes, for me the making of a film represents a single, unified work. I mean that I cannot interest myself in anything but that film, day and night. That shouldn't be considered a romantic attitude—on the contrary, I become, rather, more lucid, more attentive; I almost have the feeling of becoming more intelligent and

ready to understand. But, if you want a single answer to your question: the moment of shooting, beyond any doubt. Since it is then that all thoughts, all other moments an author experiences, come together.

In each of your films, framing plays an important role. Do you think of the composition of an image, or are you more concerned about following your characters? Or both?

Both, naturally. I always try to manage so that each element of the image serves the narrative, serves to specify a particular psychological moment. An image is only essential if each square centimeter of that image is essential.

What do you call "improvising," then, when at the moment of shooting you have written a detailed script?

You cannot help but recognize that direction today is less detailed than formerly, less detailed even than several years ago. Technical indications have virtually disappeared, also the "column on the right"—the dialogue. In my directing I have almost eliminated the numbers that used to indicate shots. Only the script girl uses them to facilitate her job. This, because it seems to me more logical to decide the angles and aspects even at the moment of shooting the scenes. That is already one way of improvising. But there are more. I seldom care to reread a sequence on the eve of shooting it. Now and then I arrive at the location where we are working and I don't even know what we must shoot. This is the system I prefer, arriving at the moment of shooting, absolutely without preparation, virginal. I often ask that they leave me alone for fifteen minutes or a half hour, on the location, and I let my thoughts wander freely. I confine myself to looking around me. I use the things around me too: they always suggest ideas to me. I have great sympathy for objects, perhaps more than for people, but the latter interest me more. In every way I find it useful to gaze at the surroundings and sense the atmosphere for a while, in anticipation of the characters. It can happen that the images I have before me at that moment coincide with those I have in my imagination, but that doesn't happen often. More often, the image in mind has something insincere, artificial.

This, then, is a way of improvising. But that's still not all. It may also happen that in rehearsing a scene I change my mind abruptly. Or I change it progressively as the electricians set up their lights and I see the actors move and talk under them. I believe it is only then that you really evaluate a scene and correct it. Speaking of improvisation also, I refer you to another thing which I have already spoken of in my answer to your fourth question.

When you are preparing and making a film, do you think of the public and does this thought influence you?

I believe I've answered that above. I repeat it: I certainly think about the public in the sense that I need someone to show what I have done, with whom I can communicate. However, I don't consider that the public influences me. If I made films for the public, shouldn't I make them for money or for glory? One makes films by thinking only about films and above all *not* about that sort of thing. I try to make films that have the greatest possibility of pleasing myself, and I am certain that, the more beautiful they are, the more they please me

Chiefly in your last films, the sound seems to have been the object of particular care. Have you any ideas about the relationship between sound and image which are uniquely yours?

I give enormous importance to the soundtrack and I always try to give it the greatest attention. And when I say "soundtrack," I allude to natural sounds, to noises, rather than to music. Music rarely reinforces the image, more often it serves merely to put the spectator to sleep and to keep him from appreciating clearly what he is seeing. All things considered, I am rather opposed to "musical commentary," at least in its original form. I feel something old-fashioned, rancid in it. The ideal would be to compose with noises an impressive soundtrack and to appoint an orchestra conductor to direct it. But then the only orchestra conductor capable of doing it—wouldn't he be the director of the film?

Which is in your career the film that seems to you, today, to be most important and why?

I have always thought that a certain amount of frivolity was necessary to answer such questions. These are questions which only aim to satisfy the curiosity of readers. It is obvious to say that all my films have as much importance in my career as in my life. Finally, I don't seem to understand how I should answer: from a critical viewpoint, certainly not, that is not my business. I would not be objective, and I would try in vain to identify the reasons for a preference among my films. From the human viewpoint, let us say, then. In this case, I would say the most important of my films in *L'avventura*, because it is the one which cost me the most, which taught me the most, which more than any other film forced me to be present to myself. In respect to that I ought to explain how it often happens that 1 am absent from myself, but we get into the realm of gossip there—and I don't enjoy that.

What are the ties in your work with that of Pavese?

Here is another embarrassing question. Perhaps (excuse me for saying this to you) it is badly worded. I could always reply that it is not for me to say, or even that no particular empathy exists beyond that of a reader for an author. I believe I have read Pavese pretty thoroughly, but there are writers I love and esteem more than I do him. What I love in *Among Women Only*, the story (by Pavese) from which I drew my film *The Girlfriends*, are the feminine characters and what goes on in their inner selves. Besides, one of these characters resembles extraordinarily another character whom I knew only too well in reality, and I wanted to speak of it, to demonstrate it. It will be said that this answer eludes the question: if it is accepted literally, the sense of it will escape you. But, frankly, I have little to add. Critics have mentioned a certain analogy between Pavese and me, recognizing in both of us our pessimism a very small common denominator. Personally, it seems to me the intellectual experiences of Pavese coincide tragically with his personal experiences. Can as much be said for me? Am I not here engaged in making a film, I would even say obstinately? And, everything added up, this obstinacy, isn't it a proof of optimism?

ANDRÉ LABARTHE

An Interview with
Michelangelo Antonioni[2]

In general, where does the original idea for your films come from?
It seems to me that no one engaged in creative activity can answer that question in good faith. Lucidity is not one of my outstanding qualities. I look at everything, avidly, and I also think I listen a great deal.

One thing is certain: ideas come to me unexpectedly. But I'm not really interested in getting to the bottom of such a question.

What does the writing of the scenario mean for you: clarifying the dramatic line, making the visual aspect of the film more specific, familiarizing yourself with the characters?
To me, the visual aspect of a film is very closely related to its thematic aspect—in the sense that an idea almost always comes to me through images. The problem lies elsewhere. It has to do with restricting the accumulation of these images, with digging into them, with recognizing the ones that coincide with what interests me at the time.

It's work done instinctively, almost automatically, but it involves a great deal of tension. One's whole being is at stake: it is a precise moral choice.

What people ordinarily call the "dramatic line" doesn't interest me. One device is no better than another, *a priori.* And I don't believe that the

2 From *Cinéma 65* 100, November 1965. Originally translated in *L'avventura. A Film by Michelangelo Antonioni*, New York: Grossman Publishers, 1969.

old laws of drama have validity any more. Today stories are what they are, with neither a beginning nor an end necessarily, without key scenes, without a dramatic arc, without catharsis. They can be made up of tatters, of fragments, as unbalanced as the lives we lead.

Familiarize myself with characters? But the characters are not strangers that I may or may not be on intimate terms with; they emerge out of me, they are my intimate inner life.

What does the fact that you work in collaboration with others on your scenario mean to you?

Every time I have tried to let others write parts of a rough script, the result, even if it was excellent from an objective point of view, was something foreign to me, something close to what I wanted without ever coinciding with it exactly. And that gave me a terrible sense of impotence. Then began the great task of selecting, correcting, even adapting—work that was as difficult as it was useless, because it inevitably led to compromise. I can never manage to be objective when I judge the work of my collaborators. The film stands between me and them. So, after trying this a few times, I ended up writing almost all the shooting scripts of my films myself.

However, I haven't ruled out collaborations altogether. I don't choose my collaborators on the basis of our affinities, but for the opposite reason. I need to have people who are very different from me around me, people with whom there can be animated, lively discussions. We talk, we discuss things for months before the film. We talk about a lot of things. Sometimes we also talk about the film, but not necessarily. What I say ricochets off them, comes back to me in the form of criticism, commentary, suggestions. After a certain time, the film becomes clear. It is only then that I begin to write the rough script. I work many hours a day, often beginning at dawn, until I'm completely exhausted.

What form does your script take in its final phase?

The shooting script is never definitive for me. It's notes about the direction, nothing more. There are no technical notations such as used to be made. The placing of the camera, the use of various lenses, the movements of the camera, all concern the phase in which the film is shot, not that in which the script is written.

I would say the same thing about dialogue. I have to hear the dialogue in the living voices of the actors, that is to say of the characters, within the scene, to decide whether or not it's right.

And then there's another factor. I believe in improvisation. None of us has the habit of preparing for a meeting to further business, love, or friendship; one takes these meetings as they come, adapting oneself little by little as they progress, taking advantage of unexpected things that come up. I experience the same things when I'm filming.

Can the choice of locations or actors influence the scenario, and if so, how?

In general, I decide upon the outdoor locations before writing the shooting script. In order to be able to write, I need to have the surroundings of the film clearly in mind. There are times too when an idea for a film comes to me from a particular place. Or more precisely, when certain locales come to mind because of the themes or characters running through my head. It's sometimes a rather odd series of coincidences.

What possibilities for improvisation do you allow for while you're filming?

Speaking of improvisation, I must add something to what I said before. If I think of the past, it's possible for me to say that I have always lived minute by minute. It's the way I live even today. Every moment of the day is important to me, every day is a new experience. And this doesn't change when I'm shooting. On the contrary, the pull of reality increases during shooting, because you're in an extremely receptive state, and because you're making new contacts, you're establishing often unexpected relationships with the crew, and these relationships are constantly changing. All that has a definite influence on my work, and leads me to improvised decisions, and even to radical changes. This is what I mean by improvisation.

How are your relations with the crew?

Excellent. I try to create a cordial atmosphere. I like to have people laughing and joking around me. People who seem to have no problems. It's quite enough that I have problems.

I admit, however, that I am very demanding. I don't allow anybody around me to show that he doesn't know his business. Or that he's unwilling to work. There is a certain laziness about crews, it's natural, inevitable. But it's what I dislike most. When I happen to scream at someone (as all directors do, it seems), I'm railing against this sort of indifference.

What are your relations with the actors?
I've always had excellent relations with actors—sometimes too good. Hearing me say that may seem odd, but it's true. Even with Jeanne Moreau, who claims the opposite, I have never—I repeat never—had arguments during filming.

I know, however, that actors feel somewhat uncomfortable with me; they have the feeling that they've been excluded from my work. And as a matter of fact they have been. But it is precisely: this form of collaboration, and no other, that I ask of them.

Only one person has the film clearly in mind, insofar as that is possible: the director. Only one person fuses in his mind the various elements involved in a film, only one person is in a position to predict the result of this fusion: the director. The actor is one of these elements, and sometimes not even the most important. There is one thing the actor can't do, and that is to see himself in the view-finder; if he could, he'd come up with a number of suggestions regarding his acting. This privilege is reserved to the director, however, who will thus limit himself to manipulating "the actor element" according to criteria and exigencies known to him alone.

There are various ways of getting certain expressions from actors, and it is of no interest to know whether or not there is a corresponding mood behind these expressions.

I have often resorted to foreign actors for practical reasons: agreements with distributors, unavailability of Italian actors, and so forth. But sometimes it was because I thought actors were better suited to the roles than those at my disposal here.

Do you prefer to record the sound on the set or to dub it afterwards?

When I can, I prefer recording on the set. The sounds, the noises, and the natural voices as picked up by microphones have a power of suggestion that can't be obtained with dubbing. Moreover, most professional microphones are much more sensitive than the human ear, and a great many unexpected noises and sounds often enrich a soundtrack that's been made on the set.

Unfortunately, we are still not advanced enough technically to be able to use this system all the time. Shooting indoors it's hard to get good sound. And dubbing also has its advantages. Sometimes I find that the transformation of a noise or of a sound becomes indispensable for certain special effects. Thus in certain cases it is necessary to change the human voice.

Who decides on the exact framing and the camera movements?

I can't imagine a director who would leave that up to other people. Excluding or including a detail, even an apparently secondary one, in the film image, choosing the angle of the shot, the lenses, the camera movements, are all decisions essential to the success of a film.

Technique is not something that can be applied from outside by just anybody. Practically speaking, technical problems don't exist. If style is there, it permeates technique. If style is missing, the problem disappears.

Do you shoot any sequences from several angles so as to have greater freedom when you edit?

Until *Red Desert*, I always filmed with a single camera, and thus from a single angle. But from *Red Desert* on, I began using several cameras with different lenses, but always from the same angle. I did so because the story demanded shots of a reality that had become abstract, of a subject that had become color, and those shots had to be obtained with a long-focus lens.

Obviously I have the editing of the film clearly in mind during shooting. And it is only when I am led by circumstances to improvise, and consequently to shoot quickly, that I try to accumulate protection takes.

How much do you have to do with the cutting of your films?

I have always had an editor at my side on all my films. Except for *Story of a Love Affair,* this editor has been Eraldo da Roma. He is an extremely able technician with vast experience, and a man who loves his work. We cut the films together. I tell him what I want as clearly and precisely as possible, and he does the cutting. He knows me, he understands immediately, we have the same sense of proportion, the same sensibility concerning the duration of a shot.

What is the role of music and the soundtrack in your hams?

I have always opposed the traditional musical commentary, the soporific function ordinarily assigned to it. It's this idea of "setting images to music," as if it were a question of an opera libretto, that I don't like. What I reject is this refusal to let silence have its place, this need to fill supposed voids.

The only way to accept music in films is for it to disappear as an autonomous expression in order to assume its role as one element in a general sensorial impression. And with color films today this is even more necessary.

Do you concern yourself with the public and its possible reactions at any stage of making your films?

I never think of the public. I think of the film. Obviously, you're always speaking to someone, but this partner in the conversation is always an ideal one (perhaps another self). If this weren't true, I wouldn't know what to base my work on, since there are at least as many publics as there are continents or human races—not to mention nations.

What phase of making a film presents the most difficulty, requires the most effort?

Each film has its own history. One will demand inhuman efforts during shooting, another intellectual tension at the scripting stage, another an iron will during the cutting or the dubbing, when you'd swear that the material you have on hand is completely different from what you wanted.

And then we each have our private lives which are not broken off during filming; on the contrary, they acquire new point and bite, giving our work a function that is sometimes stimulating, sometimes debilitating, sometimes calming, and so forth.

Do you feel that the language of film has evolved, and to what extent do you think you have contributed to this evolution?

My contribution to the formation of a new cinematic language is a matter that concerns critics. And not even today's critics, but rather those of tomorrow, if film endures as an art and if my films resist the ravages of time.

PIERRE BILLARD

Apropos of Eroticism[3]

Yor last film, Blow-Up, *was shot in London. Were you trying to avoid censorship troubles in Italy because of its erotic scenes?*

The eroticism has nothing to do with *Blow-Up*. There are some scennes where you see nudes, but these are not what's important in the film. Italian censors have passed it with very little cutting.

Was it intentional, in the scene where the photographer has an orgy with the two girls in his studio, that pubic hair apppear visible?

I didn't notice. If you can tell me where, I'll go and look.

Do you feel that moviemakers should be free to depict total nudity on the screen?

I don't think it's necessary. The most important scenes between a man and a woman don't happen when they are naked.

Is there anything you think shouldn't be shown on the screen?

There can be no censorship better than one's own conscience.

What made you choose London as the setting for Blow-Up?

I happened to be there by chance, to see Monica Vitti while she was working in [Losey's] *Modesty Blaise.* I liked the happy, irreverent atmosphere of the city. People seemed less bound by prejudice.

---

[3] From *Playboy,* November 1967.

In what sense?

They seemed much freer. I felt at home. In some way, I was impressed. Perhaps something changed inside me.

How?

I'm no go good at understanding myself. But those things I knew before that interested me now seem too limited. I feel I need other experiences, to see other people, learn new things.

Was it difficult working in a foreign country?

Blow-Up had a rather special story, about a photographer, and I followed the work of some of the more important ones, which made it easier. Also, he moved through a limited environment in London—a minority but elite group of swingers.

Apart from its setting, how does Blow-Up *differ from your previous films?*

Radically. In my other films, I have tried to probe the relationship between one person and another—most often, their love relationship, the fragility of their feelings, and so on. But in this film, none of these themes matters. Here, the relationship is between an individual an reality—those things that are around him. There are no love stories in this film, even though we see relations between men and women. The experience of the protagonist is not a sentimental nor an amorous one but, rather, one regarding his relationship with the world, with the things he finds in front of him. He is a photographer. One day, he photographs two people in a park, an element of reality that appears real. And it is. But reality has a quality of freedom about it that is hard to explain. This film, perhaps, is like Zen; the moment you explain it, you betray it. I mean, a film you can explain in words, is not a real film.

Would you call Blow-Up, *like so many of your others, a pessimist film?*

Not at all, because at the end the photographer has understood a lot of things, including how to play with an imaginary ball—which is quite an achievement.

Then you feel that the photographer's decision to join the game and forget about the murder is a positive solution. Do you think this speaks well of the way youth deals with its problems?

Certainly. There's much talk about the problems of youth, but young people are not a problem. It's a natural evolution of things. We, who have known only how to make war and slaughter people, have no right to judge them, nor can we teach them anything.

Some people over thirty seem to feel that today's youth is a lost generation, withdrawn not only from commitment but, in the case of the hippies, from reality. Do you disagree?

I don't think they're lost at all. I'm not a sociologist nor a psychologist, but it seems to me they are seeking a new way to be happy. They *are* committed, but in a different way—and the *right* way, I think. The American hippies, for example, are against the war in Vietnam and against Johnson—but they combat the warmongers with love and peace. They demonstrate against police by embracing them and throwing flowers. How can you club a girl who comes to to give you a kiss? That, too, is a form of protest. In California's "loving parties," there is an atmosphere of absolute calm, tranquillity. That, too, is a form of protest, a way of being committed. It shows that violence is not the only means of persuasion. It's a complicated subject—more so than it seems—and I can't handle it, because I don't know the hippies well enough.

Sometimes that tranquillity you spoke of is induced by hallucinogenic drugs. Does the use of such drugs alarm you?

No; some people have negative reactions or can't stand hallucinations, but others stand them extremely well. One of the problems of the future world will be the use of leisure time. How will it be filled up? Maybe drugs will be distributed free of charge by the government.

You've always emphasized both the importance and the difficulty of communication between people in your films. But doesn't the psychedelic experience tend to make people withdraw into an inner directed mysticism, even drop out of society altogether? And doesn't this tend to destroy communication?

There are many ways of communicating. Some hold the theory that *new* forms of communication between people can be obtained through hallucinogenic drugs.

Would you want to try some yourself?
You can't go to an LSD or pot party unless you take it yourself. If I want to go, I must take drugs myself.

Have you?
That's *my* business. But to show you the new mentality: I visited St. Mark's in Venice with a young woman who smokes pot, as do most young people in her environment. When we were above the gilded mosaics— St. Mark's is small and intimate—she exclaimed: "How I'd like to smoke here!" You see how new that reaction is? We don't even suspect it. There was nothing profane in her desire to smoke; she merely wanted to make her aesthetic emotions more intense. She wanted to make her pleasure giant-size before the beauty of St. Mark's.

Does this mean you believe that the old means of communicating have become masks, as you seem to suggest in your films, that obscure communication?
I think they become masks, yes.

Is alienation, then—from one's self and from others—the subject of your films?
I never think in terms of alienation; it's the others who do. Alienation means one thing to Hegel, another to marx and yet another to Freud; so it is not possible to give a single definition, one that will exhaust the subject. It is a question bordering on philosophy, and I'm not a philosopher nor a sociologist. My business is to tell stories, to narrate with images—nothing else. If I do make films about alienation—to use that word that is so ambiguous—they are about characters, not about me.

But your characters do have difficulty communicating. The industrial landscape in Red Desert, *for example, seems to leave little room for human emotion. It seems to dehumanize the characters.*

Nothing regarding man is ever inhuman. That's why I make films, not iceboxes. I shot some of *Red Desert* along a road where half the horizon was filled with the pine trees that still surrounds Ravenna—though they are vanishing fast—while the other half of the skyline was taken up with a long line of factories, chimneys, tanks, grain silos, buildings, machinery. I felt that the skyline filled with things made by man, with those colors, was more beautiful and richer and more exciting for me than the long, green, uniform line of pinewoods, behind which I still sensed empty nature.

Most of the men in your films seem to cope very easily with this new techno-logical reality, as far as their work relationships are concerned. But in their love relationships, they tend to be incapable of achieving or sustaining an emotional involvement. Compared with your female characters, they seem weak, lacking in initiative.
What do you mean—that there exists an ideal relationship between man and woman? Do you really think that a man must be strong, mas-culine, dominating, and the woman frail, obedient, and sensitive? This is a conventional idea. Reality is quite different.

Is that what you meant when you said once that women are the first to adapt themselves to an epoch, that they are closer to nature and thus stronger?
I said women are a finer filter of reality. They can sniff things.

You also said that you understand them better than men. Why?
It's only natural. I've had intimate relations with women but not with men.

Are the Italian women you've known different from those of other nationalities?
Yes, of course.

How?
This is becoming frivolous. It leads to such platitudes as that French women are calculating; Italian women, instinctive; English women, hot.

The women I like, no matter what nationality, all seem to have the same more or less the same qualities. Perhaps this is because one goes looking for them—that is, you like the type of woman and then look for her. I've always dreamed of getting to know the women of other countries better. When I was a boy, I remember, I used to get angry at the thought that I did not know German or American or Swedish women. I hope the women in my films have at least a minimal common denominator with the women of other countries, because, after all, the problems are more or less the same.

Your heroines tend to be mature in years. Do you find older women more attractive than young girls?
It depends upon the age of the woman you're in love with.

What do you find most attractive sexually in a woman?
A woman's sex appeal is an inner matter. It stems from her mental make-up, basically. It's an attitude, not just a question of her physical features—that arrogant quality in a woman's femininity. Otherwise, all beautiful women would have sex appeal, which is not so.

Do you think there can be love without eroticism between a man and a woman?
I believe it's all the same thing. I can't imagine love without a sexual charge.

In your films, though, you imply that love is more complex, that even when two people are attracted to each other, they have to struggle to keep their love alive. Why?
That love is a conflict seems to me obvious and natural. There isn't a single worthwhile work in world literature based on love that is *only* about the conquest of happiness, the effort to arrive at what we call love. It's the *struggle* that has always interested those who produce works of art—literature, cinema, or poetry. But I can't give any absolute definition of what love is, or even whether it ought to exist.

Love seems to bring little happiness to your characters. Has this been true of your own life?

I read somewhere that happiness is like the bluebird of [Maurice] Maeterlinck: Try to catch it and it loses its color. It's like trying to hold water in your hands. The more you squeeze it, the more the water runs away. Personally, I know very little about love.

How do you feel about marriage?

I'm more or less skeptical about marriage, because of family ties, relations between children and parents—it's all s depressing. The family today counts for less and less. Why? Who knows—the growth of science, the Cold War, the atomic bomb, the world war we've made, the new philosophies we've created: certainly something is happening to man, so why go against it, whi oblige this new man to live by the mechanisms and regulations of the past?

What about religion? Do you agree with those who say that God is dead?

I remember a character, in a Hemingway story, who was asked: "Do you believe in God?" And he answered: "Sometimes, at night." When I see nature, when I look into the sky, the dawn, the sun, the colors of insects, snow crystals, the night stars, I don't feel a need for God. Perhaps when I can no longer look and wonder, when I believe in nothing—then, perhaps, I might need something else. But I don't know what. All I know is that we are loaded down with old and stale stuff—habits, customs, old attitudes that are already dead and gone. The strenght of the young Englishmen in *Blow-Up* lies in their ability to throw out all such rubbish.

What besides marriage and religion would you throw out?

The sense of nation, "good breeding," certain forms and ceremonies that govern relationships—perhaps even jealousy. We're not aware of all of them yet, though we suffer from them. And they mislead us not only about ethics, but also about aesthetics. The public buy "art"—but the word is drained of its meaning.. Today, we no longer know what to call "art," what its function is and even less what function it will have in the future. We know only that it sometyhing dynamic—unlike many ideas that have governed us.

What sort of ideas?

Take Einstein; wasn't he looking for something stable and changeless in that enormous, constantly changing melting pot that is the universe? He sought fixed rules. Today, instead, it would be helpful to find all those rules that show how and why the universe is *not* fixed—how this dynamism develops and acts. Then maybe we will be able to explain many things, perhaps even art, because the old instruments of judgment, the old aesthetics are no longer of any use to us—so much so that we no longer know what's beautiful and what isn't.

Many critics have called you one of the foremost directors in the search for a new aesthetic, in changing the "grammar" of the cinema. Do you feel you've brought any innovations to the screen?

Innovation comes spontaneously. I don't know if I've done anything new. If I have, it's just because I had begun to feel for some time that I couldn't stand certain films, certain modes, certain ways of telling a story, certain tricks of plot development, all of it predictable and useless.

Was it the old techniques that bothered you—or simply the old story lines?

Both, I think. The basic divergence was in the substance, in what was being filmed—and this has been determined by the insecurity of our lives. A particular type of film emerged from World War II, with the Italian neorealist school. It was perfectly right for its time, which was as exceptional as the reality around us. Our major interest focused on that and on how we would relate to it. Later, when the situation normalized and post-war life returned to what it had been in peacetime, it became important to see the intimate, interior consequences of all that had happened.

Doesn't your own interest in the interior of external events, in man's reaction to reality, date back to before tha war? Your first film venture, a documentary, was shot in a mental hospital in Ferrara. Whay did you choose that subject?

As I suffer from nervous tics, I had gone for consultation to a neurologist who was in charge of this mental home. Sometimes I had to wait, and found myself in contact with the insane, and I liked the atmosphere. I found it full of poetic potential. But the film was a disaster.

Why?

I wanted to do it with real schizophrenics, and the director of this hospital agreed. he was a bit mad himself—a very tall man who demonstrated reactions of mad people to pain by rolling about on the floor with the rest of them. But he provided me with some schizophrenics and I chatted with them, explaining how they were supposed to move in the first scene. They were amazingly docile and they did everything in rehearsal as I asked them. Everything was fine—until we lit the klieg lights and they came under a glare that they'd never seen before. All hell broke loose. They threw themselves on the ground; they began to howl—it was ghastly. We were in a sea of them and I was absolutely petrified. I hadn't even the strenght to shout "Stop!" So we didn't shoot the documentary; but I've never forgotten that scene.

You left Ferrara to attend the University of Bologna. What made you decide not to return to Ferrara? Didn't you like it there?

I enjoyed myself tremendously in Ferrara. The troubles began later. But I didn't like university life much in Bologna. The subjects I studied—economics and business administration—didn't interest me. I wanted to make films. I was glad when I was graduated. Yet it's odd; on graduation day, I was overcome with a terrible sadness. I realized that my youth was over and now the struggle had begun.

And you went to Rome?

Yes; and the first years there were very hard. I wrote reviews for a film magazine; and when they fired me, I was pennyless for days. I even stole a steak from a restaurant. Someone had ordered it but was away from the table when it came; so I put it in a newspaper and ran out. My father had money—he was then a small industrialist—and wanted me back in

Ferrara. But I refused and lived by selling tennis trophies; I had boxes full of them that I'd won in tournements during college days. I pawned and sold them all. I was miserable, since I'd won them myself.

How did you switch from film criticism to film directing?
I went to the Centro Sperimentale di Cinematografia in Rome; but stayed only three months. the technical aspect of films—by itself alone— has never interested me very much. After you've learned two or three basic rules of cinema grammar, you can do what you like—including breaking those rules.

Then you began to direct?

No, it wasn't that easy. At first I wrote filmscripts. I did one with Rossellini, called *Un pilota ritorna* [A Pilot Returns, 1941-42]. I'll never forget Roberto. In those days he lived in a big empty house he'd found in Rome and was almost always in bed, because it was the only piece of furniture he had. We worked on his bed, with him in it. From this I moved on to other things, until I was drafted into the army. The hell began then.

Because of army life?
No, the nightmare was to work on the set of a film I had helped write—*I due Foscari*, with Enrico Fulchignoni directing—and still show up as a soldier. I used to sneak out of camp at night and crawl back at dawn, over a wall or sometimes through a hole under a hedge. It was freezing and I was paralyzed from this and from sheer exhaustion.

Why did you keep going back over the wall?
because of the excitement of working on a film, although only in a small way as an assistant. They let me experiment and I learned a lot, especially about camera movement and how to relate the movement of actors to the field of your lens.

Did you work on any other films while you were in the army?

Michele Scalera [head of Scalera films] called me in one day and asked me if I'd like to go to France to work with Marcel Carné—as his codirector—on a picture being coproduced by Scalera. I couldn't believe it—codirect with this man who was the greatest of his day—and I said yes. I had to pull strings all over Rome to get leave from the army. Then, when I got it, I was stopped at the French border. It was maddening. When I finally got to Paris, it was Sunday and I found Carné shooting in the suburbs. He looked at me like I had brought the plague. Finally, he said: "You've got eyes, my friend. Look." After that, he said nothing more to me. I didn't dare tell him I was supposed to be his codirector. I merely said I was to be his assistant; but I was never even that. We went to Nice for some exteriors and the train was so crowded I rode on the car steps, hanging on for my life. Carné spoke to me again, then—obviously scared I'd get hurt and he'd have to pay for it. At Nice we stayed at the Negresco [Hotel], where I began to enjoy myself a bit. I met the nurse-maid of a rich family and made some notes for a film on the life of a great hotel, seen from the back rooms. Somewhere along the line, I eventually lost the notes, but I'll never forget Carné. Scalera had wanted me to stay on in France and work with [Jean] Gremillion and [Jean] Cocteau, but my leave ran out and I had to hurry back to the army in Italy.

Mussolini's regime collapsed shortly afterward. How did this affect you?
It forced me to a hand-to-mouth existence. During the German Occupation of Rome, cinema didn't exist. I earned a little money by doing translations—Gide's *La Porte étroite,* Morand's *Monsieur Zero.* But then I became involved with the Action party and the Germans looked for me. I escaped to the Abruzzi hills, but they followed me there and I had to escape once more. Finally, when the Allies took Rome, we could begin again.

Did that lean period color the political or social outlook of your later films?
That had already begun, long before. When I was a boy, we often went with friends to swim in the Po, which flows near Ferrara. There were *barconi,* great river boats towed by men dragging them from the towpath.

Men pulling five or six boats, against a river's current, made a tremendous impression on me. I returned time and again to stare at them and at the people who lived on them, with their family and chickens, and washing hung out; the boat was their home. It was there that I got my first glimpse of the bad distribution of wealth. Later i began to make *People of the Po Valley*. It was my first documentary and the first time I ever handled a cinecamera.

*Yet, your first feature—*Story of a Love Affair, *in 1950—caused a sensation by breaking with the neorealist school's penchant for portraying the working class. This film and most of those you've made since are about the affluent middle class. Why?*
   I've made films about the middle classes because i know them best. Everyone talks about what he knows best. The struggle for life is not only the material and economic one. Comfort is no protection from anxiety. In any case, the idea of giving "all" of reality is overly simple and absurd. I take a subject and I analyze it, as in laboratory. The deeper I can go in the analysis, the smaller the subject becomes—and the better I know it. This doesn't prevent a return from the particular subject to the general, from the isolated character to the entire society. But in *Story of a Love Affair*, I was interested in seeing what the War had done more to the mind and spirit of individuals than to their place in the framework of society. That's why I began to make films that the French critics described as "interior neorealism." The aim was to put the camera inside the characters—not outside. *The Bicycle Thief* was a great film in which the camera remained always outside the characters. Neorealism also taught us to follow the characters with the camera, allowing each shot its own real interior time. Well, I became tired of all this; I could no longer stand real time. In order to function, a shot must show only what is useful.

Why couldn't you stand real time?
   Because there are too many useless moments. It's pointless to describe them.

Your insistence on paring the superfluous from your films is also reflected in the sparseness of your dialog. Is that why you prefer to establish the dark, cold mood of your films with a background of gray, cloudy skies?

In the early days, the films i shot in black and white were fairly dramatic, so the gray sky helped create an atmosphere. *Story of a Love Affair,* for example, was set in Milan in winter—which was correct for climate and mood. But the sun also limits movements. At that time, I used very long shots, turning through 180°; it's obvious that the sun will stop you from doing that sort of thing. So, with a gray sky you move ahead faster, without problems of camera position.

In your last two films, you've switched to color. You've kept the gray skies, but you've been known to change the colors of roads and buildings for effect. What don't you like about real colors?

Wouldn't it be ridiculous if you asked a painter that same question? It's untrue to say that the colors I use are not those of reality. They *are* real: The red I use is red; the green, green; blue, blue; and yellow, yellow. It's a matter of arranging them differently from the way I find them, but they are always real colors. So it's not true that when I tint a road or a wall, they become unreal. They stay real, though colored differently from my scene. I'm forced to modify or eliminate colors as I find them in order to make an acceptable composition. Let's suppose we have a blue sky. Who knows if it's going to work; or, if I don't need it, where can I put it? So I pick a gray day for neutral background, where I can insert all the color elements I need—a tree, a house, a ship, a car, a telegraph pole. It's like having a white paper on which to apply colors.. If I begin with a blue sky, half the picture is already painted blue. But what if I don't happen to need blue? Color forces you to invent. It's more than just a challenge, though. There are practical reasons for working in it today. Reality itself is steadily becoming more colored. Think of what factories were like, especially in Italy at the beginning of the nineteeenth century, when industrialization was just beginning: gray, brown, and smoky. Color didn't exist. Today, instead, most everything is colored. The pipe running from the basement to the twelfth floor is green because it carries steam.

The one carrying electricity is red, and that with water is purple. Also, plastic colors have filled our homes, even revolutionized our taste. Pop art grew out of that and was possible because of this change in taste. Another reason for switching to color is world television. In a few years, it will all be in color, and you can't compete against that with black-and-white films.

Besides the swithch to color, have your methods of filming a picture changed much from the early days?

I've never had a method of working. I change according to circumstances; I don't employ any particular technique or style. I make films instinctively, more with my belly than with my brain.

How does the process begin?

With a theme, a small idea that develops within me. The idea for the next film, which I want to make in America, came to me from something I can't tell you about fully, because it would mean telling the story of the film. But someone told me of an absurd little episode, saying: "Just think what happened to me today. I couldn't come for this and that reason." I went home and thought about it—and upon that small episode I began to build, until I found I had a story, growing out of a small event. You put in everything that accumulates inside you. And it's an enormous quantity of stuff—mostly from watching and observing. The way I relax, what I like doing most, is watching. That's why I like traveling, to have new things before my eyes—even a new face. I enjoy myself like that and can stay for hours, looking at things, people, scenery. Do you know, when I was a boy, I always had bumps on my head from running into mailboxes because I was always turning around to stare at people. I also used to climb onto window sills to look into houses—yes I was crazy—to peek at someone I'd seen in the window. So around the kernel of an idea or an episode, you instinctively add all you have accumulated by watching, talking, living, observing.

And then you begin to write the script?

No, that's the last thing I do. When I'm sure I have a story, I call my collaborators and we begin to discuss it. And we conduct studies of certain subjects to make sure of our terrain. Then, finally, in the last month or two, I write the story.

How long does this gestation period last?
Perhaps six months. Then I start shooting.

When do you pick your ators?
When you work on a character, you form in your mind an image of what he ought to look like. Then you go and find one who resembles him. For *Blow-Up*, I began with photographs sent by agents, throwing them out one by one. Then I went around looking into theaters. I found David Hemmings in a small London production.

Once you've cast the film and begin to shoot, do you stick to your script or ignore it?
The script is a starting point, not a fixed highway. I must look through the camera to see if what I've written on the page is right or not. In the script you describe imagined scenes, butit's all suspended in mid-air. Often, an actor viewed against a wall or a landscape, or seen through a window, is much more eloquent than the line you've given him. So then you take out the lines. This happens often to me and I end up saying what I want with a movement or a gesture.

At what point does this take place?
When I have the actor there, beginning to move, I notice what is useful and what is superfluous and eliminate the superfluous—but only then, at that moment. That's why they call it improvisation, but it's not; it' just making the film. Everything you do before consists of notes; the script is simply a series of notes for the film.

How closely do your scripts conform to to the final product?
I rewrite the scenarios afterward, when I've already made the film and I know what I wanted to do.

It's said that you insist on being left alone on the set for fifteen or twenty min-utes before beginning to shoot. true?

yes. before each new setup, I chase everyone off the set in order to be alone and look through the camera. In that moment, the film seems quite easy. But then the others come in and everything becomes difficult.

If you go on changing scenes right through the last stroke of the clapstick, it must be rough on the actors, too. Do you think that's why some of them say it's diffi-cult to work for you?

Who says so? I really don't believe that's true. I simpli know what the actor's attitude should be and what he should say. He doesn't, because he can't see the relationship that begins to exist between his body and the other things in the scene.

But shouldn't he understand what you have in mind?

He simply must *be*. If he tries to understand too much, he will act in an intellectual and unnatural manner.

Do you prefer, then, not to talk to the actor about his role?

No, it's obvious that I must explain what I want from him, but I don't want to discuss everything I ask him to do, because often my requests are completely instinctive and there are things I can't explain. It's like painting: You don't know why you use pink instead of blue. You simply feel that's how it should be—pink. Then the phone rings and you answer it. When you come back, you don't want pink anymore and you use blue—without knowing why. You can't help it; that's just the way it is.

So you want your actors to do what you tell them without asking questions and without trying to understand why?

Yes. I want an actor to try to give me what I ask in the best and most exact way possible. He mustn't try to find out more, because then there's the danger that he'll become his own director. It's only human and nat-ural that he should see the film in terms of his own part, but I have to see the film as a whole. He must therefore collaborate selflessly, totally. I've worked marvelously with Monica [Vitti] and Vanessa [Redgrave] because they always tried to follow me. It's never important for me if they don't understand, but it is important that I should have recognized what I wanted in what they gave me—or in what they proposed.

Is it true that you sometimes deliberately misdirect actors, giving them a false motivation to produce the reaction you really want from them?
Of course, I tell them something different, to arrive at certain results. Or I run the camera without telling them. And sometimes their mistakes give me ideas I can use, because mistakes are always sincere, absolutely sincere.

Have you ever worked with Method actors?
They're absolutely terrible. They want to direct themselves, and it's a disaster. Their idea is to reach a certain emotional charge; actors are always a little high at work. Acting is their drug. So when you put the brakes on, they're naturally a little disappointed. And I've always played down the drama in my films. In my main scenes, there's never an opportunity for an actor to let go of everything he's got inside. I always try to tone down the acting, because my stories demand it, to the point where I might change a script so that an actor has no opportunity to come out well. I say this for Monica, too. I'm sure that she has never given all she could in my films, because the scenes just weren't there. Take a film like *Who's Afraid of Virginia Woolf?* It offers an actress every possibility. If she's really good and has qualities like Liz Taylor, it comes out. But Liz Taylor never displayed these qualities in other films, because she never had a part like that.

Some directors claim it's difficult to direct a woman they love. Is this true with Monica Vitti?
I have no difficulty, because I forget about the relationship between myself and any actress when working with her.

Would you number Monica among the most gifted actresses you've ever seen?

Monica is certainly the first who comes to mind. I can't think of another as good as Vanessa, as strong as Liz Taylor, as true as Sophia Loren, or as modern as Monica. Monica is astonishingly mobile. Few actresses have such mobile features. She has her own personal and original way of acting.

What about directors? Have you any favorites?

They change, like favorite authors. I had a passion for Gide and Stein and Faulkner. But now they're no use to me anymore. I've assimilated them—so, enough, they're a closed chapter. This also applies to film directors. Also, when I see a good film, it's like a whiplash. I run away, in order not to be influenced. Thus, the films I liked most are those I think least about.

Are you an admirer of Ingmar Bergman?

Yes; he's a long way from me, but I admire him. He, too, concentrates a great deal on individuals; and although the individual is what interests him most, we are very far apart. His individuals are very different from mine—but he's a great director. So is Fellini, for that matter.

What do you do between films? Do you feel the same emptiness as Fellini when you're not working?

I don't know how it is with Fellini. I never feel empty. I travel a lot and I think about other films.

Are you ever bored?

I don't know. I never look at myself.

Have you ever known anyone who has understood you?

Everyone has understood me in his own way. But I would have to understand myself first, in order to judge—and so far, I haven't.

Have you many friends?

The close friends remain fairly fixed. The older I get, the more I like the people whom we call *mezzi matti*—half crazy. I like them best because they fit into my conviction that life should be taken ironically: otherwise it becomes a tragedy. Fitzgerald said a very interesting thing in his diary: that human life proceeds from the good to the less good—that is, it's always worse as you go on. That's true.

You've said your films always leave you unsatisfied. Isn't that true of the work of most creative artists?
Yes, but especially for me, since I've always worked under fairly disastrous conditions economically.

Have all the lost years—the time wasted fighting agaisnt incomprehension from producers—left you bitter?
I try not to think about it. I dislike judging myself, but I will say I would be wealthy today if I had accepted all the films that have been offered to me with large sums of money. But I've always refused, in order to do what I felt like doing.

Have you ever been tempted?
Yes, often.

As far as wealth goes, didn't the success of Blow-Up *make you rich?*
I'm not rich and maybe I'll never be rich. Money is useful—yes—but I don't worship it.

What's your next film? Do you intend to continue working outside Italy?
Quite frankly, I'd like to but don't know if I'll have the strenght. It isn't easy to understand the lives of people different from your own. I'm thinking about doing a film in the United States, as I mentioned earlier, but I don't know if it will come off.

Have you ever considered making an autobiographical film, like some of Fellini's?

My films have always had an element of immediate autobiography, in that I shoot any particular scene according to the mood I'm in that day, according to the little daily experiences I've had and am having—but I don't tell what has happened to me. I would like to do something more strictly autobiographical, but perhaps I never will, because it isn't interesting enough, or I won't have the courage to do it. No, that's nonsense, because it isn't a question of courage. It's simply that I believe in the autobiographical concept only to the degree that I am able to put onto film all that's passing through my head at the moment of shooting.

Have you ever thought about retiring?
I'll go on making films until I make one that pleases me from the first to the last frame. Then I'll quit.

I Am Tired of Today's Cinema[4]

Nowadays is not only us critics who enthusiastically support your work, as it was at the times of L'avventura *and* La notte. *A large part of the public has also shown its enthusiasm for your work since* Blow-Up *was released. How do you explain this change?*

Today, the public has matured and accepts certain themes and/or language without difficulty. As for myself, I would say that, instinctively, I might have found a way to make my films more—how can I say—Americans would say *exciting*, more interesting, but that is not the right word. More precisely, I might have found a way to be less reserved in showing emotions and feelings. Perhaps I have been able to deal with a topic more deeply and even more skillfully. I do not really know. A film—I will never grow tired of repeating it—does not need to be "understood." It is enough if the viewer "feels" it. To see a film must be an overall personal, intuitive experience, like when one reads a poem. Who would dream of being able to thoroughly explain a poem? Take *The Passenger*, for instance (I am sorry to keep returning to this film, but this is the film that everyone wants to talk about), or its last sequence, that long uninterrupted take. There is no need for the audience to understand it from a technical point of view; it is enough if they are sensitive to that slow flowing of things through the window, while the camera slowly moves onward.

---

[4] "Sono stanco del cinema com'è oggi," from *Il Tempo,* 20 March 1975. Translated by Dana Renga.

In The Passenger, *however, technique is very important, even if this is not unusual in your films.*

It seems to me that there is something unusual here. In general, I have never made camera movements that were not justified by the movements of the characters. Here, instead, the camera moves on its own, as if it had the same interest for objects, landscape, and people that the protagonist, the reporter, has. Why this? It seems to me almost arrogant to answer. I work very instinctively, and the meanings of certain techniques become clear to me only later on. For example, in reviewing *The Passenger* I ask myself: Why did I film that scene in this way? It will seem strange, but I always find an answer that I have never previously thought of. The presence of a car in a pan, apparently coming from nowhere, might have been suggested to me by the fact that a character without a past of his own, but with the past of someone who is now dead, was riding in that same car.

And I took another liberty—that of approaching every sequence with always a new attitude. If you think of it, it is possible to say that there is no technical unity in the film. Every sequence was filmed differently from the others because the content was different. At the end, however, all of these differences seem to me to find a unity of their own. This is, after all, my attitude toward the story I'm telling.

The Passenger *was released this year. Apart from the television documentary on China in 1972, your last film was* Zabriskie Point *in 1970. Why such a long break?*

Because in the meantime I prepared two films. One, *Tecnicamente dolce* [Technically Sweet], took almost two years. The script was ready, I even went location-scouting in Sardinia and in the jungle. Then Carlo Ponti, who inherited the project from other producers, eventually decided against it. He was probably scared that I would never leave the jungle or that I would start painting it.

The other film was inspired by a story by Calvino, *The Night Driver*. At first it was called *The Spiral*, and then *The Color of Jealousy*. It was an obsessive story of a jealous man who every night would leave his own city by car and go to his lover's town. In order to have a better control of the color I filmed it with a video camera rather than with a regular camera. This time I was the one who was having serious problems with the script. I could not find the right approach, and I gave up. But in the meantime, another year had gone by.

You have stated that your next film will have an Italian subject because you realized that by making films outside of Italy you began to feel uprooted. Can a frame, a language, give you roots?

We are all rooted in a language, in a culture, in an historical environment. In traveling to other countries I have assimilated parts of their culture, while at the same time losing a part of my own. It is somewhat like those writers who spend alternatively six months in the United States and six months in Europe. At a certain moment they no longer know what to write about. That is what I mean when I say that I need to find my roots. I would now like to tell the story of people born and raised in Italy. It may happen that at the last moment this country, which already makes us shiver if we look at it closely, unexpectedly will push me away and make me change my mind. I know, it is not a very original criticism, but it might be original to attempt to love this country even if you despise a part of it. And when I say "a part," I mean a large group of people, those we see in the streets, in the public places. Sometimes I think I belong to another race.

And your films?

I could answer by saying that my films are what they are because I am who I am. Some say that I am a typical elitist director. The truth is that when I come in contact with art I have a freer, less engaged attitude than most people think. Personal interests are what always move me. All of the characters in my films are fictional, but at the same time they are also real, because reality has suggested them to me. What I need is to hear a line or to see a gesture, a face, an expression, an event, a story. This grows inside of me, it becomes a sequence, the sequence becomes a series of sequences, and then I have a complete story. I'm not too sure how this happens. Maybe it has to do with the fact that I always have to make a film for someone. Not the public, but a specific person—a friend, a woman. It has always been this way, even when I used to play tennis as a young man. If I had a public, I played better. Once, in Bologna, at the final match of a tournament, practically no one was there. I lost the first two sets. Then more people came and I won the next three.

There is something else I would like to add. I wish my films were released more discreetly than the promotion requires. The publicity spots and the billboards loudly boast of how good the film is, and urge the public to go and see it and to admire it. The beauty of a film, when it is there, should instead surface almost by chance, without arrogance, since the purpose of the film is different from what advertising would make it to be.

Does autobiography play a role in your films?

There is only one way to be autobiographical: out in the open, without restraint. That is, one should not regard as private what one writes or puts in a film. One needs a certain amount of shamelessness to do this, and I do not have it. My way of being autobiographical is different, it changes depending on what people I see, what I do, what kind of light I've found on my way to work. All these things can influence the way I film or make a sequence. So if certain characters reveal something of myself, I would say that it is natural, and that it would be unnatural if it were not so.

What about tomorrow?

Cinema as it is now is beginning to tire me out. There are too many technical limitations. It is ridiculous to still have to use a regular camera, not very different from what was used thirty years ago, or to still have to go to such great lengths to transform reality to conform to our desires. We cannot completely dominate color or use it as painters do. That is why I have thought of video cameras, and I am still thinking about using them for my next film. Only with magnetic tape is it possible to avoid the compromises that the development and print laboratories impose on you. On the tape the color can be electronically corrected. It is true that there are many other technical complications, but the advantages are enormous.

You asked me: "What about tomorrow?" Tomorrow could already be today if it were not for the industrial structure of cinema that opposes it. It would be the end of film, of film development and print laboratories, of regular cameras, and of at least a third of the commercial cinema establishment. Do you think that it would be easy to destroy all of this? Among all of the arts, cinema is the one that is most solidly grounded in life, and one would have to begin to change even life. Since, the way it is now, it's not very well organized.

GIANLUIGI RONDI

THE WORLD IS OUTSIDE THE WINDOW[5]

First of all, we would like to talk about your work on the set, about what it means to live a film—that is, to live a certain period of time, to go over that kind of work that the film itself, in its final state, tends to cancel out .

For me, making a film is always a way of experiencing life. Generally, one thinks that when a director makes a film, it is just a "parenthesis" in his or her life, while waiting for the next film and the next parenthesis. In my case, at least, this is not the way things are: I go through a continuous maturation process that involves observations, experiences, reflections, which are occasionally of political and moral character. This process goes on when I am not working, but also when I am shooting. I have previously said that my way of being autobiographical does not involve representing my own personal stories, but rather having my daily state of mind reemerge within the film. In this way, for example, when I go to work in the morning, the people I meet, the things I think about, and even the light of that day can all impress themselves upon me and can influence the way I resolve, sometimes even technically, a certain sequence. It seems to me that even this is a way of being autobiographical.

But in cinema things take time. Between the initial plan and its completion, between the idea of an image and its final actualization, months can pass, even years, often not very productive.

5 "Il mondo è fuori dalla finestra," from *Filmcritica* 252, March 1975. Translated by Dana Renga.

Yes, but for me the process is different. I never try to produce images that I have thought of. I have found that if I did this I would end up with a rough imitation of my thoughts and images. Instead, when I arrive on the set, I like to feel in a state of total "virginity" toward the scene that I have to film. Sometimes—obviously this is not always possible—I prefer not to even know what I have to film. I do not want to have the time to think too much about the scene. The first idea for me is the best.

In general, what relationship is there between a take, the retakes, and the out-takes?

I never film a lot: only three or four takes per scene. I rehearse even less. I am convinced that this is better for the actors. This way they are more natural. To achieve simplicity through exhaustive preparation requires a certain amount of experience and technique. I prefer instead to have the actors in a more "unrehearsed" state when they first encounter the scene. Many times the first take is the best. But sometimes I like to shoot beyond that scene. Once the actors have done all they had to do and said all they had to say, they still keep on going, by force of inertia, until they hit what I call "dead moments." At these moments actors often commit "errors," which in some way are also part of the scene. I think that these are very sincere moments.

You create a space in which unexpected reactions can occur.

Yes, they are always different. I leave a lot to chance.

You often pressure your actors into a crisis in order to bring them to a state of "simplicity."

This also happened with Jack Nicholson, who is an expert actor, gifted with extraordinary technique.

I noticed how, during the film, Nicholson changed his way of performing, his posture. For example, in the beginning, when he nervously tried to shovel the sand from underneath the tire of the Land Rover, he seemed to not yet be under your influence, as he later would be.

I would say the opposite. It is true that in that scene he is not under my influence, but the opposite is also true. Let me explain. In that scene I was trying to pressure him into a crisis. Now, maybe I am mistaken, but I am not the type of director who explains much to the actors. I obviously explain what I think of the film and of the character, but I try to avoid letting the actor feel that he is in charge of the scene, that he becomes his own director. The actor—I will never grow tired of repeating it—is only one of the elements of the complete image, frequently not even the most important element, and it is through all of a shot's elements that I give it meaning. The actor ignores the meaning, and how I choose to express this meaning is up to me. I am the one who has to see the film in its unity. Now, to return to the scene with the Land Rover in the sand, I tried to make our relationship a bit tense so that Nicholson would enter into a state of crisis. He did not even realize it. It was a very difficult moment in the desert. With all of the wind and the sand, it was horrible being there completely uncovered, unlike the Arabs or other members of the company. When we filmed, the crisis came naturally. The weeping was natural. It was real.

This seems to happen throughout the film. It seems that Nicholson does not "play" his part, as he did in Chinatown; *the character is integrated within the actor, and he directly projects the image of a typical middle American.*

In fact I tried to control him in such a way as to produce this type. This character is not exceptionally gifted. For someone who's supposed to be an intellectual he is not very well educated; he does not even know who [Anton] Gaudí is. He is a strong man; say, like those reporters who are used to seeing it all and do not react with much emotion to the events they encounter. I lived in the United States long enough to know that there is no better way to get to know a country than to work there. My reporter has immigrated to America from England, and therefore he has had to accept changes, including some in the language. For this reason, the English edition of *The Passenger* has many nuances that have been lost in the Italian version. This reporter speaks in, let's say, a post-1968 way. That is, he is one of those young people who assimilated the language of the student protests and then ignored it when it became part of the system. And his wife, Rachel, speaks with a slightly snobbish intonation in English, so you can understand why he was so fascinated by her and why he married this type of neurotic woman, quite different from the women that he was familiar with.

And did you explain any of this to the actors?

No. One time Nicholson brought to my attention precisely this, that Rachel had this snobbish intonation. So we discussed it and came to the conclusion that it was better this way.

What about the different lengths of the several versions of the film?

This is a curious matter. I don't mean the matter in itself is curious, but that what happened was curious. The first edited version was very long, more than four hours. But this is common.

Do you edit while you film?

No, I have never done it that way. For me, editing is a creative phase of the film, and so I prefer to finish filming before starting to edit. Now, I found myself in front of all of this material, and the problem was where to cut. One of the reasons there was so much material was that I prepared the film very quickly, in not much more than a month and a half—script, writing and location-scouting included. It was the first time I made a film from a subject that wasn't mine. Mark Peploe, who's a friend of mine, had talked to me about the story from the time when it was only three pages long. Then, little by little, he developed it. We worked together on the script, correcting it and changing it always with an eye to the fact that he was supposed to make this film. When I got the project instead, I realized that the material I had in my hands had to be modified. Mark and I had to do this work in a hurry because Nicholson had given me the dates when he was available and I couldn't change them. This forced me to continue working on the script while I was shooting. And in order to solve problems for which I had not come up with a solution yet, I had to shoot much more than I needed to. I tell you all of this because I had never before ended up with four and a half hours of material.

I had the impression that you were trying to perform something of a trimming operation around a thriller or adventure story, in order to bring out its quintessence.
I wouldn't be able to say what I was trying to change.

Yes, but precisely the trimming of an ideal thriller, rather than a specific script—that is, a thriller with car chases.
There were odd scenes, dialogues that had no other purpose than to create a special relationship between the two characters of Nicholson and the girl. For me this relationship meant something different, and so it had to take up an amount of different space in the length of the film. Then I arrived at an almost normal length, two hours and twenty minutes, which seemed to me to be the perfect length for the film I wanted to make from that script. However, the producers insisted that the film be shorter, since in the United States they are very strict about this. Either the film lasts three and a half hours, like Bertolucci's film [*1900*], or it must have a normal length. To reduce its length, I had to practically redo the whole editing, shifting certain sequences. It was a grueling experience. After finishing with the editing I realized that the previous version was wrong and that this one, which was two hours and four minutes long, was the right version. I asked myself what would happen to a film if one kept on working on it for twenty years, like D'Arrigo did with his book.

In the film there are several filmed sequences, documentaries, television clips; I think all of these are introduced with a critical purpose, that is, to understand

---

* Italian writer and journalist Stefano D'Arrigo (1919-1987) enjoyed huge popularity, and divided criticism, in 1975 with the publication of his epic novel *Horcynus Orca*, on which he had been working for more than twenty years.

David's character through them. But I think that instead, one loses him right then. Is there a critical attitude on your part toward these television techniques, or even to recording in general?

I would not say so. I didn't think about it, nor did I take such a critical stance intentionally, even if I might have given this impression. It is hard to tell what emerges from what we do. There are several different ways to interpret anything, depending on one's personal articulation of the material one has at one's disposal. I included those sequences, on the one hand, to give an idea of how the character was trying to find a sense in life, even politically, through his own work. On the another hand, to capture a certain aspect of reality, even a spectacular one. It is possible that in that particular visual material you find a certain ambivalence—even a certain ambiguity, as in the execution scene—which, precisely because of what I have just said, can be interpreted in as many ways as possible. It seems to me that the effect is always the same: spine-chilling. And because of what it is, the sequence raises a political problem. To return to your question, I admit that it is plausible to think of a critical stance toward the TV images, but it was not intentional.

Critical, at least, of the illusion of being able to reproduce the "real."

Of course, it is always an illusion to believe that you can reproduce objectively the "real." Especially for a filmmaker who is interested in current events, like a reporter. I have never believed in the *cinéma vérité*, because I do not see what truth it can provide. As soon as we focus our camera on something, we must make a choice, even if we film in uninterrupted sequences, or without changing the pivot of the camera, which would seem the way to represent an event at its most realistic—

We would go further. Even if we do not "make a choice" we sense that it is not the same thing—

—it is not. Not to mention editing, where even one cut can destroy every illusion.

Have you seen much of the underground in America?

Yes, I have seen enough of it. I think that it has accomplished one thing, and that is to influence commercial, high-budget cinema. A generation of directors has been created that is different from the Hollywood ones. This is because their working spaces and tools are different. I saw the places where these people work. They are incredible, small workshops with small cameras. They make films with very low budgets, shooting in the streets, or in houses, or in their little studios. But they have extraordinary poetic intuitions. I saw many beautiful things. After all, even *Easy Rider* has shown the underground influence on the cinema, especially with the use of those quick flashes that anticipate the following sequence.

Did you like Easy Rider?

I thought it was a sincere film. I know Dennis Hopper well. He was shooting his film not too far from me, in the desert, when I filmed *Zabriskie Point*. They lived in tents and came to see me every once in a while. Behind this story there is a real America. I find it to be a skillful but genuine film. I do not know if you have the same impression.

No. For example, it used many patterns used in commercials.

That is true, but it is also true that these patterns are part of their linguistic background, and so, after assimilating and reworking them, these films are sincere in reexpressing them. America is an odd country, which offers a lot of material. You find yourself in the middle of it and you can't help but show it in your films. I think that *Sugarland Express* is much more artificial. It is a film that has a Hollywood-type gloss, and this bothers me. Much more than in *Duel in the Sun*, which is a more original idea developed with great enthusiasm, except that in the end it is far too melodramatic.

Have you also seen films that are outside of traditional commercial circles?

Yes, of course. America is an extraordinary country that offers everyone the chance to make films. It is also a ruthless country. On the West Coast, they say—they say this as a joke, but nonetheless they still say it—that those who do not succeed in New York or in Los Angeles end up in

San Francisco, where very often they end up killing themselves. In fact, the highest rate of suicide is in San Francisco. In Los Angeles there are directing schools for children from five to ten years of age. I saw films directed by six- or seven-year-old children that included scenes of missiles launching into the stratosphere—roughly done, but brilliant.

Do they use much videotape?

They probably do, I do not know. I have not been to America for some time. Well, I was in Los Angeles three months ago, but just for a month, and I did not come into contact with the underground world because I had other things to do for this film.

We heard that you did screen tests on videotape and laser disc. Do you think that you will make a complete film with either of these?

I did screen tests on videotape, not on laser disc. I have, however, seen them done on laser disc. I completed a script that was based on *The Night Driver*, a short story by Calvino. The film was called *The Spiral,* and I wanted to make it with a video camera so that I could have better control of the color. In development and print laboratories the possibilities are limited. With *Red Desert* I had to modify the natural colors which, besides being costly, is also rather limiting, especially when shooting outside. But it is not easy even for the interiors. For instance, those images that Giuliana sees on the ceiling, I would have liked to film them while they were in motion, but I had to limit myself to fixed images. With video cameras it is possible to change the color electronically. This is like painting the film. I saw a couple of films done this way, one of them by Frank Zappa. Zappa tried to achieve certain effects by carrying further those same effects that are to be found in all pop-music films, where images are a little out of focus because of the type of lights used, or rough-grained as if exposed to too much light. Nothing new. I am convinced that these methods could be used in a less coarse, more poetic way. In terms of saving money, it is wrong to think that this is possible because the tape is easy to erase. The price of the tape is low in comparison to what the necessary technicians, fifteen to twenty people, can cost. This is very expensive, at least about one hundred thousand dollars. At any rate, I think that the future of cinema can be seen only in this direction. For me, the classic camera is a very limiting tool. What we use today is not much different from the forty-year-old Debris, except for a few small modifications and better lenses.

What changes have occurred in terms of fruition and distribution?
It is very likely that we will be able to distribute by cable. Some time ago, an American company, who was working with the Japanese, tried to create this type of circuit. They consulted about ten directors, including myself and Fellini. They calculated that with a four to five-day programming they would be able to cover the production costs of a two million dollar film. Always by cable.

How clear are these images once they are projected on a big screen in color?
Once, in a theater in London, I saw a telecast of a boxing match. It was obviously a bit blurred, but we cannot judge by what we see today. Incredible experiments are being done in the lab, and when a way to distribute these images is ready, their quality will be all right. The use of the laser disc is still at an experimental stage, but what has already been done is extraordinary. I saw images of people, realistically represented, losing their physical form and turning into mere luminous shapes. Who knows what they will be able to do in the future. Anyway, all of this will not only change the technical ways of making a film or of how images are represented, but also the material of the stories that are filmed. Narrative technique will change.

In theory, one could reach a higher level of abstraction.
Of course. Because there must be something beneath what the naked eye sees, something that could give us a higher consciousness of our existence. At least, this is what I believe.

Speaking of technique, would you be able to clarify how the final sequence of The Passenger *was filmed?*

I cannot really tell you, because I promised the publisher of the book an exclusive on the pictures. I can only tell you that it involves a special type of camera, a Canadian patent, mounted on a series of gyroscopes so that it is not subject to any movement in its support. It is a machine that was being used for commercials, in 16mm, and it was difficult to convince the technicians to mount on it a 35mm. It changed the weight and it needed to be recalibrated. They wanted to give me a reel of only 120 meters, but that was not enough for me, since I wanted a six-hundred-meter reel. In the end, I was able to get three hundred meters. With six hundred, I would have been able to start the shot much earlier. It took eleven days to film the final sequence, also because of the wind that kept disturbing the camera.

So, there was no trolley?

No. It is a different system, of which I can't speak. In a certain sense, the camera was in the air. The whole village was there watching, a crowd that, as time went by, became involved with the event.

And the voices? Were they post-sync?

There was no other way. I was inside a van, in front of a monitor, supervising everything, including the zoom, by remote control. My assistant was outside and we communicated through a microphone; he then repeated my orders at the top of his voice. There was a certain rhythm and synchronicity to obtain—a terribly hard toil. We repeated it for eleven days, mostly because of the balance of light required between the indoors and the outdoors. We could only shoot between 3:30 and 4:30 in the afternoon—that is, only three or four takes a day. Only the last day it went well. This is the advantage of the monitor, to be able to control everything, even things that enter into the field by chance. I will refuse to make my next film if I am bound to find surprises during the projection. It seems absurd to me not to be able to know what the cameraman is doing, whether he is betraying what I want.

Did you use the monitor only in this long take?

Yes, only there. Buñuel always uses it.

Everyone interpreted The Passenger *in different ways but always in connection with the same idea of the imaginary, of the body, of the identity, of the projection etc. Some of us see the character of the girl as the imaginary "other"; some see her instead as the projection of the two male characters, who could also be looked at in this way. This could go on forever, until a sort of mirage effect is achieved that belongs to the logic of a generalized exchange. . . .*

These interpretations are very interesting to me. The whole film is ambiguous, but I think that it appropriates such ambiguity as its own concreteness.

Here there are none of those mystical impulses that, for instance, we see at the end of the tennis match in Blow-Up. *Instead,* The Passenger *seems to be a concrete expansion of that scene, a scene that has become the whole film—one in which the explicit relationships and boundaries between the real and the imaginary are eliminated. Moreover, the rendezvous with Daisy belongs to an awareness of death, of the end; David relaxes and waits.*

Being, says Heidegger, is being-in-the-world. When David senses the end (although probably not even he himself is sure of it), he is no longer in the world. The world is outside the window.

What makes the final scene so interesting is that we feel as if David truly remains behind the camera, truly identifies himself with his profession. He waits for death, almost looking out from behind the camera at what will happen in front of him.

Yes, a reportage of his own death.

An African "aura" is present in many of your films.

I know Africa very well. I was there as a reporter, even when World War II broke out. I went back later and visited the country extensively for long periods. More than the desert in and of itself, I always felt the need to live in a different historical context, in a nonhistorical world, or in a historical context that is not conscious of its own historicity. This is shown in the film *Tecnicamente dolce*, which I was supposed to make before this one and which should have begun in Italy and ended in the Amazonian jungle.

Would you like to say a few things about Italian cinema?

We can say that today, Italian cinema does not exist. There are directors who make good films. It is always by chance that a good film is made there or that every so often a brilliant director turns out. But there is no specific school or trend—it is all disconnected. Today, as in the past, it is very difficult for the young to assert themselves—also because, I must add, many of them were failures. Few have been able to survive.

MICHELE MANCINI
ALESSANDRO CAPPABIANCA
CIRIACO TISO
JOBST GRAPOW

Myself and Cinema, Myself and Women[6]

Tell us about the 1950s.

The way I remember it, it was a more serene and humane period in comparison with the present. Of course, people were close-minded, the milieu was provincial and dull, morality was oppressive, politics repressive, and the clericalism was unbearable. De Gasperi was prime minister and Scelba was minister of the interior.[7] The police killed workers in direct confrontations in Modena or Comacchio. The Christian Democrats tried to take over with a tricky electoral law, and censorship and moralism had the upper hand. But there was a feeling of excitement, there was hope. The only good thing that the war had left was hope—even if it was false hope, as indeed it was later deluded. However in 1950 it was still possible to live adventurously, in a way that would be unthinkable now. Not everything was at a standstill. And yet it was at that time that I made *Story of a Love Affair*. This was proof enough that someone was willing to take risks and trust other people.

[6] "Io e il cinema, io e le donne," from *Corriere della sera*, 12 February 1978. Translated by Dana Renga.

[7] Alcide De Gasperi (1881–1954) was Italy's prime minister from 1948 to 1953. Mario Scelba (1901–1991) was the cabinet's minister of Interior. Both Christian Democrats, they led their coalition government to a repressive campaign against the early 1950s turmoil originated by social protest and leftist dissent.

Was that film a risk?

Up to that time, I had only directed documentaries, which were appreciated and won several prizes, and I had attended the Centro Sperimentale di Cinematografia for three months. The war had slowed things down and I was very impatient to direct my first film, but I could not find anyone who would put up the money. I succeeded in having the script read by someone named Villani who made some money from the sale of one of his movie theaters in Turin. He did not like it at all, but he made a proposal: "Come to see me, and talk to me about the film. If you succeed in convincing me, I will finance you." So I went to his hotel room and, even if I am not very verbal and actually hate talking, I tried to present the story in the most attractive way—I went on for three hours, resorting to methods worthy of a second-rate attorney or a cheap salesman. In the end, Villani said: "I still don't like it. But since you like it so much, let's do it." Could you ever imagine anything like that happening today?

Why did you choose Lucia Bosè for your protagonist?

Because there was a romance between us. She was nineteen years old, she was marvelous, it was impossible to not fall in love with her. I had never seen such a beautiful and passionate woman. I never mixed my personal feelings with work, but she was the first person I thought of for the film. In the screen test, she revealed a dark and disturbing aura—which was very appropriate for the part. When Fausto Sarli and I started to dress her up in designer clothes and real jewelry, the girl was transformed into a real beauty. She was enchanting, intelligent, sharp, cheerful. Oh, how many blows poor Lucia had to take for the final scene! The film ended with her beaten up and sobbing, leaning against a doorway. And yet she was always happy, and it was difficult for her to pretend to be desperate. She was not an actress. To obtain the results I wanted I had to use psychological and physical violence. Insults, scolding, abuses and hard slaps. In the end, she broke down, crying like a little baby. She played her part wonderfully.

That same year Visconti made La terra trema *about Sicilian fishermen, Germi dedicated* Il cammino della speranza *to the Italian immigrants.*[8] *Italian neorealism chose the underprivileged as its protagonists, but in* Story of a Love Affair *you chose to depict the bourgeoisie. Why?*

With my two documentaries *People of the Po Valley* and *N.U.*, I already represented the underprivileged. In a way, I had to invent neorealism on my own; there was no one to teach it to me. I instinctively loved the common people. As a teenager, I would get up at dawn to get on the carts that went to the countryside so that I could talk with the carters. I spent many evenings with the customers of taverns, and with women—I have always liked them, especially the very poor ones. These were not polemical or elitist choices, but rather reflected a sincere interest. However, it would have been difficult for me to tell sentimental stories with these types of people. What I knew best was the well-off middle-class, which I knew from the inside since it was my own milieu. My mother was a factory worker and my father was a messenger in a factory; but our family, which boasted some distant relations to the Swedish royal family, had reached a middle-class status. My world, when as a teenager I was a tennis champion, was the Marfisa Tennis Club. I was surrounded by the Ferrara aristocracy and by its rich bourgeoisie from an aristocratic agrarian background. And then, after Italian cinema had analyzed characters in their relationship to society, it seemed to me that it would be more interesting to bring neorealism within the individual. For me, the bourgeoisie was a cultural obsession. I asked myself why the Italian bourgeoisie had always been mediocre, and also if its future would be any better.

During this time, weren't the intellectuals obsessed with the threat of the atomic bomb, existentialism, phenomenology, populism, and consumerism?

[8] Pietro Germi (1914–1974) started his career as a filmmaker within the so-called Italian neorealist school. To this period belongs the film mentioned in the interview ("Hope's Progress"). He is best remembered for his later "comedies Italian style," such as *Divorce Italian Style* (1961) and *Seduced and Abandoned* (1963).

I was never affected by atomic anguish. Scientific progress, in my view, is indisputable, as long as it works "technically sweet," as Oppenheimer used to say. Existentialism, and later on phenomenology, are two philosophies that I felt very close to. It is possible to see them reflected in my films, but I have never been a man of learning who interpreted everything through culture. My way of seeing is in the eye, I believe in the force of the image, of its internal rhythm. Speaking of consumerism, think of this: I have never had money. Never. Even now I do not have any. Whenever I find some money in my pocket I quickly spend it. At that time, I literally did not have a cent.

Was the film successful?
It came out when I was on a trip. As soon I returned to Rome I rushed to the theater. At the door, someone with a marked Roman accent was saying to his friend: "What a piece of trash!" I did not go in, and to this day I do not like to be present at the screenings of my films. *Story of a Love Affair* won the award at the Punta del Este Film festival; it got good reviews and made some money. Unfortunately, the agency that distributed it went bankrupt. My next film, *The Vanquished*, was financed by priests.

Is it possible to define Antonioni as "perhaps the only secular Italian director?"
Yes. That is an accurate description. And yet, the film I am now making is very close to being religious. I had refused one hundred and twenty-eight films, and I was tired of saying no. Realizing that, among the many populist directors, I was the one who knew how to portray the bourgeoisie, producers threw at me the silliest and most mundane scripts. For *The Vanquished*, which was supposed to be an edifying film about the crisis of youth after the war, I had the nicest producer that I have ever worked with. The president of the Catholic company that financed the film was Mario Melloni, who then became one of the best columnist of *l'Unità*. The themes of the "wasted youth" and the neverending "youth problem" were discussed then as much as they are today, but they did not interest me at all. I hardly took *The Vanquished* to heart. Even the subject

matter of the three episodes that take place in France, Italy, and England came directly from everyday life. The Italian episode was the story of a fascist who, out of political animosity, covered up his own suicide, making it look like a political assassination carried out by antifascists. This story was rejected by the producers, since the Christian Democrats have always been easy on the fascists. The French episode was censored because the French government did not want the story of the J3—a group of middle-class youngsters who had turned assassins—to become known abroad. Even their parents became involved in stopping the distribution of the film, which was banned from France for many years, until 1963.

Was it difficult to work outside of Italy?

Not at all. I was never bothered by petty nationalistic misgivings. I will make films anywhere, as the whole world interests me. At that time I was one of the few Italian directors to make films on topics not exclusively Italian, and since then London has been one of my favorite cities. In London, for the English episode of *The Vanquished,* I chose a girl who unfortunately turned out to be on her way to Hollywood. Her name was Audrey Hepburn. In Paris, for the French episode, from hundreds of girls, I chose three; one was Brigitte Bardot, who had only taken a screen test with Marc Allégret, the second was Jeanne Moreau, and the third was Etchika Choureau, who then made the film, but left the world of cinema soon after to marry the king of Morocco. I often have a good intuition for actresses. When Gina Lollobrigida, after signing the contract, refused to play in *The Lady without Camellias* because she said that the story was too close to her own life, I proposed to have an unknown girl I often saw in a restaurant take over the role. She was a beautiful tall brunette with splendid eyes and a wild side to her. Her name was Sofia Scicolone[9] and she was just an extra in the Cinecittà studios. The producer said no, he wanted a "name," so the film was made with Lucia, who

---

[9] The "beautiful brunette" was later to change her name to Sophia Loren.

was not the right person for the role. She was too elegant, and she did not have enough "presence," as they now say about Mangano or Pampanini.[10]

Was it interesting to make a film about the world of Italian cinema?
No. I am not narcissistic nor do I have professional fetishes. I have never been fascinated by the idea of how the cinema reflects upon itself, nor by the idea of "quoting" other films or inspiring nostalgia for past films. *The Lady without Camellias* was a failure and I do not know why. What I know is that the public did not go to see it from the very first day that it was released. Cinema audiences are a real mystery to me. I haven't seen the film since, so I do not know how it turned out. I did like some sequences, especially the one of the extras' rollcall in Cinecittà, but in general I think that it did not turn out very well. As soon as I finish a film I try to forget it. Only a few of them have left their mark on me. One of these was *The Passenger*. While I was filming it, I discovered techniques and styles that were very personal to me and that I would have liked to further develop in my next film. Instead I have not been working for three years. It's the longest break that I have ever had in my life.

After Attempted Suicide, *an episode of* Love in the City, *you made* The Girlfriends, *which was all about women. Where did this lively and unusual interest in portraying female characters come from?*
Probably from my personal history. I have always been around women. When I was young, I had many girl cousins and I was always with them and their friends. Then there was my wife with her four sisters. And then there were my female friends and all of their girlfriends, and all of the actresses and their female "entourages." The problems that are common to women have always filled my house and my life. I would like to make a film called *Identification of a Woman* to express my love for and interest

---

[10] Silvana Mangano (1930–1989) and Silvana Pampanini (1927–) were two of Italy's most prominent actresses in the 1950s and 1960s. While Mangano's career developed into international acclaim, Pampanini's remained mostly tied to popular, frolicsome comedies.

in women through the relationship of one male character with many women. Women provide a much more subtle and uneasy filtering of reality than men do and they are much more capable of making sacrifices and feeling love. While living around women, I have often had moments of complete exasperation, and I have felt locked in, suffocated, with a strong urge to escape. And sometimes I did leave. The truth is that I still like women very much.

Did you like them enough to run the risk of making a film with five lead actresses?

The story for *The Girlfriends* came from Pavese's beautiful story *Among Women Only*, which I did not follow too closely. I like the complexities of a group relationship, the mixing together of different personalities, the coming and going of people. I really did like Turin, and I can't believe how it is changed now. All of the actresses and I got along very well. They loved and respected me. Making the film, however, was very difficult, with many mixups on the set, including several that involved me. Eleonora Rossi Drago was the "diva" of the moment and felt that she had to act as such, without success. Valentina Cortese was as beautiful as she is now, and I fought epic battles with her until I succeeded in convincing her to say her lines without mannerisms, maybe for the only time in her life. Yvonne Fourneaux was good, and Anna Maria Pancani was cheerful and full of life. The most support I had to give to Madeleine Fisher, who had the least amount of experience. She was chosen at the last moment, two days before we started the film, from a photograph in a fashion magazine. She was a model and I think she now lives in a commune. The filming was suspended several times because there was no money. The same happened with *The Cry*. Money was always the problem, while it seems to me that the best memories have always to do with human relations. We were less self-concerned, more relaxed, and we used to see each other more often. Today I feel oppression, depression, closure, fear in the people around me, especially in people involved in cinema who have gone through hard times. I instead feel quite content.

Did 1957, with The Cry, *mark the end of a "first stage" and the transition, with* L'avventura, *to another creative phase?*

I would say so, if I had not written the subjects of the two films at the same time and presented them both at the same time to the producer. He chose *The Cry*, and I think that he made a bad decision. The film brought me my first success in France, but it was not well-received in Italy, and I still do not understand why. I do not know whether it was good or bad, but it seemed to be adequately concise and balanced. I liked the sequence with all the lunatics—and almost all of them were lunatics in real life. I always got along well with mentally ill people. One of my uncles was mentally ill, and when I was a child the family entrusted him to me and we got along very well. Mentally ill people see things that we cannot see. I do not believe in reason too much. Reason does not provide happiness; reason does not explain the world, or love, or anything that is important. Who knows whether there was a reason behind the commercial failures of some of my films. It is possible that they were depressing or, more simply, that they were not rhetorical or melodramatic. I have always detested melodrama more than any other thing. I have lived through many melodramatic scenes in my work and in my life. But I have always restrained myself from showing my own feelings, and why shouldn't I have restrained my characters from showing their feelings?

Is it depressing or gratifying to once again see and discuss your old films?

This may sound trite, but it is true. I have always felt like the father of my films. You have your children, they grow up, and then they leave. Every so often we see them again, and sometimes these encounters are not too pleasant.

LIETTA TORNABUONI

THE HISTORY OF CINEMA
IS MADE ON FILM[11]

After seeing your films, one would never think that Antonioni had started in cinema as a documentarist. Was the experience of making documentaries helpful to you? Did it help to form your remarkable cinematic eye?

Let's leave these adjectives out of our discussion. They don't do any good. Making documentaries was very helpful to me because I did not know whether I was capable of making films. In making documentaries, I understood that I would be able to go on to make films that were as good as anyone else's.

In reexamining your documentaries, one can see that already then you were telling stories.

This is true in a certain sense. Without even realizing it, in *People of the Po Valley* I focused more on the family that lived on the barge than on the landscape. I must confess that I was completely taken with those people. Unfortunately, I could not complete the documentary. More than one thousand meters of film were destroyed, and the way the documentary was edited, in its present form, does not emphasize enough that subtle narrative trend that emerged during the filming.

---

[11] "La storia del cinema la fanno i film," from *Parla il cinema italiano*, edited by Aldo Tassone, Milan: Il formichiere, 1979. Translated by Dana Renga.

After a first experience that was in some way "neorealist"—your documentaries and, later on, Attempted Suicide, *your episode of* Love in the City—*you took off in a different direction. Were you aware that you were entering into new territory?*

No, I was not aware of it because during that time neorealism was not an issue. Before *People of the Po Valley* in 1943, Italian cinema did not portray the poor lower classes in such a harsh way (I am referring to the final part of the documentary which was lost). At that time, documentaries used to deal with places, works of art, the Charterhouse of Parma, the Abbey of Pomposa, the paintings by Canaletto, the valleys of Comacchio carefully cleared of any sign of hardship—anything but a sort of praise of [their staple industry,] the eel. These were the products of what was then the Istituto Luce. I instead went to the mouth of the Po river, placing at risk poor Minoccheri, who was my protector within the Istituto Luce and the only one who fought to let me do whatever I wanted. Let me say it again: these images were very harsh, representing the very difficult life of the fishermen, who lived at the mouth of the river in straw huts that would flood after every sea storm. That piece of land would become a mud slide. The fishermen would put their children on top of the tables inside of the huts to keep them from drowning, and they would attach bed sheets to the ceiling to absorb the water that came pouring down. Our cinema had carefully avoided representing those situations, as the fascist government prohibited them. I do not want to sound presumptuous, but I was the first person ever to portray them. No one really knows this, noone will admit it, but the fact that I invented my own brand of neorealism gives me a certain sense of satisfaction. Unfortunately, all of the film material was taken to the North of Italy by the fascists who had remained faithful to Mussolini [after the 1943 Armistice]. When the war ended, I went to get it back and I discovered it in a warehousewas, half ruined by the humidity. Now the documentary only portrays the beginning of the storm, which is a shame because the rest was truly impressive.

"In order to save neorealism, it must be internalized." What did you mean when you said this during the 1950s?

After the war, the relationship between individual and society was the only thing that mattered. That is why the filmmakers of that period (primarily Rossellini and De Sica) have given us an accurate account of those times in the form of documentaries and commentaries. Perhaps it went like this: when I see films that I really like, I feel as if I have received a shock, and in order to avoid the trap of imitating these films, I detach myself from them. Maybe that is why I chose to examine the inner side of my characters instead of their life in society, the effects inside them of what was happening outside. Consequently, while filming, I would follow them as much as I could, without ever letting the camera leave them. This is how the long takes of *Story of a Love Affair* and *The Vanquished* came about. At the time, everyone criticized me for avoiding social themes, for turning a deaf ear to the dialectics that were developing in somewhat violent terms. But I was just acting as a mediator between these social themes and the screen.

By examining the inner side of your characters, you developed the relationship between characters and environment in a new way. The environment, instead of being meaningful background, became more and more a character on its own.
I don't know. Certainly in *The Passenger* this element is very important. It's a surface that reflects the protagonist's life within the story.

On the other hand, the protagonist of L'avventura *is an environment that is completely estranged from the characters. It is a barren island, a rocky iceberg without any sign of life, scoured by the sun and the wind. How did you come up for the idea for this film?*
In an odd way, almost mysterious. I was on a yacht with some friends going toward an island in the Mediterranean. Some time before, a girl I knew in Rome had disappeared. A thorough search was conducted, but they found nothing. She had just disappeared. The idea for the film came to me all of a sudden while we were sailing toward that island. I said to myself, "What if that girl was on the island?" And that is where the idea came from. At the outset there is always an external, concrete element. At first the film was called *The Island*.

It seems to me that the landscape was used differently here than in your previous film, The Cry.

The landscape has a different function because the stories are different. In *L'avventura*, it is more mysterious because the story was a mystery. It is almost as if the landscape had feelings.

If I understand you correctly, you mean that a subject for a film comes from an irrational, poetic intuition.

How else, if not this way? In 1962, I was in Florence filming a solar eclipse. There was a silence different from all other silences, an ashen light, and then darkness—total stillness. I thought that during an eclipse even our feelings stop. Out of this came part of the idea for *The Eclipse*. Stories come to me every night, but I don't always write them down. Laziness is my worst weakness. I could have done so much more in cinema if I weren't so lazy. This character trait comes from my origins. We from Ferrara are apathetic, we just like to do nothing.

With The Cry *you were criticized for portraying a factory worker in an unrealistic manner.*

Well—I went to tell the story of *The Cry* to factory workers around Ferrara and also in Rome. They made some comments and I took note of them. For example, in the script, the scene where Aldo slaps his wife takes place in their house. As a good bourgeois, I thought that these things should be resolved at home. I was wrong. The workers told me that a man who acts in such a way is foolish—he should slap his wife in public to prove that he is a man. So, I followed their advice and shot the scene in the village's piazza. I think that it came out much better that way.

Why did you choose an American actor to play the part of a worker from the Polesine? Maybe this is what disturbed some critics.

The distributors definitely wanted a foreigner. They thought that an American name would be more appealing to the public. But I must say that I did like Steve Cochran in the film. If no one knew that he was

American, if his name had been "Sergio Michelini," no one would have objected to him.

The Cry was not one of your most modern works, but it seemed to be one of the most distressing, well-constructed, and sincere. You could feel there the immediacy of life and the depth of your more mature works.

The idea for the film came very naturally to me within just a few minutes. The day before I had read Cortázar's story, where I got the idea for *Blow-Up,* and I was already working on it. I went out for a walk and I stopped without any reason in front of a wall, and the plot for *The Cry* came into my head—this is a mystery to me.

Let's go back to your first films. Recently, the Italian television presented a retrospective of your first works, from the documentaries to The Cry. *How did you react seeing them now? Are you still convinced that* The Lady without Camellias *was not too good?*

I reacted very strangely to this film. I always thought of it as a mistake, but instead I discovered that it has a narrative balance of its own and also that it was filmed in a curious way—a very subdued way, with characters in insignificant situations and environments, as if I wanted to ignore their psychological motivations. I thought that it was a cold film and then instead I discovered that it was very warm, and precise, both sentimentally and psychologically. I think that I am praising myself a bit too much, excuse me.

Why did you call your first film Story of a Love Affair? *Story [in the Italian sense of* cronaca, *"chronicle"], is a word à la Rossellini, and it's tied to neorealism, from which you moved away since your very first film. Would it not be better to use the word "inquiry"?*

But it is a chronicle. It is a chronicle of a love story taking place at two different times and looked at very objectively. The French spoke of "interior realism." In fact, it is the intimate chronicle of a love affair. "Inquiry" does not seem like the correct word to me. The film probes into the souls of two characters.

Your second film should have been The White Sheik, *which Fellini ended up directing. Why didn't you do it?*

The White Sheik should have been my first film. While I waited for Ponti and his associate Mambretti to approve the script I went to Bomarzo, the "villa of the monsters," to make a documentary. I got sick at Bomarzo and had to stay in bed with an intense headache. I was very ill. I could not even tolerate the daylight. It was a situation which was horrible for me, but turned out to be great for Ponti and Mambretti's company. They told me that they were in trouble because Lux [the production company] had refused a script on Miss Italy by [Alberto] Lattuada, and they needed another story. Ponti really liked *The White Sheik* and proposed to buy it from me, promising to accept another film of mine. I did not know Ponti, then. It was the first time I had even been in contact with him and so I sold him the subject for practically nothing. Later he sent me a novel to read, but it was all a pretense. I made a film with Ponti sixteen years later, *Blow-Up*.

Was your version of The White Sheik *much different from the one Fellini made?*

Not very much, but the structure was different. I have to say one thing, and I hope Fellini doesn't mind. The opening titles did not say that the story was entirely mine, as it really is. However, in my script there was no precise plot, just a series of interconnected events. It was a rather free narration, a little like Federico's own films today. At the time, Fellini and [Tullio] Pinelli criticized the fragmentary quality of my stories.

Thematically, The White Sheik *seems to develop some elements of your short film* Lies of Love.

Yes, in fact I wanted to make the film with the same two actors who played in the documentary.

Since it is impossible to talk about all of your films, let's move on to the so-called "trilogy of alienation": L'avventura, La notte, *and* The Eclipse. *Besides being sentimental stories,* La notte *and* The Eclipse *are also cross-sections of a specific social climate, the rich bourgeoisie of Milan and Rome. These films could be interpreted today as indirect commentaries on the conditioning power of money in the Italian society of the economic boom. It is enough to think of the extraordinary scene at the Stock Exchange.*

In *The Eclipse,* money is seen from the viewpoint of those who do not have any, while in *La notte* everything happens independently of money. If I had to film *The Eclipse* today, I would make it even harsher.

Is it true that you wanted to make two different films out of The Eclipse?

Yes—one from the point of view of the woman, and the other from the point of view of the young stockbroker. I made a proposal to the producers to do two versions precisely to explore the question of money. Whoever lives within the Stock Exchange sees life through banknotes. The consequence of this is that even real feelings can be filtered through the cobweb money creates around the mind of whoever is involved in it and doesn't see anything else all day long. I wanted to tell the same story through his point of view, but the producers preferred to make only one film. What I wanted to do was not the same as what Bertolucci did with *1900,* which is a two-part story. My idea was to make two autonomous films.

In The Eclipse *there is a sort of correspondence. The emotional crisis is always related to the more general crisis affecting moral values.*

Yes, this might be true.

While speaking of Antonioni as the filmmaker of alienation, critics have overlooked that, in your films, the instability of feelings is closely connected to what Fitzgerald called "the hypertransitoriness of prosperity." Even if you deal more with effects than causes, as Strick points out, one cannot deny that there is a specific social representation in your films. Why do you think this second aspect has been neglected?

Maybe because I always dealt with it in a very discreet way, and also because I never took these terms much to heart.

In the opening sequences of some of your films, such as L'avventura *and* La notte, *the conclusion of the story is already anticipated. In a certain sense, when the couple in* La notte *visit the sickbed of their gravely ill friend, this alludes to the imminent death of their relationship.*

I cannot look at my films in this way. It seems to me that the opening sequence of *La notte* places the viewer in a specific atmosphere, giving him the opportunity to view the rest of the film from the right angle. It is also as if, from the beginning of the film, the two protagonists find themselves in front of a painful yet clarifying situation. I say all of this to answer your question, since at that time I was not dealing with these problems. It is very difficult for me—I hope that you realize this—to respond to what you asked me. I do not enjoy reviewing my earlier work. The history of cinema is made by films, not by the words of their directors. Too often the interviews become pretexts for unpleasant speeches.

I still have a few more questions. Please be patient. All of your films until Blow-Up, *with the exception of* The Cry, *all center around women. Your male characters (the architect in* L'avventura, *the writer in* La notte, *the stockbroker in* The Eclipse, *the engineer in* Red Desert*) are in general less positive, more morally insensitive.*

The architect in *L'avventura* seemed to me a strong character in his negativity. He is a professional who is going through a crisis, I would say, just like the writer in *La notte*. I think that in both films, you find a woman's point of view rather than a man's. Overall I feel more at ease with female characters than with male characters. At least, I have felt this way up to a certain moment. Starting with *Blow-Up*, I began to talk about men too.

L'avventura, La notte, The Eclipse, Red Desert *are all very strong testimonials to the Italy of the "economic miracle." How do you feel about the Italy of the economic boom, now that it is only a memory?*

Well, I think that Italy will always be involved in some sort of boom. It was enough to go out at Christmas time and see what was going on in the stores. Someone might prove me wrong, but that was what it looked like. That the motivations behind it might have been more complex, is certainly possible; but that's another story. In this concept that I am trying to explain—perhaps not too clearly—is the key to my documentary on China. I portrayed China through a series of images, not through the ideas that the Chinese wanted to give me about their country. Their social structures are abstract entities that call for a different visual discourse, more didactic than my own, so extemporaneous and instinctual. They were more fragile entities than they seemed to be, if it took just two years to modify them. There has not even been the need for a second revolution.

What you say about Chinese social structures can also can also be applied to [Joris] Ivens's film How Yukong Moved the Mountains, *which today, in light of the facts, seems out of date. It seems to me that Ivens saw China through ideological lenses, while you filmed it as you saw it. Since no one likes a bare truth, your film was criticized, while no one had any reservations about the idyllic vision of Chinese reality that was portrayed in Ivens's film. When I interviewed Ivens and his wife, Marceline Loridan, at the time of the film's release, I remember that she reproached you for making a film from the outside, without knowing the people. Loridan simply concluded: "How can the director of alienation understand the Chinese?"*

I think that my documentary gives an image of China of that time, with also a "prefiguration" of the China of today. But it is not for me to judge this. I remember that one day (Mao was still alive) I asked Ivens's wife: "Do social classes exist in China?" And she responded: "Of course they exist!" I should have replied: "Then why don't they appear in your documentary?" But that would have seemed too much of a naive question. And, after all, China is a very difficult subject.

When Zabriskie Point *was released you said to me: "I will never make another film in a country that I don't know." Did you mean that it is difficult to understand a country in a short time? It seems to me, however, that you did understand America, also from what the American critics wrote about your work.*

202 / THE ARCHITECTURE OF VISION

Years ago I took a trip to Northern Europe at the end of the fall. I took a helicopter to see how the people lived on one of a group of islands in Finland. During the summer, it was a resort place, while in the winter no one was there except for the indigenous people. There were two or three men who cut wood, a few women who cooked inside of their houses, a few children who were playing. Pines, birches, ice, snow, muffled voices, children laughing: a serene atmosphere that left me spellbound and at the same time disturbed.

If I had filmed a documentary in that part of Finland on that day, what would have been my method of operation? Which "truth" would I have expressed? Probably none at all, apart from the curiosity of those people who saw us. It is the usual sense of melancholy that I feel during some of my trips: of not being able to participate in the reality that I see; of always being an outsider and, as such, condemned to seeing a reality that is affected as soon as it comes into contact with my own. It is like studying a microcosm: while you observe a phenomenon, you change it, and the particle that you try to photograph changes its course. In other words, observing reality is only possible on a poetic level.

L'avventura, La notte *and* The Eclipse *have been referred to as the "trilogy of alienation." What do you think of this classification?*

I never talked about a trilogy, much less of alienation. I do not mean that these classifications do not make sense. But, there are four, not three, of my films that touch on that same topic. *Red Desert* also deals with an existential crisis.

Actually Red Desert *completes one discourse and at the same time opens another. Not only because it was your first film in color, but because it introduced new elements: the industrial civilization, and—why not—ecology.*

Yes, it is perhaps a film that anticipated the ecological theme. At that time no one talked about it.

Red Desert, *in addition to portraying a social class, also developed a detailed and profound analysis of the relationship between the individual and the environment, and between the individual and industrial society. Was this a conscious effort on your part?*

I faced these problems in a narrative way. The ecological problem had a lot to do with the story that I telling. The neurosis of these characters originated directly from the environment.

What did you mean when you then said that "factories are beautiful"?

Factories are extremely beautiful. So much so that in many architecture competitions the first prize often goes to factories, probably because they are places that offer the imagination a chance to show itself off. For example, they can profit from colors more than normal houses can. They profit from them in a functional way. If a pipe is painted green or yellow it is because it is necessary to know what it contains and to identify it in any part of the factory.

Here, too, as in many of your films, there is a character who wants to leave, to go far away. The desire to change one's skin, to change one's place, is one of the themes that returns in many of your films. Is there a reason behind this?

I am convinced that in the soul of every Italian there is a small desire, not so much to escape, but to have an adventure. People in Italy are bored. We are not very organized in terms of amusement, which is very important, especially for the young. Opportunities to play sports are scarce. This important outlet, which in America serves to channel sexual aggression, is lacking in Italy. Don't you think that there is a gamelike component in the criminality that has infested our country? I am convinced of it. The father of a twenty-year-old accused of belonging to the Red Brigades went to visit his son in jail. Upon leaving, he said: "He is still a boy who hardly knows how to hold a Molotov cocktail in his hand."

Do you think that the violence shown in cinema has had a negative influence on everyday life?

It isn't that cinema creates violence; it justifies it.

One time, speaking of Red Desert, *you said: "If today there is still some auto-biography left, it is in color that you can find it." Would you care to clarify this statement?*

I'll bring as an example a conversation I had a few days ago. What was behind that person while we were talking? A wall? A curtain? A painting? What color were those objects? If I now try to remember all of this, I do not see neat and precise images and colors like those you can see in a film's flashback. One has to invent the distortion of memory. This is what I meant by saying that one creates an autobiography by telling the colors of one's life, not only the events.

[Andrzej] Wajda told me that spectators watch primarily, if not solely, the faces of the actors—not the objects or the setting of the scene. With a close up of Brigitte Bardot nude, no one looks at the scenery. Instead, you always give a lot of importance to objects and settings.

Of course. But if next to a nude Brigitte Bardot you place a picture of the explosion of a bomb, all red and yellow, the spectator will look at it, too.

Your research with color has advanced a lot. How did the idea come to you for a "color of the mind," in Red Desert?

I am very interested in the dynamics of color. This is why I really like [Jackson] Pollock. His paintings have an extraordinary rhythm. I have always felt the need to use color in a functional way. I would like to make my next film with a video camera. In using magnetic tape there is a better control of color, there are many more possibilities than there are in working with film in a laboratory. In *Red Desert* I had to change the appearance of reality—of the water, of the streets, of the countryside. I had to paint them with real paint and brush. It was not easy. Violating reality is easy when you are in a studio, but it becomes a problem when you are outside. It is enough for some frost to ruin everything. I tinted an entire forest gray to make it seem like cement, but it rained and the color ran off. With video cameras, all of this can be done electronically; it is like painting a film.

Is this system already in use?

It has been used a few times, but it was a bit overdone. It is a system that lends itself to fun solutions, and it is easy to let it get out of control. *Don't you think that with video cameras, which offer so many opportunities in the use of color, better images will be achieved through the "composition"?*

I have to say that from *Blow-Up* on I tried to "compose" the images in my films less carefully than before. I think that the material always needs some help in its composition. But today this is no longer a problem. Everyone knows how to "film"—if not very well, then at least decently. The problem is something else. It has to do with identifying the material—a material which, in these years of crisis hitting our Western world, has been so traumatically stirred and changed. I think that we have to find different ways to make films. This issue is two-sided: one side deals with technique, and the other deals with subject matter. I will first touch upon the latter, which is not only the most important but also the basis for, the very premise of the former.

I confess that I do not have very clear ideas about subject matter. But it seems to me that, within the political and economic turmoil that characterizes this period of time, many alarming signals have surfaced. For example, the nature of happiness, which everyone used to aspire to, has changed. Now it is more of an animal-like, wilder type of happiness. Or it could be that people no longer pursue happiness. They choose instead to pursue other satisfactions, other tensions, which can give their lives some sort of purpose, regardless of what kind. I am also under the impression that today people no longer want to "figure things out." There are too many people who feel that the reality around them is unfamiliar, and they do not even want to get to know this reality because they feel that it would not solve anything. They hear over and over again that the world lacks ideals, that it lacks family or religious values. It seems that no one in this world has any reason to be one way or another, and that science, art, and morality do not exist any longer. It comes as no surprise that this new biological man rebels sometimes with a violence that is often criminal. It depends on the level of injustice that caused him to act. The violence of the oppressed against the oppressors is a well-known, legitimate argument—and ethics can go to hell! After all, who defines the crime? And on the basis of what value? Of a higher value? Or on the basis of those historical laws which humanity should obey if it doesn't want to annihilate itself?

From within his monodic solitude, man continues to act socially, thanks to an innate calling. But it is a calling that becomes more and more difficult to respond to.

Don't be surprised if I deal lightly with such problems. I'm just trying to find a conclusion that has to do with cinema. The consequences of this ethical confusion are even verifiable in everyday events, and that's where we find subject matter. It is a fact that human relationships today are not the same as they were in the past, and the stories and their endings have changed as well.

At the same time—and also, perhaps, independently—technology advances. The symptoms are already apparent. The laser disc will signify a big step forward. I have seen incredible things done with it. Certain experiments have shown that it is possible to project an image onto a screen that is no longer a screen, but a transparent threedimensional space. In this way, one can move around it and choose ones own visual angle. I really think that the future of cinema will be in science fiction.

Then the frame will no longer make sense. Or am I mistaken?

No, you are not mistaken. The viewers will be free to choose their own frame as they wish, their own visual angle. I have to add that this will probably be only an apparent freedom, in the sense that this participation can be induced and controlled. What will change, however, is our relationship with the public.

Will this take long?

Probably years. It will involve upsetting the current industry structure. This includes the film-material industries, the development and printing laboratories, the movie theaters. But no doubt this type of evolution will occur, because the means we now have to make films are inadequate, and no longer correspond to our needs or to the needs of the public.

People talked about "phenomenology" with regard to your films. Do you accept this term?

Even Enzo Paci[12] used to say it, but it does not really matter whether I accept it or not. Just think of the names that will have to be mentioned, from [Max] Scheler to [Edmund] Husserl to [Martin] Heidegger—I do not even think about it.

What about behaviorism? This term has also been mentioned with regard to both yourself and Rossellini.

I really think it is a bit forced on the part of the critics to try at all costs to qualify in this way an attitude of Rossellini's, which for him was very natural. The stamp of his style was precisely to refuse any sort of classification because his language was free, uncontrolled, disrespectful of syntactic rules. I think that this was exactly what was needed to represent the chaotic world at which he directed his camera. This is why Rossellini is one of the greatest directors of our time, because his style—which is a lack of style—was perfectly suited to the issues of that historical period.

Can you say the same about Godard? In a way Godard continued where Rossellini left off.

The same can be said of Godard in the sense that he is ingenious, he invented many things in the cinema. His style, however, fits the facts and the characters that he portrays, which are quite often tied to a very personal vision of the world. Rossellini instead looked at things with an eye that could be defined as "public." The horizon that Rossellini looked at was wider than Godard's. Rossellini's open-mindedness is disturbing.

Speaking of Rossellini, one cannot but bring up the "chronicle" issue.

It is true that Rossellini made chronicles, but they were fundamental. To "chronicle" was necessary at that time. When we speak of the past we say: "Chronicles tell—" They are what allows us to make history.

---

12 Italian philosopher Enzo Paci (1911–1976) played a fundamental role for the sudy and dissemination of Existentialism and Phenomenology in Italy.

In a certain sense, some of Rossellini's main themes in Stromboli, Europe '51 *and* Voyage to Italy *anticipated the issues some of your own films dealt with. Do you agree?*

Yes, especially *Voyage to Italy*. However, I do not think that they are the most penetrating things that he has done. The two films by Rossellini that I like best are *Paisan* and *The Flowers of St. Francis*. *The Flowers*, in particular, is wonderful. Of his last films, the most interesting is *The Rise to Power of Louis XIV*. There, the old Rossellini and the new Rossellini, who tended to be a little superficial, happily met. From this casual and hurried encounter, a film full of grace and eloquence emerged.

Have you worked with Rossellini?

Yes. I liked him as a person, even if he was such a big and empty talker. Not so empty, however, since he always knew, when he spoke, where he wanted to get. But he was an extraordinary speaker, a real captivator of audiences.

What is your favorite film by Visconti?

The one that left the greatest impression on me was *La terra trema*. *Ossessione* is a wonderful film, visually, while the dialogues are today a bit dated. Not because they are wrong, but because they no longer fit the images. It is because today we look at those images with different eyes.

It has been said a few times that Antonioni is the only modern novelist in cinema.

And where does this leave Visconti? Or, in a different way, Bertolucci? But while Bertolucci makes "films," Visconti, with an uncommon artistic temperament, illustrates novels. An exception must be made for *La terra trema*, which is, I repeat, an authentic cinematographic work.

Overall, Visconti illustrated yesterday's novels: [Camillo] Boito, [Albert] Camus, [Thomas] Mann, [Fëdor] Dostoevskij, and [Gabriele] D'Annunzio. Rocco [and His Brothers] *is an exception. You, on the other hand, do not illustrate. You write narratives with your camera, and you always deal with novels of today, if not of tomorrow.*

Camus is a contemporary, too. But the film *The Stranger* shows that this novel was not the right kind of novel for Visconti. As for myself, I can tell you that I try to "show" stories, and in showing them I tell them. Naturally, these stories thereby become something personal, even in their form. In Visconti, instead, there is the strength of the facts, a great deal of respect for what happened to others. I do not know—if you were to ask me the same question ten minutes from now, I might answer differently.

Blow-Up came from a story by a South American writer. Why did you set the film in London?

I read Cortázar's story, I liked it, and I wrote a subject, adapting it to myself. In Italy I did not find the right environment, so I went to London. It was the period of "Swinging London." That sparkling milieu, if I can call it that, was what I wanted.

Since the film dealt with the problem of knowledge, of whether reality can be attained or not, every viewer interpreted it in his own way. Was this what you wanted?

Blow-Up is a film that lends itself to many interpretations because the issue behind it is precisely the appearance of reality. Therefore, everyone can think what he wants.

You were, without a doubt, sympathetic toward the character of the photographer. Is the film in some way your ideal self-portrait?

I like the protagonist. I like his life. When I made the film, I also lived his sort of life and enjoyed it. It was a fun lifestyle, which I led only to follow the character, not because it was my own life.

What about the idea for the tennis match with no rackets and no balls?

You are asking where ideas come from. In general, ideas have a very confusing history. They come out of nowhere and then, little by little, they become more precise. I think this is what happens in poetry: words are born in the mind of the poet, and then they put themselves into place and they become verse.

Then, in the film, is reality only appearance? Is reality equal to appearance, illusion, dreams?

I would not say that the appearance of reality is equal to reality itself, because appearances can vary. There can also be many realities, but I am not sure about this, I do not believe it. Maybe reality is a relationship. I am not in the habit of thoroughly examining the themes of a film from a philosophical point of view; that is not my job.

In thinking of Blow-Up *and* The Passenger, *I'm prompted to ask what Pirandello represents for you.*

Pirandello remains very fascinating today, although the issues he raised are a little muddled and forced. On a practical level, nonetheless, if we examined people's lives today, many of Pirandello's dramas would turn out to be true in our foolish Italian society. Pirandello is among the writers who best understood our country, those who "most saw it live."

Besides your discovery of Camus and your experience with Carné, has France meant a lot in your life?

I have to say that I thoroughly studied French literature, poetry in particular. But then, when I moved on to English literature, I put my French studies aside. Maybe because I felt that English poetry adhered more directly to life. France has been a cultural experience, while the study of English literature, especially poetry has been a life experience. I felt that those works belonged more to reality, while the French works belonged to exceptional figures of a certain reality. Mallarmé has an extraordinary mind, but it is a mind, not the symbol of its age. It is just him, that is all. But maybe I am wrong. Or maybe you are wrong by wanting me to answer these questions. *During the 1960s someone defined you, with perhaps a hint of disappointment, as "the eternal experimental director." What effect did this ambiguous opinion have on you?*

I was flattered. Being experimental was a novelty, and since I consider art to be the pinnacle of novelty and beauty, to call me an experimentalist meant to call me an artist.

*Not knowing who to compare you to (since it is easier to compare other direc-
tors to you), a French critic compared you to [Orson] Welles. Maybe because
Welles was one of the greatest innovators in the history of modern cinema.*

Or maybe because he, too, always dealt with love stories.

Truffaut maintained that Welles was a "feminine" filmmaker.

Sometimes Truffaut says strange things. I find Welles very masculine
as an artist and a narrator. He deals with stories and characters in a mas-
culine way.

*Were there any directors who were an inspiration to you, when you were start-
ing out?*

I really liked Bresson's *Les Dames du Bois de Boulogne.* I liked his way of
"dodging" the main scenes; he let you see only the consequences of the
main scenes. What also seemed extraordinary was his way of enhancing
the characters against the environment. Certain full shots of Maria
Casarés remain unforgettable. Maybe this was also because Casarés was
an actress that was gifted with a unique presence.

*Of the French directors of the Golden Age, who left the biggest impression upon
you?*

I really loved Vigo's *À propos de Nice,*[13] which I think is a fantastic
documentary. Vigo was a man who made you love him through his
films. But, I think that the greatest of them all is Renoir. I believe he
made the most beautiful films of that time in his country: *The Rules of
the Game, La Marseillaise, Grand Illusion*; and then *La Chienne, Boudu
Saved from Drowning*—it is impossible to stop naming them.

*Let's talk a little about our national cinema. After Rossellini and Visconti, is
there another director that you like?*

13 Jean Vigo (1905–1934) was one of the most promising French filmmakers. His short-
lived career is best remebered for *L'Atalante* (1934).

I never said that I only liked Rossellini and Visconti. One day, just for fun, I made a list of Italian directors worthy of that name. The list was more than one hundred names long. The best are known by everyone: Fellini, Rosi, Petri, Ferreri, Bertolucci, Bellocchio, Olmi, the Taviani Brothers, Zurlini, Brusati, Vancini, etc. Someone who is often ignored, but who actually is an unusual director, is "Citto" Maselli.[14] He leads a rather reckless life and is involved in too many things. But he's someone who brings Italian cinema back to an original sensibility.

What do you think are Fellini's best films?

8 ½ and *Amarcord*. But also *The White Sheik, I vitelloni*, and certain episodes of *Casanova* (I would place the Roman episode among the best of Fellini, like the scene on the expressway in *Fellini's Roma*.) How is it possible to speak of Fellini in a few words?

What do you think of Italian comedy? This is not supposed to be a provocative question, because I know that you are an extremely open-minded viewer.

I am an attentive viewer, but when I go to a movie I like to laugh and be moved. After all, I am a rather candid viewer. I watch films with a candid eye. If Italian comedy is funny, I laugh.

What about the critics? I have a feeling that at the beginning the Italian critics did not help you as you deserved. No one said, for instance, that Story of a Love Affair *was a striking debut.*

In the beginning, the critics were more or less benevolent, as they only accused me of being over-refined, and therefore cold. Then they changed their stance and said that I was difficult. But they also praised me a lot, in Italy and abroad. I cannot complain about the critics, even though I often think that they praise me for the wrong reasons.

---

[14] Francesco Maselli began his career as assistant director in Antonioni's early films. He then went on to make his own features, such as one of the episodes of *Love in the City* and an adaptation of Moravia's *Gli indifferenti* [The Indifferents; 1963].

Among the many, and sometimes odd, learned references put forth by critics, there was an attempt to place you within the so-called école du *regard. According to these critics, you had carried on an experiment in the field of cinema similar to the one attempted in writing by authors like Robbe-Grillet, Simon, Butor, (i.e., the new relations between subject and object, the "primacy" of things, the restraint from proposing specific meanings, etc.). What do you have to say about this comparison?*

I must say honestly that when the French began to talk about the *école du regard* for my films, I had never read a *nouveau roman*. I read them later. I have always given a lot of importance to objects. Within a frame, the object can be as important as the characters. What is important is to influence the viewers to become aware of the objects as they are of the characters.

By now everyone knows that you write very well. Were you ever tempted to become a writer?

I enjoy writing. By this I mean putting one word after another, giving form to a thought that comes to my mind—almost always in inappropriate or not-too-precise words. The pieces that I do for *Corriere della sera* are very sincere. I remember that the first time I was tempted to write was while I was reading Gide's translation of [Conrad's] *Typhoon*. There is a passage that Gide translated very freely and that is more beautiful than in the original. For me, Conrad is a more important writer than Gide, but here, however, Gide had an intuition that Conrad had not had. Many times people have called me a formalist, and I cannot deny that I have always paid a great deal of attention to form. What I cannot understand is why one shouldn't. If you transform an object into an image, it's not only a question of form, but also a more subtle question that has to do with the relationship of things to the air, of things to the world. The world of reality is the concept that is always present in an image—that is, the world of those things that are seen, and the world of all that is behind those things.

Cinema is a mnenomic synthesis, which always presupposes in the memory of the viewer what is not present on the screen, or what happened before, as well as all of the possible developments of the present situation. That is why the best way to watch a film is to have it become a personal experience. At the moment in which we watch a film, we unconsciously evoke what is inside of us, our life, our joys and our pains, our thoughts— our "mental vision of the past and the present," as Susan Sontag would say.

Are there writers who meant a lot for you in your youth? And later on? In 1961, you mentioned Faulkner, Hemingway, Fitzgerald, Eliot, Pasternak—
I often changed. I was infatuated with Gide and I read all of his work in two months. Then I moved on; he was too much of a moralist. I do not think that I mentioned only the authors that you recalled. Many others were important to me, not only the classics but also minor authors like [Paul] Nizan, [Adelbert von] Chamisso, or even [Raymond] Chandler. Don't be surprised that I mention such different types of writers. My readings are very disorderly. After all, I do not think that there should be an absolute hierarchy in literature. By reading or by seeing films or pictures or buildings, I try to fill up those empty spaces that I think all of us face now and then as an abyss that opens in front of us. In this way, it is not the choice that counts, nor its quality. What one needs is material that can be used. It is like filling up ditches that we find in our path; you throw in a lot of fertile soil, but also other things, things that are found nearby, even in the trash. What is important is to refill the hole.

It seems like a wager. You talk about how feelings change, about how conscious-ness evolves through abstraction, through a fixity in the style of—the paintings by Piero della Francesca. This might sound naive, but this is what has always struck me in your work. I am thinking of Bernard Dort's observation: "In Antonioni's films all changes and nothing is transformed."
I like the reference to Piero della Francesca. Piero is my favorite painter.

Is this almost abstract fixity something that you consciously search for? (This is an attempt to force you out of your restraint, but maybe I shouldn't insist.)
A frame is never the fruit of reason, it is an instinctive choice. But to go back to Bernard Dort's observation—it is intriguing. How many

things do they see in my films! The other day I received a thousand-page manuscript from an American on *Red Desert*. I can't understand how so much can be written on one film.

You once stated: "First I became aware of a disease affecting the emotions and then of the actual emotions." What did you mean by this?
Whenever a relationship deteriorates, emotions come under discussion. When all is going well, nobody thinks of them. I meant it in that sense.

How closely can this disease of our emotions be connected to the type of society that we live in today?
Emotions are so fragile that they can become sick very easily, like human beings. It is not that you can easily say how they could get better. They would have perhaps to live in a healthier society. But then I wonder what is meant by a "healthier" society! Give me an example of a healthy society in the world.

Both Catholics and Marxists have criticized you at times for your "resigned sadness," "bitter psychologism," a will to categorically demonstrate that "the heart of man is a cemetery of feelings."
Literature has always dealt with sickness and pain. I do not think that there exists a great work that is motivated by joy or goodness. They say that goodness has no history.

An artist's political and social obligations are discussed more than his moral ones. Assuming that this distinction makes sense, what do you think is the most important obligation for an artist? Can an artist's work be detached from an "ethical" basis?
What's important is to be at peace with your conscience. That's all. I do not know if this means reasoning in ethical or political terms. I am sure that politicians rarely reason in this way.

Will you tell us something about the latest projects you are hoping to complete? We can begin, if you don't mind, with The Color of Feelings.

This film was intended to be a kind of small treatise on jealousy, viewed from an obsessive standpoint—that is, it was the story of a man obsessed by jealousy. The story developed on three levels: the level of reality, the level of memory, and the level of the imagination. This structure gave me the opportunity to, let me say, "color" the events in three different ways, according to each of the different levels they belonged to. I wanted to make this film with video cameras so as to have a wider range of effects. In agreement with Barthes, I also used fragments of his book *A Lover's Discourse. Fragments*. I sent him the script and he wrote me a very nice letter, with pertinent and flattering observations. One day I hope to pick up this project again, if someone doesn't do it before me.

Another project was a film I was going to make in the U.S.S.R. It was called *L'aquilone* [The Kite]. I traveled all over Russia scouting for locations, and in the end I stopped in Uzbekistan, in a city called Khiva, with a medieval historical center that is practically untouched. It was supposed to be a very costly film (it was a science-fiction fable), and although the Russians were prepared to give me all I needed, they could not have given me what they did not have: a special-effects crew like the Americans and the English could provide. So I had to give it up.

In conclusion, when you make a film, what do you worry about most?

The only thing I worry about is myself. I am never happy when I film; I do not know why. One of the rare times when I was happy was during the final explosion in *Zabriskie Point*. I was very tense, but happy. The audacity of the scene was so appealing! I hope this confession of mine will not be misinterpreted. I will steal a wonderful quotation from Chekhov's diary to make myself understood: "I was happy only once: under a parasol."

ALDO TASSONE

PROFESSION AGAINST[15]

I considered refusing the Golden Lion at the Venice Film Festival, but I could not come up with a good enough reason. I would have refused it on instinct alone. I have received many awards, at almost all the film festivals—Cannes, Venice, and Berlin. The only place I have not yet won is Moscow, but that's such a particular festival that I could do without. So, when I think of another Golden Lion added to the one I already have, it is already too much. I do not know how to say it—I mean, it puts me into a situation—that is, it gives me another responsibility in dealing with the past, and this is what bothers me. I do not want this responsibility. My films are what they are, I do not know if they deserve another Golden Lion or not, and I do not want to have to talk about it. This is how I feel about that prize.

Then what made you accept it?

I did it because it is very difficult to say no to Venice. It seems a bit presumptuous for me to say: "No, I do not need another award, I am already who I am." After all, I guess it is OK to have another one.

Maybe you don't like these festivals because they show films that no longer satisfy you as they did when you filmed them, films that you have regrets about. Have you ever thought about that?

---

[15] "Professione contro," from *Il Messaggero* 31 August 1983. Translated by Dana Renga; the original title of this article is modeled on the Italian title of *The Passanger*, "Professione: reporter."

Well, in my professional life I have regrets in the sense that when I see one of my films again I do not always like it. That is, I might not like the whole film, but rather just parts of it—certain sequences, or maybe its subject matter. I would not say that I am satisfied with the entire film. There has not been a film of mine that has completely satisfied me.

Not even one? What about The Girlfriends, The Cry, La notte, Red Desert, Identification of a Woman, The Passenger?

Well, *The Passenger* would have completely satisfied me if I had been able to include all of the parts that I was forced to cut out because of its length. And let's not talk of the final version for the English-speaking market which I cannot accept, and would have removed my name from, if I could have. But even the European edition—which is the one I signed, and which I consider the only acceptable version of the film— even that version, I believe, is mutilated because the story is not well explained. For example, a sequence is omitted that explains the relationship between the protagonist and his wife, thus making it possible to understand how the failure of their marriage has an impact. If I could have included that sequence, the narrative would have been much better.

Have you met many short-sighted producers?

One example might be the brothers who produced *The Eclipse* and cut the film's ending without letting me know. The ending might have seemed a little too long, but it actually worked because it left in the viewer certain feelings, a lingering sense of the whole story that had just been told. I have written all this in one of the stories in the collection *That Bowling Alley on the Tiber*—I don't know if you have read it

Yes, I read it while I was on vacation. The story you refer to is called, if I remember correctly, "Just to Be Together."

Ah, you read it on vacation—that's good. Yes, it is that story. I mean, one should not let a film end with its ending—it has to continue further, outside the theater, where we, the viewers, live: we who are actually the protagonists of all of the stories that are told. I mean that it is necessary for the film to have a longer life than its physical projection time. It needs to stay with the viewer and the viewer should take it away with him. Then, if the film remains inside the viewer, it means that the experience that the viewer had while watching the film was worthwhile.

Once you said: "In my youth, I would rise at dawn to get on the carts that went to the countryside and talk with the carters. I spent many evenings in the taverns with a lot of different people ." What did you learn?

Well, I can only answer after racking my brain, because many years have passed since then; I would say a whole lifetime. Indeed, everything that has happened later in my life has practically erased all of these memories, which remained in what I would call the "fog of my infancy." What did I learn? I think those encounters helped me to understand people. My family belonged to the lower middle class; my father was a petit bourgeois, and my father's friends who used to come to our house were petit bourgeois. I, on the other hand, was more fond of—I had friends among the lower class. Even in my love affairs, I have always preferred women from the lower class, rather than from the middle class; I don't know why, but I liked them more. I think that what I am getting at is that I preferred poor clothes on a girl rather than rich ones. Yes, people from the lower class were more genuine, more sincere—at that time, of course. In a certain sense, I was drawn to my parent's poor origins, since also my parents came from the working class. They were, let's say, self taught bourgeois.

And what moral lessons did you get from your family?

Honesty, I would say. My father was a man who was truly honest. I think that, overall, I learned this from him. And he was a hard worker. I must say that I am less of a hard worker than he was, because in my line of work there are forced breaks that sometimes make me very nervous .. . and this is the reason why . . . I have written this book, or painted the pictures for the show that opens tomorrow at the Correr Museum, here in Venice, and then will travel to the Gallery of Modern Art in Rome. They are exclusively mountains, and I called them "The Enchanted

Mountains." They are small designs that I enlarged through the technique of blow-up. I cannot stay idle; I have to constantly be doing things. Since I work within a creative field, I continue along the same route.

You have been writing stories since you were a boy. You wrote, or began to write, a novel when you were forty. You wrote some plays. Why have you chosen to express yourself primarily through the visual image rather than through literature?

Because, instinctively, I feel more drawn toward this form of expression than towards the written word. The written word has always been harder for me, even if I more or less know how to hold a pen in my hand. I did not think I had the cultural background that was needed to become a real writer. I even had problems in school, so that from the *liceo* I had to transfer to a vocational high-school. Then, at the university I studied economics and business. So I really did not think, maybe wrongly, that I was good enough to become a writer. I then realized that, actually—this is something I realized while reading, studying foreign literatures. In America, for instance, a lot of writers come from the lower classes. They have learned to write in a style that was different from the academic teaching. Anyway, I have to say that I am more suited for the world of images than for the written word.

When you were young, did you often go to the cinema?

Oh, I don't know when I began to go regularly. Yes, when I was young, I went often and I liked it a lot. I quickly fell in love with that type of spectacle, which in the small town of Ferrara was one of the few forms of entertainment that were available.

Did you have mentors, models who inspired you when you began to direct?

I would say that the only thing I might have learned—but without realizing it at that moment—was also the only thing I liked: the refusal to have main scenes that I saw in Bresson's films. *Les Dames du Bois de Boulogne*, a film that I really liked, showed the consequences of the main scenes, the consequences of the conflicts, but it never allowed you to see the actual conflicts. I began under Carné, it was my second job as assistant director. The first one did not count, because it was with a director who was working on his first film, and he did not influence me, even if my experience with him allowed me to go to France. I went there to work with Carné because of [Ubaldo] Arata, who was the director of photography on *I due Foscari*. He spoke well of me to Scalera, the head of the production company we both worked for, and Scalera sent me to France with Carné. So my career started this way. As for Carné, I continually disagreed with what he did. The only thing I appreciated about him was how he positioned the camera, it was always perfect. But I felt that, as a persona, he was uninteresting.

You had many romantic experiences when you were a boy, and—
—also when I was older.

Even when you were older. How many of these experiences did you put on film?
Well, I think that in every film one includes always something of oneself. I would not say complete characters, since I would not know where to find, in any of my films, models that were important in my life. And yet, in all of my films, a part of these stories is certainly present—a piece of one character, a piece of another, and in the end you may even find a complete character. But I could not say which different pieces make up a specific character and, if so, which character would emerge.

In La Stampa, *Stefano Reggiani wrote: "In his maturity he still feels that his films present a challenge." Are you doing this in order to prove that you exist, like [Vittorio] Gassman?*
No, I do not have this problem. Reggiani said that after seeing the films, and I think it is true. To me, a film always presents itself to me as something to be done "against" someone, even "against" myself. The first challenge that one takes up is "against" oneself; it is a creative effort, you know? The challenge, therefore, consists of this effort. It is not easy to have to face this problem every morning while getting ready to film. I ask myself: "What should I say, what do I have to say, and how will I say it?"

Then, our everyday challenge, and—if we are sincere in trying to solve these problems, this daily problem—our autobiographical intentions, consist in this effort.

Has it ever happened that you go on the set and do not know what to say and how to say it?

When I enter the set or go on location, I prefer to arrive in a state of complete "virginity," so that I can improvise, and so that the first ideas that come to me are those that I film. If I have to think too much about a scene—which sometimes happens because I have to resolve very difficult and complex technical problems—I first have to discuss it with my cameraman, with the director of photography, with the director of production, etc. In this case I am forced to think about it first. But in general I prefer to not think about it.

Are the ideas that come to you when you improvise, always good?

Not always, not always. Indeed there are parts in my films, as I was telling you before, that today I would film in a different way. Let me give you an example. Two young men were doing a TV program on *L'avventura* and they asked me to return to Lisca Bianca—the small island where I shot most of the film, and to shoot some footage there. That's what I did in the middle of July and I must admit that the impact was very strong because . . . that island rejected me. Actually, I was the one who felt rejected; it wasn't the island. Obviously, the island wasn't doing anything; so I was the one who felt that what I was doing there at that time was totally useless and rather unbearable. I no longer wanted to be there.

Most likely, this was also due to the fact that you were dealing with a part of your life that had gone?

Well, yes, certainly. Perhaps behind this negative feeling there was also that idea: that it was a piece of my life that no longer belonged to me. So I did not see the reason why I still had to deal with it. I filmed what I was asked to do, keeping myself as removed from it as possible.

Of all the things that time takes away from you, what do you feel is the most unbearable?

In general, it is unbearable to see how, all too often, we throw away all of our feelings or we don't take care of them enough. I mean that as soon as we feel that a relationship may be ending, instead of trying to keep it going, we conclude that it is over and look for another. Sometimes things work out fine, but other times they don't. We do not find another partner and we have lost the first one. And the most unbearable part of it is that, after going on like this for a while, we feel so lonely that life becomes very painful for us.

What is it that grows old, other than your age?

I think that people feel old when they think they are old.

Is that also true for illness?

No, illness is something that either is here or is not. Even with old age, one can be physically old and yet not feel it in spirit. . . . The spirit may neutralize the physical side. With illness, however, even if you want to believe that you are not sick, once you are sick, you really are sick. Well, of course there are psychosomatic illnesses, and in this case it is evident that what counts is realizing that you are not ill.

What is it, then, that helps, as the years go by? Intellectual curiosity, interest for traveling or—?

There are still many things I want to do. If my age allowed it, I would go to the moon tomorrow. I'd really like to see these new worlds, to see what they are all about—to see, for example if they have new colors. It could be so, you know? There might even be new forms of life. It would be extraordinary! These new landscapes, these new views shown in the photographs taken by the astronauts are of exceptional interest to me. Right after finishing *Blow-Up*, I took a long trip to the States and I went to Cape Kennedy. They put on me that equipment they use to simulate lunar landings. That experience was unique. It was one of the best experiences of my life to find myself up there, pretending to land on the moon.

New things are all—
—exciting, very exciting. For example, I would very much like to experience working with laser. I know that in San Francisco there is a team that is doing it, and I would really like to follow them. That's why I made *The Mystery of Oberwald* using only electronic colors—what Coppola says he did, but instead did not do.

What angers you the most?
Obviously, I am most angered about being the age that I am—that is, seventy years old and no longer young. If I were younger, I would have more time to experiment. Anyway, I will get as far as I can.

Do you like to waste money?
Do I like to waste money? Well, I would not say that I have this problem: I believe that I spend everything I earn, but I do not think I am being wasteful. I spend for my own enjoyment, but I do not waste anything. I spend — yes, I would call it spending. Yes, I like to spend—of course, when I have the means to do so.

Cinema did not reward you too well?
Ah, no, not at all. I could have made myself rich, but I didn't. After *Blow-Up*—a film that, as you know, earned a lot of money—I had fantastic offers that I refused, because I did not agree with the subjects of the proposed films. Instead, after *Zabriskie Point*—a film that did not go over very well—I went through a difficult time. It's always like that. I could have made a lot of money from the fantastic offers that I had, and then go on to become my own producer. I did not do that. Evidently, I am not a practical man.

Do you think this is one of the mistakes you made in your life?
I would say so.

Do you regret other things?
Many. But I prefer not to think about them.

Do you feel any remorse?

I know the answer to this question, but I will not tell you—I cannot tell you. I did something evil once that could have been avoided. But I can not talk about it.

What is missing from your "adventure"?

Oh, my goodness, what a difficult question! Well, I do not even know how to respond. I cannot say that I have had everything I wanted. But I cannot complain either. I don't know what I am missing—maybe I am missing a bit of madness, that's it.

LUIGI VACCARI

Ten Questions[16]

Your first film, Story of a Love Affair, *is a love story where the individual personalities are confused one within the other, and fused within a love story.* Identification of a Woman, *besides representing your own personal quest to define different behaviors, is the story of three possibly irreconcilable personalities, each caught within a solitary search of its own. It is no longer a love story. You do not identify yourself with the lover, but with the artist.*

It would be worthwhile to discuss this type of question, which asks me to dissect two of my films (my first and my last) into so many pieces, each of them suggesting a different concept: sociological, critical, psychoanalytical, philosophical, etc. It is something I never do, something I do not know how to do. My answer, supposing that you did ask a question and not simply express an opinion, is very simple. I never identify myself with my films. I live with them emotionally, but I always observe them from that distance which is part of the function of "narrating."

Do you ever miss the way that love stories used to be lived in the past? Do you think that these are difficult times for love?

Our times are difficult for everything. But I do not miss the love stories of the past. Today, what in the nineteenth century was called a "passion" makes me smile. It is true that people still kill for love, but I am sure that if we went deeper into events of this kind, we would find that there are

16 "Dieci domande," transcript of a press conference for the presentation of *Story of a Love Affair* in Paris, 27 March 1985. Translated by Dana Renga.

many other factors involved other than love. For example, the need to find a house is part of the difficulties that a couple must deal with when they want to marry.

At certain times, it seems to me that you associates women with what is incomprehensible and with a behavior that is unintelligible to men. Is this, then, a type of association that bids woman farewell as if she were a thing of the past?
It is impossible for a man to always and completely understand the behavior of the women with whom he is involved. Let's consider for a moment the working class, to see what happens with them. The Italian working class is notoriously uncultured and scarcely educated. Therefore, they react very instinctively. I do not think that they ever deal with the problem of understanding the mechanisms, or even less the psychology, of their relationships, or the behavior of whoever belongs to their social and private environment. A member of the proletariat lives through his own stories, most of all his love stories. Nobody bids farewell to woman then, in any sense. Woman and her relationship with man have always been the basic topic of world's literature, from its beginning. In my opinion it will continue this way even when people have gone to live on other planets.

In Identification of a Woman, *there are two women. Why did you feel the need to represent one woman through two female characters? What comparisons and contrasts can be made between them? What does their behavior as women have in common?*
Wait a moment, I do not establish the identity of any woman in the film. In the film there is one character who attempts to ascertain the identity of another character. It must not be forgotten that the protagonist is a film director who wants to make a film centered around a female figure. As is usual, this figure is not clear in his own head, and therefore he confuses the models with their prototype. In other words, he confuses the women he meets in real life with those he meets in his imagination.

The two women belong to two different social classes. Do you think that social position influences how a woman will behave with a man?

How could it not influence it? Do you think that the education we receive and the environment where we grow up do not condition our psychology, our mentality? Our behavior is not something that is external to us. But these are all things that I never think about. What I say on a theoretical level is not to be taken as the gospel truth. Especially when the topic has to do with love. I am no Stendhal, nor am I Ortega y Gasset.

Once you said to me: "A woman is a more subtle filter of reality." Then, another time: "A woman has two lives, or two different epochs in her life"—(one that is tied to love and sexual reproduction, and is therefore intimate and personal, and one that is social, possibly tied to activity, to work, to the external world.) Do you think this is an advantage? Has it always been this way for women, or do you see this now more specifically? Is this a disadvantage, a problem for men?

I think that woman is inclined to have a deeper perception of what happens around her than man has. Possibly this is due to the fact (but I may be completely wrong) that she is used to "receive." Just as she "receives" man into herself and because her pleasure consists precisely in this "receiving," then I would dare to say that she is even naturally prepared to "receive" reality in this absolutely feminine way. Woman has, more than man, greater possibilities of finding solutions suitable to the circumstances. I do not think that this is to man's disadvantage. On the contrary, very often he counts on it.

What do you think of women artists? Do you think that a woman would be able to "identify a man," as you do with women? Would she want to?
Virginia Woolf did it. So did Simone de Beauvoir.

Do you think that a woman is more bound to autobiography in artistic expression, more driven to look inside of herself, to begin from within herself, than a man is?
I do not believe in these types of distinctions. Whoever is driven to self-expression through autobiography does not obey physiological urges. I want to say that it is not a question of gender. One obeys a need to be

sincere in the best of cases, or a need for exhibitionism, masochism, or gossip in the worst of them. *Identification of a Woman* is not an autobiographical film. The events that I recount never happened to me. We all have had, and still have, our own stories, whether they deal with love or not. Therefore, if anything, it is the experience that is gained during the course of these stories that we all have in common. The character of the film director and I share the need to express ourselves through cinema. I do not believe in autobiography, in the same sense that I do not believe in the sincerity of a diary. It is always the author who chooses what to say, and what prevails is always the material that is useful in giving a certain image of oneself. Whatever material is not needed is left, instinctively or deliberately, aside. Life, on the other hand, is made up of both types of material, combined together. Even if Gide did everything to appear ruthless toward himself in *L'Immoraliste*, I believe that the sense of remorse that results from the book is purely literary.

It has been said that your films are always also documentaries. Do you think that a fusion of these two types of cinema is possible or desirable? Do you think that in cinema, contemporary reality must be portrayed?

All films are more or less documentaries. Let's say that when the subject matter of the film is contemporary, the camera documents it. In the case of period films, more violence is exercised on reality, but this is legitimate in any creative operation.

One time you asked me: "Is it too sentimental to position the camera only and always where we are?" How would you now answer this question of yours? In this film, did you not position the camera exactly where you are?

I placed it nearby, as I always do. If I could, I would sleep with the camera at my side in order to document what happens while I am absent, while I am sleeping, and also what happens to me. Why not?

CONVERSATION[17]

Having seen your films, especially Red Desert, *the show of "Enchanted Mountains" didn't surprise me at all. I know you have always been a painter. Do you think there is a close relationship between painting and cinema?*

No, I think that cinema is very close to all forms of art—in a sense, it is the culmination of them all. It is a richer, fuller medium. Through cinema it is possible to tell what is true and what isn't, what is beautiful and what isn't—everything, truth and lies. The only thing that matters is to be convincing on screen. At that point there is no longer any true or false; all that's left is cinema on a blank screen, and that is extraordinary.

How did you come to painting?

I painted when I was young and I kept it up as a student; I enjoyed it. I did portraits (of my mother and father, Greta Garbo, Charlie Chaplin), I did architectural drawings. But I never had any artistic ambitions. Then, when I was working on *Red Desert,* I took up my brushes again in order to refamiliarize myself with color. And in the last few years I have gone back to painting again, taking advantage of the fact that I could not make films, since my inner rhythm is different from what the film industry requires.

But I suppose it was really curiosity that brought me back to painting. I began with abstract things. One day I was putting together the bits of

[17] From *Positif* 292, June 1985. Translated by Andrew Taylor.

a painting that had been ripped to pieces, and I realized that they were mountains. Such fun! One of those paintings, looked at under a magnifying glass, gave me a really odd feeling—I was fascinated by the material. And since I had always wanted to explore the hidden side of what appears to the naked eye, I decided to photograph it and enlarge it, using a procedure similar to what I used for *Blow-Up*. Photographic enlargement modifies some effects, changes certain relationships with the object, gives colors a different tonality. It's a bit like putting a piece of pottery into a kiln: you never know what's going to come out of it. Naturally, experience is a big help; more and more, you get to anticipate what the transformation will be. But there's never any lack of surprises! What strikes me most is that in this way one really comes to grips with the materials of the painting.

Your original paintings are very small, about the size of a postcard. Why is that?

Because my studio isn't very big! And besides, I don't like painting at an easel. Moreover, I like working with small sizes. It only increases the surprise when you come to enlarging them. I'm not a painter—more a filmmaker who paints. The finished work is not the postcard-sized piece, but the enlargement of it.

In that case, it was almost an accident that you came to work on mountains.

I love mountains, so probably my choice was instinctive. But certainly, enlargements are a long and delicate process: you have to go through a whole lot of tests in the lab before you get to the finished thing. That's why it's not possible for me to paint while I'm working on a film—I can't do two things at once. It's strange that for those little "dabblings" I got better reviews than for my films! By the way, I've also done some "enchanted valleys" which I personally prefer to my mountains (I was born in a city in the Po Valley)—but I'm not going to bore you with Antonioni's different "periods"!

Are there any painters who have particularly influenced you?

Well, I do like painting, but I can honestly say that I haven't been influenced by any one painter in particular. The same goes for the cinema too. Perhaps, at a certain time, I was influenced by one of Robert Bresson's films, though just one—*Les Dames du Bois de Boulogne*—but not by any others. When I start on a film, I try to forget everything that I've read or seen. As Wittgenstein used to say, it is very hard to see what we have in front of us. What we have to do, therefore, is to forget everything and follow what we have inside us.

That is the same advice you gave to students at film schools last March when you were at the Cinémathèque of the Palais de Chaillot. Without meaning to, you astonished everybody.

They kept talking about citations, as if cinema was something that you could learn how to do by looking at other films. "What citations do you need?," I asked. "You take the camera, you go down into the street, and you just start shooting! You can go to school later, after you've found out whether or not you have any talent." What other advice could I give to students? I was honest with them, but I don't know if they really understood what I was saying. Certainly, all of us have to acquire a certain amount of cultural cross references but that's not what really counts. As far as I'm concerned, if I see a film I like I try and forget about it as quickly as possible so that I'm not influenced by it. For an artist, imitation is death.

You photograph your miniature paintings and then enlarge them, so one could almost say that the process is in some way akin to cinema. Not even with your stories of That Bowling Alley on the Tiber *did you really abandon the style of the cinema.*

That's true. The stories are rough drafts of film scripts, which in my mind took the form of narratives — so I suppose you could say that they are "films in writing." Anyway, neither painting nor writing are activities which I would consider extraneous to filmmaking. Those stories aren't that old: I began publishing them in *Corriere della Sera* four years ago. I wrote "Four men at Sea"—the subject of *The Crew*—while driving from

Tehran to Chiraz. In the desert we ran into an incredible snowstorm, but there I was, sitting quietly and writing a story about the sea!

In that story you recall the influence of Conrad.

Conrad is certainly one of the writers whom I most admire. In my life I have had several literary love-affairs—with Gide, Camus, Pavese, Faulkner, Eliot. My passion for Conrad was among the most intense; Gide on the other hand is a lost love. I think many modern writers owe a lot to Conrad, especially Faulkner. Conrad has an extraordinarily subtle psychological insight, a very poetic style of writing, never overbearing, always quite low-key. But I loved Faulkner, too. I have to say that American literature has given me a lot. Recently I read a brilliant book by Joan Didion, a sort of documentary about El Salvador. It's called *Democracy,* and its an excellent book, somewhere between Fitzgerald and Gertrude Stein in terms of style.

In your book, you cite just one French author: Roland Barthes.

We were good friends. He wrote a short piece, "Dear Antonioni," which is perhaps the best thing that's ever been written about me. He was an incredibly sweet and sensitive person. Barthes was not just a very cultured man, he was a real artist, too. His essays are full of truly poetic insights. And that was actually his problem, the inability to be just an essayist. For a while I thought I might use some passages out of *A Lover's Discourse: Fragments* for a film about jealousy, based on a story by Italo Calvino. It wasn't going to be a film with a normal plot, but something more literary: the characters were simultaneously aware of their discussions about love and of what love is in the real world, and from this a sort of comparison of the two emerged. However, I never completed that project, and it was partially my fault. I would have needed Roland Barthes's help, but he had just recently died.

You wrote in one of your stories: "I rarely think about my youth." Is that true?

It's the future I'm really interested in. Kierkegaard wrote somewhere: "When you want to understand life, you look at the past; when you want to live, you look to the future." At my age, you've only got one option: the days to come must be better than those that have gone before, otherwise you'll just go crazy.

Much has been said about Antonioni's "sadness" and "anxiety." Now that I know you better, it doesn't seem that you are either sad or despairing.

Well, I may not be a manic depressive, but I certainly do have my little problems! In any case, my last film, *Identification of a Woman*, isn't despairing. The fact of describing in one's works the frailty of human sentiments, the supposed "alienation" and tragedy of human existence doesn't necessarily mean that the author himself is despairing or "alienated" from the human race. On the contrary, whenever people talk about alienation, they forget that there are many forms of it. There is the one that Marx talked about, then Freud's version of it, and also Hegel's. As for me, alienation is not an essay topic. In my films I don't want to prove a thesis, just tell a story, and the meaning of these stories is something that comes afterwards, at the end of the film. While I am making a film I try not to think, otherwise I would feel so strongly inhibited that I would never achieve anything.

How do you start off making a film?

From my observations of real life. This sort of observation becomes a kind of spiritual nourishment, food for thought. To create a work of art doesn't mean to invent things out of nothing, but rather to transform what already exists according to your own nature, your own personal style.

Are you against adaptations of literary works?

I don't think it matters where the idea for a film comes from: it can come from a book, from a conversation with a friend, from a short story. The fact that a film is based on a novel may help initially but after a while it becomes an obstacle. I realized this when I was working on *The Girlfriends*. "Among Women Alone," the story by Pavese that inspired this film was very literary. Pavese's images are all connected to words and

I had great difficulty in translating those literary images into cinematographic images.

Sometimes you have been criticized for not making films with a social or political message.

It's true that I've never had any social or political commitments. I think people are the most important thing in the world. Naturally, living in this society, I am partly influenced by what happens around me. But I do try to avoid being conditioned by it. Borges writes that "time is the material of eternity." On another level, you could say that men, individuals, are the material of society. One of the reasons why I do not particularly love political films is that they are made up of just "moments of strength"; I mean, events are presented one after the other with such insistence that in the end they don't seem real. Life is also made up of pauses, transitions, silences. And in political films no space is given to such moments as these. Without the "transitional moments," which as far as I can see are the most authentic part of human experience, a story loses its interest.

I know that you often go to the cinema. Which current directors do you prefer?

My tastes are very fickle. And anyway, it's the films that interest me more than the directors. (Even "great" directors can make a bad film, every now and then). Let's say—and this isn't an exhaustive list—that I'm interested in Bergman, Altman, Fellini, Woody Allen. I thought, for example, that Fellini's latest film, *And the Ship Sails On,* was absolutely splendid. It's the work of a director who knows what he wants and how to achieve it on film. Apparently, nothing extraordinary happens on board that ship; after all, nothing really unusual *can* happen on a ship. In the space of a few days the passengers get to know each other. And yet, of course, there are all sorts of things going on—from individual existential crises to conflict between social classes to political conspiracies to war. In that film you see all life represented; it caught my attention right from the beginning. It's a very perceptive work, conducted with great intelligence and "discretion," without any of the pompousness that Fellini doesn't always manage to avoid. You feel that the filmmaker is looking at the world with a great deal of respect. After *8 ½* it's my favorite film by Fellini.

You're not like those critics who, if they admire Antonioni, seem to almost hate Fellini.

Fellini is an outstanding filmmaker. Very few people work with as much skill as he does.

Even though, unlike Fellini, you never talk about your personal memories, the name of your native city, Ferrara, does occur often in your stories of That Bowling Alley on the Tiber.

Ferrara is a very funny city, beautiful and mysterious at the same time. In the fifteenth and sixteenth centuries it was one of the liveliest places in Europe. The Este Court played host to [Ludovico] Ariosto, [Torquato] Tasso, and [Pietro] Bembo (a famous poet and scholar), and to other very important architects and painters (there was a very original style of Ferrarese painting, the school of Cosmè Tura, Federico del Cossa, Ercole de' Roberti, and Dosso Dossi). It was also quite an irreligious place: in the famous Renaissance palace of Schifanoia, where—as the name suggests people went to get away from boredom—there are several paintings in which knights are shown with their hands up ladies' dresses and that sort of thing. It's a city with a very important artistic tradition. In the twentieth century, painters like [Filippo] De Pisis and [Giorgio] De Chirico, Futurists like [Achille] Funi and [Fortunato] Depero lived there. Strangely, under fascism, this tremendous cultural ferment died away, and almost nothing was left. There were three or four of us left, Giorgio Bassani, Lanfranco Caretti, and myself, who made up a sort of "literary salon." During our meetings—we were students back then—we used to read aloud what we wrote. I have to say that at the time, Bassani (who later went on to write *The Garden of the Finzi-Continis*) didn't write at all well. It used to make me mad, because I was responsible for the literary page of the local newspaper and he used to send me articles that were written in such a contorted style that I had to correct them myself. Then he became a real writer and I got sidetracked with cinema!

Caretti, one of the members of the group you just mentioned, told me that in those days you were famous for your "silences." "Everybody talked about Antonioni's silences," he said. But silences are also important in your films.

Yes, that's true. I really like keeping quiet and watching the world go by, and in films I like the moments when, apparently, nothing is happening. I also wrote a story, "Silence," in which an entire film was based on silence. It's the story of a husband and wife who tell each other just a few very intimate things, at the beginning, and after that they have nothing left to say to each other.

Reading the first story in your book, "The Horizon of Events," one notices a great curiosity for science. I really like that story.

I like it too. Yes, I have a great passion for science, pure science. Although it is very exact and concrete, science always carries with it an extraordinary element of uncertainty. One never knows anything definitively, you can never say you've "understood," there's never any end to it; every time you start to get somewhere, there's always something new, another horizon, that presents itself to you.

You also have a great passion for science fiction, I believe. Some years ago, you were supposed to be making a science fiction film in the Soviet Union, L'aquilone [The Kite].

I'm working on another one, with Ponti and Sophia Loren. The film is based on a beautiful story by an America writer, Jack Finley, and is called *Destination Verna*. It's the story of a middle-aged woman who doesn't expect anything more out of life. And then, one fine day, they say to her: "There's a seat in a spaceship going to the planet Verna, a marvelous place, a sort of earthly Paradise." And she asks: "But how do you get there?" The planet Verna is outside the solar system and the distance is such that the woman decides not to go. It is the last big opportunity of her life, but she lets it go by because it would be a one-way trip and she's afraid of burning her boats behind her. It's a very understandable reaction. If you asked the average man: "What are you doing here? Wouldn't you like to go to a Heaven-like place? This is a golden opportunity for you"—very few would have the courage to confront the unknown and drop everything, even though they might complain about their condition down here on Earth. They prefer to live with despair down here rather than confront the unknown. That's a very human feeling.

Do you keep abreast of the latest scientific developments?
I try to, whenever I have enough time left over from making films to read. Because the problem is, every time you finish a film, you always have another one in mind. And in that case, the more you read the more confused you become. That's the way it goes.

"When I begin a film, another one always pops into my mind." You wrote that in your book of short stories.
It's very true.

How many projects do you have in hand at the moment?
Four! *Destination Verna, The Crew, Two Telegrams* (its plot is taken from a story in *That Bowling Alley on the Tiber*—in the story there is just the basic situation, but in the film there will be a complete narrative with characters). And then I'm also working on a film for Italian TV about St. Francis of Assisi.

It's difficult to imagine how a layman such as yourself can make a film about the saint of "The Flowers."
On the contrary, maybe a layman such as myself has a more detached view of the man and of that period of history, and for this reason is able to be more objective and interesting to the public. In any case, real Franciscans don't like "The Flowers" because they think they are too saccharine, too romantic—in short, not authentic. Instead, I have followed some of their suggestions and have stuck closely to documented facts. (I made an in-depth study before I wrote the screenplay). Those same Franciscans appreciate that I have represented the character of Francis in opposition to the corruption of the Middle Ages and the atmosphere of violence on which it fed.

Those were the years of the wars between Perugia and Assisi. Francis, too, had taken part in one of those battles. The Perugian knights were on the Pope's side, and went into battle with beautiful golden armor, while the others were on the side of the poor people. In those days, corruption was widespread, even at the highest levels of the Church. For example, there were wandering nuns, women who, under the pretense of preaching the faith, practically became "prostitutes for God." The Pope had enormous power, but either he was incapable of exercising it thoroughly or others prevented him from doing so. For that reason, the provincial areas of his territory were out of his control. Added to that, there was the conflict between the spiritual power and the temporal one (dukes and princes). Speaking of which, there is a very picturesque episode in the film. Pope Innocent III, a man of great intelligence and sharp political acumen, happened to die while he was on a journey and his body lay in state in Perugia Cathedral. His body was covered with jewels and precious stones, but during the night thieves stole them all. In the morning, Francis arrived at the cathedral to pay his respect to the Pope who was his friend—completely naked.

Francis preached total poverty, rigorous asceticism, and there were few who could follow him; most couldn't stay the course. His philosophy was born out of opposition to the cruelty, the evil, and the corruption of the times, but also in opposition to the thirst for power and glory. Everybody then aspired to become a knight. To be part of that class was a sign of great distinction. In an age that had completely lost sight of Christ's teachings, Francis was so strict that even the Pope had his doubts about supporting him. And so he obtained approval for his order only in the year of his death, at age forty-four.

What is your opinion of Francis as a man?

Francis interests me as an historical figure rather than as a man. He was incredibly tough and, in a sense, almost harsh. He really was a "fanatic," It's not true that he loved nature, as people say. That old story about preaching to the birds just isn't true! And on the same note, I would remind you of a very famous episode. During a journey to Rome, his companions stopped to look at the view, a meadow full of flowers, and Francis told them off, shouting: "Come on! Hurry up! Get back on the road!"

"Francis of Assisi" is your only Italian project; the other three are American. What do you think of the crisis in Italian cinema?

You can't get the money to do anything worthwhile in Italy at the moment. The last interesting film that I saw was Rosi's *Carmen*, a French production. I think Rosi had a good idea in setting the movie on the streets in order to add a touch of verisimilitude to a story that is, of itself, rather ridiculous. The only serious film currently in production here is Fellini's *Ginger and Fred*, a satire about TV. The others are just light entertainment with minuscule budgets, with [Adriano] Celentano, [Massimo] Troisi, [Roberto] Benigni, Monica Vitti—all good actors, but they're bound to making people laugh at any cost. In short—the crisis is serious. And now, very late in the day, the politicians are working on a bill—the so-called "bitter law"—which was supposed to solve a bunch of problems in the cinema, but which has already been so emasculated that there is little left of its original intentions. Cinema has never interested our politicians. On the contrary, it scares them; they think it's just a tool of undermining the political process. First it was the Christian Democrats, who thought so because of neorealism; today the Socialists think that cinema controlled by directors is dangerous, and so they try to strangle it, destroy it. Today it is practically impossible to market any quality films in Italy.

After the success of Blow-Up, *you received some fantastic offers.*

An American producer wanted me to shoot a fairy tale, *Peter Pan*. Can you see me doing *Peter Pan*? He called me into his office, and on the one side there was Mia Farrow, who was to take the lead role, on the other side was the composer and the artistic director (the music and scenery were all ready), and in front of me there was this producer with his checkbook out, offering one million and three hundred thousand dollars. And then I just asked: "Since everything is ready, what do you need me for?"

Those guys never understood why I turned them down. So many of my colleagues would have accepted. I have to say that sacrifices of a material kind have never really affected me much. The sacrifices that matter have to do with our view of life, they are of the moral kind. It's when you lie to yourself, when you compromise, that you really pay for it.

You have shot a feature film and a few shorts on video: how did you find that experience?

It was a very interesting experience, even if at the time, in 1980, the techniques of transferring videotape to film weren't highly developed. The copy—on tape—of *The Mistery of Oberwald* is very beautiful. I don't understand why the French television didn't distribute it more widely. In America, the commercial I shot for the Renault 9 was judged the best commercial of the year. It cost eight hundred million lire to make. For the video I shot for the rock singer Gianna Nannini (the song is called "Fotoromanza"), I only had forty million lire to work with—and in fact I don't much like the end result. To make intelligent videos you need serious money.

I think video is the future of cinema. To shoot on video has so many advantages. To begin with, you have total control over color. The important thing is to work with a good group of technicians. Video reproduces what you put in front of the camera with almost total fidelity. The range of effects you can achieve is not even comparable to cinema. In the lab, you always have to compromise. On video, in contrast, you have complete control—you always know where you are because you can play it back at any stage, and if you don't like it you can redo it.

To turn to the subject of documentaries, everyone always talks—perhaps wrongly—about your relationship to the neorealist movement. My impression is that you don't actually have much in common with that whole "movement"—which, in any case, wasn't a real movement.

Antonioni the neorealist had a very brief career, limited to a few documentaries. When I shot my first medium-length film, *People of the Po Valley*, neorealism hadn't yet been born. While I was shooting it, in 1943,

Visconti was not far away shooting *Ossessione*, the film that marks the beginning of neorealism. It was the first time in an Italian documentary that people got to see reality, poor people. I don't want to be presumptuous, but I think I can safely say that I discovered neorealism on my own.

In your feature films you have departed from the external, social realities to concentrate instead on the study of psychology.

Well, the situation was changing. In the immediate aftermath of the war, some problems were such burning issues that the problems of the individual were relegated to the back burner. For example, it wasn't very important to know what the factory worker in *The Bicycle Thief* was actually thinking when you were coming to grips with more urgent matters, such as finding work and surviving. In the 1950s, I thought it was more interesting to study the individual and assess the psychological, ideological, and emotional consequences of the transformations brought about by the war. Besides, in my documentaries there had already been a tendency towards narrative, an opening out towards the intimate problems of the individual. In short, elements of storytelling were already present in my work.

Even when you are doing documentaries, you don't seek realism for the sake of realism.

No. I'm convinced that if you want to express your own poetic world you have to transcend reality.

You were the first European director to make use of the technique of long takes. I presume, therefore, that you knew The Magnificient Ambersons?

No, I saw it afterwards. I don't remember thinking of any film in particular when I shot my first long take. I remember getting up onto the dolly and following the actors around, filming them without cutting until the end of the scene. It was instinctive. Though you might not think so at first, it is more difficult to do a long take than to shoot and edit in the traditional way. When two characters are talking it's constantly necessary to move the camera and the actors, too, and sometimes this movement can become mechanical and artificial; to make it look natural and fluent requires a certain skill. However, I've never wanted to be associated with one technique in particular; every film has it's own style. In the scene of the Stock Exchange in *The Eclipse*, for example, it was impossible to do any long takes. If I feel the need to do short takes, I don't see why I shouldn't. Some directors such as [Rainer W.] Fassbinder, do long takes and then make cuts and insert other sequences. With that method, however, you run the risk of having variations in light, as there were in *Berlin Alexanderplatz*.

Unless I'm mistaken, you personally oversee the editing of your films.

Yes, I've always worked with the editor from the first cut to the last for all my films. For *Blow-Up*, I was in charge of the whole process; after two weeks my colleague, Eraldo Da Roma, had to leave for London and so I had to manage by myself, with the help of the assistant director. For *Identification of a Woman* I also decided to give myself the editing credit because, practically, I had done it with just the help of two assistants. *Identification of a Woman* is a film which is completely based on editing, a very nervous sort of editing with cuts that are sometimes very bold but do reflect the content of the film.

One could almost say that in this film, the editing is more important than the camera work and the relationship between people and their environment, which up until then had been the hallmark of your style.

In *Identification of a Woman* I didn't worry about the visual side of things; indeed, I tried to avoid anything aesthetically pleasing. I felt a need to remain inside the characters. It's very easy to create visual beauty, you can find that anywhere, even in the films of inexperienced directors. And I know that some films are entirely based on aesthetic beauty. For example, in *Paris, Texas*, there is some extraordinary imagery, sometimes it's almost too beautiful, considering the context.

What do you think of recent German cinema? I think that Wim Wenders owes a lot to The Cry, *to* La notte, *and to* Zabriskie Point.

German cinema has given a healthy shock to the old continent. It has woken us from our stupor. Among the young directors, Wenders and Herzog seem to me the best. Wenders has his feet on the ground while Herzog is more "inspired," in the sense that he is also slightly "mad." Just think of the types of stories he comes up with, his way of portraying certain characters who are always a little strange, on a knife-edge between reality and surrealism.

And recent Italian cinema, which has been so widely criticized?
Faliero Rosati and Peter del Monte seem to me to have their own style, which is something that other directors haven't yet found.

While you were shooting Identification of a Woman, *you said it would be the last "Antonionian" film. What did you mean by that?*
Just that I wanted to put an end to a certain kind of cinematic discourse. I want to get away from "sentimentalism" and concentrate on "facts." Contrary to what many people think, I am quite a violent person, and I want to free myself of this violence by making action films in which the facts speak for themselves. However, my next film, *Two Telegrams,* will still be about feelings.

ALDO TASSONE

IDENTIFICATION OF A FILMMAKER[18]

What place do writing and painting occupy in your life as a filmmaker?

Finding producers who will allow me to make the films I want and I feel the need to make has always been a problem for me. Sometimes, in the long periods of inactivity I have been forced to between films, I have devoted myself to writing stories, which then became a book. Some people have called them screenplays that never saw the light of day, but it wasn't like that. They are stories, notes, fragments, which I wrote down when I was in the mood.

Painting is a different matter, though. Usually, I prefer it to writing; it's less wearisome. When you paint, your hand is guided by instinct. The marks that you make with a pen are by contrast the fruit of deliberate thought. I think painting is part of the irrational world.

When did you first begin to paint?

I have no ambitions as far as painting goes and I don't consider myself to be a traditional painter. I began painting when I was very young, still a teenager, when I used to do portraits. I also did a lot of architectural drawings—that's an art that has always fascinated me. I also painted still lives, I drew trees and landscapes that I could see from my window. I kept on doing portraits for a long time—I'm obsessed by people's faces. When I'm alone in the dark, all I have to do is close my eyes and I see faces, a

---

18 From *L'Express*, 9-15 August, 1985. Translated by Andrew Taylor.

whole crowd of people that I don't know and that I can almost reach out and touch. So I took to drawing them. One day I ripped up a face that I didn't like and I put the pieces back together again as if they were an abstract painting. And out of the pieces, a mountain emerged. From then on, I started to do mountains.

Mountains which you then take and enlarge, a bit like the photographer in Blow-Up.

Sometimes they are tiny. I paint them with a very fine brush using a lens. Then I photograph them and I make successive enlargements. The result is almost always a surprise, a bit like firing pottery. Sometimes I change the colors during the printing, or make enlargements up to two meters across, or even reduce the enlargement, if I think that it will look better. Many details are so small that they are invisible to the naked eye. Thus, the subject matter of the painting, the meaning of what I am trying to do, is only revealed through the enlargement process.

In your films, places are an essential element of the narration.

That was true of my earlier films, but not of the latest one, *Identification of a Woman*, where, on the contrary, I didn't want to emphasize the relationship of the character to the environment. In this film, the choice of environment depends on the story. On the other hand, the story is itself based on chance. External elements come to bear on the life of the character, a director who is looking for inspiration. He is less subject to the influence of the environment because he is not going through an existential crisis, like the architect of *L'avventura,* or the writer in *La notte,* or the painter in *The Girlfriends* were.

What are the landscapes or places that attract your attention when you are out walking or traveling?

I've wanted to shoot films in every place I've ever been. Fortunately, I haven't! God alone knows how many bad films would have come out of that. It isn't true that everything that inspires or stimulates us has artistic value. Besides, when you are traveling without being able to remain incognito, what always happens is that you, the observer, transform and influence the phenomena you observe. I remember a trip to Finland, when a newspaper had made a helicopter available to me to visit the archipelago. It was wintertime and the view of those islands covered in snow, and the sea frozen over, was really magnificent. But as soon as we landed on one of those islands with barely three houses, the ten people living in them would all rush up to me and then the truth, the reality of the place vanished before my eyes—you see? In the end, traveling makes me sad. They say that melancholy is inevitable in maturity, but when I was younger it was the same. I think it comes from the inability of a newcomer to grasp the uniqueness of the existence of the people he meets. I would like to stay in one place, integrate myself and in turn be integrated by that reality—in short, to live it, at least for a while.

Were you never tempted to film an Amarcord *in Ferrara?*
In a way, that's a bit what I did with *Story of a Love Affair,* which has been shown again in Paris just recently. In the film you can see, for example, the tennis court where I used to play. Yes, I have often been tempted, but restraint has always prevented me. Everyone thinks that *Identification of a Woman* is the most autobiographical of my films because the main character is a director. It's not true. That director could not be more different from me. The only thing we have in common is our profession. I think that the character who is closest to me is the journalist in *The Passenger.* I say "I think," because my assessment of my films changes all the time. When I happen to see them again—which is rare—I don't look at them as films but as episodes in my life.

People say that you have a particular "way of seeing." What does it consist of?
It consists of moving from the particular to the whole. Starting with the details that strike me, I move on to the overall situation. When I like something about a place, I immediately get the idea of moving characters into that setting. As a child I used to play with building blocks; I loved making streets and squares and whole suburbs, which I would imagine full of people for whom I had a story ready. Even today, when I arrive in

a place, I make up a story. Inspired by the place, or even just based on the gestures and actions I see, I try to imagine what story may be unfolding before my eyes.

You are very interested in painting. Which painters do you feel the greatest affinity for?

First and foremost, Piero della Francesca. Even though he is concerned with religious topics, he does so with such detachment, with a such a mysterious lucidity that you can fall in love with his paintings even without having any feeling for their subject-matter. Other painters? It's always difficult to draw up lists; it implies a value judgment. I would say Paolo Uccello, Kandinskij, Pollock, Malevich, Morandi. And of course Picasso. I'm quoting names at random. For example, I have a deep admiration for Velásquez, who in my opinion is underrated. Another great painter from the past who is too little known is Cosmé Tura, the most original of the Ferrarese school. And among the lesser figures is Benozzo Gozzoli: I always take great pleasure in his work, he uses such unusual coloring—pinks, turquoises especially—and then, I also like his compositional skills. Among the contemporary Italian painters I would say [Mario] Schifano.

You shot many of your films abroad: Blow-Up *in Great Britain,* Zabriskie Point *in the United States. You have made a film about China. The* Passenger *was shot in Spain, Africa, Germany. Do you feel very Italian? Or, deep down, do you feel you do not belong anywhere?*

When I was shooting those films, I must confess that I never asked myself whether I, as an Italian, was working abroad because I liked it or because I had to. Or whether perhaps it was because I had lost a bit of my sense of identity. Thinking about it now, I would say that perhaps I had the feeling that my country was a bit too small for me, like a suit that I had outgrown, and I felt I had to "alter"it, so that it could fit my size. And I did that by making the world my home. In any case, I've always felt the need to go abroad. Already in 1952, I had done some shooting for *The Vanquished,* my second film, in France and Great Britain.

Ten years before that, you had been assistant director to Marcel Carné for Les Visiteurs du soir. *What do you remember of that time?*

Carné didn't even know that I had been hired to work with him. He got very angry. Apart from anything else, I was Italian and we were still at war. He was very unfriendly toward me. I remember one episode. We were shooting on location above Nice, and at lunch they set up just one table and passed around a huge plate. Every time the plate got to me, Carné took it out of my hands and left me with no food. Luckily, at that time I had a lot of money; the production company paid me well, and despite the difficulties and the rationing I didn't have any problem finding stuff to eat. I had worked out a system: I used to go to an Italian restaurant and start by ordering the wine, something like a Château Lafite of a really expensive vintage. After that, they would serve me anything I asked for!

Did you manage to reconcile yourself with France?

I know France really well. I'd say it's my second home, even though I'm also very attracted to the Anglo-Saxon countries. The United States and England have had a great influence on me. However, in France I feel at home, whereas there I feel as if I'm abroad. Still, I have to admit that I feel closer to Anglo-Saxon literature than I do to French writing, despite the fact that I know the latter better.

You have even translated some French literary works into Italian.

Yes, I've translated *The Narrow Door* by Gide and *Monsieur Zéro* by Paul Morand. And even something by Chateaubriand. I love French poetry. A few years ago I even wanted to make a film of *Les Fleurs du mal*. But I think English poets had a greater influence on my cultural development. I feel as if T.S. Eliot were whispering in my ear things that I already know.

You are a very good reader.

Yes, that's true. But I have to admit that sometimes I start a book and I don't finish it. Perhaps it's because the story doesn't develop or doesn't turn out the way I think it should. Then I get irritated and I drop it. One of my faults is always seeing in books things that could be turned into films; I admit it, it's almost a professional bias. Yet I think I'm a good reader; I like well-crafted prose. I took to Camus's writing immediately. And I also like Françoise Sagan. I love the way her writing has an almost Gidean quality—simple, dry, and yet intense. I've always loved Gide, even though his subject matter is often light-years away from my own world. Naturally, there have been other writers, too: Gertrude Stein, Conrad, Faulkner, Sartre.

In fact you once thought about filming Camus's The Stranger.

As soon as I started reading that book, I immediately had the idea of making a film of it. I was in Nice and I was waiting to get a visa to go to Paris to see Carné. I was living at the Negresco Hotel, in high style but with nothing to do. At that point I had thought of making a film about a grand hotel, from the point of view of the staff, of the room service staff who live on the top floor. I had managed to get the manager's permission, and for a week I was a room-service waiter. I slept with the others and had a great time. But I still had a lot of free time to spend in bookstores. One day, Camus's *The Stranger* caught my eye. I opened it and on the first page I read: "Mother died today. Or was it yesterday? I don't know. I've had a telegram from the hospice: 'Your mother passed away. Funeral service tomorrow. Best regards.'" Amazing. I read the book in one go, that night. At the time I was also working for an Italian weekly called *Il cosmopolita,* and I immediately sent them an article on Camus. I was the first to talk about him in Italy. I had really liked the book.

The weekly also asked me to do an interview with Matisse, who lived near Nice. So I went to his house. They made me wait a good quarter of an hour in his study. Probably they just forgot about me. Then a lady came in to tell me that the *maestro* wasn't at home. Was it true or not? Anyway, I had made use of that quarter of an hour to take notes: I published an interview with Matisse without Matisse, just as if I really had met him.

Let's go back a moment to the incident at the Negresco: what did you learn in the week that you were a room-service waiter?

I learned a lot about the inside operations of a grand hotel. I took pages of notes with the idea of writing a screenplay. Unfortunately, I lost them and gave up on the idea. I regret that I never used that experience.

You have also done a lot of film criticism. What type of viewer is Antonioni?

A very exacting one. Immediately after the war, I worked for *L'Italia libera*, the newspaper of the Action Party, which later became the Republican Party. In Italy under fascism, the market had been closed to American movie productions, so that after the liberation, our country was swamped by a flood of atrocious films. My position, like that of many other critics faced with such poor-quality productions, was very strict in its attempt to defend the "philosophy of good taste," which goes by the name of aesthetics. I was so strict that the daily's editor received a lot of protests from our distributors, and asked me to tone things down!

But you must have spotted a few islands of quality in amidst it all.

Yes, of course. But in those days it was almost a requirement to be "against" everything: against dubbing (although I'm not convinced it is so detrimental to the general style and narrative of a film); against commercial stories, at least most of them; and especially against the banal way of editing that was the prerogative of Hollywood productions.

A tidal wave of American films has again invaded Italy via television. Do you think that in Italy, or even abroad, it is still possible to make good, "auteur" films?

I feel a certain bitterness and uneasiness. I won't even mention "Dynasty" and "Dallas." I'm thinking of a certain type of recent American productions, which probably come out of the same mold anyway. The structure of the films is the same, the narrative always unfolds in a way that anticipates the moment of violence. It's all so predictable, there are never any surprises. Most moviegoers are not sensitive to reality in all its truth, and they prefer an artificial view of the world. As if—since they experience reality in their daily lives—they wanted to find in cinema something with which they are not familiar, something they don't already know. Obviously, aesthetics has nothing to do with that. Of course, there are also films by more important American filmmakers, from another generation. For me, Coppola is a director in the true sense of the word; few people know cinema as he does. The same goes for Scorsese, Altman, Kubrick, and a few others.

And in Italy?

In Italy there is a strong air of crisis, but I don't believe in crisis as a permanent phenomenon. I think it's cyclical, due to practical conditions: competition from television, the increasing cost of labor, and a badly organized society. The law that regulates the performing arts, including cinema, which the people in this business have just managed to get after years of lobbying, actually leaves a lot to be desired. Let's hope that my interpretation of crisis is correct.

And yet you have kept up the same curiosity, the same interest for all types of film. Last year at the Venice Film Festival you were often in the theater until three in the morning!

It's because I love my work and I'm very interested in what others are doing. I'm still capable of getting enthusiastic about things. Many French films have captivated me, too—*À nous la liberté; The Rules of the Game; Les Dames du Bois de Boulogne; Weekend; Hiroshima, mon amour;* to name but a few. It's strange, but when I see a good film, it's as if someone had given me a good slap on the face: I feel the need to do something entirely different.

You started out with documentaries. People of the Po Valley *was your first film about "poverty." Can one say, perhaps, that you were a realist before neo-realism?*

Yes, I think I arrived at neorealism on my own. Unfortunately, I had to edit *People of the Po Valley* with what was left of the reel. There were scenes of stunning violence, a novelty for Italy at that time. For example, there was a storm in the delta of the Po river, that had flooded the huts of some peasants and forced the mothers to put the cribs on the tabletops to prevent the babies from drowning. Such crude images had never been seen before in the cinema, and I still think they were sabotaged in the developing lab: they gave me the film back covered in stains. It was 1943, fascism was still in control. Then, because of the war, I lost all trace of the film. Afterwards, I found it again in a damp warehouse: it was completely ruined. It should have been a six-hundred-meter long documentary; now it measures only half of that.

Many of the issues and concerns of our times can be found in your films. What strikes you most, what worries you most about what you have called the "melting pot" of Western society?

It's not possible for anyone's view of the world, which is the most phenomenal of all phenomena, to be based solely on individual criteria. You have to take many things into account. My own is not a catastrophic view of the world. If you extend your field of vision to the entire universe, then even a nuclear war wouldn't mean the end of things. If the population growth continues at the current rate for the next century, it's likely that some epidemic or some nuclear catastrophe will—so to speak—come to the rescue of the human race. One day—who knows how many years hence—the Earth will cease to exist, burned up by the sun, or else frozen solid after the sun dies. Is it science fiction to imagine our descendants living beyond the solar system? Too rigid a view of things leads to pessimism.

In 1975, in fact, you wrote an article in L'Express *in which you insisted on the need to view the world with different eyes. You felt that there was a profound evolution going on, which could lead to the anthropological transformation of man himself. How far have you gotten with this idea?*

I still think so. Man has only one alternative. Either he dies, or he adapts. It's the theme of *Red Desert*. The film only dealt with the theme of man adapting to a certain environment—noise from cars, air pollution—and of the psychological effects of such an adaptation process. But one could imagine more radical transformations, of an anthropological nature; changes in morphology, physiology, in behavioral patterns. However, I would limit myself to saying that humans have become—perhaps not more evil, but certainly more indifferent toward their fellow human beings.

What makes you say that?

Recently, I spent a month in New York. Since mental hospitals have been closed, in the city there are two hundred and forty thousand mentally unstable people wandering the streets. They are everywhere, making loud speeches, gesticulating, stopping the traffic. And yet, the passers-by are completely indifferent to them. As if, in a way, this shows that it was right to want to close the hospitals. While, in another way, it also makes life in the city as it must have been in the Middle Ages, with the streets full of cops, vagabonds, charlatans, wandering preachers, prostitutes, and whatever else you can think of. The mentally ill must be looked after; it's as necessary for them as for their families, where it can sometimes lead to difficult, even tragic situations.

It has been said that a society can be defined by the way it treats its insane members.

No, absolutely not. It's a decision that derives from society's choice of a certain type of therapy. In Italy, legislation was influenced by the psychiatrist Franco Basaglia. In Great Britain, there was instead Ronald Laing—who, by the way later abandoned his theories. If you had to base your judgment of a society on these kinds of choices, then we would have to severely condemn Italian society for the way in which even criminals are released from jail, on the theory that they will be able to reintegrate into society quite normally. I don't agree. In most cases, the first thing terrorists do, if you release them, is to return to the circle of violence with perhaps even greater ruthlessness than before.

It seems that in Italy the phenomenon of terrorism is less dramatic now than it was a few years ago.

Terrorism has been fought ferociously and for a while it seemed that the armed struggle against the state was no longer one of its goals. But in the past few months, certain groups have reorganized themselves. Perhaps they don't have the same strength as they did before, but their revitalization seems linked to the Mafia and the "Camorra," and this is very serious. I'm not sure that in Italy we will ever be able to heal those two malaises.

Let's conclude with something more cheerful. Few people know that you are a great tennis player and a champion at table tennis.
Oh yes! I've won a lot of tournaments, and during the war I survived by selling the cups and medals that I had won. I also like soccer a lot. I watch the games on television, because they replay the goals over and over, in slow motion and from different angles.

That's Antonioni the sportsman, but there is also Antonioni the musician: you studied the violin, didn't you?
Yes, but then I got a few nervous tics, as you can still see. Unfortunately, the doctor ordered me to stop playing the violin and the piano, too. I used to study piano, too. I'm still interested in music, but I listen to it here at home. I don't like going to concerts, and I rarely go to the opera. At concerts, the image is more important than the sound. You look at the players and at the public. Their gestures, their expressions distract me. I prefer listening to records. I think I own the best recordings you can find in the world. But it is often an effort to bring myself to listen to them. Music is a lost love, there's nothing I can do about it. A love which I have not forgotten. As a child, I didn't realize it but as I got older I started feeling more and more the emptiness which the lack of music as a mode of self-expression has left inside me.

Can you talk to us about your future projects?
In the short run, there is a film which will be made partly in Italy and partly in the United States. I'm working on the screenplay with an American writer called Robert Wurlitzer.

May I also add one other thing in conclusion? You have questioned me as if I were a wise old man who over the years has reached some kind of certainty, not just about the problems of his work but about everything. Nothing fits me less than the role you have assigned me. I'm a man who is full of doubts, even in my work.

SOPHIE LANNES
PHILIPPE MEYER

INTERVIEWS ON FILMS

STORY OF A LOVE AFFAIR[1]

What experiences of "form" and "content" did you set out to achieve?

I did not begin with a "theory" in my head. I only wanted to break with a certain syntax that was, by that time, tired and old-fashioned. The game of shots and reverse shots had become unbearable for me. In this first film, I was able to free myself from it by way of very long crane movements that followed the characters until I felt the need to stop. But it was an instinctual solution, born on the set. I repeat, I did not apply any type of formula or scheme

Also with the "content" it was the same. I did not begin with the preconceived idea of criticizing a social class. The subject was born as the story of two characters, and I tried to delve into them in as much depth as I could. Naturally, these characters moved within a specific environment. Every human being represents an environment. But I did not force its description. I tried to be as objective as possible.

Then there was no engagément?

That would be a long story. There was *engagément*, in a way, but not as the existentialists mean it. I would say an *engagément* typical of a "special correspondent." On the other hand, the social climate was always in the background. And this is, it seems to me, what distinguishes *Story of a Love Affair* from other Italian neorealist films in which what matters is

---

[1] From *Il progresso d'Italia,* December 14, 1950. Translated by Dana Renga.

the social environment, while the characters are only the opportunity to represent it.

Some critics have said that it is impossible to fall in love with your characters.

I accept that criticism. But they are the characters I wanted. They are real. I can be accused of having chosen them—but this is different.

What criteria did you follow for the acting?

I changed it according to the different actors. With [Massimo] Girotti—who was adequately trained, but tended to "overexpress" himself—I mainly limited myself to controlling him, in order to even out his acting. Naturally, I gave him a few suggestions, but these were always very vague, so as to leave him in a relationship of uncertainty with his character. This might have surprised him. Anyway, it was my way to obtain what I wanted from him.

[Lucia] Bosè required a different, more involved approach. Apart from the fact that she was a beginner, the character was older than she was. She lacked the necessary experience to consciously interpret the character. It was useless to waste time explaining everything to her. I had to use a different approach, which turned out to be helpful, even if it might seem—and maybe even is—mechanical and hideous. On the one hand—by resorting to events and feelings that had nothing to do with her character—I took apart her natural and youthful cheerfulness in order to create within her a state of mind suitable to the scene that she had to act out. On the other hand, I shook her up and got her excited.

I have heard talk of slaps—is it true?

Yes. I hope that Lucia has forgiven me. I didn't like to have to do that, but there was no other way, nor did she have any other technique to rely on. I was also able to use this system because her face, unlike that of many other actors, has a great quality—it never changes, whether she smiled or cried. Anyway, I think that the end result was good, even if someone in Milan insists on not noticing it. I realized that Milan hates Bosè. But maybe this is understandable.

Did you encounter many difficulties during your filming?

I did not have what you might call inner difficulties. For me every-thing was pretty clear. Instead, it was the external difficulties that plagued us. For example, at a certain time it was necessary to slow down the production because—at least according to what the producers told me—all of a sudden the Banca del Lavoro stopped paying the minimum guaranteed installments. Only the intervention of new backers allowed us to continue with the regular schedule.

From a technical point of view, the greatest difficulty was in using a crane that was not only difficult to manage, but also not too well-suited to the particular and constant use that we made of it. This forced me to give up many of my expectations and to find emergency solutions. Another difficulty was that we lacked very sensitive film.

An then, the post-sync of the film practically drove me to despair. Apart from the dubbing, which it would take too long to discuss, I wanted to use sound in a functional, poetic way. In spite of my pig-headedness, the final effects only vaguely resemble what I initially want-ed. It has become necessary film with direct sound recording. In the next film I will put it in the contract.

But isn't there a specific law about this?

Yes, the law exists. But in practice, everyone post-syncs—or at the most they record a dialogue track. This happens for infinite reasons—to save money or time, or for convenience, etc.—and you can see what the results are!

What did you learn from this first experience?

It is difficult to say. How to do my job a little better, I imagine, and a greater understanding of my abilities, whatever they are. One thing I cer-tainly learned was to become aware of one of the most serious obstacles for a director: the ever-present and obsessive temptation to give up. When a scene does not turn out the way you want and you search in vain for a solution, when a setting is not what you had imagined it to be and a thousand other things are needed, when a camera movement does not have the hoped-for effect and so on, the temptation to give up is very strong. Instead, that's when you have to hold out and believe that the moment in which fantasy takes over and where production technicalities give in, will eventually come. One only needs to know how to wait for it.

What is your own self-criticism now that the film is completed?

I noticed that in the script—to which I remained faithful, with the exception of a few cuts and slight modifications—there were flaws. It was written in too much of a hurry. In all honesty, I am not aware of other faults in the film. Nor do I know whether certain things that I don't find convincing can be ascribed to me or to the conditions under which the film was shot.

On the other hand, it is still too early for me to be able to give a clear judgment. I do not yet know if I have a style, if I will ever have one. I do not really know. The films that I see almost always give me a sense of dissatisfaction. It is not that I am presumptuous. I am just not able to be satisfied. Like many others, I feel that cinema must change, and I search relentlessly for the right path. Maybe there are bigger mistakes in my film than there are in others. But maybe this is because I tried to rebel against certain current trends, because I purposedly did not want to touch on simplistic issues or set worn-out mechanisms into motion. For example, I abolished "the victim," "the hero," "the good guy," "the bad guy." Within my characters, I tried to maintain the complexity of the human being. In short, I did not want to play games with myself or with others.

What are your future projects?

In all probability, I will soon make another film. I would like to analyze a romantic relationship that lasts only one day and one night. It would portray a great love. There would only be two characters, the man and the woman. I also have another project that interests me a great deal. A ruthless film, with a disturbing truth. But it is too early to talk about it.

MICHELE GANDIN

THE VANQUISHED[2]

It is the first time that one of my films was better received by the public than by the critics. In a certain sense this pleases me, but it also makes me wonder. I am not yet a popular director (I confess that I would like to become one), and so for me to be able to communicate with the public is already an achievement. On the other hand, I feel perplexed by the fact that the majority of the critics did not notice certain things that were noticed by people who are not professional critics. I have attentively read almost all of the articles written up to this point, and I can say that in all of them there is a common misunderstanding of the film. I mean that with a few exceptions these writers were not inspired by aesthetic criteria. They started with the premise that the first sequence, in its way of bringing out wide-ranging ethical and social intentions, indicated and at the same time limited the meaning of the work. In this way it was easy to consider the film as not completely successful—if not out right wrong—because those problems were not sufficiently confronted, and even less resolved. Do I have to say, once again, that the beginning was imposed upon me by the producers, on the advice of various censors? I thought that this was clear enough, if you think of all of the difficulties which were involved in making the film, and of which the critics were certainly aware.

[2] From *Cinema nuovo* 30, March 1954. Translated by Dana Renga.

I am generally against certain programmatic impositions. A film is not an essay, and *The Vanquished* was not meant to become one. I wanted to limit myself to narrating three episodes, which seemed to me to be symptomatic of a particularly painful situation and from which a moral could have been drawn *a posteriori*, and not *a priori*. For me, it was important to tell the facts, to narrate *tout court*. Of course, since I am a man who lives in a social reality, it is clear that I am influenced by this reality in one way or another, just as everyone else is. It is also true that all the discussions and instigations made *The Vanquished* look more presumtuous than it really was. However, all of this does not justify the criticism that I was alluding to, because beyond the more or less openly declared goals, a film has to be appraised not so much by ethical or moral standards as by aesthetic ones. Besides, it's quite well known that one should not give too much weight to an author's programmatic premises. The work acquires its own autonomy outside of these premises and often against them. Guerrazzi[3] comes to my mind (who knows why Guerrazzi—perhaps to avoid more famous parallels!), who claimed to have placed moral and political obligations before artistic ones in his novels. In fact, his novels do not contain even a hint of this dualism.

At this point, I do not want to be misunderstood. The critics are absolutely free to say and write what they want. It is ridiculous to be offended by some negative opinion. But then, let also us, the directors, be free to express our own opinions of certain critics. For example, I quote one of the editors of *Il Messaggero* in Rome, who, not having seen *The Vanquished*, republished a passage that his editor in chief had written. So far, so good. The problem is that, out of a substantially positive review, he took precisely those ten lines that criticized the Italian episode in the version presented at the Venice Film Festival, which was radically different from the version presented to the public. He could

---

[3] Francesco Domenico Guerrazzi (1804–1873) had an intense, though scarcely successful, political and literary career. His best works are historical novels that combine Romantic elements with gothic themes and patriotic sentiments.

have at least taken the time to bring himself up to date. Now, he doesn't seem to be a very serious critic, not because his criticism was too severe, but because he misrepresented his chief's thought without bringing forth any new or genuine critical views

I was also accused of formalism. Here I cannot respond very well, because this discourse involves the relationship between intentions and results, which it is not up to me to discuss. But it cannot be denied that in my films I constantly search for certain issues, current issues with often compelling human content. I can also pride myself with being among the first, in the 1940s, to shift the focus of Italian documentaries from things to people, with *People of the Po Valley* and *N.U.* [Sanitation Department]. I feel it is my right if I want to express myself "in good handwriting," as any good writer would say. I only do it to give the cinematic discourse stronger implications. Otherwise, paradoxically, I would make good films using bad images.

I have another thing to say. In my opinion, every filmmaker has to try (as all of the great filmmakers have done) to reinvent the cinematic discourse in his own way. In cinema, things have been written in the same way, with the same technique, for a long time. Why not try to resolve in a different way the conventions of shot and counter-shot, and of cuts, all of which are such unrealistic and old-fashioned techniques? I would even suggest working to develop editing and even with framing. Why does Italian neorealism have to limit its discoveries to content?

Antonioni describes the problems that his crew faced while trying to carry out certain camera movements and to make the forest "photogenic" in the French episode: that is, cutting down trees, planting some new ones, lighting up the grass of a field or darkening the leaves of a shrub, positioning the lights so as to have different levels of depth—in short, "creating" the forest.

Can this effort be accused of formalism? It was in the forest that the drama developed and concluded; the forest was the backdrop for the crime and therefore it had to fit, figuratively, the situation. From this point of view, it seems to me to have succeeded.

But let's continue with the critics. Many said that the English sketch was perfect, but very few explained why they used that adjective. Almost no one wasted a word to discuss the film's music, the photography, the setting; and yet, with my collaborators on the music, photography, and set design I had tried to create three different environments that corresponded to the different countries where the episodes took place. I remember the efforts made by Suso Cecchi D'Amico to give the dialogue a "national" quality. The result: I heard them say that the film seemed to be directed by three different filmmakers—one French, one Italian, one English. As far as I am concerned, I take this criticism as a compliment, when I think that not even [Jean] Renoir succeeded in giving us a believable portrait of America. The only critic who recognized that the film had a stylistic unity, beyond its episodic structure, was André Bazin in *Cahiers du Cinéma* and in *Cinema Nuovo*.

Another accusation was directed to the "coldness" of the film. Once the three episodes were chosen, I do not understand why I should have put more warmth in the description of the protagonists. I absolutely did not want my heroes to be likable. It is so easy to make an individual with a pistol in his hand likable. In the Hollywood gangster films, the bad guys usually touch a sympathetic chord in the audience, even if at the end they get the punishment they deserve. But I didn't want to allow any sympathy for my characters, nor any comprehension. The detachment that I am being accused of was aimed at avoiding the possibility that the story could influence the public in a negative, even if involuntary way. Maybe because I succeeded in this, a good portion of the critics consider me a cold intellectual. Why an intellectual? Why cold? Because I force myself to find a new angle from which to represent reality, an angle which is different from—how can I say it?—different from the pietism of Italian neorealism? But when [Cesare] Zavattini says: "Let us reclaim everything to man," I am naturally in agreement with him. All there is to do is to agree on what "man" is. Some may remember the answer of that Irishman who was asked: "Is any man as good as another?" "Of course," he replied, "even better." I feel that I am standing a bit in the ironic shoes of that Irishman! To conclude on the subject, it seems to me that this criticism of coldness and intellectualism has by now become a commonplace for whoever does not have the desire or the ability to go into further in their analysis of my films.

As a conclusion, we asked Antonioni for his personal opinion of the film.

It is impossible for me to judge, since I am the director. I can only say that I am not completely satisfied. I had to endure too many discussions, too many battles; I had to accept too many limitations, too many compromises, even ideological ones, most of all in dealing with the Italian episode. What I know is that *The Vanquished*, as a whole, is quite different from the film that it could have been.

Antonioni told us that he had a particular affection for the French story, which, as we know, did not completely satisfy the critics.

What I wanted to say may not have been sufficiently clear. What I wanted to do was to narrate a crime that does not have a plausible justification, that seems more or less unmotivated, that was the tragic and absurd conclusion of a student trip to the country. The difficulty of calibrating the psychological relationships of the characters on the thread of ambiguity arises from that.

The Vanquished does not represent an in-depth development of one of the issues from which I started. It is, rather, a deviation that allowed me to clarify a series of technical and aesthetic problems, such as the relationship between camera and reality, and the way of viewing this reality. No one—unfortunately, I must say no one—noticed that in this film, as I see it, the secondary characters have a precise consistency, and they all have their say in the story. They all contribute to building a basis to the story itself and to the main characters. This, for me, is a step ahead with respect to the other films.

Antonioni has lengthy arguments about acting.

On this subject, the most original experience I had was the one I had in England. There, a director allows the actors a lot of freedom, in the sense that once the character is understood, the actor constructs him. I, on the other hand, directed the actors as I am used to in Italy—suggesting and explaining every gesture and every intonation. In England, [Peter] Reynolds is not considered a great actor and has been criticized for many shortcomings. I directed him relentlessly, making him repeat the scenes until both of us were satisfied, without ignoring any of his shortcomings. It was a very tiring job, but the result—I can say this because at least the critics all agree on it—was extraordinary. Reynolds himself has kindly acknowledged this in an interview.

I hope that I cleared up all that there was to clarify.

Antonioni said this while we parted. We agreed with him.

LINO DEL FRA

L'AVVENTURA[4]

How would you define your journey toward realism?
I think that cinema, as a form of spectacle, is destined to undergo a transformation in the near future. For years now it has been showing signs of fatigue. In many countries, cinema is no longer able to compete with television, although from the artistic point of view television is at a much earlier stage of development. This is proof that cinema has wasted time following paths which are by now well-trodden. Cinematic narrative has lost a lot of its original character, and it is less and less able to satisfy the demands of today's public. Old formulas are constantly reiterated. Despite the changes which have occurred in the last few years, directors are limited by technology. Forced to respect a series of conventions which influence his style, the director has lost his freedom over the subject of the film, over his own reality.

This is alarmingly apparent in today's films, and instances of interesting experimentation remain isolated incidents. Producers are undoubtedly the main culprits in this state of affairs. With few exceptions they are highly conservative; and they are such, if I may say so, almost by definition. At times you can still find some producers who venture onto less traveled paths to make unconventional films, but very often the lack of freedom from which cinema suffers almost everywhere dampens their initial enthusiasm. So they end up adapting to the norms and sticking to the tried and true.

---

[4] From *Humanité dimanche,* 25 September 1960. Translated by Andrew Taylor.

After the war—after years of dramatic events, of fear and anxiety, of uncertainty over the fate of the world—it wasn't possible to talk about anything else. A great French writer said: "There are moments when you don't talk about trees because you are angry with trees." There are also times when it would be dishonest for an intelligent man to ignore certain events, for an intelligence that quits is a contradiction in terms. I think that anyone who makes cinema should never lose the link with his own times. This doesn't mean however that he has to reproduce and interpret its most dramatic events. (You can laugh too, why not? As a viewer I enjoy funny films). It's a question of finding in ourselves the echo of our times. For a director this is the only way of being sincere and consistent toward himself, and honest and fortright toward other people—the only way to live.

And yet I believe that the principle of "ever-greater truth" which in its most crude form is at the root of Italian neorealism, should today be broadened and deepened. In a world that, in some respects, has become closer to normal, what counts is not so much—or not just—the relationship of the individual to his environment, but rather the individual per se, in all his complex and disturbing truth. What torments contemporary man; what makes him tick? How do we see reflected in him what is going on in the world? What can we tell about his feelings? What can we tell about his psychology?

These are the questions that we have to ask ourselves when we think about the subject for a film. Once we have chosen the subject, what are the paths that allow us to reach realism?

Perhaps I haven't exactly answered your original question. But it's difficult to focus on one's soul. It is very hard because that is always the starting point, even when it's the brain that is actually working. The spiritual life of a man follows a mysterious and unpredictable itinerary. And it's difficult to retrace it after you've covered it. What I can say is that my way of achieving realism consists of this: trying to understand what is happening inside ourselves, today. In what way? That's not for me to say.

Do you think a film should be felt rather than understood?

Yes, I certainly do. How do you expect me to "explain" my film?

Three issues emerge in L'avventura: *oblivion, the impossibility of perfect love, and the sense of loss which modern life creates in each of us. Which of these do you think is the most important?*

I don't agree with your list of issues on which *L'avventura* is based. It's obvious, for example, that the first of your three issues, oblivion, blends with the second. And in a sense, both these two in turn merge with the third. I think it would be risky to say that one is more important than another. Today, are men what they are because life is what it is, or is it the other way around? As far as I'm concerned, this alone could constitute a topic of research—an imaginative research, though, not a speculative one.

"Nowadays, even the people who aren't afraid of the scientific unknown are afraid of the moral unknown." That was something you said about L'avventura. *What did you mean by it?*

I am convinced that today the individual, who takes such pains to widen the frontiers of his scientific knowledge, does nothing to advance himself from a moral point of view. He is still bound by old conventions, by obsolete myths, despite the fact that he is perfectly conscious of this state of affairs. Why should we go on respecting the ancient commandments if we know that they are no longer relevant?

Perhaps what is holding us back is the fear of falling into the moral void, even if the void of the cosmos no longer frightens us. Why? Why do we refuse to push ourselves to the outer edges of our moral universe? These are questions to which, at the moment, it is impossible to provide any answers. But I still think it is important to ask them.

You have often been criticized for the slow pace of L'avventura *What is the reason for that?*

I hate the artificial mechanisms of conventional cinematic narration. Life has a completely different pace, sometimes fast, sometimes extremely slow. In a story about feelings, like *L'avventura*, I felt the need to link feelings to time. Their own time. The more times I see *L'avventura*, the more I am convinced that I found the right rhythm, I don't think it could have had any other pace than the one it has.

In L'avventura *one notes an almost total lack of music. Why did you make this choice and why, on the other hand, are there so many noises?*

The use of music in films, as we think of it in the traditional sense, no longer has any right to exist. You use music to provoke in the spectator a certain state of mind. I don't want music to provoke such a state of mind; I want the story itself to do it, via images. It's true that there are certain— let's say—"musical" moments in the development of a story. They are the moments when you need to pull yourself away from reality. In those moments, music does have its place. At other times, you have to use noises, even if you don't do that in any realistic way, but rather as if they were sound effects—naturally, in a poetic mode. In *L'avventura* I believed it was more appropriate to use noises than music.

Could you talk to us about your latest film, La notte?

With *La notte* I tried to carry on the same discourse as in *L'avventura*. We are fooling ourselves if we think that all we have to do is know all about ourselves, analyze the farthest reaches of our souls. That is, at most, a beginning. It is certainly not everything. In the best of cases, you achieve a kind of mutual compassion. But you have to go beyond that. The characters in *La notte* get to that point, but don't manage to get beyond it. They are characters of today, not of tomorrow.

May I ask the critic who became a director what his idea of film criticism is?

Without criticism, art would lose its strongest supporter.

Of all your experiences in the cinema, which one has fascinated you the most?

The making of *L'avventura*. While I was filming it, I lived through five extraordinary months. Extraordinary because they were violent, exhausting, obsessive, often dramatic, distressing, but above all fulfilling. And I think that in the film you notice it. The most difficult thing for me was to detach myself from all the things that could go wrong—and many things did go wrong. We filmed without a producer, without money, and without food, often risking our necks at sea in the storms.

All of that changed the relationships among us, whether they were personal or professional relationships. We watched incredibly beautiful natural phenomena. My greatest difficulty, I say it again, was to cut myself off from everything that was happening, so that only the essential filtered through to the film—so that it had its own atmosphere, separate from what we were going through in real life. I used to get up every day at three in the morning just to be alone, in peace and able to reflect on what we were doing. At five, we would get on board the boat. Often, some of the crew refused to get in because of the weather and just a few of us would leave for the cliffs at Lisca Bianca. At that point, our struggle with the sea would begin: a struggle with the wind, with physical discomfort, with everybody's bad temper, with tiredness and a strange form of emptiness, a complete lack of energy that often took hold of us. Five months like that. And let's not forget that the director is the only one who is not allowed to have any of these feelings. He always has to be clear, calm, and collected no matter what happens. Sometimes I had to grit my teeth. When the film was finished, I felt drained. And I had to begin making *La notte* almost immediately. These are the minor crises that you have to go through. I don't know whether anyone is interested in them; I only talked about them because you asked.

FRANÇOIS MAURIN

LA NOTTE[5]

Why did you choose Jeanne Moreau to play in La notte?

I first met Jeanne Moreau in 1952. I was in Paris making the French episode of *The Vanquished*, a film about juvenile delinquency. I needed a sixteen-year-old girl. So I made the rounds of the various drama schools; I looked at thousands of photos. In the end I narrowed it down to three girls, all of them unknowns. They were: Brigitte Bardot, Jeanne Moreau, and Etchika Choureau. The one who was best suited to the part was Brigitte Bardot, but unfortunately, since it was her first film, the producers delayed signing the contract and I had to resort to the other two candidates. Jeanne Moreau seemed too serious, her temperament too dramatic; so I chose Etchika Choureau.

But I had been very impressed with Jeanne Moreau. So after that, I was on the lookout for another opportunity to work with her. The first one that came along was *The Girlfriends*. I would have liked her for the role of Momina—which was then played by Yvonne Fourneau—but at the time Moreau was working on the stage. And then, along came *La notte*.

Had you been thinking about Jeanne Moreau right from the start, from the first inception of the film?

I didn't write *La notte* for Jeanne Moreau. A film should be written in complete isolation. The actors shouldn't influence its writing. In fact, it is

5 From *France Observateur*, 23 February 1961. Translated by Andrew Taylor.

difficult to fix the moment when a character definitely takes shape in one's mind. At least, that's the way it is as far as I'm concerned. I never think about the actors before I've completely finished the story. The final script of *La notte* is, for example, very different from what I wrote a year before. At some point I just knew that Jeanne Moreau would be the ideal Lidia.

Do you take part in scouting for locations, choosing the set design and other visual elements of your films?

Not only do I take part in those things, I don't understand how one could not be involved in them. The smallest object, the tiniest painting hanging on a wall, the tiniest detail of the setting is chosen by me and by me alone. The set designer makes suggestions, but I'm the one who decides. Every element of a film is important for expressing one's self. As a result, you cannot leave anything out. You have to check everything.

La notte *will probably repeat the success of* L'avventura. *In Italy, it's breaking all box-office records. What do you think of all this success?*

I'm very pleased, of course, especially since it will give me the opportunity to work a bit more. From *Story of a Love Affair*, my first feature film, right up to *La notte*, I've made one film every two or three years. Now, after *L'avventura* and *La notte*, I'll finally be able to work the way I want to. So far, I've had great difficulty in finding producers—even for *L'avventura*, which had to be taken over by [Cino] Del Duca in its later stages. In France I have just signed a contract with the Hakim brothers and I have many offers in Italy, too. I can't complain.

ANDRÉ LABARTHE

THE ECLIPSE[6]

Thirteen years ago, The Eclipse *appeared as the film that would complete the existential discourse that began with* L'avventura *and was followed by* La notte. *Their common theme was alienation and the crisis of emotions within a bourgeois context.* The Eclipse *ended with the total silence of the human voice, with man reduced to a simple object. How would you represent middle-class man today? The same way you represented him then or would you give him a different destiny?*

I would say that the bourgeoisie of that time was quite different from the one of today. From what it's possible to understand—from things that happen every once in a while, most of all in Italy—it seems to me that the middle-class is very much involved in social and political life in order to defend its privileges, but also because of an internal corruption, which will eventually bring the middle-class, I believe, to its extinction. Society is proceeding along certain channels where it's difficult to find a way out. I am neither a sociologist nor a politician, but it seems to me that—not only in Italy, but throughout the world—we are moving toward a certain type of society. The middle-class is showing signs of deterioration with its "angry" reaction to the leveling-out that is taking place in society. Therefore, if I had to make *The Eclipse* today, I would be even harder on them, more violent.

[6] From *Corriere della Sera,* 15 October 1975. Translated by Dana Renga.

In the film I directed thirteen years ago, there are signs of violence that are connected with money. Today it would be even more so. It probably would no longer be connected with the Stock Exchange, because the Stock Exchange—although it still survives—already shows signs of its ineffectiveness. Probably—but I am not sure of it—the society of tomorrow will no longer have a need for the Stock Exchange.

The changes in the price of gold, of the dollar, of the lira, the "monetary serpent" and all of these things so difficult to follow (I studied finance when I was at the University and it was so abstruse that I had to strive hard to pass the exams) are manifestations of mechanisms that are getting more and more "rusty." I could be mistaken, but on the outside, to a nonexpert like me, that's how things look. And yet the survival of the middle-class is tied to these mechanisms. I am not making a political statement, nor am I speaking as an economist of the left would. I am speaking as a filmmaker, as someone who is used to looking at reality, to drawing certain conclusions from events, from facts, from feelings. I would say that *The Eclipse* is still a modern film in that its protagonists are people who do not believe in feelings—that is, they limit them to certain things.

The Eclipse *concluded a certain discourse, but at the same time opened up another one, which you then investigated further in* Red Desert. *We are referring to a certain type of social and class criticism within an Italian context. Why, after* Red Desert *is your cinema no longer focusing on Italian society?*

Because it seems to me that all I had to show of Italian society I have already shown. Already with *Red Desert* I had slightly broadened the subject-matter. It was one of the first films (and here in Italy, undoubtedly the first) to deal with ecology. Ecology began to be discussed after 1964, when the pollution of the waters, the destruction of the forests, etc., were quite advanced. With *Red Desert* I already started to bring national issues into an international context. Then I left, because I felt that my "cinematic clothes" were becoming a bit too tight. Besides, it was impossible to situate the photographer of *Blow-Up* in Italy at that time. After *Blow-Up*, I felt I was being drawn outside of my country. I did not have the desire to return and film here.

In the future, will you return and film in Italy?

I would like to make a film in Italy now. However, I find myself faced with a conflict. To avoid certain topics (the same ones I mentioned answering your first question) would seem to me to betray the situation here, and to be untrue to myself, because these are topics I'm sensitive to, topics I would like to deal with.

At the same time, I understand that it is not possible to search in as much depth as I would like to, because there are too many things that are hidden, too many things that one can't understand. I cannot speak of them because I do not have a direct knowledge of them. I would say that, after all, everything here is happening behind the scenes. What do I know of what happens with the Mafia? It seems to me very evident that the Mafia is involved with the kidnappings that are going on nowadays. And it seems even more evident that nothing is done against the Mafia, even with an anti-Mafia commission that has been working for the past fifteen years, and whose activities are hardly known. Now, whose interest is it to keep it hidden? Which political ties are there, behind the Mafia?

I do not like to deal with topics that remain so mysterious. I would have to search in depth, and who would allow me to do so? On the other hand, when we talk about kidnapping, we don't talk about unusual things. I am trying to move from my house in Rome because it is too small. The other day, I saw that the owner of the building, under construction, where I am supposed to move soon had a gun in his coat. I asked him why, and he told me: "Right below here is where [the industrialist] Danesi was kidnapped." I saw [the jeweler] Bulgari: he, too, walks around with a gun. He is right. What should he do? Kidnapping has becomes an issue that touches us personally, and we find ourselves faced with it—in the guise of sons and dughters of kidnapped parents, of big guns, and so on.

But how can one talk about these things? I would have to touch upon them lightly, in a newspaper fashion; but that's not enough for me. On the other hand, this situation is taken for granted outside of Italy. For them, everything that happens in Italy is of no importance. In case I decided to make a film about this, it would be a film of purely national interest, without any international appeal. I am torn between the desire to make a film here in Italy in order to find my roots, and the awareness of not being able to make the film that should be made.

The Eclipse contains some sequences commonly cited as "required viewing." The ending is a sample of pure and almost abstract cinema; but there is also the Stock Exchange sequence, an hallucinatory synthesis of the madness produced by the greed for money. Do you remember where the idea for that sequence came from?

I happened to meet women who played the stock market, like the mother of Monica Vitti's character, and they seemed to be characters so odd that I felt drawn to them. So I started to investigate the matter a little further. I asked for a pass to enter the Stock Exchange and I was given one. For fifteen, twenty days I went there (I even speculated a little; I bought some shares and then resold them, miraculously earning a little money—very little, indeed) and I understood that it was an extraordinary setting, even from a visual point of view. A bit like the gestures that the men in white gloves made at the dog races in the English episode of *The Vanquished.*

I do not know how they understand each other in the Stock Exchange, as they operate with such quick gestures. It is a special kind of language, which is based—and that was what really interested me—upon honesty. The stockbrokers have to be honest with each other. "With this gesture I purchased three thousand Montedison shares, and you have to give them to me. At precisely that price." There is nothing to do about it. If someone cheats, he will no longer work in the Stock Exchange.

A bit like the Mafia's honesty—

Well—I tried to reconstruct that environment employing all of the people that worked at the Stock Exchange: operators, brokers, bankers, and others. Very few extras. All people who knew how to move there. I gave [Alain] Delon a model to follow—a certain Paolo Vassallo who, curiously enough, was then involved in a kidnapping. He worked in the

Stock Exchange helping his father. Delon went to the Stock Exchange to study Paolo Vassallo: what he did, how he moved.

If we recall correctly, The Eclipse *had a surprising success in different parts of the world, especially in Japan. In Italy, however, despite the consensus of the critics, it never became too popular. Do you think that the public, now, has become mature enough to grasp the meaning of the film?*

The success of *The Eclipse* in Japan is explained by the very slow rhythm of the film, broken only now and then by "outbursts," such as the Stock Exchange sequences. The Japanese liked that a lot, and they already knew and loved Delon and Monica Vitti. Keep in mind, also, that the film "opens" with a song by Mina.[7]

In Italy, I do not think that the public has changed to the point of being able not only to "appreciate" the film, but also to "follow" its rhythm—which, by the way, I would not give any film today. I have become a little detached from its subject matter, and also from this type of cinema, based on a relationship between two types of people who no longer exist today. The girl is from Rome, deeply bourgeois, and therefore—how can I say it?—a bit a victim of certain moral principles. Therefore she is a little scared to let herself into that relationship. Nowadays, perhaps, this type of reticence would not exist. The conclusion of the relationship could be the same, but the relationship would probably be different. It would develop in a more candid and less reticent manner; with less modesty, I would say; with fewer drawbacks.

Was it difficult for you to make a film of this kind — of a "different" kind. Did you have difficulties with the producers? Or, after L'avventura *and* La notte, *was everything fine?*

Before *Blow-Up* I never had an important commercial success. It started with *Blow-Up,* which earned a lot money and opened many

---

7 Mina [Anna Maria Mazzini] has bee one of Italy's most popular singers for the past four decades. The opening song of *The Eclipse* is called "Il twist" [The Twist].

doors for me. The producers cut the ending of *The Eclipse*. In the theaters it was shown with several cuts. In the version shown on TV, the ending should be the original one—at least I hope so.

But the reputation that you already had outside of Italy must have already contributed to give you credit with the producers. For example in France.
Yes, in France, *L'avventura* did very well at the box office. Also *La notte*. Anyway—here is a curious thing—I wanted to make two films of *The Eclipse*, one from the point of view of the woman [played by Vitti], and one from the stockbroker's. The producers instead would only allow one film. I think that it would have been interesting to make a film from his point of view, because it would have shown the world of money, where feelings have hardly any place.

There are directors who feel (or pretend to feel) almost a sense of repulsion when faced with some of their works. What is now your state of mind, your attitude toward The Eclipse?
I will not watch *The Eclipse* again on TV because I never look back, I always look ahead. Because of this, I never make period films, and I do not make films about historical characters. Fellini knows how to do this very well. He can talk of himself, he can relate events dealing with his childhood, he can take historical figures like Casanova and manipulate them in his own way. I do not think that I would be capable of doing that.

You were given the label of the "alienation director." Did you appreciate this definition, or did you find it limiting? Limiting in the sense that it did not correspond to the truth and that there were other themes, other arrows in your bow?
I do not really understand what this label means because there are quite a few types of alienation: there is Freud's, Hegel's, Marx's—there are so many! Everybody talks about alienation, but in a different way. I don't know what kind of alienation mine is. I don't want to delve into it, because I can't give an objective critical evaluation of what I do with my

films. Certainly, I have been interested for a long time in the so-called alienated relationship between human beings. But not as a type of alienation, but rather as a type of story that I can find all the time in the real world around me.

Dario Fo,[8] on his recent return from China, expressed a negative opinion on your documentary on China. What would reply to him?

For me, this controversy is closed. I just don't feel like going on with it. I would like only to add one point with regard to Joris Ivens, whom Fo mentions. He states that Ivens's documentary on China [*How Yukong Moved the Montains*] has enlightened him on the realities of that country. If Fo takes a camera and walks through the streets of Peking and through the countryside where I have been, and shoots whatever he sees, what he gets will be the film I made. If instead, he plans everything from A to Z, very meticulously, what he gets will be Ivens's film. They are two different films. I did not want to make Ivens's kind of film; I wanted to make the film that I made. By the way, Ivens could not have acted differently, because, unfortunately, he had lost his sight.

LEONARDO AUTERA
ETTORE MO

---

[8] Actor, stage director, and playwright, Dario Fo is one of Italy's best known theater personality. His four-decade career, based on an original research on comic languages and gestuality, has often been devoted to expressing strong, and dissenting, political views.

RED DESERT[9]

In *Red Desert* I used color for the first time. I don't think that's particularly significant since color is such a part of modern society. Many color films I have seen have fascinated me and at the same time left me unsatisfied. Because while, on the one hand, they gave me a more realistic picture of the external reality of people and things, on the other hand, the colors were never the right ones to fully capture the feelings generated by the relationships between people and things. I have, therefore, tried to exploit each and every narrative resource of color in such a way that it contributed to the mood of each sequence.

The similarities in certain new ways of utilizing color in modern cinema—I'm thinking for example of [Alain] Resnais and [Ingmar] Bergman—is not a coincidence. It's a need that we directors have all felt at the same time, because it's connected to expressing the reality of our times, which in my opinion is something that cannot ignore color. In *Red Desert*, we are in an industrial world which every day produces millions of objects of all types, all in color. Just one of these objects is sufficient—and who can do without them?—to introduce into the house an echo of industrial living. Thus, our houses are full of color, and our streets and public places are full of colorful posters. With the invasion of colors we have become addicted to them.

---

[9] From *Humanité dimanche*, 23 September, 1964. Translated by Andrew Taylor.

When, around the turn of the century, the world began to industrialize, factories were painted neutral colors—black or gray. Today, instead, most of them are brightly painted. Even our water pipes, electricity cables, and heating systems are colored. Behind this invasion of color lie technical causes, but also psychological ones. The walls of the factories are colored not red, but light green or pale blue—the so-called "cool" colors, on which the workers can rest their eyes.

I always thought of *Red Desert* in color. The idea for it came to me as I was going through the countryside around Ravenna. I was born in Ferrara, which is about seventy kilometers from Ravenna, and for a long time I went there many times a year for different reasons, but especially to take part in tennis tournaments. Since then, Ravenna has become the second port of Italy, after Genoa. The violent transformation of the countryside around the city has had a strong effect on me. Before, there were immense groves of pine trees, very beautiful, which today are completely dead. Soon even the few that have survived will die and give way to factories, artificial waterways, and docks. This is a reflection of what is happening in the rest of the world. It seemed to be the ideal background for the story I had in mind—naturally, a story in color.

The world that the characters in the film come into conflict with isn't the world of factories. Behind the industrial transformation lies another one—a transformation of the spirit, of human psychology. This new way of life conditions the behavior both of those who work in the factories and of those who, outside of it, suffer its effects. The characters in *Red Desert* are in close contact with the industrial world. Giuliana, the protagonist, is a neurotic. And where do her neuroses take her? To attempting suicide. Giuliana—and perhaps I didn't explain this well enough in the film—tries to cut her life short by driving her car into a truck. The "accident" that she talks about and confesses to (because she is perfectly aware of what she did) is a consequence of her neurosis, not its cause.

Giuliana cannot adapt to the new "way" of life and she goes through a crisis, while her husband, on the other hand, is content with his lot in life. And then there is Corrado. He has almost got to the point of neurosis and thinks he can cure himself by going to Patagonia.

I'm not against progress. But there are people who, by their nature, by their moral makeup, have to wrestle with the modern world and can't manage to adapt to it. And thus we witness a sort of process of natural selection: the ones who survive are those who manage to keep up with progress, while the others disappear, swallowed up by their crises. Because progress is inexorable, like revolutions. In the same way that some people suffer during a revolution, there is also a malaise connected to progress. It's life itself and there is nothing extraordinary about that.

I read somewhere that before he went into space, [Soviet cosmonaut Ermann] Titov spent the day out walking in Moscow with his wife, perfectly calm, doing a thousand little things that had nothing to do with the mission that he was about to undertake. That's an entirely new situation: a couple living in a hitherto unknown dimension of life. Progress rudely intrudes on human intimacy.

I tried to show characters who cannot adapt, because it is in them that this situation becomes a drama. Giuliana lives through a profound crisis because of her inability to adapt to the modern world. And it's not by chance that there was only one scene in which I used color "normally"— that is, leaving colors their natural hues. It is the scene in which Giuliana, having run out of stories to tell her sick son, makes one up with great simplicity and purity of heart. In that sequence, the plot is suspended, as if the eye and the conscience of the narrator had been distracted elsewhere. In fact, that sequence, in which each element—and first of all, color—tells a fragment of the human experience, shows reality as Giuliana wishes it were—that is, different from the world that appears to her as transformed, alienated, obsessive to the point of being monstrously deformed.

The electronic music, a sort of transfiguration of real noises—especially in the first part of the film, the part about the factories—finds a counterpart in the sounds that Giuliana hears. It was the only musical score that seemed suited to those images. But, how to explain the unfocused areas that highlight certain other parts of the frames? The truth is that it's only while you shoot that you find the right technique for telling a story. While I was working on my first film, I felt the need to shoot some very long takes. Only afterward did I understand why. For *Red*

286 / THE ARCHITECTURE OF VISION

Desert, on the other hand, I chose very short takes. Perhaps it was the fact that I was using color that suggested this technique to me, this deep-seated need to deal with it in large blotches, as if they were pulsations that penetrate chaotically inside the characters.

I think the background that you see as the title credits roll is very beautiful. The colors are superb. In the countryside around Ravenna, the horizon is dominated by factories, smokestacks and refineries. The beauty of that view is much more striking than the anonymous mass of pine trees which you see from afar, all lined up in a row, the same color. The factory is a more varied element, more lively, because behind it one can detect the presence of man and human life, his dramas and hopes. I am in favor of progress, and yet I realize that because of the disruption it brings, it also causes trouble. But that is modern life, and the future is already knocking at our door.

Red Desert isn't really a continuation of my previous work. Before, the environment in which my characters lived was described indirectly through their own positions, their psychology and feelings and backgrounds. What those films were most about was the personal relationships of the characters.

In *Red Desert*, I wanted to highlight more the relationship between the characters and the world around them. I tried, therefore, to rediscover the traces of ancient human feelings which are buried nowadays under a welter of conventions, gestures, and rhythms that amount to substitutes; and under a conciliatory "public-relations" jargon that hides our true feelings. It's almost like being an archeologist, digging through the dry and arid material of the modern age. If this kind of "digging" shows through more clearly in *Red Desert*, it is also because our world is slowly becoming easier to study.

FRANÇOIS MAURIN

THE NIGHT, THE ECLIPSE, THE DAWN[10]

Your three previous films, L'avventura, La notte, The Eclipse, *gave the impression of developing out of one another and standing along the same line of inquiry. And now you seem to have reached a new destination with* Red Desert. *For the woman in the film, perhaps, it is a desert but for you, it is something fuller, more complete: it's a film about the whole world and not just about the world of today.*

For the moment, it's very hard for me to talk about *Red Desert.* It's too recent a film. I'm still too close to the "intentions" that drove me to make it; I don't have the clarity of thought and the detachment necessary to judge it correctly. Still, I think I can say that this time I haven't made a film about feelings. The results that I had obtained from my previous films—good or bad as they may be—have by now become obsolete. The question is completely different. At one time, I was interested in the relationships of characters to one another. Now, instead, the main character must confront her social environment, and that's why I treat the story in a completely different way. It's too simplistic to say—as many people have done—that I am condemning the inhuman industrial world which oppresses the individuals and leads them to neurosis. My intention—and I realize that one always knows where one starts off, but very rarely where one is going to—my intention was to translate the poetry of that world,

10 From *Cahiers du Cinéma* 160, November 1964. Translated by Andrew Taylor,

in which even factories can be beautiful. The lines and curves of factories and their chimneys can be more beautiful than the outline of trees, which we are already too accustomed to seeing. It is a rich world, alive and serviceable. I have to say that the neurosis I sought to describe in *Red Desert* is above all a matter of adjusting. There are people who do adapt, and others who can't manage, perhaps because they are too tied to ways of life that are by now out-of-date. This is Giuliana's problem. What brought on her personal crisis was the irreconcilable divide, the gap, between her sensibility, intelligence, and psychology, and the way of life that is imposed on her. It's a crisis that has to do not just with her surface relationships with the world—her perception of sounds, colors, and the coldness of the people around her—but with her whole system of values (social, moral, and religious), which are by now out-of-date and can no longer support her. She therefore finds that she has to reinvent herself completely as a woman. That is the advice her doctors give her and that she tries to follow. The film, in a sense, is the history of that effort.

How does the story she tells her child fit into all this?

There is a woman and there is a sick child. The mother has to tell a story to the sick child, but he already knows all the ones she knows. So she has to invent one. Considering Giuliana's psychology, I think it's natural that for her the story should become—unconsciously—an escape from the reality of her life, a way out to a world where the colors are those of nature. The sea is blue and the sand is white. Even the rocks take on a human form, embracing her and singing to her sweetly.

Do you remember the scene in the bedroom with Corrado? She is leaning against the wall and she says: "Do you know what I'd like? To have all the people who have loved me, to have them here around me like a wall." She needs them to help her live; she's afraid she might not make it by herself.

So the modern world is nothing but a tool to reveal an ancient, deeper neurosis?

The environment she lives in accentuates Giuliana's crisis, but naturally, for a crisis to occur, there must be fertile ground in which it can take root. It's not easy to determine the causes and origins of neurosis. It reveals itself in many forms; sometimes the symptoms look like schizophrenia. It's only by putting pressure on the character, by subjecting it to a sort of provocation, that you begin to grasp the situation. I have been criticized for having chosen a pathological case. But if I had chosen a woman who had integrated perfectly normally into society, there would have been no drama; drama lies in those who don't adapt to society's norms.

Weren't there, perhaps, already traces of this character in The Eclipse?

Vittoria, the character in *The Eclipse, i*s the opposite of Giuliana. She's a calm, well-balanced girl who thinks about what she is doing. There is absolutely no symptom of neurosis in her. In *The Eclipse,* the crisis has to do with emotions. In *Red Desert,* the emotions are taken for granted. The relationship between Giuliana and her husband is normal. If someone asked her: "Do you love your husband?," she would say: Yes. Until her attempted suicide, her crisis is buried deep insied her, it's almost imperceptible.

I would like to make clear that it's not her environment that causes her crisis: that's just the trigger. You might think that outside of that environment there would be no crisis. That's not so. Even though we don't realize it, our lives are dominated by "industry." And by "industry," I don't just mean the factories themselves, but also their products. They are all over our houses, made of plastic or materials that, up to a few years ago, were totally unknown. They are brightly colored and they chase after us everywhere. They haunt us from the advertisements, which appeal ever more subtly to our psychology, to our subconscious. I would go as far as to say that by setting the story of *Red Desert* in the world of factories, I have got to the source of that crisis that, like a river, collects together a thousand tributaries and then bursts out into a delta, overflowing its banks and drowning everything.

Doesn't the beauty of the modern world also represent an answer to people's psychological problems, revealing their futility?

The drama of these individuals, who are so conditioned by society, should not be underestimated. Without this type of drama, perhaps mankind wouldn't even exist. Still, I don't think that the beauty of the modern world can solve all of our dramas by itself. On the contrary, I think that if we learn how to adapt ourselves to the new techniques of life, perhaps then we will find new solutions to our problems.

But why do you make me talk about these things? I'm not a philosopher, and these discussions have nothing to do with the "invention" of a film.

Is the robot in the little boy's bedroom a good or an evil presence in his life?

A good one, I think. Because if he gets used to that sort of toy, he will prepare himself for the type of life that is awaiting him. But we are getting back to what we were talking about just now. Toys are the product of industry, which through them exercises its influence also over the education of young children.

I am still amazed by a conversation I had with a professor of cybernetics at the University of Milan, Silvio Ceccato, who the Americans hold in high esteem, a sort of a new Einstein. He's amazing, he has invented a machine that is capable of seeing and of describing what it sees, of driving a car and writing an article from any given aesthetic, ethical, or political point of view. It's not a television, but a true electronic brain. In the course of our conversation, this man, who is so extraordinarily intelligent, didn't use a single technical term that I couldn't grasp. Well—I thought I was going mad. After a while I couldn't understand what he was talking about. Despite the fact that he was trying to speak my language, we were still living in two different worlds. Beside him was his secretary, of about twenty-four or twenty-five, a cute girl from the lower middle-class. She understood him perfectly. The people who program these electronic brains are, in Italy at least, usually young girls with an ordinary high-school diploma: for them it's very easy to deal with the thoughts of an electronic brain, while for me it's certainly not so.

Six months ago another scholar came to visit me in Rome, Robert M. Stewart. He had invented a chemical brain and he was going to Naples to a congress on cybernetics to tell them about his invention, one of the most extraordinary discoveries in the world. It was in a tiny box, mounted on a load of tubes: there were cells, made up of gold and other substances, in a chemical solution. These cells have a life of their own and have certain reactions: if you walk into a room, they take on one shape, whereas if I walk in, they take on another, and so on. In that little box there were a few million cells, but from such basis you can actually reconstruct a human brain. That man feeds them, puts them to sleep—he talked to me about it very clearly, but it was so incredible that at a certain point I couldn't follow him anymore. Yet, a child who has played with robots from his earliest years would understand perfectly; such a child would have no problem going into space on a rocket, if he wanted to.

I feel very envious of such people. I really wish I were already part of that new world. Unfortunately, we are not there yet, and for older generations, such as mine or that of people born just after the war, this is a real tragedy. I think that in the next few years we will see some major violent transformations, both in the physical world and in man's psyche. The current crises derive form this spiritual confusion, which is also moral, religious, and political. So I have asked myself: "What does cinema have to say to us today?" And that's why I wanted to tell a story about the things I mentioned before.

And yet the male heroes of your films are part of this mentality. They are engineers; they are part of this new world.

No, absolutely not. Richard Harris is an almost romantic figure, thinking of running away to Patagonia. He hasn't the least idea of what he should be doing. He wants to go away; he thinks that in this way he will solve his existential crisis. He doesn't realize that the problem is inside himself, not outside. In fact, meeting a woman is enough to make him doubt whether he really wants to leave. This encounter upsets him. I would like to emphasize one moment in the film which is intended as a criticism of the old world. When the woman, in the middle of her crisis, needs help, she meets a man who takes advantage of her and her insecurity. They are the same old things that overwhelm her. Somebody like her husband would have acted differently: first he would have tried to help her then perhaps later—but as it is, she's betrayed by her own world.

At the end of the film will she perhaps become more like her husband?

I think that after the effort of trying to find a connection with reality, she might end up by compromising. Neurotics go through periods of crisis, but also periods of lucidity that can last a lifetime. She may find a compromise, but the neurosis will stay with her forever. I wanted to hint at this idea of continuing sickness by the slightly unfocused images. She is in a static phase of her life. What will become of her? I'd have to make another film to find out.

Do you think that being conscious of modernity has any repercussions on your aesthetics, on your work as an artist?

Yes, of course. It alters my way of seeing things. It changes everything. Pop art is a proof that we are looking for something new. Pop art should not be underestimated. It's an "ironic" movement, and a conscious irony is extremely important. Apart from [Robert] Rauschenberg, who is more of a painter than the others, pop artists are well aware that the aesthetic value of their work isn't yet mature—though [Claes] Oldenburg's *Soft Typewriter* is beautiful, I like it a lot. I think it's a good thing that all this has been expressed. It can only accelerate the transformation process I talked about.

Do scientists share this awareness? Do they see the world as we do?

I put that same question to Stewart, the inventor of the chemical brain. He replied that his particular job certainly has an effect on his private life and on his relationships with his family.

And feelings? Should we keep them?

What a question! Do you think it's easy to answer something like that? All I can say is that our feelings have to change. "Have to"—I should say they are already changing, have changed.

In science fiction novels, characters are never artists or poets.

That's true, it's strange. Perhaps they think they can do without art. Perhaps we will be the last to produce completely superfluous things like works of art.

Did Red Desert *also help you to solve some personal problems?*

Filmmaking means living, and so it also means solving personal issues—issues that have to do with work, but also with private life. If people are no longer talking about the same things as they did after the war, that's because the world has changed around us, but also because we have changed. Our needs, our goals, our arguments have changed.

Right after the war, there were many things that had to be said. What counted was to show social reality, the social conditions of the individual. Today, this has already been done, already seen. The new themes that we have to deal with are the ones I have already mentioned. I don't yet know how to deal with them, how they should be presented. In *Red Desert,* I think I have at least touched upon one of them, even if I haven't treated it fully. We have just begun to confront a series of problems, of aspects of modern society, of our way of living. Even you, Mr. Godard, make very modern films; your way of dealing with certain topics reveals a need to break with the past.

When you start or end a shot of an abstract shape, of an object or detail, do you do so in the same spirit as a painter?

I feel the need to express reality in terms that are not completely realistic. The white abstract line that breaks into the shot of the little gray road interests me much more than the car which is coming toward us. It's a way of getting close to the character by starting from things instead of from her life—which, after all, is of only relative importance to me. Her character is part of the story in a way that is dependent on her femaleness, her female outlook and personality—which I think are essential to the story. That is why I wanted the part to be played in a slightly static kind of way.

On this point, too, there is a break with your previous films.

Yes, figuratively speaking, it is a less realistic film. That is to say, it's realistic in a different way. For example, I used the camera lens to limit the depth of field, which is of course an essential element in realism. What interests me now is to put the characters in contact with things, because today what counts are things, objects, matter. I don't believe that *Red Desert* is the last word; it is, rather, an ongoing piece of research. I want to tell different stories with different tools. Everything that has been done, everything that I have done up until now, no longer interests me; it bores me. Perhaps you also feel the same way?

Did shooting in color represent an important change for you?

Very important. I was forced to change my technique, although it wasn't just because of color. I was already feeling the need to make a change for the reasons we were talking about. My needs were no longer the same, and using color only accelerated the change. Color requires different lenses. Besides, I realized that certain camera movements were no longer possible: a fast pan works well if the main color is bright red, but it doesn't work if the color is olive green, unless it is meant to suggest new contrasts. I think that there is a relationship between color and the camera. One film alone is not sufficient to examine the problem in depth, but it is a problem which has to be studied. I had done some interesting experiments on 16mm film, but I have been able to put in the film only some of the effects I had discovered. Sometimes, one is just to busy.

You know that there is such a thing as a psychophysiology of color; studies and experiments have been done about it. The inside of the factory in the film was painted red; in the space of two weeks, the workers on the set had come to blows. The experiment was repeated, painting everything pale green and calm was restored. The workers' eyes need to be soothed.

How did you choose the colors for the shop?

We had to choose between warm and cool tones. For her shop, Giuliana needs cool colors, because they show off better the things she has to sell. Against a wall painted bright orange, the things would be drowned, while against a pale blue or green the objects would stand out without being overwhelmed. I was interested in the contrast between cool and warm colors; there was orange, yellow, a brown ceiling—and Giuliana realizes that for her it is no good.

Originally the title of your film was going to be "Pale Blue and Green."
I dropped it because it didn't seem to me to be strong enough. It was too tied to the idea of color. I never thought of color, per se. The film was conceived in color, yes, but obviously my main concern was what needed to be said, even though I did use color in order to express that. I never thought: "Now let's put a blue next to a brown." I wanted the grass around the hut to be colored in order to accentuate the sense of desolation, of death. I had to give the landscape a certain truth: dead trees really are that color.

So the drama is not just psychological, but also plastic.
Well, it's the same thing.

And all those shots of objects during the conversation about Patagonia?
It corresponds to a sort of "absent-mindedness" on the part of the character. He's tired of all that talking. He's thinking of Giuliana.

The dialogues are simpler, more functional than in your previous films. Perhaps their traditional function as commentary on the action has been taken over by the use of color?
Yes, I think that's it. Let's say that they have been reduced to the bare minimum, and in that sense they are linked to the use of color. For example, in the scene in the hut where they are talking about drugs and stimulants, I couldn't *not* use red. In black and white it would never have worked. The red puts the viewer into a state of mind that allows him to accept such dialogues. It's the right color for the characters—who, in turn are justified by the color—and also for the viewer.

Do you feel closer to the methods of painters or of writers?

I feel close to the methods of the *nouveau roman*, even though they are less useful to me than certain others. I'm even more interested in painting and in a scientific methodology, although I don't believe they influence me directly. In my film, the methods of the painter are not used; we are very far from the exercise of painting—or at least, so it seems to me. And of course certain pictorial needs, which in painting do not have any narrative content, find this content in cinema. That is where the novel and painting come together.

Did you take up the offer by Technicolor to enhance the color of your film in the developing room?

I never rely on the developing room when I'm shooting. I mean that I try to give things and landscapes their correct color on location, so that I don't have to touch them up in the developing room. What I try to do instead is to use the lab to make sure that the effects are faithful to the original intention. It hasn't been easy because, as you know, Technicolor requires many processes to be performed on the film. It's been an extremely long and delicate process.

Did you do color adjustment during the shootings?

Precisely. I think that you should never rely too much on what can be done in the lab. It's not their fault. It's because with color, from a technical point of view, we are still quite unsophisticated.

Do you think that Giuliana sees colors as you do in the film?

Some neurotics do see color differently. Scientists have done experiments on this subject, using mescaline, for example, to discover what they really see. I have also thought of doing this type of experiment. In the film, there is only one scene where you see stains on the wall. I had thought of changing the colors of certain objects, too, but then it seemed to me that all those "tricks" were fake, that they were artificial ways of saying something which could be said much more simply. So I cut out those effects. Sure, we can say that she sees colors differently.

It's odd. Here I am talking to Mr. Godard, one of the best and most modern directors today, and just a while ago I had lunch with René Clair, one of the greatest directors of the past. The conversation with him was rather different. He is worried about the future of cinema. We—I think you will agree—have faith in the future of cinema.

And what will you do now?

I'm preparing an episode with Soraya.[11] With this story, I want to continue the research into colors, pushing it beyond the experiments I did in *Red Desert*. And after that, I'll make a film that interests me even more. Provided that I can find a producer who will let me do it.

JEAN-LUC GODARD

[11] Iranian born Soraya Esfandiary became the Shah of Iran's second wife in 1951. After being divorced in 1958, she moved to Italy where she started an acting career, using her first name only, Soraya, as her stage name.

The American Desert[12]

What will your film be called?

Zabriskie Point. It's the name of a place in Death Valley, in the California desert.

Blow-Up represents your English experience. Will the new film deal with an analogous experience in the United States? Or aren't places important to you?

Places are important. But *Blow-Up*'s story could have happened anywhere. *Zabriskie Point*, instead, is a film about America. America is the real protagonist of the film. The characters are just a pretext.

Don't you think that the themes of your past films (incommunicability, solitude, anguish, alienation and so forth) find their greatest confirmation in Anglo-Saxon society? That is, don't you think that these themes are, after all, the real themes of the most advanced form of neocapitalism?

Yes, that's true. These themes have a clearer, more extreme, more profound resonance here in the United States.

How does the revolt of young people (students, hippies, beatniks) fit into your usual world? I mean: until now you have shown us the middle-class grappling with its problems, but you have shown us them from within, you've accepted

[12] "Il deserto America," from *L'Espresso colore*, 11 August 1968. Translated by Carmen Di Cinque.

the values of the bourgeoisie itself. Students, young people, it seems to me, deliberately place themselves outside of the system; they try, as they say nowadays, to challenge it. Does this dissent interest you?

Yes, it interests me; in fact, I have incorporated it into the film.

In what way?

I can't say. I'll limit myself to mentioning that the characters of *Zabriskie Point* are in a certain way typical of the present American situation. More than a psychological affinity they share an ideological affinity. Ideological affinity in turn becomes a means to communication, to mutual understanding.

Don't you think that something has changed in these last years? Western society seemed entrapped in the mechanism of well-being, without an escape route and, what's worse, without being aware of it. Revolt is always an indication of an attempt at consciousness raising, objectivity, explanation, comprehension. To revolt does not only mean to reject subjugation, but also to affirm one's own autonomy. In this case, it means to reject not so much society as much as the idea that man is powerless to change society, and that reality is an impenetrable mystery. What do you say?

I think so, too. Nevertheless, reality continues to be just as much of a mystery. What's new, if anything, is that young people today do not want to submit passively to this mystery. And that they use it as a springboard, so to speak, for revolt. Anyway, I don't believe that man is powerless. The change for the better that has taken place in recent years, if nothing else, proves that.

What is your relationship with America? I mean, what are the points of friction? In what ways do you feel provoked, offended, humiliated, irritated?

My relationship with America reflects the division of Americans into very distinct categories: in one camp are two-thirds of the population, irritating and unbearable people; the other third are wonderful people. The first group is the middle-class; the second one is today's youth. Among young people there is an absolute indifference toward money, there is purity, disinterestedness, revolt and change. The middle-class, instead, I would call a social class of crazy people because, after all, despite all their alienation, they are uncorrupted and well-meaning. The European middle-class, you see, is corrupt and therefore is not crazy.

Would you like to become an American director? Do you consider the American experience as the beginning of a new phase of your career?
No, I consider it a transitory experience.

Figuratively speaking, has America suggested something new to you?
Yes, in a figurative sense, America has really made a strong impression on me. It was jarring. Particularly advertising. Everything is so photogenic that you don't know where to begin.

In America, they say, there aren't classes but races. In your opinion, is this true?
In America there is everything as far as divisions go: there are races, sub-races and so on, and then there are classes, sub-classes and so on. And there's more. Their mania for inequality persists even within a democracy that should function as an overall equalizer. For example, there are these receptions where, for lack of other criteria, only people with an income greater than one hundred thousand dollars are invited.

What has struck you most in working on an American production in comparison to a European production?
Cinema in America is less improvised, less original than in Europe. Everything is more bureaucratic and more mechanical. Americans are very tied to routine.

Do you generally like your relationship with Americans? Doesn't it seem automatic, impersonal? Don't you miss the relationship you have with Italians, which is so much more irregular and sometimes even unpleasant but always personal?
I do prefer the relationship with Italians. But my relationship with the American world is an important experience.

Do the producers impose their own will? Do you have labor problems? Is your relationship with the producers smooth or difficult?

It's smooth. My real problem is understanding the country and trying to make the right film.

Is there an ideological tendency (conscious or unconscious) in the American cinematographic industry? I mean: is there a conformist barrier?

Is there? And how!

To what extent will a major production studio like Metro Goldwyn Mayer allow an art film to be made?

I would say that you can't put the question in those terms. Because MGM films have to make money. If they make money, MGM stocks go up; if not, they fall. Does an art film like *Blow-Up* make money? If it does, fine, let's make art films.

In general, does the United States thrill you or depress you?

It thrills me when I understand it. It depresses me when I don't understand it.

Have the themes of your films been enriched by the American experience?

Yes they have. Then again, novelty is always a great thing. I was tired of seeing the same people all the time, the same landscapes.

How do you explain the fact that until now no European director has managed to adjust to America?

Perhaps because they have found America to be a curious, exotic country. My greatest concern—I even lose sleep over it—is not to approach America as a curious, exotic country, but to capture its deep, authentic characteristics. On the other hand, I must acknowledge that I experience some difficulty fitting in, because, in fact, I do not want to find a point of contact with the American world beyond the realm of work. Basically, I feel a little rejected and I reject a little, too. And then the language is a problem, at least for me.

What do you think of Hollywood and underground cinema? Do you like the fact that Hollywood is capable of adopting the experiences of the underground and making them its own?

There is a lot of bad stuff; but there are also good films, in underground cinema. Underground films influence Hollywood and viceversa. For example, recently the underground has taken a few steps backwards. [Jonas] Mekas, who is more or less the ideologue, says that we need to return to the plot, to the narrative sequence. There is an osmosis between the two form of cinema.

And the actors? Where will you get the actors?

Off the street. I have already found the female lead: she is a student in San Francisco. I thought I had found the male lead the other day, in a restaurant. He was a blond hippy, handsome, very young. He was exactly what I was looking for. While I was trying to figure out what to do to approach him, the irreparable happened. A policeman showed up, looked at him; he took off, escaped, disappeared. The cop followed him but it was no use. I never saw him again. He probably ran out of there like that because of some drug problem.

You are an autobiographical director, in the sense that the themes of your films are projections of your experiences, isn't that true?

In this film I used other people's experiences. But I hope to make them my own.

Will you film in the studio?

In the studio, film crystallizes, it becomes impermeable to the unexpected. I will film on location as much as possible. If there are any riots (black uprisings) this summer, I'll be there with a camera. Also, they are demolishing an entire neighborhood of Los Angeles to build a new one. I'll film this too.

You said that you'll incorporate the young people's revolt into your film. What is it that attracts you about this revolt?

The fact that it's not tied to any ideological system, that it's anarchistic.

In your films first comes the point and then the story; or does the story come first and then the point?
First the story and then the point. For example, I only discovered the point of *Blow-Up* a month ago.

Where have you gone to scout the location for Zabriskie Point?
I traveled a lot: New York, Los Angeles, San Francisco, Palm Springs, Las Vegas, Barnstone, Death Valley, Sacramento, Miami, Cape Kennedy, Nashville, Chicago, New Orleans, Montreal, Dallas, Houston—

And which locations have you chosen?
I have decided on Los Angeles and Arizona.

How did the story come about?
I had some notes on America. The story took shape from these notes.

How long will it take?
A film takes one year. This one will take a year and a half, maybe two years.

Doesn't it seem to you that the postwar years were "lost" years? And that now everything is beginning to be more interesting?
The immediate post-war period was great. The period between 1950 and 1960 was very boring. Now things are better, it's true.

One last question: would you like to be younger?
I am younger now—younger than I will be when I am older.

ALBERTO MORAVIA

ZABRISKIE POINT[13]

Antonioni's sympathy with the young radicals was very apparent. When I asked him what kind of a reception he had received from them, he replied:

They didn't trust me at the beginning, and they were right. First of all, I walked in and said I was working for MGM, for the establishment. But after many, many meetings, and after I had started working with Fred Gardner, who is one of them, and after he explained to them what I was trying to do, they became much more open. And they allowed me to use the initials of their group, SDS [Students for a Democratic Society], which is important.

But this sympathy does not mean that he is uncritical of the movement or unaware of the problems it faces. He seemed very sensitive to the differences between student radicals in America and elsewhere.

The student movement in America is different because they are less together. There are many, many groups. They can't work together yet. You know this country is so big, so contradictory, that it is more difficult here for them to do something important. When something happens in Paris, it is happening in France. When something happens in Rome, it is happening in Italy. And the same thing for Berlin in Germany. Not here. When something happens in Los Angeles, it doesn't matter for New

---

13 From *Sight & Sound*, Winter 1968–69.

York—it has nothing to do with New York. What happened at Columbia University was important here, but as an echo. They don't have any relationship. They get in touch sometimes, but they don't work together. At least, that is what they themselves admit.

It would be misleading to overemphasize the political aspects of this film. Despite rumour, Antonioni sees it as a film about interior feelings.
 I think that this film is about what two young people feel. It is an interior film. Of course, a character always has a background.

The contemporary context, the young central characters and the setting seem crucial. I wonder which came first and how he had decided to make this particular film.
 I took two trips to America (the first in the spring of 1967 and the second in autumn). I had this idea to do a film here because I wanted to get out of Italy and Europe. Nothing was started in Europe yet, I mean this movement of youth. When I came to America, the first thing that interested me was this sort of reaction to the society as it is now—not just to the society, but to the morality, the mentality, the psychology of old America. I wrote some notes, and when I came back I wanted to know if what I had written down, the intuition, was true or not. My experience taught me that when an intuition is beautiful, it is also true. When I came back I realized that what I had in mind *was* true. I decided on this story when I came to Zabriskie Point. I found that this particular place was exactly what I was looking for. I like to know where the story is placed. I have to see it somewhere to write something. I want a relationship between the characters and the place; I can't separate them from their milieu.

But their milieu was not Antonioni's. I wondered whether he could really feel comfortable in making a film about this world which was essentially foreign to him and in a foreign language.
 I wrote this story, the story is mine. I called in Tonino Guerra, whom I have worked with before; but he doesn't speak English and it was difficult

for him to help me get in touch with people, so Tonino went back. When the script was in the synopsis stage (without dialogue or an indication of dialogue), I started to look for someone else because I could not write dialogue in Italian. You can't translate dialogue. An American answers in a different way from an Italian or Frenchman. I wanted to write the dialogue in English. I started to read a lot of plays and books, and I found Sam Sheppard, who started to work on the dialogue for the film. I did the first version of the script with him. I did many versions of the script, and then I got in touch with Fred Gardner, who is one of these young people and very cooperative. The last version of the script was written with him, but I am still changing as I am shooting.

The process of change was very apparent on location. For example it had been reported that the following week Antonioni was importing hundreds of people from San Francisco, Salt Lake City, and Las Vegas to shoot a love-in, but on the day of the interview he changed his mind.

It was just an idea, but I never saw this idea as something real. I didn't have the image, I couldn't find the key to doing it. I saw lots of love-ins in America—with groups playing and people smoking or dancing or doing nothing, just lying on the ground. But I was looking for something different—something which was more related to the special character of Zabriskie Point, and I couldn't find this relationship. I'm going to put it in the film anyway, but in a different way—just a few people and the background almost empty.

Last-minute changes have always been an essential part of Antonioni's method of working. He has never been tied to a script before, and this film is no exception. When asked how he decided a change had to be made, he replied:

A film is not one thing after another, everything in it is related. I know immediately when something is wrong. And if something is wrong here, the consequence is that it is also wrong later in the script. So if I have to change something here, I have to change something else. I can't judge a line until I hear the line said by the actor at the moment of shooting. Sometimes I shoot two versions of the same scene. I did this on one of the Mobil scenes. I shot one version and wasn't quite happy. I wanted something more ironic so I did another version of the scene. Maybe you hear a suggestion, you see a particular place, or going to the set in the morning you have an idea and you have to explore it.

The Mobil scene to which he referred is a sequence that takes place in Los Angeles. Antonioni constructed an expensive set high up atop the Mobil Building in downtown Los Angeles, which is supposed to be the plush offices of the Sunny Dunes Real Estate Company. In one shot he simultaneously has in focus a TV commercial for these land developers, the action inside the office, and the view of downtown L.A. outside the window.

When asked about his impressions of Los Angeles, Antonioni commented on the billboards:

The billboards are an obsession of Los Angeles. They are so strong that you can't avoid them. Of course, there is the danger of seeing Los Angeles as a stranger. To us the billboards are so contrary, but for people who live there they are nothing—they don't even see them. I am going to show them in the film, but I don't yet know how.

Apparently, he chose Los Angeles as a location because of its proximity to Death Valley.

This story should start in a city that is not so far from the desert. It is easy for someone from Los Angeles to come here. The desert is something very familiar to people who live in Los Angeles.

Yet there seemed to be a more meaningful connection between the two sites. When we were on location in Lone Pine looking at the dry lake bed below Mount Whitney, Antonioni observed that it had been drained because Los Angeles needed the water. It occurred to me that this was another example of Los Angeles as the consumer society. Los Angeles forces upon you an awareness of the materialistic culture; you are constantly confronted with objects to be desired, pursued, and replaced. It is both physically and emotionally draining. But Death Valley with its stark beauty merely exists without forcing anything upon you.

When I first heard that Antonioni was shooting in Death Valley, I immediately thought of the settings in The Cry, L'avventura, *and* Red Desert, *and assumed it would be linked to sterility. But once I got there and observed its beauty, I began to suspect that he might not fulfill these conventional expectations, that it might be used in a more complex way. In Lone Pine he casually remarked that Death Valley contains both the highest and lowest points in the United States. It is vast, cosmic, and varied. When I asked him specifically how he intended to treat Death Valley, he answered:*

When I came here, I had these two young people in mind. It seemed to me the best place to have them *out* of their milieu—to be free. Zabriskie Point was perfect; it was so primitive, like the moon. I'm not going to explore this landscape in the film in the same way that you see it when you come here. I want to put it in the background because otherwise it would be too strong.

This particular setting will undoubtedly affect Antonioni's use of color, for he seemed to use it quite differently in Red Desert *and* Blow-Up.

In *Red Desert* it was subjective. For the most part of the film, the reality was seen from the view of the woman who was neurotic, so that's why I changed the color of the backgrounds, the streets, everything. In *Blow-Up* my problem was completely different. I knew London because I had shot there before on one of the episodes in my second film. But when I went back to London, I found it so different. When I am visiting a town I have thousands of impressions and images. The problem for *Blow-Up* was that I had just a few exterior scenes of London, and I had to concentrate all my impressions in these few scenes. So I had to decide, more or less, what was the color of London—not for others, but for me. I changed the colors of the streets according to the story, not according to the real London. For *Blow-Up* it wasn't really London, it was something *like* London. But I didn't change the colors very much. In this new film I don't change colors; I try to exploit the colors that I have.

The changes in style are not limited to the use of color. Antonioni predicted there would be many changes, mainly because he is working in Panavision for the first time.

The technique for this film is different from *Blow-Up*. I am shooting in order to have the possibilities for choosing a style at the end in the cutting stage. I am shooting in different ways. I am talking primarily about the use of lenses. This is the first time I am shooting in Panavision, and Panavision forces you to use different techniques because the lenses are different. As soon as you get familiar with them, you have to exploit this difference. For example, I am using the sides much more than I did before because in this way you have a stronger relationship between the character and the background.

Since one of the main stylistic changes in Blow-Up *was the faster pace, I wondered whether this trend would continue in* Zabriskie Point.

In *Blow-Up* it was fast, very fast, because the character was lively and needed this sort of pace. I don't know here. In this film the plot is not so precise. In *Blow-Up* there was a beginning, and then something happens, and then you go straight to the end. Not here. The plot is much less strong in this film. The beginning of this film will be almost documentary. No plot at the beginning—but a mosaic of many things. And then the characters come out from this mosaic. So I don't know yet how fast the pace or beat will be. While I'm shooting I never think of that.

Since this is Antonioni's first experience of working in America, I was curious to discover whether there were any problems, especially in his relationship with MGM. *Although he did not feel any restrictions on his autonomy, he did express uneasiness about problems connected with the budget.*

My autonomy, I would say, is complete. They leave me free to do what I want. The only thing now is that they are starting to be worried about the budget. They ask me why the film is so expensive, but that's what I'm going to ask them. I don't know why it's so expensive, I really don't know. I have a crew that is only half the size of what is usual in America because I don't want a big crew.

It was clear that he considered the fact that they were over-budget the fault of the Americans and not his. In fact, he was horrified by the American tendency to waste money.

It seems to me I'm seeing such a waste of money. It seems to be almost immoral. I feel bad sometimes. For instance, they threw away a piece of gelatin that we used and the piece was still new. There is also a waste of film. If I am shooting with two or three cameras and I need this camera only in the middle of the scene, in Italy I would start with that camera just at that moment. Not here. They start from the beginning. It is a waste of film! They are consumers. They are used to wasting something—goods, materials, food, everything. And I'm *not* used to this.

Ironically, this tendency toward conspicuous consumption and waste seems to be one of the American characteristics under attack in Zabriskie Point.

Antonioni's crew was unusual not only because it was small, but also because it was surprisingly young for a Hollywood film. For many this was there first assignment on a feature, and most of them were very enthusiastic about working with Antonioni. The first assistant director, Bob Rubin, is only twenty-seven and his only experience is in television. Although Harrison Starr was associate producer in Rachel, Rachel, *this was his first assignment as an executive producer. The still photographs on the set were being shot by Bruce Davidson, a talented and noted artist in his own right. The press agent, Beverly Walker, who is very knowledgeable about cinema, came right from a job with the New York Film Festival. One of the electricians, Jerry Upton, is an avid film buff who has seen most of Antonioni's films several times. Since this kind of crew is unusual in Hollywood, I wondered whether Antonioni had selected it purposely. He admitted that he had tried to get as many young crew members as possible, but added:*

I have some elements of this crew who are not so young—some older people who worked, for instance, on the first film of Greta Garbo, on the first *Ben Hur*, on Stroheim's *Greed*. It's very amusing to talk to them about these things.

His problems were not limited to age; they also involved the unions. For one thing, he had tried to hire some black cameramen to shoot a sequence that takes place in a Negro ghetto but was unsuccessful because he couldn't find any black men in the union. Some of the problems with the unions were also linked with age.

I had a lot of problems with the unions, and in Hollywood this is much more difficult than in New York. The unions are so strong. There are lots of old people. You can't find what you are looking for. I needed some cameramen and some assistant cameramen—some young people used to shooting in the modern way, people who can zoom without your having to tell them the exact distance from the actors to the camera, people who can make changes on their own and who can sometimes do what they want. I *want* them to do that, to do something different from the script, maybe. At that critical moment, the assistant cameraman has to make the decision, but the American cameraman can't do this. That's why I was forced to bring some people from Italy.

Antonioni links these difficulties not only to the unions, but also the national character. He finds it much more difficult to work in America than in England.
    I don't know why, but English people are much more familiar to me. At the time I was making *Blow-Up*, at least, they were so mad—in a positive and very pleasant way—that they were almost Neapolitan (that's a joke). I like them, I like English people much more than Americans. I mean I find myself closer to them. The Americans are so cool sometimes. They need to know exactly what they are doing. Sometimes they are like Germans—fastidious, precise. This makes me upset because I like to have people around me who are more spontaneous.

This difficulty did not seem to apply to his relationship with his two leading actors—Mark Frechette, a twenty-year-old carpenter from Boston who is interested in founding an underground newspaper and who has never worked in a film before; and Daria Halprin, the 19-year-old daughter of Ann Halprin, head of the experimental San Francisco Dance Workshop. Daria is an anthropology major at Berkeley. She reminded me of a miniature Sophia Loren, with plenty of vitality, warmth, and guts. In the particular sequence I watched them shoot, Daria was in a car being buzzed by a plane (supposedly flown by Mark). The stunt pilot came so close in one pass that the plane scraped the radio antenna of the car. In the next shot the plane cashed Daria as she was running across the desert and came within five feet of her head. She was scared but kept her cool.

Antonioni seemed to select these non-professionals for their naturalness and spontaneity—which he couldn't find among actors.

I saw a lot of young people—actors and students in acting school, but I couldn't find the right people. And so I started to look for them out of the schools—out of the usual milieu of young actors; and I saw Daria in a film. She wasn't acting. There was a ballet in this film, and Daria was one of the girls dancing. I saw this face coming out from the back, and I was impressed. We made a test, and she was extraordinary. She had the best qualities for an actress. She is so sincere, she can communicate anything, everything. Finding Mark was much more difficult because I made a lot of tests of young people, students and actors before I could find anyone. One of these tests was Mark's.

He felt it was particularly fitting to use non-professionals like Mark and Daria for this film "because this story could have happened to them. They use their own names—first names and family names—in the film because the story is about them." In an attempt to preserve their naturalness, Antonioni is not allowing them to be interviewed or to see the rushes; which is probably a wise decision. The one time I saw Mark and Daria ruffled was when they read their first publicity. At first they were excited to see their names and pictures in print, but when they read the article they were angered by what was said. The writer didn't understand their respect for Antonioni, their attitude toward the film, or their sense of humour. Starring in a movie has not yet destroyed their "authenticity." And they know they are not just in any movie, but a movie by Antonioni (although Mark Frechette had never heard of Antonioni when he was first offered the part). They seem to be aware of why he chose them for their roles. Thus, they appear casual on the set while at the same time realize the implications of what it means to be acting in this film. They probably both will become stars, but this will probably be the high point of the careers.

And for Antonioni Zabriskie Point *looks as though it will also be a high point. For it deals with some of the most vital contemporary issues, it is visually exciting, and it continues his experimentation with the medium.*

MARSHA KINDER

The American Experience[14]

I think we can start with Blow-Up, *a film that for you constitutes a sort of conclusion, at least provisionally. This work appears to be a meditation on the structures of cinema, on what it means to "make films," on the value of an "artistic" experience today. It seems to be the most extreme expression of that "reflection on form" which is a constant presence in your work. Was it your deliberate intention to explore these things in* Blow-Up*?*

The answer to this question would be too long for an interview. If you have read Susan Sontag's article "Against Interpretation" you should know that she talks about form and analysis; about the new way of looking at and evaluating art that is being proposed to us, assuming that "art" still actually means something. Today, the old tools of "aesthetics" are clearly seen to be obsolete. To make a distinction between form and content leaves me a bit confused, because I don't know, in *Blow-Up*, how much content can be separated from form. Since the film deals with how an individual relates to reality, it's obvious that such a reality has to take on a certain shape, it has to be represented somehow, and thus one arrives inescapably at form.

That's really dealing with reality the way art does.

Yes, and especially because in this film there is a character who sees and yet doesn't see reality. All of this materializes in a form, an image, and that is the film, the substance of the film.

[14] From *Jeune Cinéma* 37, March 1969. Translated by Andrew Taylor.

In this film, one notices an impatience with certain traditional forms of "canonical" cinema. What worries you most about cinema as an artistic medium?

What is usually called the grammar of cinema—a certain way of shooting, of dealing with sequences by means of shots, counter-shots, preset camera movements, and so forth—these conventional techniques, which have been used to make many great films, are no longer helpful for the vitality of cinema. A film should be more fluid, more linked to particular circumstances. One can no longer be autobiographical in films today, except in as far as you succeed in transposing on film your everyday state of mind. That's why I like shooting on location, in real places that always give me new stimulations. When one talks of improvisation, one must remember that this implies changes that affect the film in its entirety. One can only write a film as it is being shot.

You have already partly answered the question about your concept of scriptwriting. Is the script something that you follow closely or that you use just as an outline while you are shooting?

I would like to answer by referring to a specific example. At the moment I am making a film in America. It is a film which is strongly tied to local current events. These events are not well known, I would even say they are almost obscure, that not even too many Americans know about them. So I have to leave it "open." At the moment, the script is only an outline; it will be completed in the fall, along with the film. Everything depends on what happens this summer. If one wants a film to reflect the real-life situation of a country, I think that this is the only way to proceed. In *Blow-Up*, the characters had their own personal histories and the place was merely a background to that. In this film, on the other hand, we are in a violent, authoritarian country, which conditions the characters to such an extent that they become living symbols of it.

It seems that the visual element in your films is taking on ever greater importance. What do you think of that? Does it imply a tendency toward a "freer" cinema, maybe even an abstract cinema?

I think that there are many of us who are tempted to make abstract films; that's nothing new. It's not even very difficult. However, as far as I'm concerned, and keeping in mind what we usually mean by the word "art" (and we don't even know what that will mean in the future), I think that there must be some kind of dialogue with the viewer. I was talking about this a while ago with Jonas Mekas, and he said that to arouse the public's interest, underground, dissident cinema had been forced to abandon that technique, which can only reach an élite and no one else. If Andy Warhol has been able to get the public's attention it has been thanks to some sort of scheming, if I may call it that. He himself said that he felt it as a duty to wish for a return to more "narrative" cinema: telling people their own life-stories—which are not the stories of traditional cinema—and also telling them with greater consistency. In short, I don't believe that abstract cinema, as we conceive of it today, is the route for cinema to take in the future. Making movies in a freer way means appealing to the viewer's sensibilities rather than his intellect; it means seeking greater and more personal involvement from the viewer. We have a much wider margin of freedom, in the sense that we appeal to a wider reality.

You have talked about the new American cinema. What interests you about it?
I don't think there are any specific tendencies that I can pick out. I have seen many films, few of which were of any great merit. The director with whom I have been most impressed has been Bruce Belley. I think his way of making films is very personal, very sincere.

As a director, you have had lots of trouble with producers. Do you think that today you have more freedom of movement, or do you still feel constricted by the production methods of cinema?
Yes, since *Blow-Up* I have been able to make films more or less as I want. Partly because the producers haven't read the script in its current form. I have had to fight hard and at MGM they are very tough, they are business people. They wanted me to take out several words that they considered coarse, and they wanted me to sign a document stating that the film didn't intend to attack the "community"; when I asked them what

316 / THE ARCHITECTURE OF VISION

community they were referring to, they couldn't answer. So I said to them: "What you mean is the business community, your own community, and in that case, I admit it, the film does attack that community; so now you know and you can decide whether you still want to make the film." Of course, there are plenty of other obstacles. In America it's not easy to do what you want. It's a mysterious country, and not just because—as any tourist can see straight away—it is full of contrasts. Even if we just stuck with what we can see, there would be many things that are difficult to overcome. For example, it's difficult to come into contact with black people and even harder to meet young revolutionary people. It's not easy to make films in America. I understand why almost all the European directors have had no success in America. In fact, I can't remember seeing even one great film among the ones made by Europeans in America—apart from the Europeans who went to live there. I'm very worried about my film. I can't see why I should succeed.

You have written that the greatest danger for people making films lies in the extraordinary possibilities that cinema offers to tell lies. But on the other hand, people say that Antonioni completely avoids mystification, that he is very clear and objective. What is your answer to all this?

Most filmmakers lie, I am deeply convinced of that. I think that you can count on the fingers of one hand the number of American directors who say what they really believe; perhaps even fewer than that. The best films are the ones made by directors of integrity, and they are very rare. It's so easy to manipulate cinema that few people today are capable of forgetting the effectiveness of the medium they are handling, and so they are not able to reject certain facile effects. Let's take for example *cinéma vérité*—which, in my opinion, is anything but truthful. What we have been seeing is a wave of films made with a portable camera, a telephoto lens, and some slight fuzzy effects. It's almost too easy to make a film like this, and a director rarely manages to say what he wanted by making films this way. So there is one case where cinema can lie. Perhaps if he adopted a different style, the director would be more honest. Blobs of color on the screen can indeed be pretty, but often they are just useless.

I'm thinking of *Boom!*, [Joseph] Losey's last film. It's the most pointless film I've ever seen. It's the whim of a director who knows how to shoot, knows what cinema is. It's so sparkling, elegant; the colors are used so gratuitously, and everything are so superficially effective, that the film really turns out to be a conveyer of lies. As I see Losey going off on these "escapades," I ask myself whether he really has anything to say. They are so obviously pleasant that I'm inclined to think that he's lying to himself, because he's not the type to indulge himself in such pastimes; he's a complex man, tormented, sick. His best films are those which express his most intimate personality, and not those which bring out the virtuoso in him.

Blow-Up gives the impression that judgment is suspended, in view of the many types of hypothetical "objectivity" that are suggested and of the ensuing ambivalence. Do you think that cinema today is something that abstains from taking any kind of stand on or from intervening in any way on reality?

No, I don't think you can say that about *Blow-Up*. Even if it is very difficult to judge one's own films, and especially the latest, the very fact that I now express an opinion about my character implies I am taking a stand. The character agrees to take part in the game, knowing full well that it is precisely a game. (I don't think there is any doubt over that.) Therefore, he is a negative character and, in stating this, I'm taking a stand. I think that today it is more necessary than ever to tell certain stories and to say what you have to say. I remember having written an article, a long time ago, in which I quoted a phrase from Kafka, who advised artists: "Lock yourself alone in a room and something is bound to happen." I once believed that it was the artist's job to do just that. Now I don't believe it any more. I think, rather, that if someone creative wants to help himself, then he should look outside, go down into the street and mingle with other people. It's the only way to grasp the essence of truth, to make films that have that flavor of truth, which cinema needs today more than in the past. The film I'm now making is this type of film, although it's certainly not a documentary. In this film, more than ever, you'll find things that have never been shown before in that way. I ask the viewer to judge them only after I've presented to him my conclusions and in the hope that he will agree with them.

GIORGIO TINAZZI

A Constant Renewal[15]

I would like to start off with a general question about what your image of America was during your formative years, the time of your artistic apprenticeship—the meaning that the images and culture of America had for you at that time.

My interest in the United States dates from the time when I was at the university. I remember that when I was a student I applied for a scholarship to Berkeley, but I didn't get it because my grades weren't high enough. It may be that this disappointment actually helped me somehow. Otherwise, I would have perhaps found myself in Hollywood or who knows where, and it is logical that under those circumstances my professional life would have been completely different. But my first contacts with America were above all literary, and quite naturally so. I say "naturally" because Pavese's and Vittorini's translations were famous,[16] and there were places in Rome during the war where you could go to find them, despite fascist censorship. We read a lot in those days, due to the fact that there wasn't a lot to do, with the curfew and everything else, and so I have to say that literature, including American literature, certainly played a very important role in my formation during my youth.

---

[15] "Un rinnovamento senza sosta," from U. Rubeo, *Mal d'America. Da mito a realtà*, Rome: Editori Riuniti, 1987. Translated by Andrew Taylor.
[16] Cesare Pavese (1908–1950) and Elio Vittorini (1908–1966) were instrumental, during the postwar years, in introducing to Italy the works of several American writers, including Melville, Faulkner, Caldwell, Steinbeck, Stein, and Dos Passos.

What major differences have you noticed between the America you read about in novels and the one you found in reality? Did you have to reconcile your abstract image of that country with what you found in reality, or did the two come together without any significant discontinuities?

The first time I went to the United States was in 1961, on the occasion of the American première of *L'avventura*, and I have to say that this first contact with a country which, after all, I did not know was for the most part a positive experience. I remember, for example, that I immediately fell in love with that great sense of freedom you feel as soon as you arrive in America. I'm talking about a freedom which is physical, too, of moving about—a characteristic that struck me immediately and that I think is typical of that culture.

So there was no traumatic upheaval. On the contrary, during that same first stay I already had the idea of shooting a film in America, a plan that I eventually brought to a conclusion in 1969 with *Zabriskie Point*.

In what way did the American experience influence your choices of subject matter for Zabriskie Point, *and also the preparation and shooting of the film?*

Actually, the subject matter and screenplay that I had originally written for that film were very different from what turned out to be the basis of the actual film. I had created a story which revolved around the figure of an imaginary poet who lived in the United States and his vision, his attitudes, were much more individual—I would almost say more abstract—than the characters in the film I actually shot. It was a substantially different story, more introspective, perhaps more suggestive. And then, while I was in Chicago in the summer of 1968, I witnessed an incident that contributed to changing the whole course of the film. I happened to see the National Guard charging against some youths who were demonstrating in front of the building where the Democratic Convention was being held.

In what way did that episode upset the plans you had made for the film?

Let's say it contributed to radically changing the original plan. On that occasion, I came into contact with a group of people from backgrounds very different from my own, people who for the most part had gone there to protest against the Democrats' policies. Among them, for instance, there was Tom Hayden, who later married Jane Fonda; there were several young people. So we got together and we rewrote the screenplay entirely, we practically came up with a different film.

I have to say, I continued to have reservations about the whole thing. Until the day we began working on it, I even thought of calling the whole thing off—and perhaps I would have done it, if it hadn't been for the thought that I would then have had to wait too long to make another film. So, since I couldn't wait to begin working on something, I decided to go ahead with that project.

American critics were rather hard on Zabriskie Point. *Some comments were harsh, if not actually berating—but undoubtedly, they influenced the public reaction to the film, which, in comparison to* Blow-Up, *was rather lukewarm.*

Honestly, I never understood why the film didn't have the success I hoped for, at least in the States. Probably, the American public interpreted it as a piece of anti-Americanism, which frankly wasn't true. Perhaps, also, there was some ambiguity over what seemed to be true in the film and what was in fact completely fictional. In that regard, it is possible that the long tradition of pragmatism which permeates American culture had a strong influence in leading the public to not pay sufficient attention to the constant interlacing and interaction of the two levels: the imaginary and the real.

I have to say that, watching your film, one has the impression that daydreams, imagination, in the end get the upper hand over a flat, prosaic, violent reality, even from a moral point of view. Couldn't it have been this message, which could be found everywhere in the film, that annoyed the public, always so sensitive to any kind of moral censure?

Yes, I think it's possible that the film can be interpreted in the way you describe, but it should be remembered that this is just one aspect of the work, which should really be seen and judged in its entirety. The most important axis of the film is its juxtaposition of reality and imagination;

I would almost say that it is entirely based on that. Obviously, since I shot the film and nobody else, it's logical that it should reflect my own sensations and emotions at that time, what I felt and thought about America. And yet, in my film, there was a story, a somewhat unusual love story between the two main characters, Mark and Daria. The development of the film should be seen precisely as the development of that plot. Now, let us take for example the final scene, which provoked many contrasting reactions. Well, in that scene I visualize the desire of a woman whose fiancé has just been killed in an anonymous way, and for no apparent reason. It is her mental reaction that I am showing, and I think it's perfectly understandable that she would want the house to explode, to blow up.

The famous scene of the explosion is repeated with insistence; and it's a scene that even the Americans, when it's taken out of context, seem to have appreciated, at least from a technical point of view.

Yes, that's true. But even in that particular case, the insistence on the explosion is due to the fact that it's part of my aesthetic vision, an integral part of it. Yes, I believe that an artist should be allowed to express what he thinks, according to his own aesthetic principles—which in my case means translating that particular story and those principles into images. After all, it may be that the Americans simply didn't feel like accepting a critical view of their country by someone who isn't American. It may be that *Zabriskie Point* had that effect, even if, personally, I regret that the film was at least partially misinterpreted. And yet, when I went back to the United States last year, I noted that the film was again showing in several theaters. I mean, that seems an encouraging sign, that maybe the American public is changing its opinion of my film.

Another film of mine, *The Passenger,* also didn't get the same acclaim that it got in Europe. In this latter case, however, I have no responsibility for the outcome of the film, since it was the head of MGM who decided, against my wishes, to make an American version of the film, different from the one that had been so successful in Europe. Two or three fundamental scenes were taken out, and the whole thing was a mystery to me, since that certainly wasn't an anti-American film. Personally, I'm convinced that if the original version of *The Passenger* were only to be rereleased, it would be a success in the United States, too. Recently, when Cornell University invited me to take part in a symposium dedicated to my films and I had the opportunity to show the original film, I had the distinct impression that the people in the audience were immediately aware they were seeing a film substantially different from what had previously been distributed throughout the United States. There was long applause and it seemed that everyone liked it—despite the fact (which both amused and pleased me) that no one could work out what technical devices I had used in the last scene. They really seemed to be in shock and they kept on asking me how I had shot the scene. So I told them. Anyway, since there is now someone else in charge at MGM, I hope to be able to rerelease the film in America and I think it will go down well there this time. We shall see.

Apart from these episodes, did your contact with America give rise to any feelings of disappointment, compared to what had been your expectations?

Perhaps this will surprise you, but I don't think it's easy to be disappointed by America, unless—and this certainly happens sometimes—one goes there with a preconceived idea of what it should be like. In that case, yes, it can be disappointing in many ways. To me it seems a very strange and contradictory country. But if you have the chance to travel, to see different places and contrasting things, then you easily realize that in America there is a huge variety of different places and cultures, which can only be stimulating and interesting. There is a lot of color, and I don't simply mean in nature, but also in the cities; and if you compare it to what there is here in Italy, then you see that theirs is much richer. And then, you can meet a lot of wacky people, and they can be interesting, too: people who, for example, live in almost complete isolation, in remote places, even in the middle of the desert. Indeed, when we were shooting *Zabriskie Point* in the Arizona desert, I saw that there were people who lived in great freedom. Do you remember the episode of a man who lives in a hut in the middle of the desert? Well, what you see in the film is an accurate reflection of reality. That man really lived there.

In the most general terms, what do you think of American culture, of their cinema, and of the relationship between that way of life and ours?

As far as American cinema is concerned, I don't think it's possible to make general comments or statements of any kind. I can tell you who I think the most representative directors are of the vitality that characterizes contemporary American cinema, even if this is unlikely a very original contribution to film criticism. Anyway, in my opinion, Steven Spielberg from his first film *Duel in the Sun,* seems to have made the most interesting experiments, managing also to achieve a wide international success, which he fully deserves. As for the others, among those who in the last fifteen years have contributed most to raising the standards and popularity of American cinema, I would name [Martin] Scorsese, Arthur Penn, [Francis Ford] Coppola, Bob Rafelson, and Robert Altman.

On a more general note, as far as American culture goes, I think the debate over its quality is still open: a few years ago, George Steiner said that one still cannot see any genuine culture in America—culture in the sense of that "deep seriousness" which he sees as an almost exclusively European phenomenon. I would say that, overall, the European tradition is still more refined and more deeply rooted than the American one is. But I would like to add that I think this holds true only as far as artistic expression and creative thinking is concerned; for, in the area of academic research and analytical criticism, I have to say that in America I have found quite a few people who are far above the European standard in these areas. I have really been impressed with the level that art criticism has reached in the United States and of course, in a way, that too is part of "culture."

I think it would be a good idea, in conclusion, to ask you as a filmmaker whether you think there is a representative image, a synthesis, which suggests and can help to visualize the sense, the hidden essence, of what America is for you.

One thing I like about America is the continual movement, the constant renewal that you notice. Now, even if this renewal is dictated by the frenetic pace of the consumer system, I think the element of change, overall, is a positive thing.

Flying low over the desert, every so often you see a cluster of houses in the middle of nowhere, abandoned who knows when, a sort of ghost town. From above, you can still see the traces of the old trails that led into the old town—and all this right in the middle of the desert, with nothing for miles and miles around. That is a symptom of change, too; that is America.

UGO RUBEO

Talking of Michelangelo[17]

"I want the Chinese to know this: during the war, as a member of the Resistance, I was condemned to death. I was on the other side!"

Antonioni's need to make this statement publicly, in discussing Chinese attempts to sabotage, the world over, the screening of the documentary that he has shot in China, indicates his bitterness—a bitterness which cannot but reflect on his works which follow. Maria Schneider, who plays in it, says that his latest film The Passenger, *is his most desperate. A film, she says, without any form of optimism.*

He had gone to China full of optimism. There he produced 220 minutes of calm, poetic footage, giving no facile answers, no scientific analysis. It is a work of perception that calls upon the sensibilities, even endurance. Certainly not a documentary which to its claim of objectivity adds a dose of attitude. That, in fact, is what the Chinese resent most.

Even if Antonioni's "other side" is less easily defined today than it was in 1943, when even anti-fascism seemed a simpler concept with enemies more readily identified, it is certainly not Antonioni who has changed barricades. It is precisely the lack of the simplistic, scientific attitude requested by the Chinese, precisely that openness and lack of bias, which represents the film's greatest value. Chung Kuo *is a film made with love, not with opinion.*

[17] From *The Guardian*, 18 February 1975.

My experience in China must be divided into two clear and separate ones. The first one was that of the shooting, of visiting certain parts of China, unfortunately not many, but more was not allowed me. That experience was of an absolutely positive nature. I found myself facing a people, a country, which showed clear signs of the revolution that had occurred.

In seeking out the face of this new society I followed my natural tendency to concentrate on individuals, and to show the men rather than the political and social structures which the Chinese revolution created. To understand those structures, one would have to stay in a country much longer. These five weeks, permitted only a quick glance; as a voyager I saw things with a voyager's eye. I tried to take the film spectator with me, to take him by the hand, as it were, and have him accompany me on his trip. Also social and political structures are abstract entities which are not easily expressed in images. One would have to add words to those images, and that wasn't my role. I had not gone to China to understand it, but only to see it. To look at it and to record what passed under my eyes.

He had not planned the documentary himself. It was born of a relationship between Italian television (RAI) and the Chinese Embassy in Rome.

One day they called me and asked if I wanted to shoot a documentary in China, I responded enthusiastically.

When the film was finished, the first persons, outside of my collaborators, to whom it was shown, were some representatives of the Chinese Embassy in Rome. The ambassador didn't show up. There was the director of the New China agency and two or three others. At the end of the screening these persons expressed themselves positively. "You," they said, "Signor Antonioni, have looked at our country with a very affectionate eye. And we thank you." That was the first reaction of certain Chinese responsible people. I don't know what happened after that. I have no idea why they changed their opinion. I can only imagine why, but it would be a useless subject for discussion.

Antonioni was accused of having associated himself with Lin Piao in denigrating the Chinese revolution.

It has been said that I did not sufficiently appreciate what the social-ist system and the dictatorship of the proletariat in China have con-structed. I reject in the most decisive manner that this be true of my doc-umentary. Seeing it you will realize this. It has been said that I am being paid by Russian revisionists. Who these Russian revisionists are supposed to be, I truly do not know, because after all—that I do know—because after all, I live on this planet and not on another, and thus what happens in other countries does interest me.

It has been said that I purposely denigrated China in many other ways: one of these is supposed to be the fact that I have used a "cool" colortone in order to eliminate the real colours of China and the Chinese land-scape. It has been said that I've denigrated Chinese children. I really don't know why. I made shots of those children while they were singing their little songs; their delicious little faces. They are really beautiful. Chinese children—If I could, I would adopt one. I don't see how I could have denigrated them.

I have been told that I showed the bridge in Nanking in a diminished way, not triumphal enough. I must say that in fact the day I went to shoot it was a foggy day and I asked to be allowed to return another day. There is a long shot of the bridge left in the film, I think, but it doesn't show the bridge in a very expressive way. I had to limit myself to take shots of the bridge from closer by, and naturally, passing underneath it, the bridge appears slightly deformed. But that is our way of looking at things, from an individualistic viewpoint. That is the point of departure that our own social context creates. When certain aspects of reality fascinate me, my first instinct is to record them. We, as descendants of Western civiliza-tion, point our cameras at things that surround us, with a certain trust in the interpretative capacities of the viewer.

I don't see what they are accusing me of now. It is really unheard of. May I add that the vulgar language of their accusations really hurts me. And that is what I mean by my second experience of China: not the experience in China itself, which was positive. The negative experience I am making concerning China is this one, this murcking about in the undergrowth of politics. Their going to the Foreign Ministry to try and stop the projection here. Their going to Sweden, as they did, to try to blackmail the Swedish government by threatening to cease having cultural relations with Sweden if Swedish TV presented the film. Their going to Greece, mind you, while the colonels were still in power, and their asking the colonels not to show the film, which happened. Their going to Germany to try and do the same thing: the Germans, unlike the Greeks, refused. Their going to France to try and do the same thing again. It is this method they use which seems too small-minded to me. This way they have of insulting me personally, calling me a charlatan, a *buffone*—that is the word. I can't tell you the Chinese original, I only read the papers in Italian.

Was there anything that he was actually kept from shooting?

Well—I remember when we were in the centre of China, in Hurlan province, we ran through a village where a free market was going on, a thing apparently widely tolerated in China. I asked to get off, but the driver wouldn't stop. I made something of a fuss; I said to the driver, look, let me off, and I opened the door of the car, and he stopped. But the people who were there to accompany me—and in this case they were eight—didn't tell me: "Don't shoot." They just said: "You may shoot, if you wish, but it displeases us."

You will see this scene in the film. What would another Italian director have done in my stead? Obviously I started shooting: then I saw that their displeasure was effectively great, and I stopped. What I want to say is that everything I did in China was done in complete accord with the people who were there to accompany me. Usually there were eight of them. In Nanking they were fourteen. Thus I never did anything that wasn't allowed and I never shot anything without their being present.

I have been accused of being a fascist. Of having fought with the fascist troops. I want the Chinese to know this: during the war, as a member of the Resistance, I was condemned to death. I was on the other side! I must say these things, once and for all, because it can't go on that these people go around insulting me in this way and I can't even find anyone to defend me.

Antonioni had to shoot quickly in China—eighty shots a day.

We had five weeks and an enormous itinerary. I could not do what I had done in the period of my early documentaries, where I studied the light for every shot, and picked the best hours of the day for shooting. I couldn't prepare much. While my early documentaries prepared me for features, this Chinese experience has prepared me for the new way in which I have used the camera in *The Passenger.* I am *not* really a good son of neorealism: I'm rather the black sheep of its family, and with this film even more so I have replaced my objectivity with that of the camera. I can direct it any way I want: as the director, I am God. I can allow myself any kind of liberty. Actually, the liberty I have achieved in the making of this film is the liberty the character in the film tried to achieve by changing identity.

In The Passenger *Jack Nicholson plays a man given the chance to change identity midway in life. Based on an idea by Marc Peploe, it shows what disasters follow this attempt at self-liberation. It is basically a film about the uselessness of human individuality and of the strife for quality in one's expressions. It is the first time that Antonioni has filmed the idea of another, but after initial perplexity he found in the story elements which intrigued him in terms of his own experience. He denies that it is an autobiographical study. But the spirit of the work is the spirit of Antonioni.* In a way, it is his own story.

My story as an artist, as a director, without wanting to sound presumptuous. In my own life, I don't know whether I shall succumb. I don't mean to the temptation to change identity; we all have that. But to destiny, since each one of us carries his destiny within himself; I do not know whether I shall succumb to that, to all those acts which at the end of a life come together to make up one's destiny. Some succumb and some don't. Perhaps changing one's identity one commits an error, one succumbs to life.

A journalist sees reality with a certain consistency: the ambiguous consistency of his viewpoint, which to him, and only to him, seems objective. Jack in the film sees things in his way and I, as the director, play the role of the journalist behind the journalist: I again add other dimensions to reproduced reality.

He did *not* seek objectivity. The dialectic of life would be missing. Films would become boring. Pretending to be objective, you annul yourself. Others talk through you but you remain extraneous. What sense would life have, then? What I say, that I have tried to be more objective, I mean it in a technical way. I no longer want to employ the subjective camera, in other words the camera that represents the viewpoint of the character. The objective camera is the camera wielded by the author. Using it, I make my presence felt.

The Passenger *is an important stage for him, mostly because it's not based on a story he wrote himself.*

When it was first suggested to me that I should direct a film based on this script of Marc Peploe's, I was somewhat taken aback, but then, rather instinctively, I decided for it, feeling that after all there was something in this story which reminded me of I-don't-know-what. I began to shoot, to work, before I even had a final script, because there wasn't much time, due to Jack Nicholson's other commitments. So I started working with a certain feeling of distance. A feeling of being somewhat removed from the story itself. For the first time I found I was working more with the brain than, let's say, with the stomach. But during the shooting of the film's beginning, the certain something that this story contained began to interest me even more. In this journalist, as in every journalist, there coexist the drive to excel, to produce quality work, and the feeling that this quality is ephemeral. The feeling, thus, that his work is valid for a fleeting moment only.

In fact no one can better understand such a feeling than a film director since we are working with a material, the film stock itself, which is ephemeral as such, which is physically short-lived. Time consumes it. In my film, when Jack feels saturated to the gills with this sentiment, after years of work, with age, a moment arrives when there is a break in his inner armor, when he feels the need for a personal revolution.

Add to this frustrations for other motives: a failed marriage, an adopted son whose presence did not have the expected effect upon his life, and another, ethnic need, which becomes stronger as he progresses. You will understand, then, how this character, in the moment that the occasion arises takes the opportunity to change identity, fascinated by the promise of the liberty that he expects will follow. That, in any case, was my point of departure. What the film tells, is the story of what happens to him after this change of identity, the vicissitudes that he encounters, perhaps the disappointments.

We have created a structure that suscitates doubts. We are all dissatisfied. The international situation, politically and otherwise, is so unstable, that the lack of stability is reflected within each individual. But I'm used to talking in pictures, not words. When I talk of man, I want to see his face. In China, when I asked them what was the thing they felt was most important in their revolution, they said it was the new man. That is what I tried to focus on. Each individual, each one creating his own little revolution, all those little revolutions which together will change humanity. That's why I insist upon a personal viewpoint, concretizing it with the camera; every change in history has always started from individuals. You can't change facts: it's the human mind that creates human action.

GIDEON BACHMANN

ANTONIONI DISCUSSES *THE PASSENGER*[18]

BETTY JEFFRIES DEMBY: *Did you do the screenplay for* The Passenger?
MICHELANGELO ANTONIONI: I have always written my own scripts, even if what I wrote was the result of discussions with my collaborators. *The Passenger*, however, was written by someone else. Naturally I made changes to adapt it to my way of thinking and shooting. I like to improvise—in fact, I can't do otherwise. It is only in this phase—that is, when I actually see it—that the film becomes clear to me. Lucidity and clearness are not among my qualities, if I have any.

LARRY STURHAHN: *In this case, were there any major changes in the screenplay?*
MA: The whole idea, the way the film is done, is different. The mood is changed—there is more of a spy feeling, it's more political.

LS: *Do you always adapt a piece of material to suit your particular needs?*
MA: Always, I got the idea for *Blow-Up* from a short story by Cortázar, but even there I changed a lot. And *The Girlfriends* was based on a story by Pavese. But I work on the scripts by myself with some collaboration, and as far as the act of writing is concerned, I always do that myself.

LS: *I have often felt that the short story is a better medium to adapt to film because it's compact and about the same length as a film.*

---

[18] From *Filmmakers Newsletter* 8 (9), July 1975.

MA: I agree. *The Girlfriends* was based on a short novel, *Among Women Only*. And the most difficult pages to translate into images were the best pages as far as the novel and the writing were concerned. I mean the best of the pages—the pages I liked the most—were the most difficult. When you have just an idea it's easier. Putting something into a different medium is difficult because the first medium was there first. In a novel there's usually too much dialogue—and getting rid of the dialogue is difficult.

LS: *Do you change the dialogue even further when you're on the set?*
MA: Yes, I change it a lot. I need to hear a line pronounced by the actors.

LS: *How much do you see of a film when you're looking at the script? Do you see the locations? Do you see where you're going to work with the film?*
MA: Yes, more or less. But I never try to copy what I see because this is impossible. I will never find the exact counterpart of my imagination.

LS: *So you wipe the slate clean when you're looking for your location?*
MA: Yes. I just go and look. I know what I need, of course. Actually, it's very simple.

BJD: *Then you don't leave the selection of location up to your assistants?*
MA: The location is the very substance of which the shot is made. Those colors, that light, those trees, those objects, those faces. How could I leave the choice of all this to my assistants? Their choices would be entirely different from mine. Who knows the film I am making better than me?

BJD: *Was* The Passenger *shot entirely on location?*
MA: Yes.

BJD: *I believe most of your other films were too. Why do you have such a strong preference for location shooting?*
MA: Because reality is unpredictable. In the studio everything has been foreseen.

BJD: *One of the most interesting scenes in the film is the one which takes place on the roof of the Gaudí cathedral in Barcelona. Why did you choose this location?*

MA: The Gaudí towers reveal, perhaps, the oddity of an encounter between a man who has the name of a dead man and a girl who doesn't have any name. (She doesn't need it in the film.)

BJD: *I understand that in* Red Desert *you actually painted the grass and colored the sea to get the effects you wanted. Did you do anything similar in* The Passenger?

MA: No. In *The Passenger* I have not tampered with reality. I looked at it with the same eye with which the hero, a reporter, looks at the events he is reporting on. Objectivity is one of the themes of the film. If you look closely, there are two documentaries in the film, Locke's documentary on Africa and mine on him.

BJD: *What about the sequence where Nicholson is isolated in the desert? The desert is especially striking, and the color is unusually intense and burning. Did you use any special filters or forced processing to create this effect?*

MA: The color is the color of the desert. We used a filter, but not to alter it; on the contrary, in order *not* to alter it. The exact warmness of the color was obtained in the laboratory by the usual processes.

BJD: *Did shooting in the desert with its high temperatures and blowing sand create any special problems for you?*

MA: Not especially. We brought along a refrigerator in which to keep the film, and we tried to protect the camera from the blowing sand by covering it in any possible way.

BJD: *How do you cast your actors?*

MA: I know the actors, I know the characters of the film. It is a question of juxtaposition.

LS: *Specifically, why did you choose Jack Nicholson and Maria Schneider?*

MA: Jack Nicholson and I wanted to make a film together, and I thought he would be very good, very right for this part. The same for Maria Schneider. She was my understanding of the girl. And I think she was perfect for the role. I may have changed it a bit for her, but that is a reality I must face: you can't invent an abstract feeling. Being a "star" is irrelevant—if the actor is different from the part, if the feeling doesn't work, even Jack Nicholson won't get the part.

LS: *Are you saying that Nicholson acts like a star, that he's hard to work with?*
MA: No. He's very competent and a very, very good actor, so it's easy to work with him. He's intense, yet he doesn't create any problems—you can cut his hair (I didn't), he's not concerned about his "good" side or whether the camera is too high or too low; you can do whatever you want.

BJD: *You once said that you see actors as part of the composition; that you don't want to explain the characters' motivations to them but want them to be passive. Do you still handle actors this way?*
MA: I never said that I want the actors to be passive. I said that sometimes if you explain too much, you run the risk that the actors become their own directors, and this doesn't help the film. Nor the actor. I prefer working with the actors not on an intellectual but on a sensorial level. To stimulate rather than teach.

First of all, I am not very good at talking to them because it is difficult for me to find the right words. Also, I am not the kind of director who wants "messages" on each line. So I don't have anything more to say about the scene than how to do it. What I try to do is provoke them, put them in the right mood. And then I watch them through the camera and at that moment tell them to do this or that. But not before. I have to have my shot, and they are an element of the image—and not always the most important element.

Also, I see the film in its unity whereas an actor sees the film through his character. It was difficult working with Jack Nicholson and Maria Schneider at the same time because they are such completely different actors. They are natural in opposite ways: Nicholson knows where the camera is and acts accordingly. But Maria doesn't know where the camera is—she doesn't know anything; she just lives the scene. Which is great. Sometimes she just moves and no one knows how to follow her. She has a gift for improvising, and I like that—I like to improvise.

LS: *Then you don't preplan what you are going to do on the set? You don't sit down the evening before or in the morning and say, "I'm going to do this and this"?*
MA: No. Never, never.

LS: *You just let it happen as you're on the set?*
MA: Yes.

LS: *Do you at least let your actors rehearse a scene first, or do you just go right into it?*
MA: I rehearse very little—maybe twice, but not more. I want the actors to be fresh, not tired.

BJD: *What about camera angles and camera movement? Do you carefully preplan in this area?*
MA: Very carefully.

LS: *Are you able to make decisions about print takes very soon, or do you—?*
MA: Immediately.

LS: *Then you don't shoot a lot of takes?*
MA: No. Three. Maybe five or six. Sometimes we may do fifteen, but that is very rare.

LS: *Would you be able to estimate how much footage you shoot per day?*
MA: No.

LS: *Just whatever you can accomplish?*
MA: In China I made as many as eighty shots in one day, but that was very different work; I had to rush.

LS: *How long did it take to do the final scene of* The Passenger?
MA: Eleven days. But that was not because of me but because of the wind. It was very windy weather and so difficult to keep the camera steady.

BJD: *One critic has said that the final seven-minute sequence is destined to become a classic of film history. Can you explain how you conceived it?*
MA: I had the idea for the final sequence as soon as I started shooting. I knew, naturally, that my protagonist must die, but the idea of seeing him die bored me. So I thought of a window and what was outside, the afternoon sun. For a second, just for a fraction—Hemingway crossed my mind: "Death in the Afternoon." And the arena. We found the arena and immediately realized this was the place. But I didn't yet know how to realize such a long shot. I had heard about the Canadian camera, but I had no first-hand knowledge of its possibilities. In London, I saw some film tests. I met with the English technicians responsible for the camera and we decided to try. There were many problems to solve. The biggest was that the camera was 16mm and I needed 35mm. To modify it would have involved modifying its whole equilibrium since the camera is mounted on a series of gyroscopes. However. I succeeded in doing it.

LS: *Did you use a zoom lens or a very slow dolly?*
MA: A zoom was mounted on the camera. But it was only used when the camera was about to pass through the gate.

LS: *It's interesting how the camera moves toward the man in the center against the wall but we never get to see him, the camera never focuses on him.*
MA: Well, he is part of the landscape, that's all. And everything is in focus—everything. But not specifically on him. I didn't want to go closer to anybody. The surprise is the use of this long shot. You see the girl outside and you see her movements and you understand very well without going closer to her what she's doing, maybe what her thoughts are. You see, I am using this very long shot *like* closeups, the shot actually takes the place of closeups.

LS: *Did you cover that shot in any other way or was this your sole commitment?*
MA: I had this idea of doing it in one take at the beginning of the shooting and I kept working on it all during the shooting.

LS: *How closely do you work with your cinematographer?*
MA: Who is the cinematographer? We don't have this *character* in Italy.

LS: *How big a crew do you work with?*
MA: I prefer a small crew. On this one I had a big crew—forty people—but we had union problems so it couldn't be smaller.

LS: *How important is your continuity girl to your work?*
MA: Very important. Because we have to change in the middle, we can't go chronologically.

BJD: *How closely do you work with your editor?*
MA: We always work together. However, I edited *Blow-Up* myself and the first version of *The Passenger* as well. But it was too long and so I redid it with Franco Arcalli, my editor. Then it was still too long, so I cut it by myself again.

BJD: *How closely does the edited version reflect what you had in mind when you were shooting?*
MA: Unfortunately, as soon as I finish shooting a film I don't like it. And then little by little I look at it and start to find something. But when I finish shooting it's like I haven't shot anything. Then when I have my material—when it's been shot in my head and on the actual film—it's like it's been shot by someone else. So I look at it with great detachment and then I start to cut. And I like this phase.

But on this one I had to change a lot because the first cut was very long. I shot much more than I needed because I had very little time to prepare the film—Nicholson had some engagements and I had to shoot very quickly.

LS: *So you didn't have time before the shooting to cut your screenplay down to size.*
MA: Right. I shot much more than was necessary because I didn't know what I would need. So the first cut was very long—four hours. Then I had another that ran two hours and twenty minutes. And now it's two hours.

LS: *Do you shoot lip sync—record the sound on location?*
MA: Yes.

LS: *What about dubbing?*
MA: A little—when the noise is too much.

BJD: *The soundtrack is an enormously important part of your films. For* L'avventura *you recorded every possible shading of the sound of the sea. Did you do anything similar for* The Passenger?
MA: My rule is always the same: For each scene, I record a soundtrack without actors.

BJD: *Sometimes you make critical plot points by using sound alone. For instance, in the last sequence we have only the sound of the opening door and what might be a gunshot to let us know the protagonist has been killed. Would you comment on this?*
MA: A film is both image and sound. Which is the most important? I put them both on the same plane. Here I used sound because I could not avoid looking at my hero—I could not avoid hearing the sounds connected with the actual killing since Locke, the killer, and the camera were in the same room.

BJD: *You use music only rarely in the film, but with great effectiveness. Can you explain how you choose which moments will be scored?*
MA: I can't explain it. It is something I feel. When the film is finished, I watch it a couple of times thinking only about the music. In the places where I feel it is missing, I put it in—*not* as score music but as source music.

ᡕ⠀ᐧ

LS: Who do you admire among American directors?
MA: I like Coppola; I think *The Conversation* was a very good film. I like Scorsese; I saw *Alice Doesn't Live Here Anymore* and liked it very much—it was a very simple but very sincere film. And you have Altman and *California Split*—he's a very good observer of California society. And Steven Spielberg is also very good.

LS: I have the impression from your films that your people tend to just appear full-blown in a particular situation, that there's not much of a past to your characters. For instance, we find Nicholson in an alienated place with no roots behind him. And the same for the girl; she's just there. It's as though people are just immediately in an immediate present. There's no background to them, as it were.
MA: I think it's a different way of looking at the world. The other way is the older way. This is the modern way of looking at people. Today everyone has less background than in the past. We're freer. A girl today can go anywhere, just like the one in the film, with just one bag and no thoughts for her family or past. She doesn't have to carry any baggage with her.

BJD: You mean moral baggage?
MA: Precisely. Moral, psychological luggage. But in the older movies people have homes and we see these homes and the people in them. You see Nicholson's home, but he's not tied down, he's used to going all over the world.

BJD: Yet you seem to find the struggle for identity interesting.
MA: Personally, I mean to get away from my historical self and find a new one. I need to renew myself this way. Maybe this is an illusion, but I think it is a way to reach something new.

BJD: I was thinking of the television journalist like Mr. Locke getting bored with life. Then there's no hope for anything because that's one of the more interesting careers.

MA: Yes, in a way. But it's also a very cynical career. Also, his problem is that he *is* a journalist—he can't get involved in everything he reports because he's a filter. His job is always to talk about and show something or someone else, but he himself is not involved. He's a witness not a protagonist. And that's the problem.

LS: *Do you see any similarity between your role as a film director and the role of Locke in the film?*
MA: In this film it may be yes; it's part of the film. But it's different in a way. In *The Passenger* I tried to look at Locke the way Locke looks at reality. After all, everything I do is absorbed in a kind of collision between myself and reality.

LS: *Some people think of film as being the most real of the arts and some think it's purely illusion, a fake, because everything in a movie is still pictures. Can you speak a bit about this in relation to* The Passenger?
MA: I don't know if I could speak about it—if I could do the same thing with words I would be a writer and not a film director. I don't have anything to *say* but perhaps something to *show*. There's a difference.
That's why it's very difficult for me to talk about my films. What I want to do is make the film. I know what I have to do. Not what I *mean*. I never think the meaning because I can't.

LS: *You're a film director and you make images, yet I find that in your films the key people have a problem with seeing—they're trying to find things or they've lost something. Like the photographer in* Blow-Up *trying to find reality in his own work. Are you, as a director working in this medium, frustrated at not being able to find reality?*
MA: Yes and no. In some ways I capture reality in making a film—at least I have a film in my hands, which is something concrete. What I am facing may not be the reality I was looking for, but I've found someone or something every time. I have added something more to myself in making the film.

LS: *Then it's a challenge each time?*
MA: Yes! I fight for it. Can you imagine? I lost my male character in the desert before the ending of the film because Richard Harris went away without telling me. The ending was supposed to be all three of them—the wife, the husband, and the third man. So I didn't know how to finish the film. I didn't stop working during the day, but at night I would walk around the harbor thinking until I finally came up with the idea for the ending I have now. Which I think was better than the previous one—fortunately.

BJD: *Have you ever wanted to make an autobiographical film?*
MA: No. And I'll tell you why: Because I don't like to look back; I always look forward. Like everyone, I have a certain number of years to live, so this year I want to look forward and not back—I don't want to think about the past years, I want to make *this* year the best year of my life. That is why I don't like to make films that are statements.

BJD: *It's been said that in a certain sense a director makes the same film all his life—that is, explores the different aspects of a given theme in a variety of ways throughout his pictures. Do you agree with this? Do you feel it's true of your work?*
MA: Dostoevskij said that an artist only says one thing in his work all through his life. If he is very good, perhaps two. The liberty of the paradoxical nature of that quotation allows me to add that it doesn't completely apply to me. But it's not for me to say.

An In-Depth Search[19]

In The Passenger, *you are particularly looking for a new relationship with reality. What lies behind this search?*

You are asking me to do some self-criticism, and that is something I always find difficult. Explaining myself verbally is not my business. I make films, and the films are there, with their own content, for whoever wants to go and see them. Anyway, I will try to answer. Behind that search there is perhaps the suspicion that all of us are giving to things—events in which we are protagonists or to which we are witnesses, social relations, and even sensations—an interpretation that is different from the one we gave them in the past. Someone might say to me that this is logical and natural, since we live in a different time and, in comparison to the past, we have acquired some experiences and notions that we didn't have before. But that's not all I want to say. I think that there is a great anthropological transformation going on, which will profoundly change our nature.

The signs of this are already to be seen, some are familiar, others are worrisome, disturbing. We don't react any longer as we would have done before to the sound of bells or to a shooting or a murder. Even certain environments, which once seemed calm, conventional, commonplace in their relationship to reality, can now be seen as somehow tragic. The sun, for example. We look at it differently than we did in the past. We know

---

[19] "Una ricerca nel profondo," from *L'Europeo*, 18 December 1975. Translated by Andrew Taylor.

too much about it. We know what the sun is, what happens up there. The scientific data we have about it have modified our relationship with it. For example, I sometimes have the feeling that the sun hates us, but this idea of giving a human feeling to something which is always the same unto itself means that this type of traditional relationship is no longer possible. I say "sun" as I might have said moon or stars or the whole universe. Some months ago in New York, I bought an extraordinary little telescope, the Questar, which is about half a meter long but shows you the stars up close in a striking way. I can see the craters on the moon really close-up and Saturn's rings and so on. Anyway, I get out of this a physical perception of the universe which is actually so upsetting that my relationship to the universe can no longer be the same as it was before. I don't mean by this that it is no longer possible to enjoy a sunny day or to take a moonlit stroll. I just mean that some scientific notions have set in motion a transformational process that will end up changing us, too—that will lead us to act in a certain way and not in another, and consequently will change our whole psychology, the mechanisms which regulate our life. It won't just be the economic and social structures that change man, as Marxism believes; rather, man will be able to change himself and these structures, too, as the result of a transformational process which involves him directly. I may be wrong of course, as far as the general nature of this process is concerned but I don't think I am wrong as far as my own individual life is concerned.

Well, to return to what you asked me about my search—that is, my profession, my personal territory—it's obvious that, if what I say is true, I must look at the world with different eyes, I must try to get to the heart of it by routes other than the usual ones. This changes everything—the narrative material I have at hand, the stories, their endings—and it cannot be otherwise if I want to bring out, to express, what I think is happening. I'm really making a big effort to find some narrative structures that are different from those of the past. I don't know if I'll succeed, because if there is anything that eludes our conscious effort, it is the act of creation.

In this film, I would say that you have succeeded. Because even in the moments when the format may seem familiar, the disturbance it causes is radically new.

I don't know. I don't know if you agree, if other viewers also agree, but in this film I have instinctively looked for narrative solutions that are different from my usual ones. It's true, the basic format may be the same, but as I was shooting, every time I realized that I was moving on familiar grounds I tried to change track, to deviate from the norm, to resolve in some other way certain moments of the story. Even the way in which I had these realizations was strange. I noticed a sort of sudden disinterest in what I was doing, and that was the sign that I had to move off in another direction. We are talking about an area which is fraught with doubts, anxieties, and sudden, enlightening flashes. The only certain thing was my need to reduce the suspense to a minimum, even though there had to be some left—and I do think some has been left, even if it is an element of indirect, filtered suspense. It would have been very easy to make a thriller. I had the pursuers and the pursued; nothing was missing, but it would have been banal. That wasn't what interested me. Now I don't know whether I have managed to create a filmic narrative that does make one feel the way I felt myself. But when you have just finished a film, the thing you are the least sure of is the film itself.

I would say that you managed to establish a new relationship with the viewer, right from the first moment. For example, my own experience on seeing the film was that something was missing.

Really? And what was that?

During the first few minutes, I sensed that something was missing, but I couldn't understand what it was. Then I realized that it was the music—and I thought that it was no accident; that in fact you were using the absence of music as something musical in its own right, as a non-music that put the viewer into a kind of emotional vacuum.

Yes, a "vacuum," as you call it—that was deliberate. In fact, I do not share the ideas of those who would use music to emphasize the dramatic, happy, or affecting moments in the film. I believe instead that in a film, the images shouldn't need musical support; they should be able to create certain suggestions in their own right. The fact that you noticed the lack of music tells me two things. First, that the image was strong enough to influence you, to give you this light, ambiguous feeling of a vacuum and of disturbance, all by itself. Second, that your ear, which is accustomed to music in other films, was disconcerted and thus helped to create the sense of something lacking that came from the images. But it's not that I consciously set out to create this effect. Rather, I was following my own idea of cinema. I use music very little. I especially enjoy music which comes from within the movie itself—a radio, someone singing or playing, what the Americans call source music. That is what you find in the film. Besides, the protagonist is a reporter, so he's quite a dry character— adventurous, used to emotions and so capable of controlling them, not easily influenced as a person. A character like that didn't need any musical commentary.

In a way, yours is an adventure film, quite a new and unexpected choice on your part. What are the cultural reasons behind that choice?
    The element of adventure is not completely alien to me. It was already there in *Zabriskie Point,* and it was especially there in another film which I wrote and scripted and prepared down to the last detail, but could never film. It was going to be called *Tecnicamente dolce* [Technically Sweet]. Now, from *Zabriskie Point* through *The Passenger,* by way of *Tecnicamente dolce,* I noticed a sort of obscure intolerance, the need to escape, through the characters in the film, from the historical context in which I and they lived—that is, the urban, civil, and civilized context—to enter another environment such as the desert or the jungle, where you can at least attempt a freer, more individual lifestyle, where such freedom could be tested. The adventurous character, the reporter, changes his identity to free himself from the self who had been ignoring such a need.

One could say that this need is the need to escape from modern life, and so also to escape from history—
    From a certain type of history.

—and that essentially the film, or at least one of its themes, is about the impossibility of escaping from history because history always ends up capturing anyone who tries to get away from it?

Perhaps the film can be interpreted in this way. But there is another problem. Let's look a little at the character. He is a reporter, a man who lives amid words and images, and in front of things; a man who is forced by his profession to be always and only a witness of whatever is going on around him, a witness and not the protagonist. The events happen far away from him, independently of him, and all that he can do is reach the place where they happened and to talk about them, to report them. Or, if he happens to be present at the time, to show them, in accordance with the artificial duty to be impartial, that is part of his profession. This, I believe, is a worrisome, frustrating aspect of a reporter's profession. And if, besides this, a reporter has—as the character in the film does—a failed marriage, a bad relationship with his adoptive son, and lots of other personal problems, one can understand that he could be pushed into wanting to take someone else's identity when the opportunity presents itself. So it is from himself that the character is escaping, from his own history, not from History with a capital "H." And this is true even to the extent that when he finds out that the man whose identity he has assumed is a man of action—a man who takes an active part in life, and isn't just a passive witness—he tries to take on not only his identity, but also his role, his political role. But this other man's history, which is so concrete, so built on action, becomes too much of a burden to him. Action itself becomes problematic.

Generally, in your films, the political dimension is simply implied. In this film however—

I think it's much more implied than explicitly presented in this case, too. Anyway, I do take an active interest in politics, I follow it closely. Today, especially, it's a moral duty for all of us to find out how we are governed, check what the people who guide our lives are doing, because there is no alternative. We only have one life each, and so we must try to live it in the best and most just way possible, for ourselves and for others.

Naturally, I am interested in politics in my own way, not as a professional politician, but as a filmmaker. I try to make my own little revolutions with my films; I try to highlight certain problems and contradictions, to bring out certain emotions in the public, to have them experience certain ways of life rather than others. Sometimes it happens that the films are interpreted differently from the way the director intended, but perhaps this isn't important. Perhaps it doesn't matter whether films are understood and rationalized; it's enough that they are lived as a direct personal experience.

You say that it's not necessary to understand your films—it's enough to feel them. Is this something that applies only to art, or can it be extended to life in general?

I may be wrong, but I believe that people have stopped asking themselves the whys and wherefores of things—perhaps because they know there is no answer. People have realized that there are no longer any sure points of reference, any values, any final arbiter to which they can appeal. They can't even rely on science any more, because the results of science are always provisional, temporary. These days you can't actually sell a computer— verybody leases them, because while you are waiting for one to be delivered, a new model is brought out which renders the old one obsolete. This type of mechanical progress, which makes owning any type of machinery pointless because there is always a better model, leads people not to ask themselves what is a machine, what is a computers, or how it works. What will do for them are the results that machines bring forth. And perhaps everything is like that. Perhaps this logic permeates everything in our lives without us realizing it. Now, this might seem to contradict what I said before, but really it doesn't, because although "knowing" about our world can change our view of it, so also can "not knowing." And in all of this there is a certain mistrust of reason. But perhaps people have realized that it's not reason that governs the lives of individuals and society. So they tend to trust instinct more, as well as other centers of perception. Otherwise, I can't explain why the instinct toward violence is currently so strong, especially in the younger generations.

Speaking of techniques that are always subject to refinement, with The Passenger *you made some tremendous achievements on a technical and expressive level. Are you completely satisfied with the medium you work with?*

No, not at all. The medium is far from perfect. I feel a little restricted by the technical limits of cinema today. I feel the need for more flexible and advanced techniques which would, for example, give us a greater control over color. What you can get from film in the developing stage nowadays is no longer enough; one needs to use color in a more functional, expressive, direct, inventive way. In that sense, the video camera is much richer than the film camera. With video you can, as it were, paint a film with electronic colors, even as you are filming it. In *Red Desert,* I made a few experiments by coloring the world directly—that is, painting roads and trees and water different colors. With video you don't need to go to all that trouble. You just push a button and you get the tone of color you want. The only problem lies in transferring the videotape to film. But even that can be done with reasonably good results.

Do you think that the use of this new technology will affect the subject matter, suggest new topics?

Probably. Today, many topics are off limits to us. Certain metaphysical dimensions, certain sensations are conveyed in cinema today only approximately, precisely because of technological limitations. Therefore, it's not a question of using ever more advanced technology to achieve prettier images, but rather to expand the content of cinema, to capture contradictions, changes, and atmospheres, better than before. Cinema on videotape is quite mature now, even if the people who have tried it have only used it for quite common, predictable effects. It can be extraordinary if used wisely, poetically.

Will the cinema of the future be made using videotape?

I think so. And the next development will be cinema that uses laser technology. Laser is truly fantastic. In England I saw a hologram—that is, a projection made with a laser—and I was very impressed by it. It was a little car projected onto a glass screen, and it didn't look like the image of a car, the representation of a car, but like a real, three-dimensional car, hanging there in space. Instinctively, I reached out my hand to touch it. The stereoscopic effect of it was incredible. And not only that: when the laser beam was shifted, the image moved, too, and you could see the sides and back of the car. A lot of time will be needed but it's obvious that laser cinema will be further developed. For now, holograms are projected onto a flat screen, but scientists experimenting with lasers think that you can project them onto a transparent solid shape placed in the middle of a room, so that the viewer can move around it, choosing his own angle to view it from.

A sort of "Morel's invention." Do you think that, at least in the distant future, we will be able to get that far? I mean, project three-dimensional images right next to us, without a screen, even images of people—live next to people who don't exist?

You'd have to ask a scientist that, or a science-fiction writer. But as far as I'm concerned, I wouldn't put any limits on this type of discovery, because I don't think there are any. I think that everything that has been imagined up until now by science fiction may even seem childish in comparison with the discoveries of the future. Now even science fiction is conditioned by the limited scientific knowledge we possess. All we can do is make little forays into a future which always has our own present as its point of reference. But in the future, who knows? It's useless to ask questions to which there are no answers. But according to our "operational" outlook, isn't it already significant to say that a question is meaningless? Then, let's take your question, too. We can amuse ourselves by thinking that maybe we will end up creating in the laboratory the situation that was imagined in the novel by Bioy Casares, *Morel's Invention*—a desert island, inhabited only by images of people who don't exist. With whatever mysterious, anxiety-producing, and ambiguous that something like that implies. But perhaps even the concepts of mystery, anxiety, and ambiguity will have changed by then.

ALBERTO ONGARO

THE DIRECTOR AND TECHNOLOGY:
"TAKE IT FROM ME, THIS IS THE FUTURE"[20]

Are you convinced that technology can be a really useful tool for man and for his fundamental need to express himself? Could it happen instead, as in 2001: A Space Odyssey *and in* War Games, *that technology takes over from man, speaking on its own, in the place of and perhaps even against man?*

I don't think so. I think that problems may lie elsewhere. I think that the advent of technology in cinema can help us confront a situation which is analogous to what happened in the world of visual arts with the advent of abstract painting. At that time, thousands, tens of thousands of people, because of the age-old need to express themselves, began to scribble color on canvas, convinced that they were artists just because they could draw circles and lines.

And it's only now, after a few years, that we know that only five or six people have really been important in this type of art, and we all know who they are. The only ones who survived are those who succeeded to make of abstract art their own, authentic form of self-expression. And the same thing will happen with technology: everybody will make films; the garbageman will pick up his bags of garbage and make films about them. But just as with abstract art, technology too will only appear to simplify the task of the filmmaker, and only appear to open it up to everybody. In the end, you will see that those who have made real contributions to

[20] "Il regista e l'elettronica: Credetemi, è il nostro futuro," from *La Repubblica*, 15 November 1983. Translated by Andrew Taylor.

cinema (and maybe this will even include films about garbage bags) will be very few.

Would you say that The Mystery of Oberwald *and Disney's* Tron *are both equally techno-movies? If not, what's the difference between the two?*

There is a huge difference in their way of using technology. *Tron*, on the one hand, is the product of computer aided design—in other words, it's computerized cinema, with flat images and only a painting-like depth. My *Mystery of Oberwald*, on the other hand, is a sort of cinema that—although it also uses technology—is still much closer to film, inasmuch as the camera was still held in front of real things, which have their precise, real-life dimensions.

Technology applied to cinema—with a director enabled, like the poets of former times, to "dazzle" his audience—might it not mean that in the future our movie screens will have room only for the spectacular, the fantastic, typical of films like Star Wars, *and that we will see the end of any type of cinema that has to do with truth and reality, with the real problems of mankind?*

The danger exists, I grant you. But it's a fact that this spectacular, fantastic cinema is also what is being made on conventional film. It will depend, above all, on the public, on whether they fall into this trap or manage to avoid it. And, anyway, if this does happen more and more in the future because of technology, there will be, I think, a saturation point: people can't always play around with fairy tales, they also inevitably need reality. And it's not true that we won't be able to tell real-life stories with these new technologies: we can do absolutely what we want with them, just as we can—and even more so than we can—on film: it's not a limiting device; it's just the opposite.

Is it going to be a revolution involving just the methods of production, or also artistic expression—and if so how exactly?

The range of possibilities which technology gives to a filmmaker is infinite. For example, it allows you to control color: I can still use "natural" colors, but by using the new "color enhancers" I can have electronic colors, if they seem to me better suited to reflect the subjectivity of the story I am telling. And again, with the new technique of "engraving," technology allows you to correct just one corner of the frame while the rest stays as it is: in the event that a take came out perfectly except for a detail of the furnishings in the room where the action takes place, I can change just that, without having to go back and shoot the whole thing again. In short, if a painting seems out of place in a certain setting, with the new techniques I can put into the same frame a whole new picture that is more suitable.

You are the eternal optimist. But how do you explain the fact that most of your colleagues and cinema operatives are all very much afraid of the advent of these new techniques?

They are scared because they aren't educated, they know nothing, they are lazy. I'd like to see Federico [Fellini] with these new machines: he'd go mad with joy and excitement, I'm sure of it.

And yet Ingmar Bergman announced recently, at the last Venice Film Festival, that if these new technologies take over and supplant the film camera, he will retire.

That will depend, I think, on what opportunities he will be offered. And if they are opportunities that allow him to improve on his type of cinema while staying faithful to it, then he himself will be the first to make use of it, despite what he said. The new technologies, for example, could allow him to use color in a more decisive way than he has been able to do until now in his color films.

These new technologies applied to other fields have been a threat to employment. Do you think the same will be true of the movie industry?

Techno-cinema will certainly not be as romantic as cinema used to be; it is already less and less so today. It will be something so technically precise and complex that it will require quite a high level of expertise on the part of all those who are called upon to work in it. It is likely, of course, that the people who work in cinema will change; in place of some of the current staff, other highly specialized technicians will be employed. But this will just be something that makes the film industry more professional, and that goes for the whole entertainment industry, too.

Will technological cinema really cost less?
Only if all the structures and the general organization are up to the level of the technology they are managing: if the cameraman, as he does today, arrives on the set an hour and a half late, well then, you can say goodbye to any savings you might have secured by using new technology.

As everybody knows, film deteriorates over time. Scorsese, along with others, made an emergency appeal to save classic cinema from the slow death that's going on in some of the film archives where the reels are preserved. Will the films made with these new technologies be exempt from such deterioration? Will they last longer and better?
Unfortunately, no. Magnetic tape deteriorates, too, just like film. However, it's easier to see that in the future there might be ways of salvaging magnetic tapes from ruin, unlike film, which is fated to disappear completely.

Why are these things so little discussed yet in Italy?
Because, after all, it's useless. The coming of technology to cinema, our Italian cinema, is not dependent upon our efforts. We in Italy can't even take part creatively and productively in any of this; it all goes on outside and above us. Either we will be given the means to make this new cinema, or we won't be at all able to be part of it. And that would certainly be the end of us, because one day, not via a revolution as many people think, but via a slow and inexorable evolution, cinema will be completely, one hundred percent dominated by these new technologies, and on that day I do not believe there will be any room left for conventional film.

ANNA MARIA MORI

A FILM BASED ON CONFLICT[21]

The fact that the main character of this film is a film director gives the story a particular relevance, I guess. Wouldn't this be, by chance, another Passenger, *with a director as protagonist?*

Right from the beginning—the original idea for *Identification of a Woman* dates from a few years ago—the main character in the story was a director. This doesn't mean that it's an autobiographical film: the main character is forty-four years old, and besides, the things which happen to him never happened to me, except in as far as we have all had romantic experiences. It's not even a film about the profession of the main character, because in *Identification of a Woman* there is very little talk about cinema. In one scene, the main character explains to a colleague, a screenwriter, what is it that he hopes to achieve. It's rather a vague idea, which hasn't yet emerged clearly. After having heard him talk, the other guy asks him a question: How can you tell it's a female character if you have no real idea of what you want to do? "Rather than having an idea of this film, I have a feeling about it, and it feels like a woman," the main character replies. The difference between the main character and myself lies also there: the director in the film, Niccolò, is not making a film about the identification of a woman, nor does he want to make it, because he "knows" that I am the one who is making that film.

[21] "Un film sui conflitti," from *La Repubblica,* 15 May 1982. Translated by Andrew Taylor.

The main character subsequently gets involved with two very young women. Are they twin aspects of today's kind of woman? Of the same woman?

The two girls are not two aspects of the same, ideal woman, even though in the film the ideal woman is indeed brought up. They are two very modern women, but I never set out to draw a portrait of today's woman. Be that as it may, feminists could even be satisfied with the way in which I portray women in the film. Mavi is an aristocrat, Ida a petit bourgeois. Their different social origins give rise to different types of behavior. In their love relationships, for example, the aristocrat is more reckless, she has fewer inhibitions than the other has. In short, there is a different type of sensuality. There are three erotic scenes in the film. It's the first time I've shot such scenes; I forced myself to do it, as they were necessary to describe the aristocratic character. I did shoot a love scene with the second girl, too, but I cut it out; her type of eroticism comes out in other ways.

Through his search for the female character, doesn't the main character also try to explore his own identity?

This need to find one's own identity, at least initially, is not to be found in the film. The main character, unlike my other male characters, is not going through an existential crisis—not even a crisis of artistic inspiration. In fact, he's already working on an idea for a film and he has a producer willing to back it. The novelty of *Identification*, compared with my previous films, lies in the fact that there are no crises for the characters, but rather conflicts between them. Only when they erupt, do such conflicts find a solution.

How do reality and imagination interact in the mind of the main character?

The heart of the story lies in this dialectic between the real and ideal characters, between the women in his life and the women in his mind. At a certain point they so overlap that the director—this isn't made explicit, but you can guess it—is no longer sure whether he is looking for a woman for himself or for his film. The protagonist is someone who looks at what is happening to him with a professional as well as emotional outlook. The two are almost inseparable. It's obvious that he is a man who makes films, as well as a director who lives his stories as a man.

Identification [of a Woman] *is your first film set in Italy since* Red Desert. *Is it a specifically "Italian" film, too? What do you think has changed since the 1960s in Italian society?*

It is a very Italian film, and a very Roman one, too—not just because you see Rome, but because cinema *is* Rome, and the main character has the mindset of a movie professional. What has changed in Italian society? How can I say answer in a couple of sentences? In the 1960s one could still feel the strong aftershocks, sentimental and sociological, of the immediate postwar period. Today these forces are spent. In this situation of stasis, it's natural that everyone should turn in on themselves. If you don't know where to go for help, what else can you do but rely on yourself?

In what sense, during the shooting, did you mean that Identification of a woman *was the last film "Antonioni style"?*

In the sense that I would like to free myself of the restrictions of emotions to concentrate more on facts. I feel the need to move in a different direction. In my last film, for example, I made it a rule right from the beginning to leave out certain formal aesthetic pleasures in composing the images; and I intentionally left out the relationship between the character and his context or physical environment. In my previous films, the link between what surrounds the characters and their psychological situation was much tighter. I tried to be as linear as possible, concentrating on the characters and following the thread of their story.

Where does this need to move in a different direction come from?

In these past years of enforced silence, I have had more time available to observe, and to live. And now I feel more mature than I did twenty years ago. Perhaps I'm a little too mature!? If I were a few years younger, it might be better; but so far, age doesn't bother me.

The Italian entries for the Cannes Film Festival seem quite rich this year. In Paris they are saying: "This year the Italians will walk away with everything." Do you also think that the recent "crisis" has helped to improve Italian cinema?

I have had a strange experience. Some days ago, a producer came to me with an extremely serious, dark, sad novel, and asked me to film it. As he was a producer who by his own admission is commercially oriented, I was stunned. "How come you, of all people, are proposing me to do this?" I asked him. He replied that he had recently seen *Blow-Up* again on television; and also that, in his opinion, next year there will be a change in public tastes. What made him think that? "The success of *Anni di piombo* [The Lead Years] and [István Szabó's] *Mephisto*" he replied. Maybe he's right. That something is happening in the film industry is undeniable. At Cinecittà there are eight films being made. And apart from that, the movie theaters are getting full again. The other night I went to see the latest film by [R. W.] Fassbinder, a director who was once the preserve of the élite—the theater was full. Evidently, people are going back to the movies.

What do you think of Fassbinder and of what was once called the "new" German cinema?

German cinema gave a therapeutic shock to the old continent. It woke us up. In my view, the best among the new directors are [Wim] Wenders and Herzog. Wenders has his feet on the ground. Herzog is more "inspired," in the sense that he's a little mad: just think of the type of stories he comes up with, his way of characterization, always a bit unbalanced, on a knife edge between reality and surrealism.

What do you think of the young generation of Italian cinema?

Faliero Rosati and Peter del Monte seem to possess a personal style that the others are still trying to find.

And the Americans?

The young directors are brilliant, but they give up their vocation a little too quickly. Because you have to have a vocation to film something like *Duel in the Sun,* while you don't need one to make *Star Wars.* I think the best American director is still Altman. He's a bit mad too: sometimes he shoots stuff without worrying about his audience. I don't think he's as sincere as he was when he made *Quintet.* It's a game to him, a challenge, and sometimes you can lose a challenge.

In Italy they complain about the lack of bold producers, and sometimes they give as examples American producers. What does the most international of all the Italian directors think of this comparison?

Certainly the departure of Ponti and De Laurentiis has left a gap. They had class, they could deal with the Americans as equals. The producers of today still haven't learned how to deal with other people. I wouldn't say though that American producers are more dynamic: they always travel the most formulaic and predictable routes. They are less bold and less— less imaginative than the Italians are.

And what about RAI?

The biggest enigma on the Italian scene.

ALDO TASSONE

IDENTIFICATION OF A WOMAN[22]

Why have you been so silent since The Passenger?

In the meantime I have finished *The Mystery of Oberwald,* and made a film on videotape based on Jean Cocteau's [play] *The Two-Headed Eagle,* although nobody has bought it in France. It's a melodrama and it's very different from my usual genre, but I'm happy I could make this experience. The videotape technique allows a greater mastery over the image than is possible with conventional film.

It certainly cannot be said that in Identification of a Woman *you have neglected the visual aspect. Did you work much on color?*

No, I didn't at all. I wanted to make a complete departure from any issues over color or setting. This time, I wanted to focus attention on the characters. If there is some visual beauty, then it's due to the truth value of the emotions I have given the characters. Before this film, I gave too much importance to the setting. But now it's become too easy to make pretty movies. Everybody is doing it.

There is a long scene in the fog which is particularly disturbing. Do you mean that the whole world is also in a fog?

Some very important things are going on in the world, and to a certain degree they are quite mysterious things. There is a sort of backlash.

22 From *Le Matin du Festival,* 24 May 1982. Translated by Andrew Taylor.

After the war, there was a feeling of solidarity, and Sartre even said: "Man is he who acts." Today man is no longer what he was, but we have to continue to have faith—and anyway, we can't really do anything else.

Your attitude seems much less hopeless than when you made L'avventura *or* La notte.

And yet, I feel I'm in the same place I was in twenty years ago. As far as creative freedom goes, it's still very difficult. Every day you have to come up with ideas and techniques, invent gestures, compose images. And then, there are no more producers like De Laurentiis, Ponti, Grimaldi, who were willing to take a risk on really creative work. This is the age of the formula.

In a way, you seem very much affected by what is going on in the world around you. Don't you think that one of the main characters in your films is fear?

I have never directly dealt with social or political issues, but I am just like everybody else, I cannot get away from the times we live in. I am bombarded by hundreds of pieces of information. The world is afraid, and I am, too—and obviously this comes through in my films. Still, I did nothing to put the concept of fear into *Identification of a Woman*.

Speaking of woman, how has she changed in the last twenty years?

I'm not a psychologist, nor a sociologist, but I think that women are clearer about what they want, they think more about themselves, and this has been troublesome for men. You can see this in certain behavior patterns, certain gestures, certain expressions. Ida, in the film, is well-balanced. Her wisdom consists in living in her own environment, surrounded by nature and by her horses. Mavi, on the other hand, is a lost soul, trying to escape her bourgeois little world, to actively take part in politics. Mavi looks for freedom in failure. And for man, she is the most attractive character.

What about sex? In Identification of a Woman, *the sexual act is shown with great clarity and technical mastery. How do you explain that?*

Sex is very important, it lies at the very heart of any love story. Without sex there can be no love. In a story by Jack London, two lovers decide to retire to a desert island and choose chastity to try and keep their relationship together. Their love is ruined. Apart from that, I don't know whether I show sex any differently than other people do. I'm not a voyeur. You have to do such things, not watch them. Love doesn't have too much to do with images, it's something far more important. However, I should say that if there is anything in the film which is autobiographical it's the sex.

The scene in the fog was partially filmed in a closed set. Are you, too, following the trend of filming indoors?

No, I feel very ill at ease in the studio, whether I'm shooting there or just seeing other films that have been made that way. With *Hammett*, Dean Tavoularis did a splendid job, but throughout the film I felt sort of claustrophobic.

Why did you use the cliché of Venice for the lovers, but distort it?

Intellectuals like to take refuge in conventionality. I got married in Venice. The couple in the film, on the other hand, goes to Venice in the winter to be alone and face their problems. The screenwriter is aware of this need for isolation. By contrast, I need to be surrounded by other people, watch them, listen to them.

How was it to work [on the scrrenplay] with Gérard Brach?

Despite his very particular personality, he's an interesting man. He lives in his room, he needs to get away from the outside world, but after one conversation, he's immediately able to relate to any creative suggestion. I need to work with people like him, who reflect my own ideas back to me in a fresh, detached way. Both of us really want to work together again. Tonino Guerra, with whom I have been working for ages, gave a more Italian touch to the dialogue.

At the end of Identification of a Woman, *the hero decides to write a science-fiction film. Are you also toying with the idea?*

While I'm shooting, I always think of the next film. Actually, there is a science-fiction film in the works but I'm not entirely happy with it yet. I would like to, though—who knows? Perhaps one day. Most likely, we'll still come up against the same problems.

NICOLE CORNUZ-LANGLOIS
JEAN-DOMINIQUE BAUBY

My Method[23]

To begin with, we want to ask a very simple question, the same one that the child asks Niccolò in Identification of a Woman*: "Why don't you make science-fiction films?" Let us ask you the same thing.*

A question like that isn't for you—it's OK for a child like the one in the film! You know well that I haven't been able to do everything that I wanted to do. I suggest ideas, but it is the producer and his distributor who make the decision. It's very difficult today to make suggestions for films, especially for a science-fiction film; they immediately make comparisons with what the Americans are doing in this field, even though we don't have access to the same resources as they do. It's useless to try and compete with them; we have to do something different. In the end credits to *Blade Runner,* there were at least forty technicians. There aren't that many in the whole of Italy! And even if there were, they would cost too much to hire.

I thought your film was trying to be an answer to American science fiction films—an answer to E.T. *and* Blade Runner, *a European version of these things, dealing with everyday issues.*

Perhaps. What you say is interesting. Why did you think that?

The character of Niccolò—the director— eems very interested in everything to that has to do with science. The telescope allows him to approach the farthest his

23 From *Cahiers du Cinéma* 342, December 1982. Translated by Andrew Taylor.

human eye can reach. And then there is the issue that recurs throughout the film: the issue of otherness, be it a woman or other objects. Or perhaps the "other" is extraterrestrial?

That's interesting. I like interpretations, a film is always open. You can interpret it any way you want. Seeing a film is always a personal experience. I would like to make a science-fiction film, but to do so in an Italian style isn't easy. It's such an alien mentality to us. Still, I did write a script for a science-fiction film: it's half classic science fiction, with extraterrestrials; but then that format gives way to a different type of science fiction, where you find yourself inside the characters, who are all characters from science fiction. It was interesting, but I wasn't satisfied with the production deal so I didn't go ahead with it.

The difference between the Europeans and the Americans lies in the fact that while the Americans live in daily contact with science, with technology, and with the future; the Europeans live with their own culture—especially the Italians and you in particular. In Europe there isn't the same proximity to the issue of science, which is nonetheless a constant presence in your films.

In Italy there is no research being done. There is a Center for scientific research, but it hasn't any money and can't do anything. In the (mostly private) laboratories of the United States, they have the greatest scientists in the world. Research serves to develop ideas which are destined to be sold on the world market. In Italy, not even students have any contact with science, other than in their textbooks. The scientific games that American children have don't even exist here.

But that is also a cultural phenomenon. I have just come back from Japan, and despite the fact that there is a lot of technology there, too, there isn't the same interest in science fiction as in the United States. The Japanese feel little interest in other possible worlds. Do you think we will ever get to explore them?

The Japanese are very practical. For them, technology only serves an immediate purpose, making things that are useful to mankind and can be sold abroad, not things that are useful to go into space.

What meaning can we give to the yearning that moves Niccolò, since in your films—unlike those of Bresson—religion and the divine order of creation seem to have been replaced by a "common-people" investigation, rather than a theological one. Do you mean to say that an artist is a kind of lay scholar?

You are giving me explanations of what I have done. Naturally, you can do that, but I must tell you that I have never thought about it. I have only thought about a character, and he came out of my imagination in the way I wanted him to. He's a sort of sculpture. I can't answer your question, I would need the detachment that only a critic or a viewer can have. I am still too involved with him; I can't answer.

Independently of this film, are you interested in religion?

They asked me to do a film about St. Francis of Assisi, but for bureaucratic reasons I don't think it will be possible. At RAI [the Italian state TV], they're late with their contracts, and in any case, I have signed up to do two films, so at least for the moment I can't do anything about it. We'll see. The second of the two films, in a sense, has to do with religion, but seen through the eyes of a layman. I think that because of a professional bias we tend to seek out all those who can help us understand the world in which we live and tell stories about it. The religious spirit is there, it's a real fact, so why not talk about it or even try to capture it? In the case of this film, it's a matter of a man trying to understand why a young girl has shut herself up in a convent. His inquiry has a practical basis: he wants to understand. He doesn't mean to get into the question of religion; he wants to see why others do, in such a profound, total way that it changes their lives completely. It's a sort of scientific research project. For this film, I visited fourteen convents, and I have to say that I had very strong feelings about them. It really impressed me to meet nuns who were so serene, so happy. I met some very special, very intelligent women. One of them had been inside the convent for fifty-five years.

Recently I spent a month in the United States. It's very difficult to get Italian newspapers (in Los Angeles, not in New York), and when you do find them, they are a week old, practically useless. So you forget newspapers, you forget Italy and all its problems, and when you come home and open the newspaper, it's as if you'd been gone only a day: the same names, the same politics, terrorism, crime.

But is it the world that doesn't change any more, or is it you who are no longer attuned to the changes?

Yes, that's true, it's us. You even get used to crimes and scandals, to the hypocrisy and corruption, to everything. It's very serious.

Wasn't it like that when you started out in cinema?

No, there was a certain amount of honesty then, at least people tried to be honest. Nowadays, people are as cruel as they were in the Middle Ages. Two days ago, some bandits killed the security guards at a bank. They were on their way out, they had stolen everything, the guards were lying on the ground. They stopped for a few seconds and killed them just like that, for no reason at all. It's crazy!

To what extent is the character Niccolò autobiographical?

He's a film director like me. We have a few things in common, but his story is different; what happened to him never happened to me. And besides, I don't believe in autobiography. One always has to make choices in order to draw a self-portrait, and there are instinctive inhibitions which lead to all authors drawing the same basic two or three types of self-portrait. A film is autobiographical to the extent that it is authentic and, in order to be that, it has to be sincere.

Do you use the same method that Niccolò uses to create his characters?

No, I don't think so. First of all, I have to admit that I have no method of creating [the story for my] films; a film simply occurs to me. *The Cry* occurred to me while I was looking at a wall, *L'avventura* while I was on board a yacht, heading toward an island. A girl that I knew, a friend of my wife's, had disappeared and I wondered if she could be on that island. That's how I thought of the story for *L'avventura*. In short, there is no fixed method.

What do you think of Niccolò's method? Will his film turn out well?

I hope so, for his sake. Perhaps I should make another film for him. Yes, I think his is a good method. When you begin to think about a film you always start from a sort of chaos in your mind and from there you choose a particular thread that leads you in a particular direction. A director's work is a bit like a poet's: before writing a poem, isolated words float around in your head, and then they join together, one, two, three at a time, until you have a whole line.

Niccolò says he feels the shape of a woman in his mind. That's a good beginning; he feels he has to build the film around a female character. He doesn't yet know who she is—anything about her. His affairs with the two girls complicate matters for him. When you are in love and you respect the woman with whom you are having an affair, it's the natural thing to do to take her as your model. At that point, you don't know any more whether you're looking for a woman for yourself or for the film.

There is a word you use very often, the word "chaos." Should we take it in its scientific or political meaning?

No, in its literal sense of disorder. The disorder of ideas. Once I finish shooting a film, I always allow myself a period of rest, after which I immediately have to think of another film. This way, I begin to look, read all the newspapers, listen, go for walks, waiting for an idea to come to me. It may happen that this occurs in the space of two days, but sometimes a whole year can go by. Naturally, it's impossible for the material that I collect during this process to take on a coherent form right away. Diverse elements have to emerge from the chaos and stand out, so that I can begin to see whether my character will be a poet or an architect, a man or a woman. Naturally, I know that other directors work differently, read novels, prefer to keep their feet on the ground.

It's a little like a photographer who allows the portrait to develop bit by bit. You travel a lot. What role does traveling have in your conception of the world?

Travel makes the creative process more difficult because it's distracting. I'd love to shoot a film in every place I go. Fortunately, I don't do it, it wouldn't be good for me, but I am tempted. What holds me back is that when you're traveling, you rarely have the chance to examine carefully the reality of the place; you can only give it the fleeting glance of a tourist, and I don't like that. I hate being a tourist, you don't get to understand anything. One day I went to Finland; a helicopter was put at my disposal, so we went to a little island inhabited by about a dozen people. It was an interesting situation, ten people on this little island off Finland, covered with snow. But when the helicopter landed, they all rushed up to us. That was the end; there was no reality any more except for those people who were so curious to see me. The same goes for any phenomenon in a microcosm: once you put in an observer, the situation changes, and then how can you have a true representation? On the other hand, when you work in a country, you know its problems, you're in direct contact with the people and their reality, you speak the same language. Besides, any journey is always a little sad: as soon as you fall in love with a place, it's already time to leave. I couldn't care less about memories. I couldn't care less about being able to say: "I've been to Afghanistan." But when I'm actually there, how do I feel? Seeing things, problems, and not being able to reach out and touch them makes me feel frustrated. If I can use the images to make a film, it's different. But if I don't use them, despite the fact that the experience has of course been useful, then I have to say that my relationship with Afghanistan is over. Finished.

So you only have a relationship with things while you are actually in the presence of them?
Certainly, and the same goes for the past. The past doesn't interest me, my only alternative is the future. All I have in front of me is the future.

I think you are the only important Italian director never to have made a costume film.
Yes I have—*The Mystery of Oberwald,* even if it wasn't completely my own project. And then, I was supposed to do a film about St. Francis of Assisi—but probably nothing will come of it. I thought of doing a period St. Francis, a St. Francis of his own time—which, by the way, was an extremely violent, crude age; at the time there was a war between the

people of Assisi and the nobles of Perugia. With his ideas about peace, St. Francis was everyone's enemy. He was alone, a voice crying in the wilderness. That's how I wanted him to come across—ahead of his time. For example, the idea of the convent was born at that time. Nuns used to sleep with anybody; and to restrain them, they invented the convent. They were times of extreme cruelty. Think of the relationship between society and lepers. In order to declare someone a leper and send him out alone into the world, they organized whole ceremonies. The leper had to announce his arrival by ringing a bell. St. Francis met one and gave him a kiss. Now that's a great story.

We also find it in Rossellini's The Flowers of St. Francis.

That's a good film, but from the historical point of view it's not a very serious contribution.

And Pasolini's The Hawks and the Sparrows?

Pasolini is more of a poet, that was a beautiful film.

Do you think there are any similarities between the age of St. Francis and our own age?

All things being equal, perhaps that will be what the world is reduced to in twenty years' time. Maybe worse.

Since we are in a pessimistic frame of mind, were you surprised that a young director like Wenders asked your opinion at Cannes on the death of cinema?

No, but I have to say that I'm not as pessimistic as he is about that. It's true that children are so used to television that they are incapable of having an independent thought these days. They are completely conditioned, they study by computer as they watch television. One day, a boy came to my house and immediately noticed that the television wasn't on. He wasn't used to silence. They need noise, even if they don't listen to it. I think we will have to adapt, they are already ready. We are asking what cinema will be like in ten or twenty years, but it is they who will make it. They will make films according to their views, their psychology, and among their generation there will certainly be some bad directors, but there will also be some poets.

When you and the other directors of your generation were younger, did cinema have any rival equivalent to what television is now?

Radio. But it wasn't as strong. Unlike television, which is very popular with young people, for the most part it was older people who listened to radio; they stayed at home and listened. It's a sort of mystery. I remember when I was a child, my parents' bedroom was next to the living room; my mother listened to the radio and I always asked her to turn the volume down because I couldn't get to sleep. It annoyed me, but for her it was a quiet time with a voice talking. And it did have a strong impact on the imagination: when you hear things, you automatically create in your mind pictures to visualize the things you have heard, to give a shape to the words. Television, by contrast, is like a photograph, everything is already given.

Rossellini thought television was a great tool for educating people. What do you think of that?

Yes, I agree, I think it's already being used in schools. I think it is very direct—it goes straight to your brain via your eyes. I don't know much about it, but I think it's a good tool. However, you need to make educational programs, invent a new method of teaching, and that is not easy. I could never make a film like that, I'm not capable of it.

In a way, you are very up-to-date in terms of your grasp of the language of modern cinema. You are careful to frame your shots, your use of lighting and color is deliberate, and yet at the same time your films are concerned with a certain part of the "in" society, the bourgeoisie, the aristocracy in Rome. The characters in your films are often directors, architects.

They are characters who are part of the daily life of Rome; I don't think that to make a thoroughly modern film you have to choose a boy who knows about electronics or can solve the Rubik's cube in ten seconds flat—that's not a valid criterion. Of course, nowadays a boy like that is someone important. Anyway, for my next film in the United States, since the main character will be American, I've found an American partner to review the script: he's a very intelligent guy, very up-to-date, he has just written a screenplay for Spielberg based on these young electronic geniuses. I really like his whole view of the world. We have in common an interest in everything around us; only, he understands everything, too, while I don't necessarily. His way of writing is very different from mine. He uses words I don't know—even though I do speak English—and I like that, it's a very fruitful collaboration.

Does Identification of a Woman *describe one character's investigations of the world around him, or are you using the film as a vehicle for investigation?*

Both. My films teach me a lot, not because I make them, but because they are the sum total of experiences which I otherwise would not have had. Talking about this society, this reality, is for me a way of understanding them more profoundly.

American cinema is becoming more financially healthy by aiming at the children's market, while European directors like you still aim at an adult audience. Do you think that cinema today can count on a large adult audience?

Adults also go and see *E.T.* It's an extremely intelligent film, but very old, full of nineteenth-century sentiments. Spielberg's great idea was to make the little monster capable of love. That's the novelty of the film, and children aren't interested in it, only adults are. Feelings are too old for children—the petit bourgeois, the family, the mother, the intruder.

Let's take another example: *Blade Runner.* That's quite an interesting film. I like the idea—which, by the way, comes from a novel—of the Earth being on the point of dying. Everything is in a terrifying state, some of the scenes are extremely beautiful. The technological side of the picture is marvelous, too: a world full of light and noises, very modern. And at the end, a man asks a woman: "Do you love me?" And what does that mean?

Their films end where yours begin.

Yes, but they are passed off as being artistically avant-garde and it's not true.

They are popular because they signal the return of both the spectacle and meta-physics. For fifty years, America has had a monopoly on speaking to the future and the next world. It's something that the Europeans aren't interested in. That is why we asked you to talk about religion. When Europeans take an interest in the invisible, whether it's from a scientific or religious point of view, they look for it around them. In your film, one has the feeling that the camera is sometimes a microscope and sometimes a telescope.

You will remember the image of the sun. It's quite a rare image, because it was taken by shooting directly at the sun. The images of the sun you get in the observatory's telescopes are, instead, the image of the sun reflected onto a screen. The sun is seen on a white screen in a context other than its own. In the film, what you see around the sun is really the sky, filmed directly. I had an adapter built with the right focal length and we shot the sun directly, using filters. It had never been done before. I love science, it used to be a great interest of mine.

Do you think that human emotions counterbalance science? In your film we see them both.

As creative moments, yes, but not—I would say—in real life. For example, *The Mystery of Oberwald*, in my view, was a hateful story. I didn't like it at all. And yet I felt relieved by it. At last I was able to let myself go and use certain techniques. It wasn't "my" film, it was just "directed by" me.

What did you learn in making that film?

I learned to film without being personally involved in it, being completely detached, and I also learned how to work with videotape. The range of possibilities which videotape offers is extraordinary. I enjoyed myself a lot. There's a machine called color enhancer. It's a great toy. It made me want to color one of my black-and-white films, *The Cry* or *L'avventura*.

Is the average viewer of Identification of a Woman *the same age as Niccolò? What is the profile of the typical cinema audience today? Does everybody go to the movies?*

No, today there are more young people than there used to be.

How do they manage to understand your films?

I don't know, that's a good question.

I read in an interview that many of your friends are young people.

Of course, that's natural. There are my assistants, for example, or the friends of the woman I live with. She's very young, too. I'm surrounded by young people. And yet, it's a strange thing; with friends who are my age, we don't talk the same language any more. I don't feel comfortable with them. It's worse than with sixteen year-old kids; we have nothing in common any more. But with someone who's twenty-five or thirty, there's a dialogue there, we like the same things. For example, one thing we both have in common is violence. I'm ready to do anything, face any situation. Sometimes I do dangerous things. For example, during the shooting of *Zabriskie Point* I had to make a forced landing. I was in a small plane with my cameraman, who was really scared and had turned completely silent. The pilot was going crazy, too. I was the only one who stayed calm and organized everything. It made me laugh—who knows why? It was crazy. I said we had to throw out everything in order to lighten the plane, get rid of the gasoline so there would be no explosion, and I did everything myself. The pilot managed to land and we were safe!

To hear you talk, it sounds like being in a war film by Hawks, although the manly world of war and heroism is completely alien to your films. You seem more interested in the female world.

And yet I did do that sort of thing. For Lattuada's *The Tempest,* I shot some battle scenes with thousands of horsemen. I shot them as if they were love scenes with Silvana Mangano. I enjoyed it a lot. It was like going to the movies. It wasn't tiring, like the movies I usually make. In fact, I'm fed up with making this type of film. A phase is coming to an end, a long phase which has lasted almost all my life. From now on, I'll do something different.

Are you making a change because you're fed up, or because you've found something else?

Of course, if I have found something else it's because I was tired of those issues, of that conception of life. For example, I would like to make a thriller, if I could find something realistic, because all those thrillers, even Hitchcock's, aren't at all real. They have an amazing format, great suspense, but they aren't realistic. Life is also made up of pauses, of impurities; in both content and its representation there is a sort of dirtiness (in the same way that we say a painting is dirty), and that should be respected. The rhythm of films in which one sequence is closely linked to the next one creates a false movement, which is not that of real life. Why do you think that *L'avventura*, in its day, caused a scandal? Because it had a rhythm that was more true to life.

You use the terms "dirty" and "clean." I don't think that in Identification of a Woman *there is anything that could be said to represent the dirtiness of life. I think, rather, that in your films and your characters there is a certain natural aesthetic pureness.*

That's not true as far as the characters are concerned. What matters is the spirit.

Sometimes Niccolò seems grotesque, just a little bit. Was that deliberate?
Sometimes, yes.

Whatever the equivalent might be in women for this grotesque element, I think that, almost by nature, women cannot be grotesque.

I don't think you can make generalizations. The two women in this film aren't. Niccolò sees them as grotesque, and for that reason they aren't. Although the film is generally objective, this is his view of the world. Well, perhaps that's what links us, him and me, this view of the world. I take women seriously, too—perhaps too much so. And for that reason I make films especially about women, and I know them better than I know men. I've never been to bed with a man, so I know them less intimately. I know myself, but not other men.

During the whole film, it is Niccolò who directs the situation. But when, at the end, Ida tells him she's expecting a child by another man, he's completely lost, his film slips away from him.

Yes, but then there's the sequence about science fiction. In that he takes control of the film again and writes his screenplay.

Do the advances made by feminism, and the fact that the social status of women has changed, make women more difficult to understand than before, or has little really changed?

I think that you have to make a distinction between the real feminists and the rest of women, who are another thing altogether. Perhaps we are struggling to understand feminists, but we do understand the others— and they are the majority. Feminists are the ultimate expression of a need for liberation; today however, we are seeing a kind of backlash.

The Lady without Camellias *dealt with the theme of the alienation of a woman who aspires to become a star.*

It's a film that the feminists loved. I don't know whether they will appreciate the latest one.

Did you get the commission to work on the project in the Soviet Union?

One year I went to the Moscow Film Festival with Tonino Guerra, one of my partners. There he met the woman whom he later married. So he wanted to go back to Russia, and I did too. I was very happy to go. They said that if I wanted to make a film they would give me everything I wanted. So we thought about a science fiction story. We made four trips, and visited many of the Soviet republics, but then we weren't able to make the film. I needed technicians who weren't available there, at least not at the time. So we would have had to pay some Americans or some British to do it—an assistant director, a cameraman—and where was the money going to come from? They would only give me rubles. It was impossible! And for a film with Russian actors, the distributors wouldn't give me an advance. And on top of everything, the Russians would have wanted to develop the film there, and I wanted to do it in Rome. The new Kodak film had just come out and it wasn't easy to develop.

Had you already written the screenplay?

Yes, the book will be published in the Soviet Union and in Italy. I wrote it together with Tonino and it's illustrated by a Russian painter.

Does the Soviet Union interest you?

No, that's the point. It would have been a completely abstract film. They had asked me to do it that way. And I said: "If I put a camera here, inevitably it will film something of your reality. And what else am I supposed to make it say? That your reality is just that? I can't do it!" I would have had to film in Uzbekistan, in ancient, out-of-the-way cities. The peasant costumes were quite different from the way they dressed in Moscow! No one knew in what period the film was supposed to be set, and I didn't like the idea of going to Russia to make a film that didn't show anything.

But the film about China was another matter.

Yes, but the Chinese are more candid than the Russians. The Russians wouldn't allow me to even glance at their reality.

Why are you about to shoot another film in the United States? After Zabriskie Point *you said you'd have some reservations about doing it again.*

This time there will be no problems. The story takes place mostly at sea, on board a yacht. The theme will be the relationship between one character and his crew. I met some producers who asked if I had any projects in mind. I made a proposal and it was accepted. In Italy I had been asked to do an adaptation of a novel which I didn't like, and besides that, the producer was terrible, I couldn't work with him. So I accepted, for practical reasons, but I have to say that I also wanted to shoot a second film in the United States. I like America a lot; I don't want to start any polemics. I will shoot in [Miami,] Florida—rather a nice place where everything is static, where everybody is wealthy, and the poor are there too, but they are Cubans and Puerto Ricans.

Why Miami?
Because it's right for the story. Anyway, I'll be filming very little on land.

Is it a major production company or an independent one?
It's a French-American production company with a budget of nearly eight million dollars. It's the most expensive film I've done to date. In America, with the unionized system you can't make films cheaply. The actors are Robert Duvall, Joe Pesci, perhaps [Vittorio] Gassman, and another famous actor whose name I can't reveal. There will also be a woman. The title is *The Crew.* It will be quite a crude film, but humorous, too—a strange story.
Can we talk about Italian cinema?
What is Italian cinema today? It doesn't exist. There are a few comedies made with the advances given by distributors. But in Italy these days they can't afford films which cost more than four hundred million lire!

Did you ever want to do any shooting in France?
I have to say no to that. I've never really courted the producers. French television made me an offer two months ago, but to do a TV movie—no, I prefer cinema. French production companies like Gaumont have never made me any offers.

Did you write this story with an American?
No by myself. I took my inspiration from a news report; then I invented a story and wrote the screenplay with Mark Peploe, the author of *The Passenger.* Currently we are tidying it up. We'll begin shooting at the beginning of March. I admit that I'm having trouble getting away from

Identification of a Woman, with the New York Film Festival, the subtitles in English and French, the dubbing, sales promotions—

It makes me curious to hear you say that you are ending a phase which has lasted all your life, and that from now on you will do different things.

Still, it's what I think. I don't know how much of the old me there will be in my next film. Anyway, the conflicts will arise from natural situations, the sea, storms. No intellectuals.

And your violent side?

I hope to make a film which is violent and less realistic.

SERGE DANEY
SERGE TOUBIANA

INTERVIEW[25]

I was thinking of asking you about the "thriller" form in your films. That format, already present in Story of a Love Affair, *surfaces also in other films, and in* Identification of a Woman *it leads us astray again.*

What do you mean, "it leads us astray"?

The mysterious man who carries out threats is a classic character from a thriller. At the end of the film, we have not found out anything about him. The famous sequence in the fog hides a mystery, something unexplained. That's already a classic technique.

In the film, the threat is more important than the person who carries it out. By the same token, what happens in the fog is what counts, not whatever it was that started that sequence. Who is the man who fell in the river? It's irrelevant. What matters is that someone fell in. It's not a thriller, it's a film based on the events of everyday life, and it brings together characters from that reality. It will be the characters themselves who explain what the story means. The life of each character is made up of elements that he or she encounters in daily life. It's not important where each element comes from. Only the stories matter, not the explanations of them. It's very simple!

[25] From *Positif*, 263, January 1983. Translated by Andrew Taylor.

You like observing on mysteries. For the character, it is a very short step from observing the sun to observing, spying on other people, women—

That's a sort of professional bias, the character is a film director. This job makes you look at everything. For example, [Richard] Avedon, who is a photographer, took some photos of his father as he was dying and did some extraordinary things with them, I don't know if you saw them. Or even the film by Wim Wenders on Nicholas Ray.

So there is no ethical question?

No, absolutely not. It's a matter of one's view of reality—or rather, of non-reality, the appearance of reality. The classic theme of philosophy is the relationship between reality and its appearance. But that wasn't a real question, right?

What I meant to say was that you go beyond what you call a "professional bias." By telling me it's a question of philosophy you have answered my question. I should say that you have a way of observing things in depth that actually touches on philosophical questions and that, at the end of the film, finds an answer in the child's question—"And then what?"—that leaves the whole issue open. But there is also a continuous visual search. What role do you assign to the painting of Rome, which we see so often, or to the decoration of the wall of Ida's home?

They have no function, they are just natural decorations for those characters. I found that little house just as it was in the film, and I thought it would be the perfect decoration for a woman like her, who lives the same banal life that all the girls live who are into alternative theater. She also has some other interests, like horseback riding and having relationships with different people. I find her quite an interesting woman, and I think it's consistent for her to have such a painting in her house. It's not banal at all.

In this film, did you perhaps further explore the possibilities of color, renewing and pushing forward the experience you had with your previous film, The Mystery of Oberwald?

No, not in this film. I tried to get away from "beautiful images." If there are any left, I didn't intend them to be there.

I think there are!

Well, all the better. But I really wanted to concentrate on the character, rather than the setting or landscape. Naturally, any character lives in a certain context. But I didn't choose to put them against a specific setting.

In this relationship with space, there are often stairs, as well. Mavi is linked to that spiral staircase, where in the end [the protagonist] finds her with her girl-friend. When Ida arrives at his house, there is also a certain relationship with stairs, but of a completely different type.

Well, the stairs are different. The decision to put a character on the stairs rather than in a room was instinctive. Often the most important scenes of our lives are played out in places which are anything but important. A staircase has no intrinsic importance, it has value only as the means of communication between two places. It's interesting because what one says on the stairs, the things one talks about actually nullify the stairs. I don't know if that makes sense: a staircase is such a transitory place.

Still, when Mavi goes up to the fashionable soirée and meets her father, it's a stressful entrance because we don't know yet that it is her father. We have the point of view of Niccolò, who is asking himself who that man is. Thus we experience a certain anxiety. When he finds her again, when he spies on her from above, there is a kind of void; he gets vertigo. In short, the stairs do say something.

Well, you see, it was an old house, there weren't any elevators! No, joking apart, in movies there are also practical reasons for doing things.

Mavi's stairs suggest anxiety, breakdown, they act on the unconscious. While for Ida, the stairs only have hidden implications—roses are left on them, scenes of pettiness happen there, rational things. For Mavi, by contrast, they aren't rational.

You just proved my point: what counts is the character's psychology.

I am keen to know, however, how you express that.
Through the character, certainly not through the stairs which—I say it again—are a completely secondary element. If they occupy an important place in the film, that means I made the right choice.

Can I try you a bit harder?
Of course!

I was disappointed by the two female characters. Your previous films had made us accustomed to other things. The fact that love is not resolved brings with it a simplification of the female characters. One chooses homosexuality, the other chooses motherhood. I think that's a bit simplistic.
Let's look for a moment at the two characters that you think are simplistic. The first is a girl from an aristocratic family, a countess or something like that—anyway, a blue blood. Like all the girls from that environment, she tries to rebel against her origins, tries to build her own, different, independent life. But it's not easy for people like her. They aren't familiar with the working world, they have trouble getting a job; and then, what job should she choose? So she lives in a house, by herself or with a friend, tries to do things that really aren't important. People like that are frustrated. They seek their own identity in vain. They try to live and give the impression of having a definite plan, a personality, ideals, but it's not true. Mavi manages to find a sort of relaxation, an escape, only in sensuality. Now, do you still think she's not very complex?

What I can't stand is that Niccolò takes pity on her.
That's not true. Niccolò is in love with her. Someone like her interests him, he's in love with her out of professional curiosity. He's seduced by her—he doesn't feel pity for her at all. Why do you say that?

It's just a feeling. The same goes for Ida, too: his gaze when he looks at either of them really cuts me to the quick.

He's just older than they are: his gaze is passionate and fatherly at the same time.

Is Niccolò a character who disappears? When he looks for Mavi and arrives at her house, there's the scene on the stairs, and then Mavi goes home to her girl-friend. She looks at Niccolò from the window. He's down in the street. She's upset; she turns away for a minute, and then goes back to the window, but he's gone.

And you think he feels sorry for her? No, Niccolò walks away. It's he who leaves her. He saw her crying and decides not to worry about it. I would like you to tell me, now, whether you're still convinced that Mavi is a simplistic character?

I think that you, Michelangelo Antonioni, have a simplistic view of women. That doesn't mean that they themselves are simple. Ida, for example. For the first time in one of your films, we have a pregnant woman. And—what a sur-prise—her pregnancy makes love impossible. In your films you have often exam-ined the theme of the impossibility of love, but never because of pregnancy.

But the girl says she's happy with the child's father.

No, she just repeats what Niccolò had said about the two terrorists.

She says: "We're happy together, too." As far as she's concerned, the director is just a whim, he doesn't interest her.

Why does she cry, then, if he's just a whim?

One always cries in situations like that. She feels that a breakup is near, and that makes her sad.

In this film you have a harsh view of women, something that you had never had previously.

My film tells a different story from what you think you have seen in it. You talk about a man who is willing to accept a child who isn't his own. That's not what I wanted to say. You can't ask yourself: "Why isn't the film like this?" or "Why is Madame Bovary not different?" These are "whys" which have no right to be asked. When Pirandello was asked certain questions, he used to say: "I am the author".

Who is the child?
Niccolò's nephew.

Niccolò gives him some stamps. Does that imply a sort of handing on of culture?
Yes.

Niccolò is trying to find his own identity, but he's also looking for a female character—from whom, however, he distances himself in order to concentrate on his relationship with the child. Does culture have to be handed on from man to man? The sun represents a scientific, nearly philosophical curiosity. For the child it's an elementary mystery, for Niccolò it's much more complex.
Exactly. It's the sun that counts, not the child. The child is only an intermediary between Niccolò and the mystery of the universe. You shouldn't overestimate the importance of the child. His role is only one of mediation on a purely formal, narrative level.

The mysterious quality of the nest is very different from the one that emerges from the fog scene with the gunshots.
Perhaps you have to be Italian to understand the film properly. The scene in the fog is completely banal for an Italian. Recently, coming out of a friend's house, I happened to hear a noise. It was a bomb and I knew it, but it didn't upset me. There was no mystery there. Who threw the bomb, why they did it—these questions are part of our daily life. It matters little whether it was a terrorist, the Mafia, or a common criminal. And yet there is a mystery: why a bomb, why the nest, why the fog? It's the same mystery that pervades the whole of human life. The nest is simply an object of an organic nature, apparently devoid of any mystery. But why is it there?

For you the most important thing is to ask questions?

Yes, but I've never given answers to them. I've always worked like that.

You told L'Express *that* Identification of a Woman *is an optimistic film. Can you explain how?*
Niccolò is an optimist. His intellectual work reaches a dead point. He fails, because he hasn't managed to give expression to his idea of the ideal woman, because he has had these two relationships with real women. There is no happy ending. So he has another idea which will allow him to continue his work of "identification." He thinks up a film completely different from the previous one, and that is positive. It's creative. Something comes out of the nothingness he was in. "As long as the seed doesn't die—" Gide used to say. The process continues; he will carry on in his own intellectual and emotional life and if the film gets made at the end, he will come to love it.

Are you planning to make a science-fiction film?
I would love to. I've already written a science-fiction story line. No, I'll do a film in the United States. It will be very different from my previous films. There will be no women in it. The conflicts will not derive from the characters, but from the situations they find themselves in—that is to say, at sea, where nature can be extremely calm but also very violent, and naturally the behavior of the characters will be conditioned by that.

FRANÇOISE AUDÉ
PAUL-LOUIS THIRARD

ABOUT THE AUTHOR

Michelangelo Antonioni was born on 29 September 1912 in Ferrara, an old city in the Po Valley, of well-to-do parents. In 1935, he graduated from the University of Bologna with a degree in Economics, and in the early 1940s moved to Rome. There he met his first wife, Letizia Balboni, whom he married in 1942. After separating from her, he had several relationships with other women, including one with Monica Vitti, the actress who shared with him the international success of his 1960s films. He married his present wife, Enrica Fico, in 1986.

Antonioni's interest in cinema found its early expression in the film reviews he wrote first for the local Ferrara paper, *Il Corriere Padano*, and later, during his early stay in Rome, for the important magazine *Cinema*. He enrolled for some time at the Centro Sperimentale di Cinematografia and collaborated on the script of Roberto Rossellini's *Un pilota ritorna* (A Pilot Returns). In 1942, the production company Scalera hired him as scriptwriter and assistant director for Enrico Fulchignoni's *I due Foscari* (The Two Foscaris). Scalera then sent him to France as codirector of the Italo-French coproduction of Marcel Carné's film *Les Visiteurs du soir* (1942). In spite of Antonioni's admiration for him, Carné was rather unimpressed by young Italian.

Returning to Italy, Antonioni started shooting his own first work, the documentary *People of the Po Valley*. The documentary, which was completed only after the war, in 1947, focused on an enviroment the director knew well and on people whose problems and hardships he strongly sympathyzed with. In 1950 he directed his first feature film, *Story of a Love Affair*, which addresses topics that will be a constant presence in his early works—the "crisis of emotions and of moral values" within the context of Italian bourgeois society. With *L'avventura* (1960)—and the other two films that immediately follow it, *La notte* (1961) and

The Eclipse (1962)—Antonioni established himself as one of the most talented, innovative, and technically accomplished Italian filmmakers.

But his quest for the new did not stop. With *Red Desert* (1964), he experimented with the use of color as a key element in the portraying of characters and landscapes. From the mid-1960s on, Antonioni undertook even more ambitious projects involving the exploration of different cultures and societies. After the London success of *Blow-Up* (1966), he obtained an MGM contract for shooting *Zabriskie Point* (1970) in the United States. In 1972 he completed *Chung Kuo: China*, a documentary on Chinese society commissioned by the Italian state television, and in 1974 *The Passenger*, an international coproduction shot in North Africa and Spain.

Antonioni's interest in technical innovations brought him to experiment with a video camera for *The Mystery of Oberwald*, (1980), a film based on a play by Jean Cocteau. With *Identification of a Woman* (1982), Antonioni returned to Italian characters and situations. In 1995, after years of silence due to illness, he codirected with Wim Wenders his "comeback" film, *Al di là delle nuvole* (Beyond the Clouds). In the same year, Antonioni was awarded an honorary Oscar for his lifetime commitment to the cinema.

FILMOGRAPHY

1942 *I due Foscari*, feature film by Enrico Fulchignoni:
      Antonioni participated as scriptwriter and assistant director.
      Les Visiteurs du soir, feature film by Marcel Carné:
      Antonioni participated as assistant director.
      Un pilota ritorna, directed by Roberto Rossellini:
      Antonioni participated as scriptwriter.

1943-47 *Gente del Po (People of the Po Valley)*, documentary.

1947 *Caccia tragica (Tragic Pursuit)*, feature film by Giuseppe De Santis:
      Antonioni participated as scriptwriter.

1948 *N.U.* (Nettezza Urbana; *Sanitation Department*), documentary.

1949 *L'amorosa menzogna (Lies of Love)*, documentary.
      Superstizione (Superstitions), documentary.
      Sette canne, un vestito (Seven Reeds, One Suit), documentary.

1950 *La villa dei mostri (The Villa of the Monsters)*, documentary.
      La funivia della Faloria (The Funicular of Mount Faloria), documentary.
      Cronaca di un amore (Story of a Love Affair), first feature film.

1952 *I vinti (The Vanquished)*, feature film in three episodes.

1953 *La signora senza camelie (The Lady without Camellias)*, feature film.
      Tentato suicidio (Attempted Suicide), episode of *L'amore in città (Love in the City)*, a six-episode film directed by Antonioni, Fellini, Lattuada, Lizzani, Maselli, and Zavattini.

1955 *Le amiche (The Girlfriends)*, feature film, based on the novel *Tra donne sole* by Cesare Pavese.

1957 *Il grido (The Cry)*, feature film.
      Scandali segreti [Secret scandals], a play written with Elio Bartolini and directed by Antonioni at the Teatro Eliseo in Rome.

1960   *L'avventura* [The adventure], feature film; Special Jury Award at the
        1960 Cannes International Film Festival.

1961   *La notte* [The night], feature film.

1962   *L'eclisse* (*The Eclipse*); Special Jury Award at the 1962 Cannes
        International Film Festival.

1964   *Il deserto rosso* (*Red Desert*), feature film; Golden Lion and Cinema
        Nuovo Award at the 1964 Venice Film Festival.

1965   *Il provino* [The screen test], episode of the film *I tre volti* [Three Faces].

1966   *Blow-Up*, feature film based on the story "Las babas del diablo" by Julio
        Cortázar; Palm d'Or at the 1967 Cannes International Film Festival.

1970   *Zabriskie Point*, feature film.

1972   *Chung Kuo: Cina (China)*, documentary.

1974   *Professione: Reporter* (*The Passenger*), feature film.

1980   *Il Mistero di Oberwald*, (*The Mystery of Oberwald*), feature film based on
        the play *The Two-Headed Eagle* by Jean Cocteau

1982   *Identificazione di una donna* (*Identification of a Woman*), feature film.

1983   *Renault 9*, publicity spot.
        Ritorno a Lisca Bianca [Return to Lisca Bianca], short documentary for
        the TV program *Falsi ritorni* [Fake returns].

1984   *Fotoromanza*, a music video made for the song of the same title by
        Gianna Nannini.

1989   *Kumbha Mela*, documentary.

1990   *Roma*, documentary for the TV program *12 autori per 12 città* [12
        authors for 12 cities].

1992   *Noto, Mandorli, Vulcano, Stromboli, Carnevale*, documentary on Sicily.

1995   *Al di là delle nuvole* (*Beyond the Clouds*), with Wim Wenders.

SELECTED BIBLIOGRAPHY

SCREENPLAYS

Il grido [by Antonioni, Elio Bartolini, and Ennio de Concini]. Ed. E. Bartolini. Bologna: Cappelli, 1957.

L'avventura [by Antonioni, Elio Bartolini, and Tonino Guerra, based on a story by Antonioni]. Ed. T. Chiaretti. Bologna: Cappelli, 1960.

L'eclisse [by Antonioni, Tonino Guerra, Elio Bartolini, and Ottiero Ottieri, based on a story by Antonioni]. Ed. J.F. Lane, Bologna: Cappelli, 1962.

Screenplays [*The Cry, L'avventura, La notte, The Eclipse*]. With an Introduction by Antonioni. New York: Orion Press, 1963.

Il deserto rosso [by Antonioni and Tonino Guerra, based on a story by Antonioni and Guerra]. Ed. Carlo di Carlo, Bologna: Cappelli, 1964.

Sei Film [*Le amiche, Il grido, L'avventura, La notte, L'eclisse, Il deserto rosso*]. Turin: Einaudi, 1964.

Blow-Up [by Antonioni and Tonino Guerra, based on a story by Julio Cortázar]. Turin: Einaudi, 1967.

Blow-Up, New York: Simon and Schuster, 1971.

Zabriskie Point [by Antonioni, Fred Gardner, Sam Shepard, Tonino Guerra, and Clare Peploe]. With an introduction by A. Moravia, Bologna: Cappelli, 1970.

Il primo Antonioni [*Gente del Po, Nettezza Urbana, L'amorosa menzogna, Cronaca di un amore, I vinti, La signora senza camelie, Tentato suicidio*). Ed. C. di Carlo, Bologna: Cappelli, 1973

Chung Kuo: Cina. Ed. L. Cuccu, Turin: Einaudi, 1974.

Professione: Reporter, ed. C. di Carlo, Bologna: Cappelli, 1975.

The Passenger [by Antonioni, Mark Peploe, and Peter Wollen, based on a story by Peploe]. New York: Grove Press, 1975.

Tecnicamente dolce. Turin: Einaudi, 1976.

Il mistero di Oberwald [by Antonioni and Tonino Guerra, based on a play by Jean Cocteau]. Ed. G. Massironi, Rome: ERI, 1981

Identificazione di una donna [by Antonioni, Gerard Brach, and Tonino Guerra, based on a story by Antonioni]. Ed. A. Tassone, Turin: Einaudi, 1983.

WRITINGS BY AND INTERVIEWS WITH ANTONIONI

"Ritratto." *Corriere Padano*, 18 December 1938

"Il problema del colore." *Bianco e nero*, 1948.

"Antonione risponde a Chiarini." *Cinema nuovo*, 15 May 1953.

"Colloquio con Michelangelo Antonioni." *Bianco e nero*, June 1958.

"Fare un film è per me vivere." *Cinema nuovo*, March-April 1959.

"Questions à Antonioni." *Positif*, 30 July 1959.

"Ho una storia vera che non posso girare." *Successo*, February 1961.

"Dichiarazioni di Michelangelo Antonioni sul *Deserto rosso*," *Cineforum*, December 1964.

"Antonioni parle." *Cinema '70*, June 1970.

"An Interview with Antonioni," with CT. Samuels. *Film Heritage*, 5 (1970).

"Conversazione con Michelangelo Antonioni," with M. Mancini et al. *Filmcritica*, January–February 1973.

"Quel bowling sul Tevere e inoltre Il deserto dei soldi." *Cinema nuovo*, March–April 1976.

"Appunti per un film da fare o non da fare." *Cinema Nuovo*, November–December 1977.

Aquilone: una favola del nostro tempo. Rimini: Maggioli, 1982.

Quel bowling sul Tevere. Turin: Einaudi, 1987.

That Bowling Alley on the Tiber. New York-Oxford: Oxford UP, 1987.

Fare un film è per me vivere, Scritti sul cinema. Eds. Carlo di Carlo and Giorgio Tinazzi. Venice: Marsilio Editori, 1994.

I film nel cassetto. Eds. Carlo di Carlo and Giorgio Tinazzi. Venice: Marsilio Editori, 1995

CRITICAL WORKS ON ANTONIONI

Aristarco, Guido. "L'universo senza qualità," *Cinema Nuovo*, May-June 1962.
—. "La donna nel deserto di Antonioni," *Cinema Nuovo*, January–February 1965
Arrowsmith, William. *Antonioni: The Poet of Images*. New York-Oxford: Oxford UP, 1995.
Baldelli, Pio. *Cinema dell'ambiguità*. Rome: Samonà e Savelli, 1971.
Brunetta, Gian Piero. *Forma e parola nel cinema*. Padua: Liviana, 1970.
Cameron, Ian and Robin Wood. *Antonioni*. London: Studio Vista, 1970.
Chatman, Seymour. *Antonioni, or the Surface of the World*. Berkeley: UCal. Press, 1985.
Cowie, Peter. *Antonioni, Bergman, Resnais*. London: Tantivy Press, 1963.
Cuccu, Lorenzo. *La visione come problema. Forme e svolgimento del cinema di Antonioni*. Rome: Bulzoni, 1973.
Di Carlo, Carlo, ed. *Michelangelo Antonioni*. Rome: Edizioni Bianco e Nero, 1964.
—. *Michelangelo Antonioni, 1942-1965*. Rome: Ente Autonomo Gestione Cinema, 1987.
—. *Les images d'Antonioni*. Rome: Cinecittà International, 1988.
Fallaci, Oriana. "Visite à Antonioni." *Positif* 44 (1962).
Fink, Guido, et. al. *Michelangelo Antonioni. Identificazione di un autore*. Parma: Pratiche Editrice, 1983.
Hamilton, Jack. "Antonioni's America," *Look*, 33 (1969).
Huss, Roy, ed. *Focus on Blow-Up*. Englewood Cliffs: Prentice-Hall, 1971.
Kauffmann, Stanley. "Antonioni." *The New Republic* 167 (1975).
Kinder, Marsha. "Antonioni in Transit." *Sight and Sound* 36 (1967).
Leprohon, Pierre. *Michelangelo Antonioni: An Introduction*. New York: Simon and Schuster, 1963.
Lyons, Robert J. *Michelangelo Antonioni's Neo-Realism: A World View*. New York: Arno Press, 1974.
Mancini, Michele and Giuseppe Perrella. *Michelangelo Antonioni. Architettura della visione*. 2 vols. Rome: Coneditor Consorzio Coop., 1986.

Miccichè, Lino. "La solitudine esistenziale di Antonioni." *Avanti!*, 2 November 1982.

Micheli, Sergio. *Il film, struttura, lingua, stile: analisi di alcuni campioni di cinema italiano: Antonioni, Scola, Visconti, Taviani.* Rome: Bulzoni, 1991.

Nowell-Smith, Geoffrey. "Shape Around a Black Point." *Sight and Sound* 33 (1963/64).

Perry, Ted. "A Contextual Approach to M. Antonioni's Film *L'eclisse*." *Speech Monographs* 37 (1990).

—. "Men and Landscapes: Antonioni's *The Passenger*." *Film Comment* 11 (1975).

—. and René Prieto. *Michelangelo Antonioni: A Guide to References and Resources.* Boston: G.K. Hall, 1986.

Renzi, Renzo. *Album Antonioni. Une biographie impossible.* Rome: Cinecittà International, 1990.

— "Cronache dell'angoscia in Michelangelo Antonioni." *Cinema nuovo*, May–June 1959.

Rifkin, Edwin Lee. *Antonioni's Visual Language.* Ann Arbor: UMI Research Press, 1982.

Rohdie, Sam. *Antonioni.* London: British Film Institute, 1990.

Salinari, Carlo, et. al. "Le idee e il linguaggio di Antonioni." *Il Contemporaneo* 49 (1962).

Strick, Philip. *Antonioni.* London: Motion Publications, 1963.

Tailleur, Roger and Paul-Louis Thirard. *Antonioni.* Paris: Editions Universitaires, 1963.

Tinazzi, Giorgio. *Michelangelo Antonioni.* Florence: Il Castoro Cinema, 1974.

Wollen, Peter. *Signs and Meanings in the Cinema.* Bloomington: Indiana UP, 1972.

INDEX

The Tempest (Lattuada), 375
That Bowling Alley on the Tiber, 218, 232, 236, 238
La terra trema (Visconti), 187, 208
Thomas, Dylan, 59
Titov, Ermann, 285
Troisi, Massimo, 240
Tron (Lisberger),353
Truffaut, François, 211
Tura, Cosmé, 236, 248
Turin, 191
Two Telegrams, 238, 244
The Two-Headed Eagle (Cocteau), 158, 361

Uccello, Paolo, 248
United States, 177, 223, 249, 298, 301, 319-ff, 366, 367, 378-79
Upton, Jerry, 310

Valéry, Paul, 54, 103
Vancini, Florestano, 212
The Vanquished (*I vinti*), 5, 31, 71, 73, 188, 189,195, 248, 263-ff, 274, 279
Vassallo, Paolo, 279-80
Vedova, Emilio, 44
Velasquez, Diego, 248
Venice, 363
Venice Film Festival, 217
Vigo, Jean, 211
Visconti, Luchino, 10, 35, 65, 187, 208, 209, 212, 242
Vitti, Monica, 32, 41, 42, 66, 78, 83, 90, 148, 164, 165, 240, 279, 280, 281
Vittorini, Elio, 319

Wajda, Andrzej, 204
Walker, Beverly, 310
War Games (?), 352
Warhol, Andy, 315
Welles , Orson, 211

Wenders, Wim, 243, 244, 359, 371, 382
The White Sheik (Fellini), 198
Who's Afraid of Virginia Woolf (Polanski), 164
Wittgenstein, Ludwig, 232
Woolf, Virginia, 228
Wurlitzer, Robert, 255

Zabriskie Point, 92-ff, 102, 169, 179, 201, 216, 224, 243, 248, 298-ff, 304-ff, 320-ff, 347, 375, 378
Zappa, Frank, 180
Zavattini, Cesare, 71, 137, 266
Zinnemann, Fred, 10
Zurlini, Valerio, 212